SAN FRANCISCO AND T

SAN FRANCISCO AND THE LONG 60s

Sarah Hill

Bloomsbury Academic
An imprint of Bloomsbury Publishing Inc

B L O O M S B U R Y
NEW YORK • LONDON • OXFORD • NEW DELHI • SYDNEY

Bloomsbury Academic
An imprint of Bloomsbury Publishing Inc

1385 Broadway	50 Bedford Square
New York	London
NY 10018	WC1B 3DP
USA	UK

www.bloomsbury.com

BLOOMSBURY and the Diana logo are trademarks of Bloomsbury Publishing Plc

First published 2016

© Sarah Hill, 2016

Cover art inspired by Trips Festival poster © Wes Wilson

All rights reserved. No part of this publication may be reproduced or transmitted in any form or by any means, electronic or mechanical, including photocopying, recording, or any information storage or retrieval system, without prior permission in writing from the publishers.

No responsibility for loss caused to any individual or organization acting on or refraining from action as a result of the material in this publication can be accepted by Bloomsbury or the author.

Library of Congress Cataloging-in-Publication Data
Hill, Sarah, 1966–
San Francisco and the long 60s / Sarah Hill.
pages cm
Includes bibliographical references and index.
ISBN 978-1-62892-421-3 (pbk.: alk. paper) – ISBN 978-1-62892-420-6 (hardback: alk. paper)
1. Popular music–California–San Francisco–1961–1970–History and criticism.
2. Popular music–Social aspects–California–San Francisco–History–20th century. I. Title.
ML3477.8.S26H77 2015
781.6409794'6109046–dc23
2015025736

ISBN: HB: 978-1-6289-2420-6
PB: 978-1-6289-2421-3
ePDF: 978-1-6289-2422-0
ePUB: 978-1-6289-2423-7

Typeset by Deanta Global Publishing Services, Chennai, India
Printed and bound in the United States of America

*For Elena Dôn and Onwy Siân,
my half-American beauties*

History will show, I believe, that the San Francisco dance renaissance played a key role . . . in the socio-cultural and political revolution in which we are involved.

[Ralph Gleason, "Perspectives: San Francisco and the Stars," *Rolling Stone* 14, July 20, 1968, p. 10.]

San Francisco started out as a Spanish mission. But when they discovered gold, people came from every corner of the world, one at a time. Therefore San Francisco is the only place I know of that was built on the individual. Maybe that is its core secret. What makes it so different from everywhere else?

[Marc Arno]

But the practical question remains: why San Francisco? When the studios, the companies, and the heavy music traditions are all plugged in and anchored in New York, Chicago, and Los Angeles, why a comparatively tiny town on a bay? The answer . . . is something like this: "We don't dig recording as much as playing live music; we don't need or want to sign ourselves away to a record label unless and until we're ready; and fuck tradition."

[Ben Fong-Torres, "San Francisco Going Strong In Spite of Bad-Mouthing," *Rolling Stone* 20, October 26, 1968, p. 1.]

CONTENTS

List of Illustrations	viii
Acknowledgments	xi
Preface	xiii

1	**Introduction: Ripples**	1

The Short 60s

2	Prelude: *City Scale*	21
3	Into "The 60s"	25
4	1965	31
	"Laugh Laugh"	54
	"The Only Time Is Now"	57
5	1966	61
	"Sing Me a Rainbow"	107
	"Someone to Love"	110
6	1967	115
	"Hello Hello"	185
	"Section 43"	188
7	1968	193
	"Summertime Blues"	223
	"The Fool"	227
8	1969	233
	"Everyday People"	261
	"White Bird"	265

The Long 60s

9	Psychedelia and Its High Other	273
10	Postlude: *The Dharma at Big Sur*	295
11	Hippies, Inc.	301
12	Gatherings of the Tribe	315
13	The Grateful Dead Archive	325

Notes on Interviewees	333
Bibliography	337
Index	349

LIST OF ILLUSTRATIONS

The Short 60s:

Cover:	Grateful Dead in the Park © Jim Marshall Photography LLC	19
3.1	Ralph Gleason in the newsroom	26
	© Mike Alexander/San Francisco Chronicle/Corbis	
4.1	The Seed: The Charlatans at the Red Dog Saloon	42
	© George Hunter	
4.2	Bill Graham in the Mime Troupe office	45
	Photograph by Gene Anthony	
	© Wolfgang's Vault	
5.1	Trips Festival Poster	62
	© Wes Wilson	
5.2	Chet Helms at the Avalon	67
	© Mary Anne Kramer	
	San Francisco History Center, San Francisco Public Library	
5.3	Diggers feeding people in Golden Gate Park Panhandle	92
	© Ted Streshinsky/Corbis	
5.4	Newspaper seller	93
	San Francisco History Center, San Francisco Public Library	
5.5	Kesey speaking from the bus	94
	© Ted Streshinsky/Corbis	
5.6	Psychedelic Shop bookstore in San Francisco	96
	© Gordon Peters/San Francisco Chronicle/Corbis	
6.1	Lying on Haight Street	116
	© Jim Marshall Photography LLC	
6.2	Be-In announcement	118
	Oracle 5, p. 2	
6.3	KMPX ad	129
	Oracle 7, p. 46	
6.4	Tourists take pictures of hippies on the Gray Line Bus Tour through the Haight-Ashbury district	134
	© Arthur Frisch/San Francisco Chronicle/Polaris	
6.5	Allen Ginsberg and Gary Snyder at the Houseboat Summit	138
	Oracle 7, p. 15	
6.6	Dancers in the Panhandle	141
	© Jim Marshall Photography LLC	

List of Illustrations

6.7	Chet Helms letter to *Ramparts*	145
	Oracle 7, p. 23	
6.8	Summer announcement	149
	Oracle 8, p. 32	
6.9	A Hill for Hippies	154
	San Francisco Chronicle Sunday Entertainment page	
6.10	Straight ad	156
	Oracle 7, p. 47	
6.11	Vicki & Marlene	160
	© Baron Wolman	
6.12	Motorcyclists riding in a funeral procession	161
	© Bettmann/Corbis	
6.13	Straight dance	163
	© Jim Marshall Photography LLC	
6.14	Death of Hippie	164
	Oracle 10, p. 22	
6.15	Birth of Freeman	165
	Oracle 10, p. 23	
6.16	A sunrise funeral ceremony in Buena Vista Park to mark the "Death of the Hippie"	167
	Peter Breinig/San Francisco Chronicle/Polaris	
7.1	Lew Welch benediction	194
	Oracle 12, p. 24	
7.2	Haight-Ashbury residents	200
	© Bettmann/Corbis	
7.3	Bill Graham, with the marquee of his Fillmore West Nightclub, formerly the Carousel Ballroom	208
	© Peter Breinig/San Francisco Chronicle/Corbis	
8.1	Altamont map	247
	San Francisco Chronicle, December 4, 1969	
8.2	The Jefferson Airplane perform at Altamont Speedway	250
	© Sam Emerson/Polaris	
8.3	Stragglers and trash at Altamont Speedway	253
	© Bettmann/Corbis	

The Long 60s:

Cover:	Big Sur Folk Festival 1969 © Jim Marshall Photography LLC	271
9.1	Columbia Records ad	276
	Berkeley Barb, November 22, 1968	
9.2	Carlos Carvajal with Dancers Jocelyn Volimar and Bruce Bain	279
	Museum of Performance + Design, San Francisco	

List of Illustrations

9.3	Dancer Michael Rubino	280
	Museum of Performance + Design, San Francisco	
9.4	Pigeons in Union Square	283
	San Francisco History Center, San Francisco Public Library	
10.1	A Buddha at Esalen	297
	Photograph by author	
11.1	1967-era hippie map	309
11.2	2008-era hippie map	310
11.3	Ben & Jerry's at the Haight/Ashbury corner	311
	Photo courtesy http://philip.greenspun.com	
11.4	Wavy Gravy with Ben & Jerry, Union Square	312
	Photograph by author	
12.1	Joyfest hippies	320
	Photograph by author	
12.2	Artista mural	321
	Photograph by author	
12.3	Evolutionary Rainbow mural	322
	Photograph by Tim Kerns	

ACKNOWLEDGMENTS

First on my list of people to thank is my friend Vicki Leeds, who graciously opened her address book and put me in touch with some wonderful people she knew "on the scene" in the Haight back in the 1960s. Even the people she didn't introduce me to seemed to know her anyway. Hers is one in a long list of names of Haight folk whose words are included in these pages, but there were many others who do not appear here. I would like to thank all of my hippie interviewees once again for sharing their memories with me.

Research for this project was made possible by generous grants from the Arts and Humanities Research Council (AHRC) and Cardiff University. The *Music and Letters* Trust provided financial assistance for the reproduction of some of the photographs in these pages. For their local assistance I would like to thank the staff at the Newspapers & Microforms Library and at the Bancroft Library, both University of California, Berkeley; Kyra Jablonsky and Supriya Wronkiewicz at the Museum of Performance and Design, San Francisco; and Jonathan Manton at the Stanford University Archive of Recorded Sound.

For their many acts of kindness I am indebted to my colleagues at Cardiff University, most particularly Ken Gloag, Amanda Villepastour, Keith Chapin, David Beard, and Clair Rowden. My colleagues in the Severn Pop Network have provided necessary perspective, and I must thank Lee Marshall, Justin Williams, and Katherine Williams for their always timely advice. Finally, my deepest thanks to my colleagues on the editorial board of *Popular Music*. Though I do not wish to single any one of them out, I must mention Allan Moore, Dai Griffiths and Nanette De Jong for the many and varied ways that they have helped me during the writing of this book.

For the right chats at the right times I would like to thank Fred Lieberman, Patrick McGuinness, Sara Cohen, Tia De Nora, Philip Bohlman, Simon Frith, Joe Bennett, David Shumway, Tom Irvine, Tim Perkis, Tim Hughes, Dave Oprava, and especially the late Dave Sanjek. For their comments on earlier drafts of the manuscript my thanks go to Drew Buchman, Alexandra Apolloni, Ian Inglis, and the two anonymous reviewers. Further away, Nicholas Meriwether at the Grateful Dead Archive has been remarkably generous with his time and expertise. For entirely nonacademic reasons I offer my love and thanks to Claire Connolly, Paul O'Donovan, Kaite O'Reilly, Phillip Zarrilli, and Gerald Tyler. Finally, a very special thanks to my editor at Bloomsbury, Ally-Jane Grossan, for shepherding this book these last twelve months.

The greatest pleasure of this project has been the opportunity to spend extended periods back home in Oakland. Some of my friends have been involved with this project at different junctures, and others have helped in more practical ways: Kent

Acknowledgments

Sparling, Tim Kerns, Ben Moseley, James and Jules Pelican, Jane Hodges, Alex Coronfly. My sisters, Elizabeth, Anne, and Martha, have taken part in this project as well, whether by talking about music, joining me at events, accompanying me on field trips, or simply babysitting their favorite nieces. My husband, Jon Gower, has been my constant, endlessly enthusiastic, companion, and though he is not cited in these pages, his presence is most certainly there. Our daughters have been eager, if baffled, research assistants on this project throughout their entire lives, so it is only right that I dedicate this book to them.

Images from The San Francisco Oracle (The Psychedelic Newspaper of the Haight-Ashbury) provided courtesy of the estate of Allen Cohen and Regent Press, publishers of the SAN FRANCISCO ORACLE FACSIMILE EDITION (Digital Version) available online at www.regentpress.net.

Lyrics to Grateful Dead songs by Robert Hunter, copyright © Ice Nine Publishing Company. Used with permission.

Every effort has been made to contact copyright holders for text and images used in this book. If there are any inadvertent omissions we apologize to those concerned, and ask that you contact the publisher directly so that we can correct any oversight as soon as possible.

Arts & Humanities Research Council

PREFACE

What follows is a brief history of a small neighborhood in San Francisco. It is not a biography of famous musicians; it is not a tale of illicit sex and hallucinogenic drugs. It is an account of a community that coalesced in the 1960s in search of a new way of living. There are many voices that contribute to this history—contemporary journalists and underground press reporters, music critics, musicians, people who lived in San Francisco in the 1960s, people from elsewhere who found the Haight community, people who have embodied the Haight for the last fifty years. From newspaper reports and published accounts about it, through public celebrations of it, to personal recollections and musical communication, *San Francisco and the Long 60s* interprets a cultural moment and traces its enduring legacy.

1. INTRODUCTION: RIPPLES

There used to be a store in north Berkeley, California, called Black Oak Books. In an industry overrun with corporate predators, for many years Black Oak was part of the empowered minority of independent booksellers in the Bay Area. Historically, the ethos of this network was embodied by one shop: Lawrence Ferlinghetti's City Lights Bookstore in North Beach, San Francisco, which opened in 1953. In 1955 Ferlinghetti established City Lights Publishers and the Pocket Poets Series; their publication the following year of Allen Ginsberg's epic *Howl* led Ferlinghetti through an ultimately vindicated ordeal of obscenity charges and censorship. Black Oak never boasted the biggest or best selection of books in the Bay Area, but it did offer local color, which, for residents of Berkeley anyway, was a far more important thing.

For most of Black Oak's existence, there hung on the few patches of wall not otherwise covered by bookshelves a series of framed prints celebrating what seemed to be the essence of the place.[1] Among others—a poem by Gary Snyder and one by Richard Wright, an excerpt from Salman Rushdie's *The Jaguar Smile: A Nicaraguan Journey*—was the following, by Robert Hunter:[2]

> If my words did glow with the gold of sunshine
> And my tunes were played on the harp unstrung
> Would you hear my voice come through the music
> Would you hold it near as it were your own?
>
> It's a hand-me-down, the thoughts are broken
> Perhaps they're better left unsung
> I don't know, don't really care
> Let there be songs to fill the air
>
> Ripple in still water
> When there is no pebble tossed
> Nor wind to blow
>
> Reach out your hand if your cup be empty
> If your cup is full may it be again
> Let it be known there is a fountain
> That was not made by the hands of men

There is a road, no simple highway
Between the dawn and the dark of night
And if you go no one may follow
That path is for your steps alone

Ripple in still water
When there is no pebble tossed
Nor wind to blow

You who choose to lead must follow
But if you fall you fall alone
If you should stand then who's to guide you?
If I knew the way I would take you home

To one browser, this poem would have been a delicate message of hard-earned wisdom, or simply a supportive word from poet to reader. To another browser, this poem would have been a lyric of spiritual enlightenment, and of community ethos, profoundly resonant with the voice of Jerry Garcia, who set the poem to music and sang it with the Grateful Dead. Poet Robert Hunter wrote "Ripple" in London in the early summer of 1970. The Dead first performed "Ripple" live at the Fillmore West in San Francisco that August, and then recorded it for release on their 1970 studio album *American Beauty*.

There are three levels to "Ripple" worth exploring here. The first is "Ripple" as poetry. Unlike some other songs written around 1970,[3] these lyrics actually work as a separate entity, as that disembodied poem hanging on the wall in Black Oak Books. There is no obvious meter or established rhyming scheme to the lyric. The poet addresses the reader directly, optimistically, almost conversationally. There is a refrain—a quasi *haiku*, consisting of seventeen syllables, 6+7+4 (rather than the traditional 5+7+5)— that grounds the poem in a mystical sort of spirituality. The refrain brings a stillness to the lyric, encouraging the reader to reflect on the wisdom in the verses. The verses themselves adhere to a rough syllabic pattern, with the occasional alliterative link between lines or verses (own/broken; care/air; follow/alone; follow/alone) but no predictable scansion. The lyric's symbolism suggests a wide frame of reference, from Psalm 23 ("The Lord is my shepherd, I shall not want . . . /He leadeth me beside the still waters/ . . . /Thou annointest my head with oil, my cup runneth over") to the Tao Te Ching ("And, desiring to lead the people, One must, in one's person, follow behind them") and Walt Whitman's "Song of Myself" ("Not I—not anyone else, can travel that road for you,/You must travel it for yourself");[4] yet is not so oblique as to obscure the underlying message. There are conceptual similarities between the first and final, and penultimate and final verses, but otherwise, the musical references in the first two verses—"and my tunes were played on the harp unstrung," "let there be songs to fill the air"—are the only obvious acknowledgment of its ultimate context. The lyrics, in other words, may be divorced from the music and read, as an autonomous work, without any obvious or subconscious sense of pulse or melody.

The second level to "Ripple" is musical. As often happened in the Robert Hunter/Grateful Dead partnership, the lyrics and music for "Ripple" were not composed collaboratively. In this case Robert Hunter's lyric fit perfectly to a tune that Jerry Garcia had already been forming.[5] With this tune Garcia had tapped into the continuum of an American musical vernacular and channeled something as familiar and comforting as a folk song. There is an unfussiness about the song: melodically, each halting musical phrase covers rarely more than five syllables of text, and harmonically the song never strays from a solid G Major tonality. It is restrained, thoughtful music, the understated, loping shuffle evoking Saturday morning cowboy films and long evenings rocking on the front porch. The melody is simple; it weaves in and out of itself, potentially infinitely. It is uncluttered enough to allow for Hunter's shifting syllables, with spaces wide open for the graceful interplay between Garcia's guitar and David Grisman's mandolin.[6] Yet without Hunter's lyrics, Garcia's melody would suit another text, or work purely as an instrumental, with enough room for improvisatory exploration.

The third level to "Ripple" is its performance. According to one searchable Grateful Dead setlist archive,[7] "Ripple" was only performed forty times between 1970 and 1995, so a performance of "Ripple" would have been something of an event. Although the band's audience faithful generally maintain that the live Dead was the "authentic" Dead, for reasons of brevity I need to stress here the primacy of the band's studio recording of "Ripple," for it lays bare a basic truth about the group. Garcia's voice was unique, though never the most forceful of instruments, so he generally relied on his guitar to do most of his singing for him. In "Ripple," where his voice is tentative in the first verse, he is joined in the second by band members Phil Lesh and Bob Weir, by David Grisman's mandolin in the refrain, and so on until the end of the final verse, when the voices of various friends and passersby carry on the wordless melody in a kind of campfire singalong. The performance then becomes the embodiment of the lyrical message itself. Despite the individual strengths of the words and music, the message of "Ripple" really comes across in this performance, and it goes beyond a simple "this is a difficult road you have to travel through life, but support is where you need it." It is about the Grateful Dead as an extended family—musicians, lyricists, crew members, partners, children, audience—and the values upon which their community was based.

To understand the Dead phenomenon it is important to note a few things about their evolution. From their beginnings in 1965, the Grateful Dead were known locally in San Francisco as a live band. They lived communally in a house at 710 Ashbury Street, in the Haight district of San Francisco, and played innumerable free concerts for neighbors and friends in nearby Golden Gate Park and elsewhere. Like other contemporary Bay Area bands in the mid-60s—Big Brother and the Holding Company, Jefferson Airplane, Country Joe and the Fish—in their formative years the Dead did not have a contract with a major record label, and enjoyed a certain freedom to do whatever they pleased.[8] The Dead and their contemporaries grew organically out of the student and dropout populations in the Bay Area, were integral members of the Haight community, served that community and others through performances at the major dance halls—the Fillmore, the Avalon, Carousel, Winterland—and helped to define the mid-60s San Francisco popular music "scene."

When eventually the Dead ventured beyond the Bay Area, their reputation as psychedelically enlightened messengers from the Left Coast attracted increasingly larger audiences across the United States. The reason that this reputation preceded them is by now the stuff of legend, but bears summarizing briefly here.[9] In 1965, the members of the Grateful Dead fell into company with author Ken Kesey and Neal Cassady, immortalized by Jack Kerouac as Dean Moriarty in *On the Road*. Along with their larger group of friends and Kesey's Merry Pranksters, their excursions into the underground world of LSD grew into the Acid Tests, a kind of open call to freaks in the Bay Area and beyond to converge on a given location and share in a total, communal, sensory experience.[10]

The writer Tom Wolfe shadowed Kesey and the Merry Pranksters and in 1968 published *The Electric Kool-Aid Acid Test*, an account of their exploits.[11] In the following extended excerpt, Wolfe attempts to recreate the atmosphere and the pulse of December 4, 1965, the night that the Grateful Dead performed at the second Acid Test, in San Jose:

> The Dead had an organist called Pig Pen, who had a Hammond electric organ, and they move the electric organ into Big Nig's ancient house, plus all of the Grateful Dead's electrified guitars and basses and the Pranksters' electrified guitars and basses and flutes and horns and the light machines and the movie projectors and the tapes and mikes and hi-fis, all of which pile up in insane coils of wires and gleams of stainless steel and winking amplifier dials before Big Nig's unbelieving eyes. His house is old and has wiring that would hardly hold a toaster. . . .
>
> They come piling into Big Nig's, and suddenly acid and the worldcraze were everywhere, the electric organ vibrating through every belly in the place, kids dancing not *rock* dances, not the frug and the—what?—*swim*, mother, but dancing *ecstasy*, leaping, dervishing, throwing their hands over their heads like Daddy Grace's own stroked-out inner courtiers—yes!—Roy Seburn's lights washing past every head, Cassady rapping, Paul Foster handing people weird little things out of his Eccentric Bag, old whistles, tin crickets, burnt keys, spectral plastick handles. Everybody's eyes turn on like lightbulbs, fuses blow, blackness—wowwww!—the things that shake and vibrate and funnel and freak out in this blackness—and then somebody slaps new fuses in and the old hulk of a house shudders back, the wiring writhing

and fragmenting like molting snakes, the organs vibro-massage the belly again, fuses blow, minds scream, heads explode, neighbors call the cops, 200, 300, 400 people from out there drawn into The Movie, into the edge of the pudding at least, a mass closer and higher than any mass in history, it seems most surely, and Kesey makes minute adjustment, small toggle switch here, lubricated with Vaseline No. 634-3 diluted with carbon tetrachloride, and they *ripple*, Major, *ripple*, but with meaning, 400 of the attuned multitude headed toward the pudding, the first mass acid experience, the dawn of the Psychedelic, the Flower Generation and all the rest of it, and Big Nig wants the rent.[12]

That night, the Grateful Dead became the *de facto* house band for the Acid Tests, and from that point onward their philosophy of performance—and their audience's experience of it—was informed by a kind of higher group consciousness. In many accounts, this consciousness approached inter-band telepathy. For the Grateful Dead, this meant that their inevitable free-form group improvisations—the influence not only of Free Jazz, but local experimental art music[13]—often ended in unplanned yet spontaneous segues into an original number or a rock 'n' roll standard. With each of the band members operating on the same wavelength, their awareness, in each moment, of the direction their music would take was unspoken, telepathic.[14] Acid, in other words, was the key to the Dead's artistic vision.

The role of acid and other hallucinogenic drugs in the creative process has been theorized elsewhere;[15] the simple wonder of the drug was perhaps best summarized by Jerry Garcia, who said:

When LSD hit the streets finally, that was like, "You're looking for more? Here it is. This is more. This is more than you can imagine." . . . After that, for me, in my life, there was no turning back. There was no back, not just a turning back, but the idea of backness was gone. It was like all directions were forward from there.[16]

The Dead's live performances were deeply encoded with this psychedelic experience, this forward momentum into the unknown,[17] and the audience's understanding of the musical, visual, and lyrical codes was aided by their own hallucinogenic consumption. But it was an experiment that did not last long unadulterated. By late 1966, the sense of vitality in the San Francisco Bay Area musical scene had already been the subject of exposés in the mainstream press; "hippies" had entered the public consciousness; tour companies began to haul busloads of frightened out-of-towners through the Haight-Ashbury in search of flower children. In October 1967, the end of the Summer of Love, members of the head community staged a symbolic funeral for the hippie. Many of the local bands, whose presence had long provided the soundtrack to the neighborhood, left the city and began to live rural lives across the Golden Gate Bridge in Marin County and further afield. The Haight began to turn ugly. Those hippies still grasping at remnants of the dream in 1969 found themselves in a waking nightmare at the Altamont Speedway. That forward momentum established in the vital years 1965–66 had dissipated. So what happened to the music?

Needless to say, because the Dead performed upwards of 150 concerts a year, they continued to compose new material, some of which they recorded in the studio. The problem they had was in trying to capture their essence on vinyl. Their early studio recordings—*Anthem of the Sun* (1968) most notably—simply attempted to replicate the live Dead experience. By mixing together four separate live performances, in *Anthem of the Sun* the band played with the idea of subverting the listener's subjective sense of time and equilibrium, as well as the very definition of "studio performance."[18] But in contrast to their live performances, with those intangible moments of higher consciousness and that enveloping sense of one-ness, their studio albums from 1970 onward betrayed a certain nostalgia, both lyrically and musically. And this is where historicizing the Dead, and historicizing the 1960s, becomes somewhat problematic.

The dawn of "country rock" coincided with a general countercultural motion "back to the land." Toward the end of the 60s, albums such as *Buffalo Springfield* (1967), Dylan's *John Wesley Harding* (1967), the Band's *Music from Big Pink* (1968) and *Crosby, Stills and Nash* (1969) heralded this new direction in popular music.[19] Generally speaking, the music revealed little or no evidence of mind-altering chemicals,[20] and was characterized above all else by the use of acoustic instruments and the prominence of tight vocal harmonies. This roughly termed "country rock" was a rediscovery of roots, a simplification of music and ideas, an almost willfully dated sound and style.

The life of the rural hippie demanded a shift in musical approach, an antidote to the "urban hippie" sound of hour-long space jams and psychedelic noodling. As Dead manager Rock Scully commented at the time:

> After all these years of mind-gumming psychedelics we are all actually beginning to *crave* the normal. We need something to ground us—our hair is talking to us, our shoes have just presented a set of demands, the walls are alive with the sound of intergalactic static. Please remind us whereof we come? Our home planet is what?[21]

This prompted a more general shift in the Dead's musical aesthetic, and soon they were crossing Crosby, Stills, and Nash terrain, emphasizing the voice over the "space."[22] Robert Hunter's return to the fold enabled the Dead to speak more clearly to their fractured and dispersed community, in an idiom appropriate to their new musical direction.

There are two Hunter songs written on either side of this musical shift that illustrate this point: "Dark Star" and "Uncle John's Band." Written in 1967, "Dark Star" was the centerpiece of the Dead's live repertoire, and over the band's thirty-year performing career, was never played the same way twice. This makes it the quintessence of the Dead experience, an Acid Test remnant. When asked, in a 1971 *Rolling Stone* interview, to talk about "where 'Dark Star' comes from," Jerry Garcia famously remarked:

> You gotta remember that you and I are talking about two different "Dark Stars." You're talking about the "Dark Star" which you have heard formalized on a record, and I'm talking about the "Dark Star" which I have heard in each performance as a completely improvised piece over a long period of time. So I have a long continuum of "Dark Stars" which range in character from each other to real different extremes. "Dark Star" has meant, while I'm playing it, almost as many things as I can sit here and imagine, so all I can do is talk about "Dark Star" as a playing experience.
> Reich: Well, yeah, talk about it a little.
> Garcia: I can't. It talks about itself.[23]

Forever existing in that incomprehensible space, "Dark Star" is an example of the Dead's inter-band telepathy, of their philosophy of performance, and of the openness with which they shared their musical freedom with their audience. Though the lyrics and the musical germ were constant in each performance—the song was based on a two-chord theme,[24] for which Robert Hunter wrote the lyrics in the studio—the places that "Dark Star" took the Dead and their audience, in any given moment, were unpredictable.[25] But any performance of "Dark Star," such as the one captured on *Live/Dead* (1969), is still only one of 222 possible points on that "Dark Star" continuum.

Hunter invokes a cosmic terminology in this lyric that is grounded in the 1960s search for universal truth, clear in the song's first section:[26]

> Dark star crashes
> pouring its light
> into ashes
>
> Reason tatters
> the forces tear loose
> from the axis
>
> Searchlight casting
> for faults in the
> clouds of delusion
>
> Shall we go,
> you and I

while we can?
Through
the transitive nightfall
of diamonds

Perhaps the most notable aspect of this lyric is its form. Under most conventional rules, this would not be read immediately as a "pop song." There is no distinction between verse and chorus, no sense of refrain,[27] and even the regular syllabic pattern of the first stanza (4+4+4) is disrupted in the second (4+5+4), returning partially in the third (4+4+5), only to disappear entirely in the last (3+3+3+1+6+3). This allows the vocal passages and musical backing to exist interdependently:[28] the voice is not welded to the musical germ, nor does it disrupt the flow of the instrumental passages when it emerges from the texture; rather, the lyrics situate the Dead's musical journey within the larger cosmic questions explored by the hippies more generally outside of the band's orbit.

By contrast, "Uncle John's Band," written two years later, is much less opaque. Here Hunter's lyrical expression suggests a grounding in earthly, rather than celestial, verse forms:

My purpose in writing song lyrics, besides having nothing better to do and making a living, is the exaltation of my spirit through other spirits. Traditional tools and forms are often apt for the purpose, such as the "Come All Ye" forms so popular in sailor songs and union ballads. When I recommend others "come hear Uncle John's Band," I verbalize . . . one of the ongoing agendas of life, the coaxing and cajoling of the forces of generational unity. I don't say *we* . . . are Uncle John's Band . . . —the truth is that we as a group also wanted to come hear "UJB," [*sic*] and to come home, too, if it's not too much to ask.[29]

Well, the first days are the hardest days,
Don't you worry anymore
When life looks like Easy Street
There is danger at your door
Think this through with me
Let me know your mind
Wo-oah, what I want to know is are you kind?
. . .
Come hear Uncle John's Band
By the riverside
Got some things to talk about here beside the rising tide.

The affective differences between these two songs should be obvious. Musically, "Uncle John's Band" firmly embraces the country-rock aesthetic; the psychedelic remnants of "Dark Star," both musical and lyrical, however, are firmly embedded in another, earlier, moment in time. That is what I will call "the short 60s":[30] the period of psychedelic experimentation that, for some, came to define an entire era. But for San Francisco bands such as the Dead, that psychedelic moment only lasted a couple of years, from the Acid Tests of 1965 to the Death of the Hippie funeral in 1967. LSD was a central component, of course, and it established a direction—"forward"—for self-perception, community awareness, popular music, and cultural meaning. To illustrate, the lyrics of "Dark Star" hint at an experience to which many hearing the song today would not have immediate and personal access. For those people, this song might "mean" the 60s, but it would mean a very short 60s.

For that same audience, "Uncle John's Band" is much more accessible, lyrically and musically. Though both songs involve direct address—"shall we go, you and I" and "let me know your mind"—it is the latter which holds perhaps the more universal meaning,[31] and which has the longer-lasting cultural impact. I call this "the long 60s": the perpetuation of an ideology beyond the confines of geographical or temporal space. In this sense, and specifically in the case of the Grateful Dead, the 60s have already lasted fifty years.[32]

"Uncle John's Band," while not self-referential, is nonetheless evocative of the Dead themselves.[33] The end of each verse marks a kind of passing of time—the passing of the short 60s—by posing direct questions to the listener: asking "are you kind," "will you come with me," "how does the song go," "where does the time go," and so on. By the closing verse there is a palpable sense that a community has formed, of people whose understanding of the band's motives and common experience will allow them to carry on with the unfinished project established at the beginning of the short 60s. The long 60s, the continuation of that ideology, in part begins here. And this is where "Ripple" comes back in.

"Ripple," recorded in the same year as "Uncle John's Band," is a multilayered representation of the long 60s. As an autonomous poem once hanging on the wall in Black Oak Books, it existed to codify the tenets of a particular philosophy, and served to remind the local community, Deadheads and otherwise,[34] of a brief moment in Bay Area history, the short 60s. The deeper significance of the lyric is in its very title. In physics, according to the OED, a ripple is "a wave on the surface of a fluid the restoring force for which is provided by surface tension rather than by gravity, and which consequently has a wavelength shorter than that corresponding to the minimum speed of propagation." In terms of the hippie community, the period 1965–67 was one of enormous social awakening and creative freedom in the San Francisco Bay Area. To stretch a metaphor, 1965 was the seismic moment of initiation, the Acid Tests the initial "plop" in the cultural water. The ripples emanating from that point demarcate later moments of enunciation—the Trips Festival, the Human Be-In, the Death of the Hippie—and suggest a certain cause and effect.

The contemporary Haight-Ashbury community, shaped by the simple desire to care for the people in one's immediate environment, had become unsustainable by 1967. There were too many people making too many demands on the community's limited resources for it not to implode. It needed to become a virtual community, a kind of Brigadoon that would emerge at certain moments—a Dead concert, a commemoration, a gathering of the tribes—only to disappear again almost without a trace until the next time. In other words, the surface tension of the straight world would be disrupted by the emergence of the virtual community, more of those ripples emanating from 1965. To an outsider, stepping into that Brigadoon could be like stepping back into the 60s, a kind of exercise in ideological time-travel. In the everyday material world, for outsiders browsing the shelves at Black Oak Books, "Ripple" was just a small insight into a protected, yet welcoming, other world, the wavelengths of which have been undulating for half a century.

When Robert Hunter wrote "Ripple" that sunny day in London, his geographical and temporal distance from the ideal Haight community of the mid-1960s enabled a clear vision for the continuation of its legacy. This kind of backward glance, from deep within the long 60s, is a ripple in itself, an idealization of history. Nostalgia is inherent in the song's lyrical form, and in its evocation of the passing of time—"it's a hand-me-down/the thoughts are broken"—but this is not to suggest that everything Hunter wrote referred in some way to the Haight or the Dead community; on the contrary, his lyrics are grounded in much deeper traditions. Like the Dead's brand of country-rock, Hunter's use of American folk poetry forms simply eases the audience's access to his lyrical message. Sometimes that message is couched in metaphor; sometimes it is unmistakable, as in "Scarlet Begonias" (1974):[35]

> As I was walking round Grosvenor Square
> Not a chill to the winter but a nip to the air
> From the other direction she was calling my eye
> It could be an illusion but I might as well try
>
> She had rings on her fingers and bells on her shoes
> And I knew without asking she was into the blues
> She wore scarlet begonias tucked into her curls
> I knew right away she was not like other girls

"She" could be a flower child right out of Golden Gate Park, circa 1966, tripping the light fantastic, leaving the gentlest hint of patchouli as she goes;[36] or she could be a proof that a 1960s ethos was alive and well even outside the American Embassy in London in the early 1970s, an earthly embodiment of the long 60s.

To consider the "short" and the "long" 60s is necessarily to consult historical accounts of the time and to talk not only to the people whose experiences have not yet been recorded, but to revisit those whose experiences form part of the historical palimpsest. The hippie community generated a great deal of interest in the mid-1960s, both journalistic and sociological. Journalistic interest in the hippies from outside their culture perhaps began with Tom Wolfe and *The Electric Kool-Aid Acid Test*, continuing with Joan Didion's *Slouching Toward Bethlehem* (1968) and Nicholas von Hoffman's *We Are the People Our Parents Warned Us Against* (1968), and in mainstream magazines such as *Time*, *Life*, and *Variety*. Journalistic interest in the community *from within the culture* found a voice in, among others, the short-lived psychedelic newspaper *The Oracle* and *Rolling Stone* magazine. These papers provide the key source documents for the local community, representing as they do both the short 60s (*The Oracle* published 12 issues between 1966 and 1968) and the long 60s (*Rolling Stone* was founded in San Francisco in 1967, and has now published well over 1,000 issues). Both of these journals are rooted in a specific time and place, and despite *Rolling Stone*'s defection to New York in the 1970s, its political bent, nurtured in late-60s San Francisco, has remained sharp through the many musical changes of the ensuing decades.

Sociological interest in the hippies is an interesting phenomenon. Academics, firmly rooted in the "straight" world of the 60s, immersed themselves in the Haight community, logging countless hours of interviews with merchants, students, street people, civic leaders, and others, and reported their findings back to their learned readership. These studies—Burton Wolfe's *The Hippies*, Leonard Wolf's *Voices from the Love Generation* (both 1968), and Helen Swick Perry's *The Human Be-In* (1970), among others—provide a valuable insight into the culture as it was in process. The authors are not uniformly impressed by the lifestyle and ideals of the new generation, but they do provide the earliest source documents of the hippie ideology in the act of its articulation. Significantly, some of the subjects interviewed in those early studies have been interviewed again, by others, at successive moments of inferred import—the 10th anniversary of the Summer of Love, the 25th anniversary, and soon, inevitably, the 50th.

The idea of historical palimpsest is embodied by many of the characters who inhabit the following pages. For example, Teresa Tudury is a singer-songwriter whose name pops up in the acknowledgments of some oral histories of the 60s. She grew up in North Beach during the beatnik 50s, found her voice in the coffee-house folk music circuit of the early 60s, fronted a band called the All-Night Apothecary at the height of the San Francisco "scene," then fluttered off to communal life in Big Sur, wandered around Europe, and was eventually brought back to the States under the protection of her friend, Leonard Cohen. I interviewed her before I had seen her name in print, and I have yet to find in any of those histories a quote directly attributed to her. She's a shadow, in other words, whose experiences of the 60s typified the kind of lifestyle and recreational mind expansion readers expect from accounts of the time. Her "short 60s" were the formative years of her life, but she has no need to embody them outwardly.

At the other extreme is Wavy Gravy, hippie supremo, clown, humanitarian, ice cream flavor. His presence is guaranteed in any history of the counterculture, and I was eager to interview him for this one. Early in the summer of 2005 he presided over the memorial concert for promoter Chet Helms at the Great American Music Hall in San Francisco. At one point during the concert Wavy Gravy said to the assembled throng, "We're still a tribe. We'll *always* be a tribe. We are the Hip-Eye Nation." The continued and unproblematic usage of the term "tribe" is something that intrigues me, so when I met him a few weeks later I asked him to riff on it—and he referred me to the Woodstock movie. Then I asked him where he was between 1965 and 1967:

> WAVY GRAVY: I left the Committee [the SF-based improvisational theater group], gave away all my stuff and went to live with the Hopi Indians. It was written in the book of the Hopi that during conditions of emergency, people would gather together on these Mesas and await instructions from the spirit world. Well, these Hopis kind of took pity on me. They said, hey, you're pretty early. They took me in for a while, and then I went to LA.

While in Los Angeles Wavy Gravy hooked up with Ken Kesey, was involved in the Watts Acid Test and out of that experience formed the Hog Farm Collective. It's a good, if familiar, story, one in a string of anecdotes that he repeated to me that day, almost verbatim, from his book *Something Good for a Change* (1992). I am certainly not going to fault Wavy Gravy for repeating himself once or twice; the man has fifty years of often brilliant interviews behind him. The problem is that his memories are not so much a palimpsest as a carved stone tablet. When I tried to steer him off course, as it were, he referred to what he calls "the train wreck of the mind"—those gaping holes in memory where data just disappears: a black hole, a dark star.

Wavy Gravy lives up the road from where Black Oak Books used to be. I asked him if he ever noticed the framed print of "Ripple" hanging there on the wall. He said that at Camp Winnarainbow, the summer camp he runs in Mendocino County, the children learn two songs: "Ripple" and "Teach Your Children," by Crosby, Stills & Nash. Every year since the camp was founded children have been taught these two texts, these two folk songs.[37] Singing these two songs connects the children to an ideology codified in the aftermath of the short 60s, and encourages them to live by the codes offered in them. Wavy Gravy said that, rather than making him nostalgic for the 60s, this makes him nostalgic for the future. Then he left me this image:

> I see us in our old folks home, that that part of Black Oak Ranch is gonna turn into, and we'll all be in our rockers singing "Ripple" like those Confederate veterans were singing the Battle Hymn of the Republic.[38]

Just as musical codes can suggest altered states of consciousness, so can lyrical codes act as a call to collective memory. In considering some of the lyrics Robert Hunter wrote for the Dead in the early 70s, a distinct pattern emerges: moments of nostalgia, moments of recognition, moments of regret. An online keyword search of the Dead lyric database might reveal a large number of occurrences of the word "sunshine," for example, or "love," or "home"; and a cursory reading of the lyrics in the Dead's 1970s studio albums, *Workingman's Dead*, *American Beauty*, and *From the Mars Hotel*, reveal clear thematic tendencies. There are references to blues tropes, American folklore, the Dead themselves; there are stories about gambling, driving, meeting the Devil; in short, there is a plundering of the vaguely familiar. Musically, in their 1970s studio albums the Dead remained faithful to a kind of country-rock aesthetic, occasionally dipping into jam band territory. In contrast to early recordings such as *Anthem of the Sun* and *Aoxomoxoa* this later music does not try to replicate the psychedelic experience; it does not attempt to recreate that transcendent moment of total unity, the forward leap into another dimension of consciousness. In the long 60s, the Dead's music was neither progressive nor psychedelic—the direction might not have been "forward"—but the residual hippie ethos was.

Though live performances provided arguably the more "authentic" Dead experience, the band's early 70s studio artifacts offer insights into that moment when the 60s became an *idea*. To consider these artifacts many decades later is necessarily to consider local history, community formation, and the power of the written and sung word. The little home truths that Robert Hunter spun are rich with the personal experience of mid-60s San Francisco, and can be read as such. But it is the unquestionably unfashionable way in which Jerry Garcia set those truths to music that poses the challenge to popular music historiography. It demands the suspension of disbelief; it demands an allowance for that one cultural anomaly to ripple occasionally; and it demands that a 60s aesthetic be sustained through an essentially anachronistic musical style. Maybe the Dead's long 60s were all about recuperating from the short 60s; maybe "Ripple" is just a nice tune about nothing in particular; but fifty years of ideological undulations suggest that in some cases, the linear progression of history is secondary to the prolongation of a moment.

Notes

1. Black Oak Books opened its Shattuck Avenue store in 1983. After two decades of community presence, compelling calendars of events, and welcoming opportunities for late-night browsing, the original owners sold the business. With the sale of the store in 2008 came a shedding of Black Oak's visual identity: the new owners stripped the walls of their broadsides, and turned the "new" shop into something much more generic and closely aligned with its corporate competitors. After just over a year in its new incarnation, Black Oak Books left its Shattuck Avenue premises in May 2009. Black Oak currently operates a retail space on San Pablo Avenue in West Berkeley, around the corner from Fantasy Studios.
2. "Ripple," words by Robert Hunter; music by Jerry Garcia.

3. There is a minefield awaiting one who suggests that song lyrics should "equate" to poetry, but there are some contemporary lyrics of Bob Dylan, for example, which are structured in a similarly free style and are generally held to possess a certain uncommon "artistic" sensibility. Mention should also be made of the lyric to "Teach Your Children" by Crosby, Stills, Nash and Young, not only as a testament to universal generational (and intergenerational) concerns, but because the version that appears on CSNY's album *Déjà vu* (Atlantic, 1970) is enhanced by Jerry Garcia's guest work on pedal steel guitar.

4. For an exhaustive analysis of "Ripple" and the rest of the Dead canon, see David Dodd, *The Annotated Grateful Dead Lyrics* (New York: Free Press, 2005), or its online predecessor, arts.ucsc.edu/gdead/agdl/, from which these references are drawn.

5. As Jerry Garcia noted, "'Ripple' is one of those things of having two halves . . . come together just perfectly. Bob Weir had a guitar custom-made for himself and I picked it up and that song came out, it just came out. . . . [Then the] next time I saw Hunter he says, 'Here, I have a couple of songs I'd like you to take a look at,' and he had 'Ripple' and it just . . . all of a sudden, just bam, there it was, it was just perfect." In Jerry Garcia, Charles Reich and Jann Wenner, *Garcia: A Signpost to New Space* (Cambridge: Da Capo Press, 2003), pp. 53–54.

6. "Ripple" was not composed with Grisman's mandolin in mind. David Grisman was invited to join the Dead's *American Beauty* recording sessions, having recently seen Garcia playing in an informal softball game between the Dead and Jefferson Airplane. Grisman and Garcia had met in the mid-1960s, and formed a bluegrass group, Old and In the Way, in the early 70s. Garcia's last musical project before his death, a recording of Jimmie Rodgers' "Blue Yodel #9," was recorded at Grisman's studio. Some of their early 90s informal jam sessions were filmed by Grisman's daughter and released as the documentary film, *Grateful Dawg* (dir. Gillian Grisman, 2000).

7. www.setlists.net.

8. This is a freedom of self-expression they steadfastly maintained even *after* signing a contract with Warner Brothers, a fact that caused no end of stress to the label's executives, and that served to highlight the philosophical fissures between the musical communities of San Francisco and Los Angeles. See *Anthem to Beauty* (part of the *Classic Albums* series, Rhino Home Video, 1998) for Bob Weir and Phil Lesh's reflections on this issue.

9. A complete account of the early days of the Grateful Dead may be found in Dennis McNally, *A Long Strange Trip: The Inside History of the Grateful Dead* (London: Transworld Publishers, 2002).

10. Lysergic acid diethylamide-25 (LSD-25) was first produced by Albert Hofmann at the Sandoz Laboratories in 1938 as part of a research project into ergot alkaloids. Five years later he synthesized the "relatively uninteresting" LSD-25 for further pharmacological tests, and it was then that Hofmann accidentally took the first acid trip: "a not unpleasant intoxicated-like condition, characterized by an extremely stimulated imagination. In a dream like state, with eyes closed. . . . I perceived an uninterrupted stream of fantastic pictures, extraordinary shapes with intense, kaleidoscopic play of colors. After some two hours this condition faded away." LSD-25 had great potential for psychotherapeutic research—in the treatment of migraines, alcoholism, psychosis—and was the basis of experimentation through the 1950s. The US military saw LSD as a potential counterespionage tool, and began conducting experiments of its own; one of the subjects of these experiments at the Menlo Park Veterans Hospital was Ken Kesey. Over at

Harvard, two members of the Psychology faculty, Timothy Leary and Richard Alpert, began controlled but nonclinical experiments into the effects of LSD on consciousness; one of the first subjects of these experiments was the poet Allen Ginsberg. See Albert Hofmann, *LSD: My Problem Child*, trans. Jonathan Ott (Sarasota: Multidisciplinary Association for Psychedelic Studies [MAPS], 2005), Peter Connors, *White Hand Society: The Psychedelic Partnership of Timothy Leary and Allen Ginsberg* (San Francisco: City Lights Books, 2010), and Martin A. Lee and Bruce Shlain, *Acid Dreams: The Complete Social History of LSD* (New York: Grove Weidenfeld, 1985).

11. A contemporary review of Wolfe's book dubbed it "a very odd kind of masterpiece," and added that while "there has probably never been a Literary Biography" like it, "there has seldom been this kind of reporting. Wolfe works INSIDE, so far back there that the normal dicta of his craft—the things old journalists set great store by—are forgotten. Like driving from San Francisco to Santa Cruz on the Harbor Freeway, for goshsake." Wolfe captured a *feeling*, in other words, if not in a verifiably accurate kind of way. See Donald Stanley, "A Kandy-Kolored Look at Ken Kesey," *San Francisco Examiner*, August 18, 1968, p. B4.

12. Tom Wolfe, *The Electric Kool-Aid Acid Test* (Farrar, 1968), pp. 210–12.

13. This is an issue to which I return in Chapter 9.

14. See McNally, *A Long Strange Trip*, pp. 102–06.

15. See, for example, Marlene Dobkin de Rios and Oscar Janiger, *LSD, Spirituality and the Creative Process* (Rochester, VT: Park Street Press, 2003) and Bernard Aaronson and Humphry Osmond, *Psychedelics: The Uses and Implications of Hallucinogenic Drugs* (Garden City: Anchor Books, 1970).

16. Jerry Garcia, quoted in McNally, *A Long Strange Trip*, p. 104.

17. For more on psychedelic coding and music of the 1960s, see Sheila Whiteley, *The Space Between the Notes: Rock and the Counterculture* (London: Routledge, 1992). The Grateful Dead do not figure significantly in her study, but she rightly notes that the San Francisco "hippy" scene had effectively ended by the time the mainstream press and music industry had spread the notion of the countercultural ideology beyond its local (and, some would say, natural) habitat.

18. As Jerry Garcia said, '*Anthem of the Sun* was like a chance for us to try a lot of things, and to see what things might work and might not. Actually, when we mixed it, we mixed it for the hallucinations. And . . . Phil and I performed the mix . . . as though it were an electronic music composition. You know, he would do things and I would do things, we were working over each other, bringing these faders up and those down, and switching these things around. And it was pretty intense. And we performed each side all the way through. . . . The original tapes, our first stereo master tapes, preserved some of that quality when you had a good enough playback system to really hear, but . . . when the disc came out, it sounded muddy and it was terrible, and . . . you know, all the things that we put together so carefully [just] didn't make it across.' See *Anthem to Beauty*.

19. For more on late 1960s communes, see Jerome Judson, *Families of Eden: Communes and the New Anarchism* (London: Thames and Hudson, 1974). See Greil Marcus, *Invisible Republic: Bob Dylan's Basement Tapes* (New York: Picador, 1997) for a study of the "old, weird America" accessed in the 1968 shift to country rock.

20. Lyrically, however, there are still occasional suggestions of expanded consciousness and other recreational pursuits.

21. Rock Scully, quoted in McNally, *A Long Strange Trip*, p. 319.
22. The 1969 formation of New Riders of the Purple Sage is also emblematic of this shift.
23. Garcia, Reich, and Wenner, *A Signpost to New Space*, p. 58.
24. See Phil Lesh, *Searching for the Sound: My Life with the Grateful Dead* (New York: Little, Brown, 2005), p. 101.
25. Graeme Boone has published a comprehensive and insightful series of analyses of "Dark Star." See in particular his "Tonal and Expressive Ambiguity of 'Dark Star'" in John Covach and Graeme Boone, eds., *Understanding Rock: Essays in Musical Analysis* (Oxford: Oxford University Press, 1997), pp. 171–210. David Malvinni's exploration of "Dark Star" is an important addition to the literature on psychedelic music. See his *Grateful Dead and the Art of Rock Improvisation* (Lanham: Scarecrow Press, 2013).
26. "Dark Star," words by Robert Hunter; music by Garcia, Kreutzmann, Lesh, McKernan, and Weir.
27. When the voice returns for the second section it becomes clear that "shall we go/you and I while we can . . ." acts as a refrain across the longer span of the song. Though the second section follows the same line structure as the first, the syllabic pattern is different: "Mirror shatters/in formless reflections/of matter//Glass hand dissolving/to ice petal flowers/revolving//Lady in velvet/recedes/in the nights of goodbye//Shall we go,/you and I/while we can?/Through/the transitive nightfall/of diamonds."
28. On *Live/Dead* the vocal passages emerge at 6:04–7:02 and 21:26–22:25.
29. Robert Hunter, "Introduction," *The Annotated Grateful Dead Lyrics*, pp. xix–xx. "Uncle John's Band," words by Robert Hunter; music by Jerry Garcia.
30. The notion of the 1960s as a chronological block has been debated at length elsewhere, for example, in Fredric Jameson's "Periodizing the 60s," in his *The Ideologies of Theory: Essays 1971-1986*. Vol. 2: *The Syntax of History* (Minneapolis: University of Minnesota Press, 1988), pp. 178–208, and more recently in Jeremy Varon, Michael S. Foley, and John McMillian's editorial, "Time is an ocean: The past and future of the Sixties," in *The Sixties: A Journal of History, Politics and Culture* 1/1 (June 2008): 1–7. What I aim to do here is problematize the "short" and the "long" in locally specific terms, substantiated in the following chapters. I am aware of the irony in the fact that the "short 60s" here are longer than the "long 60s." The chronicle of events in the years 1965–69 take a finite amount of space, however, while the "long 60s," I argue, are still being written.
31. The greater "accessibility" of "Uncle John's Band" should not deny the immediacy of the reference in "Dark Star" to T. S. Eliot's "Love Song of J. Alfred Prufrock," which is, needless to say, understandable even without the assistance of hallucinogenic drugs.
32. Though the Grateful Dead officially disbanded after the death of Jerry Garcia in 1995, as this book goes to press they are preparing to celebrate their fiftieth anniversary with "farewell" performances in Chicago and Santa Clara. I return to this point in Chapter 13.
33. Perhaps the most autobiographical song in the Dead canon is "Truckin" (*American Beauty*, 1970), which recounts a number of run-ins with the law that the Dead endured during one of their US tours.
34. The term "Dead Head" was first used on the inside cover of the live album *Grateful Dead* (Warner Brothers, 1971) in an invitation for fans to get in touch.
35. "Scarlet Begonias," words by Robert Hunter; music by Jerry Garcia.

36. Robert Hunter actually admitted that this song was written for his wife. See *The Complete Annotated Grateful Dead Lyrics*, p. 231.
37. The fact that children are taught these songs at Camp Winnarainbow, that they are in a sense passed from generation to generation, justifies my use of "folk" to suggest a music "of the people" in a contemporary oral tradition.
38. Black Oak Ranch is the name of the Hog Farm property in Laytonville where Camp Winnarainbow is held.

THE SHORT 60s

We wore white t-shirts with nothing on them. There was never anything on those t-shirts. Never anything. If you were creative, you rolled the sleeve of the t-shirt up. You know? Everyone wore 501 Levi jeans and hi-top Keds sneakers. That was the 50s. That was it, you know? You look at a tie-dyed shirt, you look at a white shirt. The white shirt was a decade of Dwight Eisenhower and everything for me—and then the tie-dyed shirt. And that was just like, yeah, ok, this is gonna be fun.

[Country Joe McDonald]

2. PRELUDE: *CITY SCALE*

> Whether we dig Instant Theater or not doesn't really matter. What matters is that San Francisco, with its Mime Troupe, Tape Music Center, Contemporary Dancers and far-out Happenings, is becoming an exciting creative playground as well as a cultural one.[1]

It is a hand-drawn "score," stretching across thirty-six inches of paper, outlining the main events in a six-hour "happening" that took place in San Francisco on March 9, 1963.[2] It has no absolute coordinates, street names, directions, tempos, or timing; stipulations for performance include "time: weekend night" and "full moon." It is site-specific, stretching out from the home of the San Francisco Tape Music Center at 1537 Jones Street. *City Scale* was conceived by Tape Music Center colleagues, composer Ramon Sender, playwright Ken Dewey, and visual artist Anthony Martin. Their intention was to utilize the environment around them for what Sender imagined "would sensitize the viewers, the audience, to look more carefully at everything" around them, and to play "with that sort of chaotic edge, that is between order and chaos. Isn't that where all the good stuff happens?"[3]

Both order and chaos were divided into clear sections: opening, development, return, then coda.

I. Audience arrives at the Tape Music Center, unaware of the evening's program. As they enter a small enclosure they are asked a simple question: "How do you get by?" Their answers, spoken into a microphone, are recorded on a machine in another space. Outside the enclosure are a number of suspended metallic objects, the sounds of which are recorded on another machine. The audience moves quickly into a larger space, where they are invited to draw or write or paint on the butcher paper hung on all the walls of the room. Finally, audience members tear paper into their own shape and are ushered out, passing "a taker of the shapes," described in the score as "a somewhat terrifying personage." The audience is directed toward one of two routes comprising the second section. Meanwhile, the composer begins preparing a sound collage from the recordings to play back at section III.

II. The events in section II should "appear quite natural and unprepared." The score is dotted with encircled numbers, each indicating an event that the audience witnesses: an undressing model; "a parked car, radio on, man eating celery"; two pairs of lovers, in two different places; a man and his wife in a convertible, stalled in a particular intersection, arguing. The audience moves to "an elevated view of city" for the reappearance of the Shape Taker. From this vantage point on Russian Hill the audience would overlook a "car ballet": in the North Beach grid below, cars move in a prearranged choreography. The audience would become gradually aware of this organized movement, as the cars, gels on their headlights, then "lined up in front of Coit Tower facing the audience; and . . . blinked their headlights with firecrackers going off in the bushes under [the audience]."[4] All the while, a "hidden but hearable" band is stationed in the nearby Broadway Tunnel.[5] In the transition to section III the audience walks past a soprano singing in a storefront window, wearing a dressing gown, her accompanist dressed in tails.

III. The audience reassembles at the Tape Music Center to hear a playback of the sound collage. Refreshments are served. The audience is then transported in two trucks, each with its own hostess, and driven to a desolate park where the audience inflates weather balloons. The vans take the audience to a number of specific sites: a coffee house, where the Shape Taker is again stationed; City Lights book store, where the audience "returns" books, "preferably in Arabic," handed to them en route; walks past the arguing couple; then proceeds to the nearby Wells Fargo Bank, where a movie is being projected onto the building's side wall. The celery man returns. And here begins the coda. On paper, the score fades into an impressionistic cityscape scribble with two indications: "a list of spots, places throughout the city is provided for either individual or small group journeys"; and more intriguingly, in much larger print, "THE EVENING SHOULD GET MORE AND MORE EXPLORATIVE." The piece ends at dawn.

City Scale was the final performance in a season that explored the relationships between audience and performer. Tony Martin described the work as an opportunity for people "to express themselves [and] to exchange feelings, thoughts, and expressions between each other."[6] Some "performers" in *City Scale* had no direct audience contact:[7] for the trombonist in the tunnel, the musicians in the shop window, the couple arguing in the car, their individual spaces were contextualized not by their surroundings, but by their actions. For the non-audience passersby—residential neighbors on Jones Street, the drivers of the cars in the tunnel, shoppers at City Lights—their spaces were utilized in a conventional sense, for their intended purpose. The encroachment of "theatre" into the everyday, into the otherwise normalized nocturnal environment of the city, necessitated a reimagining of the individual's place in the collective.

City Scale was one of many "happenings" in the early 1960s that blurred the lines between audience and performer, and acts as a symbolic opening of the "short 60s" in San Francisco. It was the first time Ramon Sender had encountered liquid light projections, which soon gave the experimental electronic music of the Tape Music Center a vital visual dimension. In a very short space of time, liquid lights, experimental music, and a dismantling of the fourth wall between "stage" and "audience" defined the new musical culture that coalesced in the city's ballrooms, a new soundtrack for this new creative playground. From this point onward, everything did indeed get "more and more explorative."

Notes

1. Merla Zellerbach, "The Meaning of What's Happening," *San Francisco Chronicle* April 4, 1964, p. 35.
2. The score for *City Scale* was published in *Tulane Drama Review* 10 (Winter 1965), and reproduced in Mariellen R. Sandford, ed., *Happenings and Other Acts* (London and New York: Routledge, 1995), pp. 142–50, and David Bernstein and John Rockwell, eds., *The San Francisco Tape Music Center: 1960s Counterculture and the Avant-Garde* (Berkeley: University of California Press, 2008).
3. Ramon Sender, quoted in Bernstein, *Tape Music Center*, p. 63.
4. Ibid.
5. On this particular night, trombonist Stuart Dempster: "There was a lot of traffic [in the tunnel], I remember, and there was that little kind of a sidewalk where you can walk along and do whatever I did. . . . I think I just . . .played with the echo and amused myself as I pretty much wished to." Stuart Dempster, quoted in Ibid., p. 255.
6. Tony Martin, quoted in Ibid., p. 153.
7. See Sender's introductory remarks to the score in Sandford, *Happenings*, p. 142.

3. INTO "THE 60s"

The year 1965 opened inauspiciously enough. On New Year's Day the San Francisco *Chronicle* published a report suggesting that there were 80 million "drinking Americans." It was an odd headline, considering the paper's increasing focus on the subterranean world of mind expansion and illicit drug use. Four months earlier the *Chronicle* had reported that Union Square "was filled, as usual, with pensioners, pigeons, evangelists, tourists, after-church strollers and marchers for marijuana."[1] This was the first event organized by Lemar ("Legalize Marijuana"), and was attended by about fifty "friends of marijuana" who defended their right to smoke the herb "in terms of civil liberties, health, beauty, freedom, morality and simple pleasure." The protesters stressed that the fear and hypocrisy surrounding marijuana were the result of a lack of education about the "wholesome" nature of the herb. And among the protesters interviewed for the *Chronicle* piece was Chet Helms, "a soft-spoken 22-year-old poet, [who] said laws against marijuana 'violate our Constitutional guarantee to the pursuit of happiness.'" When next Chet Helms was asked about the pursuit of his happiness it was another story altogether.

For a few years the *Chronicle*'s pages had been peppered with reports of the "new" era of drug experimentation, and efforts of the California state narcotics agents to stop it. These stories range from the quaint (Bicycle Benny's "special" cake delivery service[2]), to the considered (a mental health director defending the work of Timothy Leary's International Federation for Internal Freedom[3]), to the confessional (regular columnist Merla Zellerbach, who was convinced by Aldous Huxley to try LSD, much to her ultimate regret[4]), to the creepingly self-evident (news that San Francisco was soon to become the "pot heaven" of the West). The paper even offered an overview of the current market conditions:

> The SF marijuana market yesterday was quoting the following prices:
> One kilo (2-1/2 pounds) was going for $175 to $225. . . .
> A tobacco tin or "lid" . . . was selling for $20, while a pair of penny matchboxes filled with the stuff could be had for $5.
> A kilo can be rolled into more than 1000 cigarettes, enough to supply a man and his friends for a year.
> Most small sales of "the weed" are made among friends, with little or no profit.
> "There's more pot in the city now than there's been for years," declared one bearded devotee of the weed.[5]

A return to alcohol was actually almost quaint.

What the *Chronicle* somehow failed to notice, however, was the multicolored 1939 International Harvester School bus careening its way from rural La Honda to New York in June 1964, driven by Neal Cassady and filled with Ken Kesey's Band of Merry Pranksters.[6]

But there was more in the news than drugs. In December 1964 the *Chronicle*'s pages were consumed by the Free Speech Movement protests across the Bay in Berkeley,[7] and foreshadowed darker political currents ("New Support for Reagan as Governor"; "Gallup Poll: Most Americans Still Favor Draft");[8] meanwhile, the *Chronicle*'s Women's Pages ("Your Frigidity May Backfire"; "Where Did You Bury Your Femininity") were honored for their content. A magnified mixture of the social, cultural, and political was to be exploited in the years to come, as the *Chronicle*—and its underground complement—sought sense in it all.

The clearest indications that there were changes afoot came in *Chronicle* jazz critic Ralph Gleason's regular column. Gleason's ear for the musical, and eye for the sartorial, noted every modulation, every progression in jazz and popular music from his first *Chronicle* column in 1950 to his death in 1975.[9] His columns provide snapshots of San Francisco's nightclubs and city streets at crucial points in her countercultural history, and frequently espouse a political viewpoint more aligned against the establishment than with it.

In early 1964 Gleason bemoaned the creeping loss of the vibrant North Beach club scene, seeing every bar competing for a place in the "brawling, chintzy, tinseled collection of G-string parlors" in what had been a local jazz scene to rival that of 52nd street in New York.[10] The club names that pepper Gleason's 1960s columns—Enrico's,

3.1 Ralph Gleason in the newsroom.

the Jazz Workshop, the hungry i—evoke a moment of transition between eras, from the Beats to the hippies, from political comedy and jazz to psychedelia, and his wry commentary on the people of San Francisco suggest a deep and abiding love for the city and its local color:

> The . . . best show is free these days. It's the crowd on the sidewalk.
> Sit in Enrico's and watch them. It's fabulous. The other night, blindly butting his way through the mob, came a little old man in Bermuda shorts, his gnarled knees pumping away. He had his head deep in a newspaper held out before him, oblivious of the crowd. It was a copy of Pravda.
> Better show than in most of the clubs THAT night anyway.[11]

Earlier in that same column he suggested that "it won't be long before somebody gets smart enough to open up a good club somewhere else and prove it will work." Gleason was there when this was realized in 1965; but in 1964 the greater story of imminent cultural change was happening across the San Francisco Bay.

> In the face of a university which abandoned its nerve center to armed police, on the first university campus outside Mississippi to be taken over by the cops . . ., in the face of a torrent of apoplectic outrage from the elders of the tribe who felt their positions threatened, this generation has stood up and continued to speak plainly of truth.
> "When you go in, go with love in your heart," Joan Baez said. Those words, and Mario [Savio]'s eloquent speech, remain the only rhetoric of these ten weeks that history will remember. Literature, poetry and history are not made by a smooth jowl and a blue suit. They are made with sweat and passion and dedication to truth and honor.[12]

For Gleason, the Free Speech Movement highlighted a fundamental generational divide wherein the alternatives to mainstream thought, from Lenny Bruce to Ken Kesey to residents of the Haight-Ashbury, were demonized.

Berkeley was a magnet for radical and progressive politics, and San Francisco State College was also quietly attracting "an ever-increasing number of misfit exiles from staider institutions." This was the formative ground for the nascent hippie culture:

> Informed participators, rather than bookbound scholars, they became a large enough minority to earn for the college the reputation of a "swinging campus." Perhaps because, for nearly a decade, there was no continuous leadership from on top . . . diversity flourished. The effect on the student body, and on the surrounding city, was all to the good: probing eccentricity, responsible dissent, and individual creativity emerged as possible alternatives to the intellectual passivity of the fifties.[13]

What was now emerging was one in a line of many transitions, a new emergent pattern greeted by mainstream society at first with fear, then skepticism, then acceptance; co-opted, then jettisoned in time for the next wave of fear, skepticism, and acceptance. In 1958 the Beat generation became simply "beatniks" when *Chronicle* columnist Herb Caen's playful descriptor became shorthand not for the poetic agents of the San Francisco Renaissance, but for the "bearded cats and kits" who flocked around them.[14] The beatnik was not *On the Road*, or eulogized in *Howl*; the beatnik was now a caricature, dressed in black, sitting in a smoky coffee house, snapping along to jazz. In 1964, when the *Chronicle*'s Question Man wandered through North Beach asking "What Ever Became of the Beatniks?" he was told "they've gone to Big Sur," "they just faded away," "most of them flipped to Mendocino," and "they have been obliterated by the altered perceptions of the masses and the critics whose narrow views created them in the first place. They are now on another level of figmentation."[15] As it turned out, some of them just traded their berets for beads and headed on over to Haight Street.

Gleason often expressed a musical taste at variance with the mainstream. A weekend at the Monterey Folk Festival led him to state that "folk music IS dull,"[16] but for local musicians the scene was far more vivid:

> TERESA TUDURY: There was this funny little coffee house in Burlingame—one of those American, cocktail party, suburban places. And these musicians were showing up from all over the Bay Area: singer-songwriters and guitar players, people who could play Travis Pick. I started to play there, then would sneak up to San Francisco as a kid [age 14 in 1964], looking for people there to emulate and learn from. The places that were happening in North Beach were the hungry i, the Purple Onion, Enrico's, the Coffee Gallery, a lot of places to play, a lot of places to hang, a lot of open mics and hootenannies. It seemed that there was a congruent consistent aesthetic of the tall, lanky guy in the Pendleton shirt and Levis playing incredible old Martin guitar. Sometimes people were paired off, and the songs would come from all over the country. A lot of bluegrass. And these guys that used to hang out at the Coffee Gallery, old Wobblies, would get up and sing and play.[17] A lot of harmonicas, banjo players, and just pickers everywhere. Then by 1965 I got into a folk-rock band called The All-Night Apothecary.

That shift in 1964–65 from bluegrass to folk-rock reflects the bigger cultural shifts—from the Peninsula to the city, beats to hippies, politics to psychedelia, underground to overground—that hinged on a sleepy western neighborhood out by Golden Gate Park.

Notes

1. Robert Graham, "S.F. Dope Parade: The Far-Out Protest," *San Francisco Chronicle* [hereafter *Chronicle*], August 31, 1964, p. 1.

2. "[When Benny] was slicing up his latest batch of goodies, the agents nabbed him. They found three pounds of marijuana, seven capsules of peyote and two books on drug addiction in his apartment." "The Dope Pedaler," *Chronicle*, May 25, 1963, p. 1.

3. As the paper explained, "The furor revolves around a drug called LSD, which induced hallucinations and has been termed extremely dangerous. It has also been used experimentally to produce symptoms that mimic extreme forms of mental illness." Dr. Joseph J. Downing defended the controlled experimental use of LSD, though admitted that Leary "has something of a messianic feeling about [LSD] and believes the drug should be generally available." But Leary and his colleagues "are dedicated and able people who are convinced . . . that that this LSD experience can have a major potential for positively influencing human behavior. They are not charlatans." "Hallucination Drug Research," *Chronicle*, July 3, 1963, p. 22.

4. In her regular column, "My Fair City," Merla Zellerbach covered cultural and society events. LSD was an issue which she approached initially with some detachment, publishing letters from readers contradicting her position ("LSD cured my migraines"; "LSD cured me of my homosexuality"; "I found God through LSD"), then finally "outing" herself in the column quoted here as a one-time experimenter. It was clearly not an illuminating experience: her LSD-induced hallucinations were "about as rapturous as seeing a string of scenic postcards. Being 'far out' meant losing consciousness, and having 'increased perception' meant having so many disconnected thoughts that nothing registered." Worse yet, "[the] after-effects of the drug were equally potent. It took 24 hours for my skin to lose its reddish cast, three days for my appetite to return. Colors jumped at me from everywhere and for weeks, a doorbell or a telephone would ring like an alarm clock in my brain." See Merla Zellerbach, "The Toxic Side of Reality—LSD," *Chronicle*, September 27, 1963, p. 39.

5. Birney Jarvis, "It's Easy in S.F.: Big Marijuana Kick," *Chronicle*, August 29, 1964, p. 1.

6. For a thorough, if idiosyncratic, series of recollections of the Pranksters' cross-country trip, see Paul Perry, *On the Bus: The Complete Guide to the Legendary Trip of Ken Kesey and the Merry Pranksters and the Birth of the Counterculture* (London: Plexus, 1990). *Magic Trip* (Magnolia Pictures, 2013, dir. Allison Elwood and Alex Gibney), drawn from documentary footage of this trip, is a revealing and important resource for both contemporary cultural context and firsthand recollection of the Merry Pranksters' 1964 adventures.

7. "The Faculty 'Revolts': UC's War Spreading," December 4, 1964. For more information on the chronology of the Free Speech Movement, see its Digital Archive at the Bancroft Library of the University of California, Berkeley: http://bancroft.berkeley.edu/FSM/index.html.

8. On December 2, there was a brief notice that Ronald Reagan was gaging public interest in his potential run for governor. "New Support for Reagan as Governor," December 17. The Vietnam War was kept out of the headlines during the Free Speech Movement, though the statement that "Most Americans Still Favor Draft" (December 26) was soon challenged by the editorial, "Why We're Losing Vietnam" (January 10, 1965, p. 13).

9. Gleason was a full-time critic for the *Chronicle*, publishing five columns a week and occasional features until 1970, when he began contributing only a weekly Sunday piece. While still writing his "Perspectives" column in *Rolling Stone*, he began working for Fantasy Records in Berkeley, which at that point was busy promoting its hottest act, Creedence Clearwater Revival; his position there was "Minister Without Portfolio."

For a sense of his influence and importance, local and national, see "Ralph Gleason in Perspective," *Rolling Stone* 191, July 17, 1975, pp. 38–49 and Don Armstrong and Jessica Armstrong, "Dispatches from the Front: The Life and Writings of Ralph J. Gleason," *Rock Music Studies* 1/1 (2014): 3–34.

10. See Ralph J. Gleason [hereafter RJG], "A Creeping Case of Rock 'n' Roll," *Chronicle*, April 22, 1964, p. 47. The title might suggest that Gleason was not a fan of the "new" music, but his complaint was with the "bad imitations of good rock 'n roll performers and some of the worst local performers you can find." It is as much an indictment of the commercialization of North Beach as of the lack of a viable, organic, alternative.

11. Ibid.

12. RJG, "The Tragedy at the Greek Theater," *Chronicle*, December 9, 1964, p. 49.

13. Leonard Wolf, *Voices from the Love Generation* (Boston and Toronto: Little, Brown, 1968), p. xix.

14. See Herb Caen, "Pocketful of Notes," *Chronicle,* April 2, 1958. For background, see Michael Davidson, *The San Francisco Renaissance: Poetics and Community at Mid-Century* (Cambridge: Cambridge University Press, 1989).

15. O'Hara, "Question Man: What Ever Became of the Beatniks?," *Chronicle*, July 17, 1964, p. 34.

16. And he continued: "For if there is one thing the weekend demonstrated, it is a trend toward adulation of Appalachian music, with a dash of cowboy and a dash of blues. A sort of Grand Ole Opry, Saturday night fish fry, basically monotonous, conforming to rigid standards of antiquarianism and producing, except for rare instances, no performers with a genuine electric quality and high emotional communication. It's the cult of the primitive, the sublimation of big city anxieties in ersatz rural dress, behavior, accent and songs. A substitute for reality." See "The Boredom of Folk Music," *Chronicle*, May 21, 1963, p. 37.

17. Wobblies were members of the Industrial Workers of the World, the radical labor union founded in Chicago in 1905.

4. 1965

Yes, it is true that we have an opera, a ballet, a symphony, North Beach, beatnik Haight-Ashbury, jazz, Golden Gate Park, museums, private galleries, and an intellectually aware citizenry. In fact, we have more than that. We have chauvinism. This is the City with an ego. Surely, as long as metropolitan patriotism flourishes, San Francisco shall not enter a dark age. But avoiding a dark age is not the same as carrying the torch and leading the way towards the 21st Century.[1]

And what with the plethora of new rock groups cooking away all over the place, San Francisco may really become the Liverpool of America as well as one of the most important cities in the jazz world.[2]

There is nothing inherently magical about the year 1965. There was no enormous upheaval or political crisis, no revolution to upend the establishment. There were just quiet ripples set in motion on the outskirts of the city, gentle signals of bigger changes to come; a slow circulation of the cultural waters, from La Honda, to Virginia City, to Santa Cruz, to the Marina, to the Mission, spiraling toward an epicenter somewhere around the corner of Haight and Ashbury streets.

What was happening at the beginning of 1965 was a marking of new territory in the center of San Francisco's cultural life, mapping the coordinates to uncharted experiences. Ravi Shankar performed at the Masonic Auditorium on January 23, and the reviewer, quite unaccustomed to the sound of Indian classical music, noted the sitar's "remarkable characteristic [of] sustained resonance," effecting "quietude and passivity, as if one's blood flowed slower than usual and one's perceptivity were not numbed but attuned to more distant wave lengths than those of which one is usually aware."[3] This is not the type of language normally found in contemporary *Chronicle* music reviews, but it is the type of language found in personal recollections of psychedelic awakening. Yet the *Chronicle*'s regular depictions of "otherness," whether cultural, spiritual, or pharmacological, were generally less forgiving. And they were not alone in reporting that the nation's youth were being led astray: the *New York Times* syndicated an account of a promising young student at the Juilliard School of Music, of all places, "representative of the increasing number of young people from . . . the sophisticated and the educated families of the city and its suburbs who are using marijuana, barbiturates and addictive narcotics," whose sullied innocence was meant to act as a warning to upstanding families across the nation.[4]

Closer to home, the New Age Community Church, "otherwise known as the salvation of the North Beach beatnik,"[5] had for some months been the target of unwanted press attention and in January 1965 faced closure by the San Francisco Health Department. In its report of a marriage ceremony performed at the church's Last Exit Coffee House on 355 Broadway the *Chronicle* noted that the presiding clergyman intoned: "Here we have no theocracy—only the sharing of the love that is in all mankind."[6] The simplicity of that message would soon be a central tenet of the local lifestyle, but here it was reported cynically in juxtaposition with the image of the congregation, "drawn from the bearded and sandled ranks of North Beach bohemia." From this distance, it is clearly a vision of rites to come rather than an insidious dismantling of Christian tradition. Because not far away, at Big Sur Hot Springs, a public seminar was being advertised that would explore "ways in which the psychodelic [sic] drugs may be used in conjunction with meditation, sensory awareness, Gestalt therapy, encounter groups and other methods of psychological growth."[7]

Esalen was established in 1963 as a space to explore human potential, and to counter the conservatism of mainstream 1950s America in all its social and religious manifestations.[8] The Eastern philosophical and spiritual traditions that underpinned Esalen's founding were also an important component of the local counterculture, just not yet common currency to the readers of the *Chronicle*. Indeed, when columnist Merla Zellerbach went to Big Sur looking for beatniks in April 1965 she found an indefinable group.[9] When finally she put a label on them it was to bemoan their lack of respect for American institutions:

> The hip ones belong to a cult of pseudo-rebels who embrace Pop Art because it scorns such sacred American institutions as cowboys and Campbell's soup.... The hipsters' main delight is demolishing symbols: "The eagle's not a bold, brave bird, it's a vicious, predatory creature...." The hippies may demolish us all.[10]

This is perhaps the first use of the term "hippie" in the *Chronicle*,[11] but it is also merely a continued reaction against what most people still assumed were beatniks. Zellerbach was not the only one to notice a general disregard for established social mores: the San Francisco Mime Troupe's production of *Candelaio* received much negative press in 1965 for its use of "objectionable" language. Though street theatre was not a new artistic form, the Mime Troupe's cultural and political activism was a vital, if initially unwelcome, element of the city's new artistic community.[12]

The palpable tensions in the first half of 1965 between conservative mainstream society and the nascent counterculture were primarily expressed in the *Chronicle* via sensationalist reports of "intellectual programs" run by key figures in Esalen, and of local appearances by celebrity psychologists who attracted "North Beach types and earnest seekers-of-the-truth."[13] These were contrasted with reports of raids on the squalid apartments of LSD rings and drug kingpins, stories of innocent undergraduates slipping quickly from smoking marijuana to shooting heroin, and the efforts of law enforcement to maintain control. Some of the information relayed to the daily readership of the paper was perhaps exaggerated: in a raid on the narcotics ring labeled "The Swingers," officers discovered "marijuana in an urn and sugar cubes laced with LSD in a refrigerator." It was believed that the street value of the marijuana was $2,500—customers buying the marijuana would apparently roll their own joints and leave a dollar bill in the urn—and that the LSD-laced sugar cubes were sold for $50 each.[14]

LSD was legal in 1965, but the Federal Drug Agency branded it "a dangerous drug," a move criticized by academics and medical professionals who advocated increased research into its use and effects: at this point black market users of LSD "know more about certain aspects of it than the duly constituted authorities." Furthermore:

> The deleterious effects have been conclusively demonstrated from alcohol and tobacco, but we hold that the individual should be free to take the risk. The obvious irrationality of the reaction to the psychedelics offers a clue to the underlying psychodynamic process.[15]

These types of stories were published almost weekly, sharpening the distinctions between legal drugs such as nicotine and alcohol and the newer drugs that were increasingly being sought as a means of experiencing an amplified world. The scaremongering was occasionally tempered, as in the extended and considered exposé of Dr. Stanislav Grof, whose controlled use of LSD in psychiatric treatment acted "as a means to accelerate and intensify the psycho-therapeutic process."[16] Yet the paper's citation of academic insight into the psychological potential of hallucinogenic drugs was also deeply cynical: more frequently the paper relayed personal experiences of hallucinogenic drugs by naïve young students, the presumed "next generation" of academics.

In March 1965, Berkeley's student newspaper, the *Daily Californian*, published an extended rumination praising LSD as "a journey to heightened awareness and improved consciousness." This was intended to spark an open dialogue among readers, whose comments the *Daily Californian* would publish in future issues. American society had "lost its sense of wonder," and "to appear 'sane,' we grownups cannot smell the color of grass; we cannot wonder about the infiniteness of the universe; we cannot display our emotions in a public place." LSD provided adults with "an avenue, however temporary, which bypasses social structure."[17] Shortly after this story was published, the findings of a study conducted by a postgraduate at San Francisco State College showed that around 60 percent of the student population had tried illegal drugs—"mostly pep pills"—and that the number of student LSD users was growing monthly. The situation, according to the report, "is much worse in Berkeley."[18] These findings were duly corroborated elsewhere in the same issue by the head of the police narcotics bureau, who confirmed that "a serious marijuana problem exists in at least one San Francisco high school and possibly in several others."[19]

San Francisco and the Long 60s

When drug busts took place around the Bay Area's universities they served to engender fear among the "straight" readership of the *Chronicle*. In one example, a "Mr Big" told undercover agents that "all of [his] sales are on the [Cal] campus. That's the best place to do business." The paper helpfully listed the "drug-buying rendezvous at such places as the rear of the UC stadium at midnight, a bar near San Pablo and University avenues, and a rustic frame apartment house at 2528 Ellsworth Street." This latter location was the site for a transaction involving $600 and "144 small glass ampules of a drug known as DMT."[20] In the wake of this bust, officials at the University of California were quick to confirm that they had "been aware for several years that students on the Berkeley campus were taking drugs."[21] Berkeley had already become the byword for student activism and radical politics; the stories of a seedy underground drug culture only consolidated the image of a dirty East Bay in the minds of the *Chronicle*'s genteel readership.

There was also one very convenient scapegoat: Ken Kesey, arrested in April at his home in La Honda for drug possession. He and his friends had known they were under surveillance, and they told the *Chronicle* that any drugs found on the premises had been planted there by the police; the police countered that they found Kesey flushing marijuana down the toilet.[22] In a subsequent extended interview, Kesey showed a reporter bullet holes in the mailbox and in the hood of his pickup truck: evidence of the harassment he had experienced in his two years in La Honda. What bothered Kesey "more than anything is to be called a beatnik. I'm not a beatnik and neither are my friends. We're working, all of us."[23] Kesey and his friends were in fact working on a feature-length film based on their cross-country bus trip when the police arrested them.[24]

For over a year stories of Kesey's rise to literary fame and his subsequent fall appeared in the *Chronicle* as a multipart cautionary tale. Kesey's lawyers charged that the raid on the author's home was prompted by hearsay: the San Mateo Deputy Sheriff had not read either of Kesey's novels, but believed what he was told by "anonymous clerks at two bookstores he had phoned"—City Lights in San Francisco and Kepler's in Menlo Park—who suggested that *One Flew Over the Cuckoo's Nest* and *Sometimes a Great Notion* referred in some way to drug use.[25] Despite Kesey's insistence that he had neither advocated nor used drugs, the case was taken to trial at the end of the year. The very well-documented experiences that Kesey did have with LSD, and the very public events at which Kesey and his friends enjoyed it, nonetheless failed to filter down to the *Chronicle* readership. Any publicity about something called "an Acid Test" could easily have gone unnoticed.

The Acid Tests

[The Acid Tests were] one of the truly democratic art forms to appear in this century. The audience didn't come to see us, they came to experience something altogether different. So we had the luxury of being able to experiment freely in a situation which didn't require anything of us. It didn't require that we be good, it didn't require that we repeat a song, it didn't require that we be intelligible on any level. I mean, for a musician, that's like *carte blanche*, you know. That was great fun. But that Acid Test experience gave us glimpses into the form that follows chaos. You know, that if you throw everything out, and lose all rules and stop trying to make anything happen on any level, other stuff starts to happen. And that became a key to the way we dealt in an interior way with our music.[26]

Ken Kesey and the Merry Pranksters returned to La Honda from their cross-country bus trip in the summer of 1964. To keep the trip alive, the La Honda house became the spot for weekend Prankster parties. As more and more people began gravitating to La Honda, they attracted the attention first of the police, who raided the house in April 1965, and then the Hell's Angels, who enjoyed a fabled weekend visit there in August 1965. The mixture of the Angels and the Pranksters also piqued the interest of the police:

The cops stood out on the highway and looked across the creek at a scene that must have tortured the very roots of their understanding. Here were all these people running wild, bellowing and dancing half naked to rock-'n'-roll sounds piped out through the trees from massive amplifiers, reeling and stumbling in a maze of psychedelic lights . . . WILD, by God, and with no law to stop them.

Then, with the arrival of the Hell's Angels, the cops finally got a handle—a *raison d'être*, as it were—and they quickly tripled the guard. Kesey had finally gone over the line. A bunch of beatniks and college types eating some kind of invisible drug was a hard thing to deal with, but a gang of rotten thugs on motorcycles was as tangible a menace as the law could hope for.[27]

Kesey ultimately decided that the parties should move off his property, and suggested that they meet somewhere else: at Ken Babbs' "spread," down the coast in Santa Cruz.[28] They advertised the party cryptically, inviting their friends to The Acid Test on Saturday, November 27, 1965, 7 p.m., featuring The Warlocks.

The "uncontrolled chaos" that ensued was too much for Babbs, so the Acid Tests became a movable party: San Jose, Mountain View, Muir Beach, inching closer and closer to the straight society around them. Though some Acid Tests were held in rural spots in 1965, they were never very far from suburban neighborhoods.

CHARLES JOHNSON: I would hear rumblings every now and then from the parties that I attended on the Peninsula—all that stuff was going on two or three miles from where I grew up. It was just a passing frenzy that was going on in the hills behind us, and I didn't know what was going on there until I got introduced to these people further along in my life.

Tom Wolfe's novelized account of the Acid Tests is vibrant with detail, and his efforts as an outsider to understand the idea of an Acid Test reveal the artistic sensibilities of the mid-1960s Bay Area:

> [Kesey] talked about something called the Acid Test and forms of expression in which there would be no separation between himself and the audience. It would be all one experience, with all the senses opened wide, words, music, lights, sounds, touch—lightning.
> "You mean on the order of what Andy Warhol is doing?" I said.
> . . . pause. "No offense," says Kesey, "but New York is about two years behind."
> He said it very patiently, with a kind of country politeness, as if . . . I don't want to be rude to you fellows from the City, but there's been things going on out here that you would never guess in your wildest million years, old buddy.[29]

It was "all one experience": a band may have been playing, but so was everyone else in the room. There was no absolute focus for audience attention; actions simply begat reactions. And senses were "opened wide." There was free and unrestricted use of LSD, and the sonic revelry that had soundtracked the Pranksters' bus trip. There was freedom in the moment.

When the Warlocks joined that first Acid Test in Santa Cruz, they were not there to perform in any conventional sense of the word; they were there to react to the movement around them, to play off the energy that the room was radiating. This would have required fairly astute sensitivity and an innate understanding of musical sense. Not logic; sense. Acid was the common ingredient that enabled the inter-band telepathy that ultimately defined the Grateful Dead's performing style, though in the moment it might not have been clear exactly what was happening:

> Entering, we find ourselves in darkness, relieved only by the blinding flashes of strobe lights (carefully timed to be out of sync with one another and the music). What seems like several hundred people are variously milling about, dancing strenuously, or puddled in the corners, against the walls, and on the floor, all clad in colorful and exotic clothing. . . . Several projection screens are showing vastly different sequences of images, film clips, or full-color quasi-protoplasmic blobs moving in time (or not) to the music. The music itself is manifesting not from silence, but from a bed of ambient sound created by . . . Möbius loops of microphones and speakers, and is enhanced by interjections of what we called "Prankster music"— loud, incomprehensible, jagged, and not exactly lyrical—and punctuated by shrieks, moans, expostulations, cries, murmurs, and laughter emitted spontaneously by the assembled freaks.[30]

Not everyone who assembled at an Acid Test was necessarily a freak, but an Acid Test experience would surely have been transformative.

> Art Rogers: All these throbbing things—you know, you're trying to make sense out of it. And I think what happened is, you just want to try and relax and go with it and let it be what it was, and then you got it. So it's just a bunch of people making crazy noises, making music—look what I can do with this guitar!—doing lights, having colors, jumping up and down, one big throbbing room, and not worrying about being threatened or hurt, you know? I always felt safe. Now, I was a naïve kid, too, but I felt safe.

The Muir Beach Acid Test on December 11, 1965 was notable for appearances by two people: Hugh Romney, then involved with The Committee in Berkeley and soon to become Wavy Gravy, and Owsley Stanley, the elusive "Acid King." By all accounts it was a wild night but it was also Kesey's last Acid Test.[31] Kesey would fake his suicide and disappear to Mexico,[32] and Ken Babbs and the Pranksters took the bus down to Southern California to hold Acid Tests there, landing at Wavy Gravy's rented cabin in Sunland en route. His landlord summarily evicted them, so Wavy Gravy and his friends moved to a nearby farm to slop hogs in exchange for rent: an ideal spot to set up a commune.[33]

Wavy Gravy's experiences at the Acid Tests in northern and southern California provide an important counterpoint:

> Wavy Gravy: You know, Kesey and I kind of had a falling-out. I was not necessarily in favor of giving people psychotropics when they were not expecting it, although at that point, who wasn't? Duh! We put together the Hog Farm and Friends: an open celebration, where we did not supply the stuff.[34] You had to bring your own head, and we supplied a palette, where the audience becomes the star of the show, which is part of what the Acid Test was about also.

Ultimately, what the Acid Tests were about, and the "format" they designed—"sensual immediacy," turning people "inside out into the moment"[35]—morphed in 1966 into the Trips Festival and onward into the regular dance concerts around the city. And Kesey, Wavy Gravy, and Owsley continued to orbit lysergically around some of the "more and more explorative" events of the short 60s.

**

Amid the sensationalism there was still the fact that an untold number of people in the Bay Area were simply looking for something *more*. Some people felt it inwardly; others showed it outwardly. Some found it close to home; some found it in Esalen:

> "One of the key aspects of the program," [says Esalen founder Michael Murphy], "is the teaching of sensory perception—being more alert in observing, seeing,

feeling . . . learning to dilate the mind as an eye doctor dilates a pupil so it will see more; and hence be more interested in what it beholds." . . .

And the music programs which vary from Asiatic dances to the folk singing of Joan Baez? Here the aim is to re-awaken the sense of hearing with new and vivid experiences. "Music develops a kind of sensitivity as it requires concentration in a language of its own," says Murphy.[36]

This idea of heightened sensory perception and the "vivid experience" of music were central to the Acid Tests, and became a fundamental element of the new expressive culture emerging in San Francisco. Ralph Gleason understood this, and wrote about contemporary music in its urgent social contexts. After one May weekend he drew a beautiful and radical parallel between spirituality and political action, in reviewing local jazz pianist Vince Guaraldi's improvisational Choral Eucharist at Grace Cathedral and Norman Mailer's speech at the Vietnam Day Protest in Berkeley: "Both were concerned with truth, both with salvation and both with the link between the here and now and posterity."[37] The "here and now" was a singular dimension at the Acid Tests, and Gleason saw that the need to live authentically in the moment was a guiding principle of the new hip community.

Political activism in the Bay Area was the purview of the *Berkeley Barb*, which published its first issue on August 13, 1965. The imminent Vietnam Day Committee's march through Oakland was the source of some anxiety, as the Hell's Angels had threatened to counter-demonstrate against what they perceived as an "un-American" protest. Allen Ginsberg's two-hour public debate with a representative of the Angels on the right to protest was reported in the *Barb* with due seriousness; by contrast, the *Chronicle*'s report began with the image of Ginsberg "ringing a tiny silver Buddhist bell and chanting a prayer for five minutes 'to protect everybody from evil.'"

> [Finally], asked what his VDC marchers would do if they were attacked by the cyclists during the November 20 march, [Jerry] Rubin had this simple answer:
> "If we're attacked, all we're going to do is bleed."
> Ginsberg added his comment: "The big problem for us now is how we can start to groove with the Hell's Angels instead of getting into fights with them."[38]

The *Barb* printed Ginsberg's lengthy list of suggested activities for "turning marchers onto their roles." He felt the demonstration could become a happening: "masses of flowers," musical instruments and children's toys available "to distract attackers," opportunities for "sit down, mass calisthenics" to alleviate the stress of conflict, members of the San Francisco Mime Troupe dressed in full costume, San Francisco bands transported on sound trucks along the parade route, and "an imaginary Ladies Corps to pull down Hell's Angels Pants" and "a (theoretical) Corps of Trained Fairies to Seduce them in Mid-Battle."[39]

The Hell's Angels ultimately decided not to prevent the Vietnam Day Committee's march through Oakland:

> "Although we have stated our intention to counter-demonstrate at this despicable, un-American activity, we believe that in the interest of public safety and protection of the good name of Oakland, we should not justify the VDC by our presence."
>
> Asked what they would do instead, [President Ralph (Sonny)] Barger replied:
>
> "Probably what we'd do on an ordinary Saturday—go to the bar and drink a few suds."[40]

The *Barb* offered a platform for alternative political viewpoints, but its first issue also coincided with an event that marked the emergence of a new musical scene in San Francisco: the opening of the Matrix nightclub.

The Matrix

> The twang of folk song in SF has, in the past, been largely limited to accompanying the gurgle of grubby espresso machines, poetry mouthing and do-it-yourself insurrection plots.
>
> But with the recent opening of the Matrix at 3138 Fillmore, all that is changed. [The] Matrix is almost exclusively dedicated to music, both from the listener's and the performer's standpoint. The club is presently featuring a new group called the Jefferson Airplane Thursday through Saturday, and a variety of supporting performers.[41]

> The club is rather like the old Tin Angel. Blues singer J.C. Burris and other performers share the stage and the different night's programs with The Jefferson Airplane, and the young crowd is sophisticated and hip. It's a shame there isn't dancing, but in SF's archaic manner of handling this sort of thing, it's hard to get a dance permit.... There's a modest door charge and the atmosphere is groovy.[42]

The Matrix opened for business on Friday, August 13, 1965. Musician-artist Marty Balin saw the site's potential as a new kind of club, and convinced three investors to pay $3,000 each for a shared interest in the business in partnership with his new band, the Jefferson Airplane.[43] Earlier in the year Balin began auditioning musicians who he felt would help him appeal to young people more than the long-standing local folk scene did. No one seemed sure what to call this new kind of music; Balin called it "social blues," but John Wasserman described it as

> not folk music, nor blues, nor rock 'n roll, yet there is something of all these forms in the Airplane's sound. Elements of Bob Dylan, the Byrds, the topical,

"White" urban blues all assert themselves at one time or another and, although there are but hints at this time, it is entirely possible that this will be the new direction of contemporary American pop music.[44]

Ralph Gleason's understanding of the group's sound was that it was "not really a rock 'n roll group. Few are any longer. It's a contemporary-popular-music-folk-rock unit and we have no less cumbersome phrase to use so far."[45] The music would attract other, easier descriptors within the year.

The act of building an environment around this new music had been a fundamental feature of local underground musical life since the Acid Tests, and the merging of music and solid space in a northern corner of the city was a definitive step toward establishing an overground locus for the performance and consumption of this new sound. Balin's idea for the Matrix was to situate his music amid political folk and comedy in the same way that clubs in North Beach operated. But unlike clubs such as the hungry i, Balin designed the Matrix "from the stage out, with performers in mind."[46] It featured Balin's own paintings and an enormous collage wall—immortalized as the background of the cover photo for the Airplane's 1967 album *Surrealistic Pillow*—and a simple divided floor plan: the bar along one side of the room, a railing separating a split-level arrangement of tables at the far end of the room, and the performers' dressing room behind that. There was a sound and light booth suspended above the entrance, and in an act of providing optimistically for posterity, most of the shows at the Matrix were recorded.

The Matrix was built around the Jefferson Airplane, and though they played there most weeks in the last months of 1965, they also opened their doors to blues musicians and to local bands Quicksilver Messenger Service, the Charlatans, and the Grateful Dead. The opportunity for a band to play a weekend or weeklong residency in the same club meant not only building name recognition and a local audience, but fine-tuning their live show in one hall, with the same engineers and room acoustic, working toward a much more polished performance by the end of the run.[47] This was an important developmental step for local rock music.

The Matrix met the same fate as many of the ballrooms in San Francisco—a club located in a residential neighborhood, with a lack of adequate soundproofing and an increasingly electrified rotation of artists would always attract unwanted attention from the city's law enforcement—but in its first few years it marked radical new cultural territory. As Ralph Gleason remarked, "Something is going on here in the popular music field which bears watching,"[48] and from this point onward his gaze turned almost exclusively to the new San Francisco rock sound.

Though the opening of the Matrix was welcomed by the *Chronicle* critics, they seemed unaware of the musical scene that was slowly being transplanted from Virginia City back to the city. And it was in the sleepy Virginia City that the real innovation had been happening all along.

The Red Dog Saloon

> RUSTY GOLDMAN: It's about the beginning. It's about how the San Francisco ballroom scene began, how a feller by the name of Mark Unobsky, who inherited a lot of money from daddy, wanted to open a cowboy bar up in Virginia City. They were playing some board game high on acid and he had this epiphany to open this cowboy dancehall in Virginia City.[49] So they went up there, secured the Red Dog Saloon, and rebuilt it. They had a group of people who would come back and forth from San Francisco to Virginia City. Sometimes they were paid in guns; sometimes they were paid in weed. There was a kitchen. There was a group of people who were the founding fathers and mothers of the San Francisco ballroom scene where people didn't just go and listen to music, but actually got up and danced. And it was wonderful. It was something new, a renaissance. And it was revolutionary.

Virginia City is nestled in the hills north of Carson City and south of Reno, right on top of the Comstock Lode in Nevada. It was the most important city west of Chicago during its silver mining boom years: in its heyday, around 1874, the population of Virginia City reached about 25,000. By the turn of the century most had moved away, and in 1961 it was declared a National Historic Landmark—not the most obvious pilgrimage site for a crowd of prototypical hippies looking for a good night of live music.

But San Francisco was also once a frontier town: it owes its existence to the Gold Rush and the spirit of individual freedom. Out in the Haight, an area that grew between the Gold Rush (1849) and the Great Earthquake (1906) from sand dunes to Queen Anne houses, the romance of the neighborhood's nineteenth-century past leaned itself naturally to a certain time-travel.[50] An architecture student named George Hunter had been hanging around the neighborhood long enough to know the power of an image. He formed a band called The Charlatans that would cultivate a "look" steeped in the Old West: distinctly San Franciscan, not based on the still-fashionable British Invasion model.[51]

Charlatan Mike Ferguson worked at The Magic Theatre for Madmen Only on Divisadero Street, a head shop/vintage clothes/antiques boutique that had opened in 1964. Chandler Laughlin, a regular shopper, bought curtains and antiques and occasionally weed from The Magic Theatre to furnish a new saloon he was helping set up in Virginia City. The Charlatans, now managed by Phil Hammond, had attended to every detail of their look without actually bothering to master their instruments or book a gig. Hammond traveled to Virginia City with Bill Ham, an artist who was hoping to sell a new light machine to Mark Unobsky,[52] and before long all the key ingredients were in place for the opening night at the Red Dog Saloon.

> ALBERT NEIMAN: It was a cowboy bar but they were tired of shit-kickin' music, you know. So Michael Ferguson and George Hunter produced a poster for June 21, 1965. Unfortunately the band wasn't quite ready, so they did another poster and changed the date. It's called the Seed, and it's considered the first psychedelic rock poster.

4.1 The Seed: The Charlatans at the Red Dog Saloon.

The saloon had plenty of period musical details as well.

> WILLIAM MAGINNIS: There was a piano there like the one that Irving Berlin had. He could only play I think in the key of C or something, so this piano had a gear shift on it: he could play in C and then just shift this thing and it would come up in F Sharp or whatever.[53]

The Saloon may have been ready for raucous honky-tonk piano and can-can dancers, and the Red Dog owners may have been expecting the acoustic folk of the San Francisco coffee houses, but the music that the Charlatans played—"1920s country-folk music with something done to it"[54]—was electric and got everyone dancing.[55]

Whereas in the days of the Old West a big night at the Saloon might have meant drinking the bar dry and maybe a gunfight or two, the young freaks who gathered at the Red Dog were stoned, not drunk. As concert promoters in San Francisco soon discovered, the liquid refreshment in demand at rock concerts was not alcoholic, but rather revivifying. Things had changed.

For three summers the Red Dog drew Bay Area freaks and the locals. More importantly, it inspired the nascent San Francisco dancehall scene:

> 'Cause after the gigs at the Red Dog Saloon, we all came back to the city, and there was nothing to do. So myself and Luria Castell and Ellen Harmon and Jack Towle [calling themselves the Family Dog] got together and said, "Let's see if we can throw some dances down here".[56]

The people who had thrown together the first night at the Red Dog Saloon saw the scene progress, but it came as a shock to the young people of San Francisco who had not been to Virginia City that summer:

> LIANNE GRAVES: In the summer of '65, The Charlatans played at the College of Marin and myself and two of my girlfriends went. It was like, "wow, this is not our mother's music. This is not the way, you know, people look. This is great." And that just led us into the Haight-Ashbury.

From the Red Dog to the Haight, the most important element was community:

> ALBERT NEIMAN: It wasn't like dances in the past, which were more like concerts, and there was a wall between the musicians and the audience. It was them and us. But with the Red Dog Saloon and with the Family Dog, it was just us.

Meanwhile, something had been happening on the streets of San Francisco:

> SAM ANDREW: I was walking down Page Street, and really admiring this beautiful Victorian mansion, when I heard this guitar coming out of a window

high above. I went and shoved the door open—this is the 60s, and everybody was young; I don't think you would do that today—and shoved the door open and walked to the top of the stairs, and there was Peter Albin. And I said hey, do you want to form a band? And he said no, or uh-uh, or something, he backed up right away, which he does to this day. But we started playing in the basement of that mansion, which had a proscenium arch. It was really beautiful. That's in 1965, in the spring. And we started playing in that basement, and people started coming by. The Haight was a working-class neighborhood, so just a lot of really disparate people—there were students and black people and plastic people and beach bums and all kinds of people, really a mix. They were curious. And our friend Chet Helms came by and he said, there's just getting to be too many people here. Let's keep the riff-raff out, so let's start charging admission. Let's charge 50 cents. And then we made up a poster—but it backfired; it made everybody come. And Chet went hmmmm. . . . So those were the first rock concerts.

By October 1965 Ralph Gleason was reporting regularly on the emerging rock scene. One wild weekend in particular he began at the protest marches in Berkeley, attended by Kesey and his Pranksters, featuring poets Lawrence Ferlinghetti, Robert Duncan, Michael McClure, and Allen Ginsberg, and ended at the Longshoremen's Hall:

The Family Dog, a group of people organized to present rock 'n roll dances and concerts . . . presented a hippy happening . . . which was delightful and signified the linkage of the political and social hip movements. SNCC buttons and peace buttons abounded, stuck onto costumes straight out of the Museum of Natural History. Russ Syracuse of KYA was the emcee and the evening was a "Tribute to Dr. Strange" of comic book fame.

The crowd danced all night long to a succession of rock bands—The Great Society, The Marbles, The Charlatans . . . and the Jefferson airplane [sic]. I mean they danced. The bar did no business and the coke machine ran out. That's where it was at. Long lines of dancers soaked through the crowd for hours, holding hands. Free-form improvisation ("self expression") was everywhere. The clothes were a blast. Like a giant costume party.

They all seemed to be cued into Frontier Days and ranged from velvet Lottie Crabtree to Mining Camp Desperado, Jean la Fitte leotards, I. Magnin Beatnik, Riverboat Gambler, India Imports Exotic and Modified Motorcycle Rider Black Leather-and-Zippers, alongside Buckskin Brown.

It was a gorgeous sight. The lights played over the floor, the bands wailed out their electronic music, and the audience had a blast! One spectator danced by himself at the edge of the bandstand. . . .

4.2 Bill Graham in the Mime Troupe office.

> The dances were variations on everything of the past decade: the Hitch-Hike, the Jerk, the Dog, the Hully Gully, all improved on and individually performed for self-expression.
>
> Dixieland trumpet player Bob Scobey once said that dancing was "only an excuse to get next to a broad." Since the New Morality supplies that need elsewhere, the dance floor is no longer the scene of the sexual expression it was. Now it is becoming a training ground for the free-est [sic] generation this country has seen and they dance beautifully.[57]

A few days later Gleason published an interview with Family Dog member Luria Castell, who said that "San Francisco can be the new Liverpool."[58] The potential was manifestly there: an excited audience, the Acid Test template, the Red Dog experience, the Matrix, the Family Dog. Perhaps the scene would have coalesced without a formal structure, but the accidental introduction into the mix of a canny and driven businessman formalized the scene and revolutionized the local music industry.

The Mime Troupe

Bill Graham began working as a promoter for the San Francisco Mime Troupe during their 1965 run of *Il Candelaio*. The Troupe had clashed with the city's Parks Commission that year and lost their permit;[59] at a performance of *Il Candelaio*, in Lafayette Park in April 1965, Mime Troupe founder Ron (R.G.) Davis was arrested onstage in front of an audience of roughly one thousand.[60] Davis was tried and convicted of performing without a permit, so to alleviate the costs of his legal battle,

San Francisco and the Long 60s

on November 6, Bill Graham held an appeal at the Mime Troupe's Howard Street loft. He did not, however, expect it to be quite so well-attended.

> People lined up in the street for the party. Huge hoards of people. Thousands of them. Legally, the loft held maybe six or seven hundred. I'd say we had fifteen hundred in there at one time. It was this cross section of people who had *never* come together before. A mixed group. It was amazing. In San Francisco, you could turn over seventeen different parts of the city and the worms under each rock would represent one neighborhood. That night, all the worms got into one pot.
>
> It wasn't psychedelic yet. There was a little weed but nothing heavy. But I saw things that were firsts all night long. I saw people come in and instantly start dancing with other people and only then did I realize that they didn't know each other. They just started dancing. I'd never seen that before. It was like instant cousin-ship. They became a one. It was like when you look under a microscope at protoplasm. All the cells were touching and bubbling at once. That night, they were *all* in the play. It was theater-in-the-round.[61]

The extraordinary success of the first Mime Troupe benefit showed Bill Graham that there was a good business to be carved out of concert promotion. He organized two more Mime Troupe benefits, on December 10 and January 14, 1966, at an old hall called the Fillmore Auditorium. For the people in Graham's orbit, what they saw at the Mime Troupe benefits was the dawn of the 60s, "a cultural revolution going on. Not minor. *Grand*. [The] towering cultural events leading to the Haight-Ashbury."[62]

Ralph Gleason had suggested the Fillmore Auditorium as a suitable site for Graham's shows, and attended the December benefit himself. His review is nothing short of exuberant:

> The benefit . . . Friday night at the Filmore Auditorium . . . was a rousing success. Over 3500 people paid $1.50 apiece to be there.
>
> But it was a great deal more than a benefit. It was substantiation of the suspicion that the need to dance on the part of a great number of residents of this area is so great it simply must be permitted.
>
> The Friday night affair was basically a rock 'n roll dance such as the ones the Family Dog put on at the Longshore Hall. . . .
>
> At 9:30 there was a double line a block long outside the Fillmore Auditorium. At 1 a.m. it was still there, the individuals were new but the packed house still existed.
>
> Inside a most remarkable assemblage of humanity was leaping, jumping, dancing, frigging, fragging and frugging on the dance floor to the music of the half dozen rock bands—the Mystery Trend, the Great Society, the Jefferson

Airplane, the VIPs, the Gentlemen's Band, the Warlocks and others. The costumes were freeform Goodwill-cum-Sherwood-Forest. Slim young ladies with their faces painted a la Harper's *Bazaar* in cats-and-dogs lines, granny dresses topped with huge feathers, white Levis with decals of mystic design; bell bottoms split up the side. The combinations were seemingly limitless.

At each end of the huge hall was a three foot high sign saying LOVE. Over the bar was another saying "No Booze," while the volunteer bartenders served soft drinks. Alongside the regular bar was a series of tables selling apples! The only dance (outside of Halloween) I've ever been at where they sold apples. Craaaazy! In a corner past the apple table was a baby in a carriage, sound asleep with a bottle and a teddy bear clutched in his (her?) arms. . . .

Although it was a benefit for the Mime Troupe . . . there were thousands there who never heard of [them] or at least never had been to one of their shows. . . .

They were there for a multitude of reasons, and the reasons bear examination. Some were there because the Mime Troupe represents . . . a battle for creativity in the arts. Others, and more I suspect, were there because the Mime Troupe's park use hassle dramatizes another aspect of the struggle of US against THEM.

Still others were there as part of the rock revolution. They don't need booze. . . . All they need is the sound of the guitars. They get high on decibels alone. And they are hurting to dance.

San Francisco has been hell on dances for years. The police obviously regard mass proximity of the sexes to the sound of music as a hazard equal to a time bomb. But I suspect this attitude will have to be tempered. The actual demand for dances is going to increase. The whole rock revolution points to dancing, the music ineluctably moves one to move.

Another thing about The Friday night revel. There were no guards inside. There was an absence of uniforms and there was no trouble.[63]

After the success of the benefits Bill Graham left the Mime Troupe and began holding regular concerts at the Fillmore Auditorium. But the importance of that first benefit cannot be overstated. There was a community of people in the city who were "hurting to dance." There was an underlying tension of "US against THEM" brewing. And the demand for dances was not going away. More importantly: "It was a revelation. Not just for me. For everybody. That night, we *all* found each other."[64]

Notes

1. Tom Caylor, "New Face of Culture," *Chronicle*, September 19, 1965, p. II.3.
2. RJG, "A Good Year for S.F. Musicians," *Chronicle*, December 27, 1965, p. 39.
3. "Sounds of Another World," *Chronicle*, January 25, 1965, p. 43.
4. "New Social Problem: Good Kids on Dope," reprinted in *Chronicle*, January 4, 1965, p. 1.

5. Jonathan Root, "Guitar and Handbills: Ceremony in a Beat Church," *Chronicle*, February 8, 1965, p. 5. Narcotics officers finally succeeded in shutting down the New Age Community Church—"but not because they are a bunch of untidy bohemians." No, apparently the reverend "sold a pound of cocaine for $250 to [a police officer] who infiltrated the congregation. . . .," though no one in the SFPD knew "for certain whether the white powder in that package is hard-core cocaine." "Cops Move In on The Beat Church," February 25, 1965, p. 1.
6. Root, "Guitar and Handbills."
7. "Seminar on LSD and Personality," *Chronicle*, February 14, 1965, p. 30.
8. For a comprehensive history of Esalen, see Jeffrey J. Kripal, *Esalen: America and the Religion of No Religion* (Chicago and London: University of Chicago Press, 2007).
9. See Merla Zellerbach, "Beatnik Research Without Any Beats," *Chronicle*, April 9, 1965, p. 42.
10. Merla Zellerbach, "Patriotism—What Hippies Never Show," *San Francisco Chronicle*, August 16, 1965, p. 46.
11. The first appearance of "hippie" is often taken to be Michael Fallon's article on the Blue Unicorn coffeehouse, "A New Haven for Beatniks," September 5, 1965; dating its provenance in the local or national press is less important than noting the general trend toward acknowledging this shift from beatnik to the next thing.
12. See R. G. Davis, *The San Francisco Mime Troupe: The First Ten Years* (Palo Alto: Ramparts Press, 1975) for a full chronicle of this period.
13. Jack Lind, "The Drug that Peels the Psyche," *Chronicle*, November 3, 1965, p. 5. Richard Alpert and Timothy Leary were colleagues at Harvard and along with Ralph Metztner collaborated on *The Psychedelic Experience* (1964), the influential "guide" for the use of psychedelic drugs based on the Tibetan Book of the Dead.
14. See "2 Narcotics Raids—Big Haul, 7 Held," *Chronicle*, February 19, 1965, p. 3.
15. Donovan Bess, "Drug Expert: 'Medical Apathy Toward LSD,'" *Chronicle*, February 22, 1965, p. 2.
16. Dean St Dennis, "LSD Under Control: A Simple Tool for Psychiatry," *Chronicle*, June 7, 1965, p. 7. Stanislav Grof was one of the early researchers into psychedelic therapy. Among the techniques he developed is Holotropic Breathwork, which he refined while Scholar-in-Residence at Esalen.
17. See "A Plug for LSD in the Daily Cal," *Chronicle*, March 9, 1965, p. 2.
18. Ron Fimrite, "A Shocker on the Use of Drugs at S.F. State," *Chronicle*, May 29, 1965, p. 1.
19. "Police Report: S. F. High School Dope Problem," *Chronicle*, May 29, 1965, p. 8.
20. Paul Avery, "UC Surprise: Big Campus Dope Case," *Chronicle*, June 12, 1965, p. 1.
21. Donovan Bess, "A UC Doctor Tells of Students on Drugs," *Chronicle*, June 13, 1965, p. 16.
22. See "Dope Raid: Author Arrested with 13 Friends," *Chronicle*, April 25, 1965, p. 1. The article notes that one of those arrested was "Neal Cassaday [sic], 29, [who] attained some sort of celebrity status as the inspiration for one of Jack Kerouac's central characters in *On the Road*. Cassaday [sic] also served under the name of Speed Limit as the driver of Kesey's fabulous bus that toured the United States last year."
23. Jonathan Root, "The Emnity of a Community: Dope Raid Author's Story," *Chronicle*, April 27, 1965, p. 18.
24. That film, in a much-edited form, was finally released as *Magic Trip* (dir. Alison Elwood and Alex Gibney, Magnolia Pictures, 2013).

25. See "Ken Kesey Lashes Back in Drug Case," *Chronicle*, August 25, 1965, p. 2. For a thorough history of Kepler's and its connections with the counterculture via Joan Baez, Jerry Garcia and Phil Lesh, see Michael Doyle, *Radical Chapters* (Syracuse: Syracuse University Press, 2012).

26. Jerry Garcia, quoted in *Grateful Dead—Anthem to Beauty* (dir. Jeremy Marre, Isis Productions, 1997). This quote echoes Ramon Sender's comment about *City Scale*, that "the chaotic edge . . . between order and chaos" is where "all the good stuff happens."

27. Hunter S. Thompson, *Hell's Angels: A Strange and Terrible Saga* (New York: Ballantine Books, 1995), p. 229. News of the parties at La Honda spread across other chapters of the Hell's Angels, and soon Kesey's house became the magnet for Angels from all over northern California, who "would arrive unannounced, usually in groups of five to fifteen, and stay until they got bored or ran out of LSD, which only a few had ever tried prior to the Kesey hookup." (p. 232)

28. This Acid Test is tied into the Hip Pocket, a paperback bookstore in Santa Cruz opened by Peter Demma and Ron "Hassler" Bevirt, members of the Pranksters' outer orbit. The Hip Pocket ran into some trouble for selling nude magazines, and for displaying photographs of nude men on the shop's walls. The handwritten notice for the November 27, 1965, Acid Test was posted at the Hip Pocket and the nearby Catalyst Coffee Shop, hangout of the nascent local psychedelic community.

29. Tom Wolfe, *The Electric Kool-Aid Acid Test* (New York: Farrar, 1968), p. 8.

30. Phil Lesh, *Searching for the Sound: My Life with the Grateful Dead* (New York: Little, Brown, 2005), pp. 68–69.

31. See McNally, *A Long Strange Trip*, pp. 107–19.

32. This period is covered in greater detail in the next chapter.

33. See Wavy Gravy, *The Hog Farm and Friends* (New York: Links Books, 1974).

34. These were the regular Sunday-afternoon parties at the Hog Farm that attracted crowds from all over, including on one occasion Charles Manson and his "wives," famously the only people to have been kicked off the property.

35. Ram Dass, quoted in Paul Perry, *On the Bus*, p. 149.

36. "Battle of Big Sur: College of Far-Out Knowledge," *Chronicle*, California Living, October 3, 1965.

37. RJG, "Two Moments in a Revolution," *Chronicle*, May 24, 1965, p. 51.

38. "The Hell's Angels' Debating Debut," *Chronicle*, November 13, 1965.

39. Allen Ginsberg, "Demonstration as Spectacle, as Example, as Communication," *Berkeley Barb*, Friday, November 19, 1965, p. 1.

40. Bob Robertson, "They'll Miss the Parade," *Chronicle*, November 20, 1965, p. 1.

41. John Wasserman, "The Matrix: Social Blues Via the Jefferson Airplane," *Chronicle*, August 29, 1965, Datebook p. 5.

42. RJG, "Jefferson Airplane—Sound and Style," *Chronicle*, September 13, 1965, p. 49.

43. When asked what the band's name meant, Balin replied that it was "a whole new idea. The mammal field has been exhausted. Jefferson Airplane means nothing in music, but it's very identifiable with us. Jefferson Airplane is what we do. . . . It fits us." See Wasserman, "The Matrix."

44. Ibid.

45. RJG, "Jefferson Airplane."

46. Ibid.
47. See Darby Slick, *Don't You Want Somebody to Love?* (Berkeley: SLG Books, 1991).
48. RJG, "Jefferson Airplane."
49. Rusty is referring to the fabled evening when Unobsky, Chandler Laughlin, and Don Works were cabin-bound in Zen Mine, Nevada, during a blizzard with only LSD and "a pretty heavy Risk game" to help them pass the time. They landed on the idea of opening a folk club in Virginia City and ended up inadvertently beginning the psychedelic dancehall scene instead. These and other anecdotes are recounted in the documentary *Rockin' at the Red Dog: The Dawn of Psychedelic Rock* (dir. Mary Works, Monterey Video/Sunset Home Visual Entertainment, 2005).
50. For an evocative pictorial history of the Haight, see Katherine Powell Cohen, *Images of America: San Francisco's Haight-Ashbury* (San Francisco: Arcadia Publishing, 2008).
51. The Charlatans featured Hunter (autoharp, vocals), Mike Ferguson (piano, vocals), Mike Wilhelm (lead guitar, vocals), Richard Olsen (bass, clarinet, vocals), and Dan Hicks (drums, rhythm guitar, vocals).
52. Bill Ham's prototype kinetic light show was fairly simple, but revolutionary. For each sound range (low, middle, and high) there was a corresponding color (red, blue, yellow) that would react to it. The colors would appear, then mix, and change constantly as the music was playing.
53. Bill is referring to a "transposing keyboard," the earliest examples of which date from the early sixteenth century. Irving Berlin had a number of transposing keyboards built, as he could only play in the "black note" key of F#.
54. George Hunter, quoted in Gene Sculatti and David Seay, *San Francisco Nights* (London: Sidgwick and Jackson, 1985), p. 29.
55. The story of the Charlatans' subsequent career is inevitably one of "lost promise": though they appeared fairly regularly in the dancehalls of San Francisco, their recording career was stalled on an MGM subsidiary label, Kapp, and they watched as other local bands signed big-money contracts with other major labels and found their way to the national charts. For a sympathetic retrospective, see Geoffrey Link, "The Charlatans," *Rolling Stone* 52, February 21, 1970, pp. 30–32.
56. Alton Kelley, quoted in Michael Goldberg, "The San Francisco Sound," *Rolling Stone* 585, August 23, 1990, pp. 91–6.
57. RJG, "Wild Weekend Around the Bay," *Chronicle*, October 18, 1965, p. 51.
58. RJG, "The Family Dog—Liverpool in S.F.," *Chronicle*, October 22, 1965, p. 51.
59. The show in question, *A Minstrel Show: Or, Civil Rights in a Cracker Barrel*, will return in Chapter 9. Its initial positive review did suggest that the play was bound to alienate those whom the Mime Troupe normally alienated. See John L. Wasserman, "A Funny Minstrel Show or 'Jim Crow a Go-Go,'" *Chronicle*, July 2, 1965, p. 30.
60. In discussing the charges of "objectionable language," the *Chronicle* reported that "Bill Graham, another member of the Troupe, defended the use of four-letter words, particularly in a free show. Graham said he paid $4.50 for a ticket to LeRoi Jones' *The Dutchman* and *the toilet* at Marines Memorial Theater, where he 'heard the same "objectionable" word used 147 times that night.'" See "Banned, Unbowed S.F. Mime Troupe," *Chronicle*, April 5, 1965, p. 2.

61. Bill Graham, quoted in Bill Graham and Robert Greenfield, *Bill Graham Presents: My Life Inside Rock and Out* (New York: Dell, 1992), pp. 123–24.
62. Peter Berg quoted in Ibid., pp. 124–25. Another significant connection between the Mime Troupe and the "dawn of the 60s" was the emergence of the Diggers, who reemerge in the following chapters.
63. RJG, "Lesson for S.F. in The Mime Benefit," *Chronicle*, December 13, 1965, p. 47.
64. Bill Graham, in *Bill Graham Presents*, p. 126.

SOME NOTES ON SONGS

For each of the years in the short 60s I have chosen two songs to act as markers of local style and musical aesthetic. These may not have been the most important, most influential, "best," or best-known, recordings of those years, but they are the songs that I have chosen to trace two trajectories, the commercial and the experimental, that flowed through San Francisco from 1965 to the end of the decade. "Commercial" and "experimental" are not intended as value judgments, either; on the contrary, they are merely keywords that suggest much deeper currents that could only have been tapped in the dancehalls and psychedelic culture of the Bay Area in the short 60s.

THE BEAU BRUMMELS, "LAUGH LAUGH"

(Ron Elliott)
Produced by Sylvester Stewart
7" single (Autumn 8) released in December 1964; highest chart position #18
From the album *Introducing the Beau Brummels* (Autumn Records, 1965)

Ron Meagher: bass guitar
John Peterson: drums
Dec Mulligan: guitar
Ron Elliott: lead guitar
Sal Valentino: lead vocals

In the early nineteenth century, Beau Brummel was a style icon, a Regency dandy, a man whose impact on British men's fashion permeated even the early development of popular music in England.[1] The suit and tie, often (mis-)attributed to Brummel himself, was a mainstay of early British beat groups: a sharp uniform expressing class distinction or aspiration, collective identity, and propriety. This is most evident in the Beatles who, in their shift from rock 'n' roll leathers to tailored suits, presented the respectable face of popular music, influencing men's fashion on both sides of the Atlantic, and changing the sound of popular music in the process.

Early publicity photos of San Francisco's Beau Brummels show a clear Beatles influence, as would be natural in the wake of the recent British Invasion:[2] matching suits, Chelsea boots with Cuban heels, floppy haircuts. Ron Elliott and Sal Valentino (né Sal Spampinato) were high school friends in the late 1950s, and sang together as a duo. Elliott went on to study music composition at San Francisco State College, while Valentino became a fixture on the North Beach coffee-house scene. In 1964 they were joined by Meagher, Peterson, and Mulligan, and began playing together as the Beau Brummels in small venues on the Peninsula. There they were "discovered" by local disc jockey Tom Donahue and Bob Mitchell, who were launching the Autumn Records label. "Laugh Laugh" was Autumn's first hit.

Mulligan left the Beau Brummels in late 1965. A brief notice in the *Chronicle* about the split reveals the level of success the band had reached:

> In an early example of dissonance in the local music scene, Declan Mulligan sued the other Beau Brummels for damages totalling $1.25 million, stating that the other four band members had excluded him from their profits for over a year. According to the statement, "Laugh, Laugh" had sold more than 500,000 copies and was particularly successful in England.[3]

"Laugh Laugh"

The band continued to record for Autumn through March 1966, but the label went bust shortly thereafter. The seven singles and three LPs that the Beau Brummels released with Warner Brothers did not have the impact of their early singles, however, and by 1969 the band had dissolved. All the individual members of the Beau Brummels remained active with other projects and solo work; they reunited in 1974, and again in 2013.

"Laugh Laugh" chimes with the sound of Merseybeat: the harmonica intro recalls the Beatles' "Love Me Do" (1962), the melody recalls the Searchers' cover of "Love Potion Number 9" (1965); but the vocal harmonies also foreshadow the folk-rock sound made popular by southern California bands, the Byrds and the Mamas and the Papas. "Laugh Laugh" therefore strikes an interesting balance between the West coast of the United States and Liverpool, a contemporary sound that Autumn Records packaged for international distribution. Although the "San Francisco sound" is a difficult idea to substantiate, this record suggests that the Beau Brummels are the earliest component of a rich musical lineage.

"Laugh Laugh" follows a simple verse-chorus structure:

0:00	Instrumental intro	4 bars
0:09	Verse—verse—chorus (:39)	8 + 8 + 12
1:01	Verse—verse—chorus (1:31)	8 + 8 + 12
1:53	Instrumental break (based on intro)	4
2:00	Verse—verse—chorus to fade-out	8 + 8 + 10

The lyrics of the song are directed at a woman seeking love advice from the singer. Not an unusual theme in itself, but here an interesting inversion of the singer-as-mediator in songs like "She Loves You."[4] The first line of the song ("I hate to say it but I told you so") puts the listener in an awkward position, eavesdropping on a series of admonitions that erupts in an odd celebration of *schadenfreude* at the chorus:

> Laugh laugh, I thought I'd die
> It seemed so funny to me
> Laugh laugh, you met a guy
> Who taught you how it feels to be
> Lonely, oh so lonely.

The shift between the solo delivery of the vaguely moralistic verses and the harmonies of the chorus intensifies the basic musical tension of the song, between minor and major. This tension is apparent from the introduction, which pits a static harmonica against a subtle progression in the guitars and bass. The placement of the various sounds also contributes to this tension: in the opening bars the harmonica pans from left-right, at a pace of two bars each, before settling at the center with the vocal entrance at :09. The harmonica traverses the sound field without changing pitch, while the bass and guitar walk by semitone underneath it, finally settling into minor tonality for the first three lines of every verse, then major for the fourth line and chorus. This helps the listener sense an "arrival" at the chorus, with the final line ("lonely, oh so lonely") a kind of "payoff" at the end. The listener cannot exult in the chorus, however, as "Laugh Laugh" ultimately fades out mid-phrase.

The Beau Brummels were the first San Francisco pop band to enjoy international fame.[5] In addition to their chart success, the band achieved the singular honor of appearing in an episode of *The Flintstones*: in the guise of the Beau Brummelstones, they performed "Laugh Laugh" on *Shinrock*, the prehistoric pop show, suitably dressed in matching tunics and moptop haircuts.[6] But this early example of San Franciscan pop is also significant for the studio behind it. Tom "Big Daddy" Donahue had been a trusted disc jockey on AM radio station KYA before he left the station to launch Autumn Records, open a short-lived prototypical psychedelic nightclub called Mother's in North Beach, present big concerts at the Cow Palace and the Beatles' final performance at Candlestick Park, and ultimately invent progressive FM radio with the launch of KMPX in 1967. In 1965, however, the success he enjoyed with the Beau Brummels' first single was due in part to his staff producer, nineteen-year-old Sylvester Stewart.

When Stewart joined Autumn Records he was already performing around the Bay Area in various bands, working as a disc jockey on local station KSOL, and building a name for himself as Sly Stewart. When his performing career finally gelled with the formation of his Family Stone, he took the "San Francisco sound" out of the short 60s and into new musical realms. But in 1965, Sly Stone captured the Merseybeat vibe with the Beau Brummels and helped establish San Francisco as a vibrant center for popular music.

THE GRATEFUL DEAD, "THE ONLY TIME IS NOW"

(lyrics Jerry Garcia/Dave Parker; music Garcia/Kreutzmann/Lesh/McKernan/Weir)
Recorded as The Emergency Crew at Golden State Recorders, San Francisco, November 3, 1965
Produced by Tom Donahue & Bobby Mitchell
Unreleased; appears on *The Birth of the Dead* (Rhino 74391, 2003)

Jerry Garcia: lead guitar, vocals
Ron "Pigpen" McKernan: organ, harmonica, vocals
Bob Weir: rhythm guitar, vocals
Phil Lesh: bass, vocals
Bill Kreutzmann: drums

> Jerry Garcia, their lead guitarist, is an interesting soloist with a wild surge of inventiveness and the band gets a groovy ensemble sound from the electric organ, lead and rhythm guitars, bass and drums.[7]

This is one of the first known recordings of the Grateful Dead, and it sounds nothing like them. Despite glimpses of familiar three-part harmony, the overriding sense of restriction on "The Only Time Is Now," of trying to cram too much into a two-and-a-half-minute single, is definitely not a hallmark of their later style. And it is difficult to imagine a thirty-year life story emerging from this particular recording.

The most interesting dimension of "The Only Time Is Now" is its history. The band had been playing together on the Peninsula and around the city for about five months before recording a six-song demo for Autumn Records: four original compositions, one arrangement of a traditional tune, and a cover of Gordon Lightfoot's "Early Morning Rain." Though they were known locally as the Warlocks, they were not the only Warlocks out there, so they recorded their demo under the name The Emergency Crew; within a few weeks they had chosen the name The Grateful Dead, which they used at the second Mime Troupe benefit and at the San Jose Acid Test. So "The Only Time Is Now" sits on an interesting fault line: a transitional moniker, a live band struggling with studio performance, the very idea of "liveness" changing irreversibly.

The Acid Tests may have given the Warlocks a glimpse of the "form that follows chaos,"[8] but "The Only Time Is Now" is all form, and no chaos. There is a sense of liveness to this performance—ragged at the edges, unedited mistakes, uneven balance—which gives "The Only Time Is Now" a sense of excitement, but not a complete picture of what the song might have contributed to the full-sensory experience of an Acid Test.

"The Only Time Is Now" follows a simple verse structure: a six-bar introduction plus four sixteen-bar verses, each separated by a four-bar instrumental vamp:

```
0:00   intro
0:09   verse 1   Oh I know there is no place . . .
0:35   vamp
0:41   verse 2   Oh well strange is the story . . .
1:07   vamp
1:19   verse 3   Oh I come to you . . .
1:46   vamp
1:51   verse 4   So forget about your yesterdays . . .
```

The vamp between verses two and three (1:07) is notable for a minor train wreck—no vocals enter as expected in the fourth bar, one voice enters accidentally in the sixth, the bass wanders momentarily in the seventh, then normal business resumes as usual in the eighth—but otherwise there are no solos, no breaks, no diversion from the pattern. Each verse ends with a refrain—"the only time is now"—which further adds to the sense of rigidity. Loosening things up somewhat from the margins of the mix, the tambourine provides an almost intrusive imprecision.

There are intimations here, however fleeting, of the musical culture from which the Grateful Dead emerged. The disjunct nature of the melody, its wide range, the coarse vocal delivery, and close backing harmonies, seem to reference a bluegrass aesthetic—in verse 1 at the phrases "there is no place you can go" and "come walking in the sun," then at similar points in each subsequent verse.[9] The echo-laden guitars and heavy backbeat, however, are more reminiscent of the Beatles' "Ticket to Ride" (1965): as with "Laugh Laugh," the Autumn Records desire to appeal to the fans of British beat music is clear in "The Only Time Is Now."

The lyrical message is fairly straightforward on the surface: the singer is offering his love to a woman who appears to be sad and alone. This could be the beginning of any relationship—boy sees girl on campus, at a coffee shop, at a park—and there is nothing to suggest that his intentions are anything but honorable. There are intriguing hints at geography here—"come walking in the sun" is easy to do in the Bay Area; "while dancing we will sing" is easily done at a pop concert—the context for which would be a pre-Acid Test peninsula, where the Warlocks regularly played.

Though its sentiment is simple, the florid lyric is redolent of much older music, of the type one might have heard in a Victorian parlor:

So forget about your yesterdays of sorrow
And forget about the darkness you have seen

For there's only you and me
At the edge of an endless sea
And remember that the only time is now.

What is interesting here is the recurring line, "the only time is now." The underlying message, *carpe diem*, seize the day, slowly shifted in the short 60s to the mindful, "be here now" aesthetic propounded further down the coast at the Esalen Institute, and into the long 60s via the teachings of Ram Dass.[10] "The Only Time Is Now" may be an invitation to dance at Magoo's Pizza Parlor,[11] but it is also a suggestion of a much deeper philosophical current: the song ends with unresolved dissonance at the fade-out, suggesting to the listener that there is much still left unsaid.

> GLENN HOWARD: What did the Warlocks sound like? Well, they were pretty good. Pigpen was fabulous and the whole secret of that early Dead thing is it's his band. Pigpen was the shit. He only took acid a couple of times; he got dosed once. It just wasn't part of black culture and he was part of black culture. I still have some of Pigpen's records that have little marks next to a song title, or something that's really good, that no one will ever know. But they're in his handwriting, so I'll have to check them out.

If the Warlocks were driven at the beginning by Pigpen, "The Only Time Is Now," with Phil Lesh on lead vocal, foreshadows the Dead's much later material and the problems that they encountered with studio recordings. It is easy to hear this Autumn record as the first of many in which the Grateful Dead felt unnaturally harnessed to a format that did not suit them, aesthetically, musically, or philosophically. Yet it is also easy to imagine a place for "The Only Time Is Now" on compilations of the period, or in the lower half of 1965's Top 100 chart. In a live setting, the Dead would certainly be capable of taking a song this straightforward, this unchanging, and expand it horizontally and vertically into a much different musical product; but the capacity of contemporary recording technology to capture, and the preparedness of the listening public to *hear*, something closer to the Grateful Dead of the Acid Tests was still a few years off.

Notes

1. For a study of the connections between Beau Brummel and contemporary popular culture, see Stan Hawkins, *The British Pop Dandy: Masculinity, Popular Music and Culture* (Farnham: Ashgate, 2009).
2. The British Invasion describes the flood of pop music from the United Kingdom, particularly from England, to hit the US pop charts, beginning with the Beatles' extraordinary run of Top 5 singles in 1964.

3. "$1.2 Million Rift Between Rock-Rollers," *Chronicle*, May 5, 1966, p. 4.
4. "She Loves You" (Lennon/McCartney) was the biggest-selling single in the United Kingdom in 1963, and topped the US charts in 1964.
5. Mention should be made here of the influential local band the Kingston Trio, who enjoyed enormous success with their hit, "Tom Dooley" (Capitol, 1958). I am beginning this series of case studies with the Beau Brummels because of their musical style and because of the placement of Autumn Records in the history of the "short 60s" in San Francisco. For more on the Kingston Trio, see William J. Bush, *Greenback Dollar: The Incredible Rise of the Kingston Trio* (Lanham: Scarecrow Press, 2013) and Warren Bareiss, "Middlebrow Knowingness in 1950s San Francisco: The Kingston Trio, Beat Counterculture, and the Production of 'Authenticity,'" *Popular Music and Society* 33/1 (February 2010): 9–33.
6. The episode, "Shinrock-a-Go-Go" (Season 6, episode 12), was broadcast on December 3, 1965. In the brief clip featuring the Beau Brummelstones, Wilma and Betty are seen initially sitting politely on the sofa watching the show, then dancing along, then screaming and clapping—all very familiar sights for fans of American pop shows of the 1960s.
7. RJG, "A Great Weekend for Dancing," *Chronicle*, May 9, 1966, p. 51.
8. Jerry Garcia, in *Grateful Dead—Anthem to Beauty*.
9. This is what Alec Palao calls "hootenanny-with-a-backbeat." See liner notes to the reissued original mixes of Country Joe & the Fish's *Electric Music for the Mind and Body* (Vanguard, 2013), p. 6.
10. Dr. Richard Alpert went on a spiritual pilgrimage to India in 1967 and returned to the States as Ram Dass, a name given him by his guru, Neem Karoli Baba. In 1971 Ram Dass published *Be Here Now*, a central book in countercultural spirituality.
11. Magoo's Pizza Parlor in Menlo Park was one of the sites for the Warlocks' early concert appearances.

5. 1966

Something is happening [in the Haight-Ashbury] which is far more significant than the merchant's association, the police or any of the other adult groups blinded by stereotype reflexes are able to see.

The lovely, benign and beautiful atmosphere of the Free Fair in the Panhandle at Oak and Ashbury, with the colorful costumes, the banners, the painting, the poetry and the music, is exactly the sort of thing which San Francisco—and San Francisco alone—can produce in this age of mass media and orthodoxy.

The city fathers ought to endorse it, the police should nurture it and when they come around, hand out smiles instead of parking tickets....

The main characteristic of the crowds that attended the Free Fair, that weekly attend the Fillmore and Avalon dances, is their happiness and the absence of any hostility. We may be cynical and say these people do not mean it when they talk of love, but that says more about us than about them.[1]

OUT is the negative screeching rhythm in music, art, people, love . . . IN is the positive ecstatic orgasmic rhythm everywhere stabbing relentlessly at THE ESTABLISHMENT and the deathtrap of inhibition and progress-stifling tradition. . . . Most of all . . . it's in to be yourself.[2]

The new year dawned with the annual rain of confetti on the Financial District. Among those in a small parade were Stewart Brand, Ben Jacopetti, and Ramon Sender calling to the crowd through a loudspeaker: "It's a beautiful thing you are doing to this street—be aware that you're in a parade and you'll be as beautiful as what you do." They then began distributing leaflets publicizing something called a "trips festival," to be held at the end of January in Longshoremen's Hall. The handouts, largely incomprehensible to most recipients, promised that the weekend event "will try to give the audiences far-out, hallucinogenic experiences somewhat like those induced by such drugs as LSD." Some of the workers standing nearby were more perplexed by the appearance of this "band of young urban gypsies," including the stevedore "of Genovese descent [who] growled, 'They look like damned Sicilians.'"[3]

The Trips Festival generated both buzz and perplexity in the daily papers.[4] Long-time science reporter George Dusheck attempted to explain the event's "three-day Sensorium or electronic trip . . . a drugless psychedelic experience, a kind of electronic satori or Zen revelation."[5] The issue of drugs still garnered column inches,

5.1 Wes Wilson's iconic design.

of course, both sensational and satirical: Charles McCabe attempted to temper some of the more outrageous claims, stating "that while it is probably a bad thing to take drugs, it is beyond any doubt a bad thing to talk nonsense on the subject."[6]

Poster boy for the perils of recreational drug use was still Ken Kesey, who was sentenced to six months in the County Jail, a $1,500 fine, and three years' probation—"on condition he use no narcotics, marijuana, or other dangerous drug prohibited by law."[7] On the eve of the Trips Festival Kesey broke parole: he was arrested in the early hours of January 19 on a North Beach roof—"in the heart of the warren-like district that sheltered so many of the unwashed in [its] beatnik heyday"—along with Carolyn "Mountain Girl" Adams.[8] Stewart Brand, a resident in the building, had given them permission to spend the night on the roof; Kesey was arrested for possession of marijuana, assaulting a police officer, resisting arrest and trespassing. The coincidence of Kesey's court appearance and the imminent Trips Festival was certainly not lost on the *Chronicle*, whose conflation of Kesey's and Adams' sartorial style, their choice of transportation to the county court (the Prankster bus), and the idea of "trips to the outer limits of consciousness," only amplified the distinctions between straight San Francisco and the growing population of local freaks.[9]

And then the happening happened:

> There is nothing to say about [the Trips Festival] precisely because that's what it's all about: you are either with it or you are not, and if you are with it you don't have to say anything (you KNOW) and if you are not with it, what is there to say?[10]

The *Berkeley Barb* didn't dig it much:

> If you really want to get high get high. So you know what it looked like? For all the world like the Stardust ball room. Yep. Except they were frugging. The projection on the ceiling spilled over and guess what—just like effect of makebelieve stars from lights in Roseland on dancers. Where's the trip? Dance city? Some of the projection interesting but the rock and roll interfered. Man, they even had a borsht [sic] circuit mc [sic] who told everybody what a good time they were having.[11]

There was more to the Trips Festival than dancing and lights, of course.

The Trips Festival

> For the acid heads themselves, the Trips Festival was like the first national convention of an underground movement that had existed on a hush-hush cell-by-cell basis. The heads were amazed at how big their own ranks had become—and euphoric over the fact that they could come out in the open, high as baboons, and the sky, and the law, wouldn't fall down on them. The press went along with the notion that this had been an LSD experience without the LSD. Nobody in the hip world of San Francisco had any such delusion, and the Haight-Ashbury era began that weekend.[12]

> There were five movie screens up on the wall and projectors for the flicks and other light mixes spread around the balcony. . . . A huge pair of red and yellow traffic lights blinked constantly. Stroboscopic lights set at vantage points beamed down into the crowd and lissome maidens danced under them for hours, whirling jewelry. A man played a penny-whistle for one of the dancers.

San Francisco and the Long 60s

> On stage a succession of good rock 'n' roll bands, The Grateful Dead, Big Brother and the Holding Company, produced the kind of sonic high that big bands used to, only the rock groups do it quicker and for more people. A platform in front of the stage was for dancers who free-form twisted all night long. On the main floor, people stood around and watched or danced and the balcony was jammed. [Saturday and Sunday nights] were huge box office successes but only Saturday produced things like the solitary male who spun around in circles gazing at the ceiling and the guy who held his head in his hands and danced, bent over with his face to the floor.[13]

There were few events in San Francisco's short 60s more significant than the Trips Festival. For the straight society, it came out of nowhere and meant nothing; for the burgeoning hip community, it was the first real gathering, the first mass experience of the new consciousness. It had its origins in a number of different quarters—the San Francisco Tape Music Center, the Acid Tests, the Red Dog Saloon—that existed individually, on the fringes of the mainstream, but for the heads taking part in any one of the individual scenes, the Trips Festival weekend gave a sense of inexorable momentum:

> SAM ANDREW: At first we thought this scene was only happening in 1090 Page Street. And then we went to the Trips Festival and thought "oh, this is city-wide, this phenomenon." We thought it was happening in ten living rooms at the most, you know. Then it was a city-wide thing. And then roughly a year later we realized that it was worldwide.

Each scene had its own idiosyncratic code of conduct. One tension that arose at the Trips Festival and continued throughout much of the decade was that between order and disorder:

> I remember the Merry Pranksters were there and they were pretty spaced out. Very decent people but just *out there*. I had not yet seen the acid thing in full force. That night, I did. It shocked me. They might as well have been offering hand grenades to people. When LSD exploded inside a body, how did they know how much damage the shrapnel could cause? They had ices spiked with acid, available to all, children as well. There were big tubs on the balcony and downstairs for anyone to consume. From the outset, that has always been my one ongoing argument with Ken Kesey. There *has* to be a warning. If people don't know, how can you assume that their body can take what yours can? How can you know that?[14]

This limited tolerance for flagrant public drug use contributed to Bill Graham's reputation as an outsider to the hip community.[15] He was certainly not the only person to object to the mass dosing of unsuspecting persons,[16] though some recipients of acid charity at the Trips Festival remember it fondly:

> GLENN HOWARD: I was 18 and I had a sweet tooth from hell. And I think it was ice cream—it might have been cake—and they had a whole bunch of it around. I pigged out and it was spiked. So anyway I didn't make the second night of the Trips Festival. I was up all night and mostly hung pretty close to the floor. But it was—you know, it was far out.

Others were unaffected:

> RAMON SENDER: I was probably the only person at the Trips Festival who wasn't stoned. If I'd had time to figure out where the LSD and the ice cream was—I heard later it was in the bus—I'd have partaken, but . . .
>
> WILLIAM MAGINNIS: That would have been the first place to check, on the bus.

There is footage from the Trips Festival that hints at the weekend's colors,[17] that offers a glimpse into another world, but its technicolor hue remains vivid primarily in the memories of the people who were there:

> ERIC CHRISTENSEN: The Trips Festival wasn't as much about music as it was about this incredible mix of sensory things. I mean, I remember it visually more than I do musically. And what was interesting about that event was, it was staged, but it was one of the first events I went to where the line between what went on onstage and the audience was blurred. People were their own performance artists out in the audience, and what was going on onstage was almost tangential.
>
> LIANNE GRAVES: I had no idea, no clue. I can still see myself sitting in the Longshoremen's Hall completely blown away. I couldn't believe that there were people like this and just so much excitement and energy and color and feathers and smoke. It was insane.
>
> Everything was going on at once. There was no focus of attention. Everybody was just partying furiously. . . . I mean, there was just *incredible* shit going on. Plus, it was like old home week. I met and saw everybody I had ever known. Every beatnik, every hippie, every coffeehouse hangout person from all over the state was there, all freshly psychedelicized. And it was just *great*.[18]

A common theme here is community: an audience of like-minded people gathering together in the Longshoremen's Hall, from every hip corner of the Bay Area, to participate in free-form sensory exploration. As Sam Andrew said, no one had a sense of how many countercultural pockets there were. Progressive musical expression had been a hallmark of the San Francisco Tape Music Center, however, and this connection between experimental art music and rock music is a key aspect of the Trips Festival:

> RAMON SENDER: Stewart Brand said, "Kesey's in the area doing the Acid Test with the Grateful Dead and the Merry Pranksters and he wants to do a weekend called a Trips Festival where you bring together all the various folks doing interesting things in the one venue. Are you interested?" And I said sure. The Tape Center name got on the program, and Bill Maginnis got involved and Don Buchla got involved building the PA System. My idea was to run Big Brother through the Buchla Box and just very gradually turn up the ring modulators so the sound would imperceptibly get weirder and weirder till they were way out in space. But that never really happened. There was this double stage, one lower and one a little higher. The Dead were up on the higher one and I think Big Brother were down on the lower one and my job was to take the electricity with these two huge knife switches open and just go crunch like this. Change the electricity from front stage to back stage. The only place I had to rest my head was on this built-in kind of a reflector cabinet made out of hollow core doors. So this thing was vibrating and when the Dead was playing I was sitting right below Bill Kreutzmann with these two switches and I couldn't get out of there. And that's why I'm deaf. That's my excuse.[19]

Though Ramon's memory of the Trips Festival publicity drive is somewhat hazy,[20] his recollection of its administration reveals the spirit of collaboration, and the endearing simplicity with which the business side of the enterprise was run:

> RAMON SENDER: Stewart called me in a panic and said, "You know the energies are building and we don't have our tickets, our posters aren't ready. Who's going to manage all this stuff?" And I said, "Well there's a guy named Bill Graham who just did a benefit for the Mime Troupe and it was a big success. Maybe we ought to call him." So we did, and here Stewart remembers it one way and I remember the other, but whichever way it was, one of us said to him, "Would you do it?" and he said, "Of course." And I said, "How much money do you want?" He said, "Pay me what you think it's worth afterwards." I said, "Well I'm taking $200 and Stewart's taking $200." He said, "Well pay me afterwards." So Bill came in, God bless him. He did the posters, he did the tickets, he got everything organized. He handled the door and when it was all over we met in a little cafeteria down near the Fillmore Auditorium. And he came in with these paper bags full of cash and we counted it all up and it was about $14,000. We'd never seen that much money in our lives. And then he got this weird look on his face because he says, "The count's short. The count's short." And he went

racing out—there was one paper bag left in the trunk of his car. I said, "Well what are we going to do with the rest of the money?" And we looked at each other and thought, "Well let's give it all to the Merry Pranksters; they did most of the work." So that's what we did.

Bill Graham's reputation as a businessman was now set, the multisensory musical event now had an audience, and the corner of Haight and Ashbury streets became the gravitational center of the new psychedelic community. Between February and May 1966 Bill Graham and Chet Helms held dances at the Fillmore Ballroom on alternate weekends. According to popular lore, Bill Graham secured the continued lease on the Fillmore and Chet Helms took the Family Dog operations elsewhere, to the Avalon Ballroom, located at 1268 Sutter Street, on the upper floors of a former dance academy.[21] For the rest of the short 60s, there were dedicated sites for the new musical culture, and an ever-growing community ready to partake in it.

5.2 Chet Helms at the Avalon.

A high school dropout from San Leandro was strolling barefoot through the Panhandle with a friend late one night, and the two were questioned by police. When the girls took the police to the house where they were staying, the police discovered "a rambling . . . pad bursting with beatniks and heavy with the sweet smell of freshly smoked marijuana." Marijuana cigarettes, hypodermic needles, very little furniture, and enough straw sleeping mats and mattresses around the place to accommodate the fifteen men, nine women, and assorted animals living there. The residents were brought into the police station under charges of contributing to the delinquency of a minor and being in a home where narcotics were used. The local officers were aware of what was by then a common arrangement:

> "The word is out that San Francisco is the place for the far-out crowd," Park Station Captain Dan Kiely said after the raid. "I think they're coming here from all over the country."
> And for the last several years, the far-out crowd has been flocking into the Haight-Ashbury District, "the low-rent places," he said.
> "One will get a place and 30 or 40 more will move in—and then the one who rented it moves out," the captain said. . . .
> "But they stay pretty much to themselves. They're interesting to talk with—they have funny phrases—they call us 'the agents of the establishment,' or 'the agents of the power structure' . . . or 'the fuzz.'"
> The "disturbing factor" of the beatniks' continuing influx into the district is the narcotics problem and the attraction of the "far-out" crowd "to kids."
> "And we're alert to that," he said.[22]

The Haight was indeed attracting "the far-out crowd," who contributed to the neighborhood's new colors and soundscape.

The Haight

> KURT "CROWBAR" KANGAS: Everybody has a different experience. There were hundreds and hundreds of scenes going on in San Francisco. There is not just one scene; there were many of them. Every block had five communes on it and each one had 20 or 30 people in it. And that's why every time you read about the Haight-Ashbury you're going, "I didn't see that." Well that was because there are many stories.
>
> CHARLIE MORGAN: The feeling on Haight Street was just magical. People were playing music out on the street. People were so happy they were inviting you into their house. People who are into quantum mechanics talk about how there's always this unlimited potential in every moment, and that's really what

you felt. It was magic, and people were very kind to each other. Most people were just doing pot and maybe some mushrooms or LSD and mescaline. It was really rich.

Art Rogers: I didn't understand what was going on. I thought these people were crazy—"they're running around being happy for nothing!" And what is the big message? That joy is; you just have it. It's not how much stuff you have. In the long run, what brings you happiness is that peace of mind, that center, your faith. Your faith. Maybe that's something everybody can understand.

Vicki Leeds: I put a lot of miles on Haight Street. It was a very social thing to do, just walk up and down the streets, visit with your friends, have a cup of tea or share a joint. There were all sorts of things that would happen in the Park, too. We'd go and have picnics, listen to music, and just hang out. We had friends who owned the shops: there was Bobby's Boot Hook, which sold custom-made shoes, and our friend Steve's hippie style general store. There was the Russian bakery where we ate piroshkies and there were the cafes. We didn't have a lot of money to spend, but I never missed a meal and I ate quite well. It was so colorful. A lot of us took care of each other; we really didn't see the dark side of what was going on—you know, the bad trips. That just wasn't part of our reality and it never seemed to exist around us.

Banana: See, I never was very aware of what was going on in the Haight. I was not aware of what was going on in East Marin, let alone over the bridge. So from my point of view the scene was the Avalon and the Fillmore and the Carousel Ballroom and the Matrix, and as far as all the hanging out and who was in the scene and who wasn't, or all those fabled houses and all that stuff? I'm just completely clueless. I never saw it, I never really heard much about it, I didn't hang out with the people who were part of it. I would see them at gigs, if they were in a band that was playing at the same gig we were, but other than that, I don't know where they lived, I don't know what they did, I don't know what they liked for dinner, anything.

Jhiani Fanon: It's funny how it happened. The corner of Haight and Ashbury is where most people gathered. We just stood around there, and you know, smoked weed, talked about the nature of what we were experiencing, the nature of just being. And we did this daily.

Teresa Tudury: I remember walking up and down Haight Street, or Oak, near the Panhandle, and just walking into houses I'd never been in before. People would just say, come on in. It was like an open house all over that neighborhood. And there were these great coffee houses where people were hanging out, exchanging ideas, playing music. It was unbelievable. Doing a lot of dope, of course.

LiAnne Graves: In 1963 I started surfing, so for me it was the surfers that brought me up into the Haight. Everyone was on the street, involved, connected. If you had enough gumption and whatever you could jump right in the mix. And my confidence was in surfing and so I paralleled both of them—you know, I'd go dance at the Fillmore at night and then go surf all day and then go back and dance again.

David LaFlamme: I'd been performing in Berkeley at the New Orleans House and the truck broke down. A wheel fell off of it, right on the corner of Haight and Divisadero. So I was desperate to get to this engagement and I literally ran out in front of a young fellow in a Volkswagen bus on Haight Street and stopped him. And went around to the side and told him this desperate situation I was in, that I was trying to get to this gig in Berkeley and my truck had broken down. And if he would take me and my amplifier and my instrument to this engagement that I would make sure that he got dinner, all the beer he could drink and probably even get him laid after that. He took us and a bunch of stuff over to the place in Berkeley and I'm afraid I kind of disappointed him—but I did get him the beer and the pizza.

New residents of the Haight were now attracting unwanted police attention: "Bohemians (or beatniks, or beats) complain of police bullying, of being pestered at their 'pads' by plainclothesmen seeking narcotics and stopped and searched on the streets 'just for wearing sandals and long hair.'"[23] Other folks actually enjoyed opening their doors to strangers. Over in Berkeley, an intrepid reporter attended "one instance of a new and growing fad among the Bay Area's swinging way-out set": the nude party. Berkeley should not take credit for the fad, however, as according to the reporter "the custom actually got going in San Francisco some time ago." The party began with guests dancing, drinking red wine, and talking about politics, and by the end of the evening the reporter witnessed something that "the Sexual Freedom League likes to call 'a sheer undiluted orgy.'" The primary message behind these gatherings is a search "for a guiltless, 'free' attitude toward sex," which many in the Sexual Freedom League believed would bring an end to the world's problems.[24]

If there were a musical-political divide between the city and the East Bay, it found its expression in "The Folk Scene," a regular column in the *Berkeley Barb*. Here there was a definite bias toward "authentic" folk and blues acts as opposed to what was perceived as the "business" of the emerging "rock":

> Almost unnoticed in the midst of this year's wave of acid bands, Frisco's largest rock label seems to have gone bankrupt—at least some of Autumn Records' masters have gone under the hammer in a recent auction to satisfy debts. The acid bands themselves have gotten much more publicity than money, and the only real success they had, the Trips Festival, was merchandised as a head trip

not a musical concert. They too are on their way out, unless I misjudge the signs, for the young and ignorant hippies are climbing on the bandwagon. Starting in joy they are ending in greed, just as rock itself did.

Rock has had a long lingering death. Let's hope the final crisis comes rapidly so that the money boys will quit and the survivors can get to the business of making a real music with a real audience.[25]

Fillmore dances attracted a different kind of unwanted police attention. Having subleased the Fillmore, Bill Graham decided to apply for his own dance permit. District police surveyed local business owners about Graham's use of the hall, and twenty-seven individuals complained, including Rabbi Elliot Burstein of nearby Congregation Beth Israel.[26] Graham countered that the fourteen dances he had run at the Fillmore were free of incident, and that he had been investing back in the neighborhood by improving the auditorium, cleaning the streets, and cooperating with the police on patrol. His application for a temporary permit was nonetheless rejected, as he said, out of "fear of the unknown. . . . They don't like white beatniks in a Negro neighborhood, people who come in my place and take off their shoes to dance. But is this against the law?"[27] No manager of any other dancehall in the city encountered the same problems. Yet.

Meanwhile, the chief of the SF Police narcotics division agreed with the Senate investigating committee that LSD should be labeled a dangerous drug. Lieutenant Norbert Curry confirmed that the drug was "readily available . . . for $5 for a small capsule" and that he had seen that the drug "causes behavioral changes which result in temporary insanity and can lead to violence."[28] The Attorney General soon added his voice to the chorus, announcing plans for a statewide, two-day conference on the control of hallucinogenic drugs, involving a wide range of participants including "young people themselves to consider the entire scope of this new drug problem." He maintained that "we have increasing reports of severe mental injuries resulting from indiscriminate and uncontrolled use of hallucinogenic drugs," including suicidal or homicidal tendencies, though he was unable to provide figures on such injuries or crimes committed while under the influence of LSD.[29]

Sandoz Pharmaceuticals had been providing LSD-25 to legitimate institutions for medical experiments, but in the wake of US government restrictions, informed the Federal Food and Drug Administration that they were withdrawing their investigational drug application due to "unforeseen public reaction."

> Dr. Craig Burrell, medical director for Sandoz pharmaceuticals, said "We brought it (LSD) in from Switzerland for experimental purposes and released it only to highly qualified clinical investigators. Our stuff hasn't gone into the black market but the impression does persist among some people that it may have gone there."[30]

In the wake of Sandoz's decision to stop distributing legal LSD, the fear of a rise of "bathtub" LSD was growing. The FDA contacted all universities, informing officials of the dangers of hallucinogenic drugs and the fact that such drugs can be made in college chemistry laboratories. The administration of UC Berkeley refused to comply with the FDA's request to report students caught taking illegal hallucinogenic drugs on campus, however, stating that such information was generally passed upward from local police departments in official reports.[31] Three days later Stanford announced that they would not be complying with the FDA's request either, as doing so would violate doctor-patient confidentiality.[32]

A pilot study showed LSD's positive effects on creativity and problem-solving,[33] and the *Berkeley Barb* showed that positive and enlightening LSD trips were possible with some basic preparation; yet the local papers devoted less time to the experiences of casual LSD seekers and more to the polar extremes (Timothy Leary, suicidal teenagers).[34] In May, the *Chronicle* published an editorial in support of the State Assembly's refusal to criminalize possession of LSD for personal use. According to the head of the student health service at UC Berkeley, LSD can be a dangerous drug, but the real problem was with its sale and manufacture:

> The lesson learned years ago from Prohibition should not be lost. LSD, like bathtub gin, is too easy to make to try to prohibit it. What are needed are stricter controls over the manufacture and sale of LSD under license for legitimate research. Such controls are contained in a Federal law which will take effect May 17 and which is well designed to catch the drug's illegal distributors.[35]

Yet the State Assembly "gave swift and overwhelming passage" to the legislation ending private use of LSD. The bill rendered possession or use of the drug a misdemeanor carrying a $1,000 fine or one year in jail; repeated violations would result in prison terms of up to five years. The manufacture, transportation, possession for sale, or sale of LSD would be deemed a felony, punishable with up to five years imprisonment on first offense and up to ten for repeated offenses.[36]

The FDA then proposed strict controls on two chemicals used in the manufacturing of LSD: lysergic acid and lysergic acid amide.[37] Amid this noise, the *Chronicle* published a considered, five-part exposé on "the Facts of the LSD World," in which Donovan Bess accompanied LSD users and their "guides" into the ritualistic use of the drug.[38] While Bess presented the users' experiences as generally positive, he did close the series with a summary of a recent editorial in the *New England Journal of Medicine* stating that "no one can be sure that ingestion of this drug will not harm him immediately or in the long run."[39]

Despite the moral panic surrounding LSD there was still recognition of more considered opinion. The UC Extension ran a week-long conference on LSD, with speakers representing equally the pro- and anti-acid perspectives, intending to probe questions relating to the future of LSD as a social issue.[40] Unsurprisingly, there were warnings about the enormous problems of enforcement facing the state when LSD was made illegal in the fall; that there would be an unprecedented underground market for the drug; and that the drug would be transportable via unconventional means—under postage stamps, on fingernails, on the lapel of a coat. Richard Alpert provided details about the number of "hits" in a gram of LSD, and estimated that

> from 85 to 90 percent of the current rock 'n' roll groups, "from the top down," use psychedelics. Rock 'n' roll, he said, is a "social institution that comes out of the psychedelic experience."[41]

The symposium also offered theatrical spectacle—a demonstration consisting of film, stills, music, strobes, miscellaneous noise, much like the Trips Festival, staged for a straight audience by Stewart Brand and Gerd Stern:

> The idea . . . was to flood the sense-receptors of the audience to the point where time sense warped, emotions ran free and love of the world suffused each spectator's body.[42]

Timothy Leary, in "ecstatic dress" also took part in the symposium, saying that LSD was "best understood as a religious pilgrimage . . . the LSD kick is best understood as ecstasy, and the LSD panic is nothing short of a spiritual crisis." LSD was "part of a revolutionary social complex . . . called 'the psychedelic style.'"[43]

A voice from "square" academia, representing Stanford's Institute for the Study of Human Problems, described the controversy over LSD in the context of mainstream American drug culture, "from the aspirin and sleeping pills in the medicine chest to the martinis and cigarettes of the social hour":

> From the standpoint of use, let us keep drugs within the domain of their demonstrable effectiveness; from the standpoint of man, let him express himself directly, without the pretense that it is a chemical and not himself which gives him depth or joy.[44]

In an unrelated seminar for business and government executives, Dr. Huston Smith, professor of philosophy at MIT, author of *The Religions of Man*, and final keynote speaker for the UC Extension symposium, suggested that the religious conversions many associated with the use of LSD would require follow-up studies, to determine the lasting effects of such changes "which are indistinguishable from [those] that occur naturally." He noted that young people were "making a balancing right end run around . . . the church to link up with Zen, Meher Baba (a Sufi spiritual leader), parapsychology or pharmacological mysticism via LSD."[45] At the end of the symposium, the *Chronicle* declared that the "question whether LSD is a curse or a blessing remained unanswered."[46]

LSD as a "religious pilgrimage," the alignment with Eastern spiritual practices, and the question of the drug's long-term effects, were common themes in contemporary discussions of drug use, and continue to resonate today with members of the Haight community.

The psychedelic experience

CHARLIE MORGAN: I wouldn't romanticize it all. There were a lot of withdrawals from drugs, there were a lot of downsides to all that, but that's how we learn. You know, we kinda followed the watchwords of Richard Alpert, Ram Dass, who said, after a while the idea is to be high, not to keep getting high. So we went for the cleanup trips. We went for Eastern religions, started to investigate how to get to a place that felt good, and was kind of elevated, without having to come down all the time.

ART ROGERS: Many cultures have taken psychedelics for many years: peyote in the Southwest, psilocybin mushrooms down in South America, Central America—LSD was just another manifestation of those. It was the same thing. *The Psychedelic Experience* showed how to take this drug, whether it be LSD or peyote or psilocybin or mescaline or whatever, as a ritual for a spiritual journey. It was a translation of the Tibetan Book of the Dead, which was a guide written by the Tibetan monks to help their fellow monks through the death process, to help guide them through the different portals, the different levels of consciousness, to release, to go back to God. You know, it's all the same, you all go back to the source, whatever you want to call it: God. I'm not saying it was a good thing that happened, but for many of us, it was a path to understanding spirituality and enlightenment and a guide for our lives. And it was all about love. That's where all of that came from: to make good choices.

TERESA TUDURY: There was a sense of sacredness about the use of drugs. I know that sounds maybe ridiculous in retrospect because of how far out it went, and how uncontrollably bad it got, but I do recall people having a great sense of responsibility too, toward changing the world. We really felt—it was probably some arrogance too—that there was something very important about sensitizing the generation before us about what was going on in the world. It was something to do with our spiritual lives as well. And through that time people started to practise yoga, meditation, Zen—it was all a piece.

TERRY HAGGERTY: The collective experience is a very ancient one, a very tribal one. LSD really dissolved your sense of identity. And if you approached it from a reverent place, and had a conscious death with the experience, unbecoming, letting go of the glue that holds your personality together, you could actually come back in and get a vision of yourself that would allow you to let go of the things you wanted to, change the things you wanted to. And death was such an important part of it, because that's an ancient slot that all beings go through, and there's great power and support in consciousness and things that lead you to it, if you're willing to be part of the great mind. But if you have to be an individual, then these things are unavailable.

Linda LaFlamme: The thing is that as soon as marijuana and LSD came along it was just remarkable. It changed your whole way of thinking. All of a sudden you weren't thinking about getting a straight job as a waitress or a secretary or anything like that; you were thinking of creating something different for yourself.

Art Rogers: As you choose your good, you define your evil. You experience something like this and you go to a place where the paradoxes disappear and everything is, you know, "one." And then as you come down, in a state of oneness, you're enlightened. You're pure joy. Everything is wonderful. And I see this as a spiritual experience, this lifting of weight, this alignment with one-ness—so as you come down from this god-like state, this beautiful, beautiful state, you start having paradox enter, the knowledge of good and evil rears its head, and you have to make some choices, of what is good and what is bad. And if you're too hard on yourself, if you define too many things that you have to live up to? I think the golden rule puts it pretty simple: that's pretty straight. You come down and say, I'm just gonna do good, you know. It's not about me. It's not about me.

Kurt "Crowbar" Kangas: You know, a drug is a gateway to opening your mind to certain things. Like LSD, we were told that you had to die and be reborn again. By taking LSD you lose your ego, you get naked and you're free. And that's what we did at that time. But I was very, very serious about searching for truth and finding something. I didn't know what I was looking for; I just needed something that felt good and that was true and honest.

Charlie Morgan: LSD taught people that what's going on inside you has a lot to do with how you perceive what's going on outside you. You know? It was a road to enlightenment, if you can call it that. And I'm still on it. I still feel like there's a long way to go, and there are many lessons to learn. But it kinda keeps life fresh and new, to still be examining it.

Jhiani Fanon: LSD is not like a drug at all. It alters your perception. It changes something about you. If I could describe it, it's like you've been in this room, and you've been in the dark all your life, and all of sudden you turn on the light. That's what it seemed like to us.

Kurt "Crowbar" Kangas: One thing about LSD though, was that you go on the ride up, and you get to a certain point and then you level off. And it's the going up that's the scary part. That's when things rush at you and the hallucinations and the weirdness and everything. Once you plane out then everything stabilizes and you become very cerebral—where everything you've learned in your life is right there.

Dickie Peterson: LSD opened doors of perception that made me aware of myself, of the cosmos, of my relationship in it, you know. Now, there are people that would never pick up on this, and I think an LSD trip would be good for anybody, but there needs to be supervision. You can't just drop this on somebody, because your whole reality changes. And if somebody is not ready for it, it's going to be a nightmare. I would never dose somebody on acid. I think that's just horrible, and I don't think that's fair to do to people. So, I think LSD will do wonders for anybody, if it's done in a constructive manner, but that's the way it is with anything.

Eric Christensen: The idea was consciousness. We weren't doing this to obliterate the reality; we were doing it to fine-tune and experiment with consciousness. And a lot of people found, well ok, we don't have to do this by rolling a joint or dropping a pill; we can study. And the real smart people that came out of it didn't become victims to drugs. A lot of people did. A lot of people had addictive personalities and became controlled by the substances. But then a lot of us went on to do very creative things, and very spiritual things. So there was that kind of crossroads there too, how that whole acceptance of mind-altering substances hurt a lot of people, but also changed a lot of people in positive ways.

Ramon Sender: I'm still a believer in better living through chemistry. I just don't think we've got it sorted out quite yet.

Kurt "Crowbar" Kangas: We all have these tremendous and wonderful stories of exploration. I tell people that we are the petri dish of the sixties. And some of us came through unscathed and others came through very wounded.

Suzi Young: I never believed that taking LSD was a way of life. I believed, along with Timothy Leary, that acid wasn't a drug that you take every day. It was something that you took to get a glimpse of what the possibilities were, but with the clear understanding that if you wanted to get there, you had to do it under your own power. That this was a glimpse, but not a shortcut. So I never thought of drugs as a way of life. I guess I was really lucky, I was never tempted or involved with a drug that I could become addicted to. I was always more interested in the psychedelics, in acid or peyote or mescaline or something to get closer to that enlightened state. And then after I saw that those things were possible I learned to meditate. And now I chant, and it's that same enlightened state. But I knew that there's no shortcut to the work. You have to do the work. Once you realize what the path is, you have to do the work, which is always the hardest part of all.

GLENN HOWARD: Now with LSD you get bounced out of those ruts which actually are controlling you even though you don't realize it. Because you're controlled by things of habit. Any time you believe exactly what you were taught by some sort of machine you'd better rethink it, which is one of the things that psychedelics are great for, and the best psychedelic is LSD.

ERIC CHRISTENSEN: I think I had a pretty healthy attitude toward it, and had a pretty healthy experience with it all. I never liked to be out of control; I would always make sure that I was in a good space with good people. And that's why there was a certain irresponsibility of some of the psychedelic rangers, of Ken Kesey's Pranksters, of dosing people and wanting to turn people on. And I'd argue that to this day, that this should be a conscious choice that people make in a very sane environment, and that some of these big events, where people were getting dosed, there were a lot of negative consequences of that. And fortunately there were groups like the Hog Farm and other people who would take care of people who got a little too out there.

CHARLES JOHNSON: Acid is an outdoor drug, where you're out at the beach. More so at the beach than the woods. Because things lurk behind trees in the woods, but at the beach you can see it coming.

TERRY HAGGERTY: I was born and raised in Marin County. I mean, the thought of taking acid and going to the city was bizarre. Not when you had all these beautiful lakes, you could get naked, and swim in the water, and lay under the tree. Go to the city, honey? Holy smokes!

JHIANI FANON: I really, honestly felt that I could do my part in saving the world. And if you got everybody high that would make them peaceful, right? Didn't quite work out that way! But you see, I guess it's written that you find what you're looking for. And if that's what you're looking for, if you're looking for peace and love and all of that, and you're 19 or 20, as we were, then that's what you find.

MARC ARNO: You know, if I ruled the world I wouldn't make everybody take it at least once. But I would sure make it readily available for spiritual purposes. Not recreational. In fact one of the most dismaying experiences was watching people decide that it was a disco biscuit that you could mix with alcohol or speed or anything else. A lot of people just related to it as another high, not connected to the spirit at all.

LIANNE GRAVES: If I hadn't taken acid I can't imagine the person I would have become.

JHIANI FANON: If I was going to recommend that anyone took LSD, they would be in a quiet, comfortable, safe place, with no distractions. Because to tell you to take it and go to a dance or a party? It's too much. In fact, it defeats the whole purpose, because the knowledge is inside; it's not external.

Rusty Goldman: I think most stable-minded people who are on a journey of self-discovery or enlightenment should be taken on a guided tour of that dimension. That dimension of LSD is happening as we speak—it's all around us. The way Leary used to describe it, it's like going to a pond in the park and putting your finger in, watching a drop of water drip. There's a whole world that exists inside that drop of water, but you can't see it unless you have the right tool, which in this case would be a microscope. You put that drop on the lens, my god, there is a world going on there—a world all in itself. It's very far out. Well, the dimension of LSD is much like that, and the microscope you use to find that psychedelic dimension is LSD. LSD can be a really good thing, really help you see, not only yourself, but the world around you. Now, there are places to do it and there are places that I advise people not to do it. And especially you want to have an experienced guide with you.

Dickie Peterson: If a band is going to take drugs, you all have to take the same drug. You can't have this guy on an upper, and this guy on a downer, and this guy on something else altogether. You will not work. Our philosophy was, we all had to be stoned on the same thing. That's necessarily true in this day and age.

Sam Andrew: Like, when I would take acid and play with Big Brother, I would go through this whole thing in my mind about how the guitar came to be. You know, it's like this piece of wood, and they cut this tree down over here, and they put the steel bands on, that metal was brought from over here. This real concrete thing, how did this guitar happen, how did the drums happen, and how did this all happen to be played together? And then on the theoretical level I'd go through it too. You know, why are we playing a C chord, how did that happen? And then the overtone series and nature and Pythagoras, and all this stuff, going all the way back to the beginning, you know. So really focusing, even in the acid experience, on being a professional musician, understanding what we were doing—all that stuff was going on in my head while we were playing. So as you can imagine, every now and then I'd go, what key are we in?

Terry Haggerty: San Francisco bands couldn't tune their instruments. I mean, that was the first and foremost thing that could not be denied. Could *not* tune their instruments. And if you ever tried to tune an instrument on acid, or even unwind a guitar chord on acid, you realize how absolutely twisted and hard it was to play in tune. And we'd listen to that San Francisco stuff and we'd just go, holy Jesus, you know, that's far out! They're covering like a tone and a half in both directions, like, and I guess that's an E chord, you know?

DICKIE PETERSON: I mean, we took a lot of acid. We took lots. I mean, we took a *lot* of acid, you know. Now, what is psychedelic music? Psychedelic music is any music that you listen to; I don't care what it is. I mean, drop a tab of acid and listen to Bach. Drop a tab of acid and listen to Mothers of Invention; it doesn't matter. When you hit that psychedelic consciousness, it's all psychedelic. You know?

The *Chronicle* published an editorial in support of Bill Graham's quest for a dancehall permit. Calling the decision by the Police Department and the Board of Permit Appeals "misdirected and highly unfair malevolence," the paper surmised that the only distinction between Graham and the tenants of the Fillmore Auditorium readily granted dancehall permits was the type of crowd drawn to rock 'n' roll shows. Citing critic John Wasserman's description of Graham as "the best entrepreneur of public entertainment in San Francisco," the editorial proceeded to dismantle the "bureaucratic fear, prejudice and instinct for censorship" at issue in this case. By this point Graham had secured written testimonials from neighboring merchants and numerous witnesses to Fillmore concerts, who "found them interesting, exciting, and completely orderly and harmless. . . . Though [participants in the revels] have long hair, and some wear beards, and few adhere to [contemporary codes of] fashion . . ." The editorial closed:

> It is not disputed that the dancing is chaste and sexless, that the dancers are peaceful and happy, that there are no drunks . . . and that a good time is had by all. The police, formerly besought by Graham to list their objections, have failed to respond and it must seem that they have no case against him. On advice of counsel, he proposes to conduct business at the old stand pending a new appeal—fortified by written testimonials and best wishes from all segments of the Fillmore community. Further refusal of his dance-hall permit cannot be justified in the absolute absence of cause.[47]

This editorial had unexpected ramifications for Graham's Fillmore operations. The following Friday, police began rounding up patrons under 18 then stood them on the street and frisked them like criminals with their hands against the police van. Two officers presented Graham with a copy of the *Chronicle*'s editorial, calling it "a direct affront," according to Ralph Gleason, who was present:

> Meanwhile in the same police precinct, the Avalon Ballroom went merrily on. No SF police officer entered the hall, no minors were hauled away. An announcement was made of what had happened at the Fillmore and those under 18 were urged to leave. Some did. Others did not. At the Longshore Hall, the dancers were uninterrupted by the law also. And at the Fillmore, not everyone who looked young enough to be eligible for illegality was taken away.

The Fillmore Ballroom has been having these rock 'n' roll dances intermittently since January. This is the first time such a police raid has occurred. The only reason I would not allow my own teen-age daughters there without me now is the fear that they would be treated like criminals by the police. For being under 18.[48]

Nonetheless, the following weekend police arrested fourteen young dancers at the Fillmore as well as Bill Graham, charging them with violating Section 558 of the Municipal Code which proclaimed it "unlawful for a minor under 18 to visit a public dancehall, or for a proprietor of a dancehall to admit such minors." Despite Graham's deliberate checking of patrons' identification at the entrance to the Fillmore, three police officers went in and began checking identification cards anyway. Several eyewitnesses to the arrest saw members of the police force carrying copies of the *Chronicle* editorial denouncing them.[49]

The fallout surrounding the Fillmore arrests was visible all over the *Chronicle*, from the front page to Gleason's column. One reporter spoke to the parents of the young people arrested at the Fillmore, who raised concerns about their children having juvenile police records despite their not having violated any law. The probation officer's admonition that the parents "just remember to keep your kid away from controversial places" seemed less like sage advice and more like a threat of further action.[50]

And the fallout continued. By this point attorneys were looking into the history of Section 558 and determined that the law in question had been enacted in 1909:

"In those days, a 'public dance hall' was a saloon certainly, a house of prostitution probably, and in any event a place where no parent would want his children to be," [Attorney Dan L. Garrett's] letter [to the SF Board of Supervisors] said.

A properly supervised dance, where no alcoholic beverages are served, does not fall under the intent of that law. . . . Garrett asked the Supervisors to study "that now anomalous bit of legislation" and substitute "proper regulatory measures" that would allow teen-age dancing.[51]

The mayor and a dozen city officials agreed that the dancehall ordinance was "outdated and needs rewriting." Mayor Shelley recognized that teenagers "have to have an outlet . . . [and] need someplace to go," and that their primary concern was the environment surrounding the consumption of popular music. Only the Board of Supervisors could modify an existing ordinance, however, and the mayor urged the board to draft a new and fairer law.[52]

The charges against Bill Graham were dropped, just in time for him to host Andy Warhol's Exploding Plastic Inevitable featuring the Velvet Underground at the Fillmore.[53] One more weekend in the ever-varying expressive culture at the San Francisco dancehalls.

Dancehall concerts

These [local] bands represent a cultural flowering, not a freaky turn in the top 40 material; and it is time, the sense of your own people on the bandstand, the thought of musicians who share your outlook and thoughts, and whose music is all the more into it because of the vast common ground between artist and audience, this which makes the music real. This cannot be recorded. Hip bands are like blues bands, they gain much from context, and no record company has figured out how to give the listener the sense of being in the Avalon or the Fillmore surrounded by 2,000 beautiful people, some watching, others tripping out swaying and bouncing, others dancing. . . . Anyway if this culture, if the people in the Haight-Ashbury and Berkeley . . . have anything to say, it is these rock bands which seem to be the way it will be said.[54]

I don't know that when we go to church we know exactly what it is that we experience. The question is whether an experience is provided that gives one any of the feelings of unity with one's fellow man, any feelings of openness, safeness, trust, a loving perception of the environment, the beauty of the environment, a chance where a group of people can get together just to be together in a very good feeling. And anybody who has been [to the Fillmore or the Avalon] knows that these transcend dances in the common, ordinary sense by such a discriminable degree, and they approach at times a moment of ecstasy. And ecstasy has always been a central experience of every religion. That's how I see it now.[55]

The two main dancehalls at the beginning of the San Francisco scene were the Fillmore Auditorium, run by Bill Graham, and the Avalon Ballroom, run by Chet Helms. The differences between the two venues are usually attributed to personal stereotypes: Bill Graham was an entrepreneur with a keen business sense, while Chet Helms was a hippie who never had a business plan. Whatever distinctions existed in levels of professionalism, in loyalty, in approach, and in psychedelic participation, the Fillmore and the Avalon established an aesthetic template for the consumption of, and participation in, musical experience, that spread from the short 60s in San Francisco to the present day. The recollections of musicians and audience members, poster artists and sound technicians, provide vivid snapshots of the new musical culture and the transformative experience of popular music in the short 60s.

Sensory environment

ALBERT NEIMAN: When you break down that fourth wall you create a ritual. It's more like a religious rite. And the experience itself can be very transcendental. Then when you throw in a light show, where you break down the barriers between what's up and down, where the walls are and where the floor is and where the ceiling is, that can be even more transcendental. You can even have trouble walking or talking. Just the experience of that theatrical milieu, that excitement, and everything's going on at once, can make a very psychedelic experience without drugs.

DICKIE PETERSON: You know, when you walked into it, you didn't have to take a pill to be stoned, you could walk in there and when you walked out, you were high, because you were just experiencing sensations and things that you had never even dreamt existed, and that made the whole art scene, not just the music scene; it was all conglomerated. Look at the posters from the 60s. Look at the artwork. This was very psychedelic art; it was very musical art. You look at this stuff and you can listen to music while you look at it; it fits, you know. It was a great time to be a musician. I don't know that that could happen again.

ERIC CHRISTENSEN: Well part of the attempt at those things, at least as I view it, was to create a psychedelic experience. Now, whether it was to enhance the psychedelic experience, or to give you an altered experience when you weren't high, that remains a question. But you could go to those events, watch a light show, listen to live music and certainly that would alter your consciousness, whether you smoked anything or not.

KURT "CROWBAR" KANGAS: Just by knowing certain people, we were connected by proxy. You'd go in and you'd party, and nobody really considered themselves anything special; we were all just a bunch of hippies in a room who liked to smoke pot.

CHARLIE MORGAN: You know, for the first time we all danced as a group. We'd just get out there when someone was ripping up a good song, and you didn't wait on the sidelines—everybody jumped out there and started to dance. And I remember feeling like we were stoned, the musicians were stoned, it was like everything was kind of—what's the word—*effected*.

KEN IRVING: The other thing was the dope. There was so much of it that you could go work a rock concert and all you'd see was dope passed back and forth. I don't think anyone was listening to the music anyway, no matter how bad it was.

MARC ARNO: You know what is interesting about the Avalon and the Fillmore? It was the first time in history black blues artists actually got paid. They would sit up there or stand up there on stage and look at all these long-haired freaks squatting on the floor, laying on the floor. Freaky guys over in the corner under the strobe light. And at the end of the song they would scream and howl and yodel and whistle.

Poster art

Not since Montparnasse has serious art—here, conveying in two-dimensional visual terms the multi-dimensional experience of an evening with the Family Dog—served commercialism with such coruscating originality. And what is entirely new in this art is its pyrotechnic calligraphy, particularly in the work of Wes Wilson, where lettering itself takes on the music's beat.[56]

The hippie canvas has no center of interest. It spreads outward, lacking form or direction, and its essence is not the whole, but the subtle interaction of parts. Thus, the content of a poster advertising a rock concert is secondary. The insinuation of the design is what matters.[57]

WES WILSON: It had something to do with design and the color choices for sure. But a lot of people assume that certain people could do things while they had LSD. And that's just not the case. Just after the fact, these things were learned. And then they were applied.

RUSTY "PROFESSOR POSTER" GOLDMAN: Much like the Moulin Rouge in Paris where you had artists of the time, rock art is the art of the times. You'll see in today's artwork the influence that psychedelic art has had on commercial art. It's amazing. It's not just amazing: it's history repeating itself, it's life repeating itself, and for the good.

WES WILSON: Bill Graham and I would get together and go over to his place and we'd go get a coffee downstairs or something, kind of a once a week. And I'd get the info for the next concert. And I delivered it myself on Fridays before the opening night. And then they'd give away free copies of the posters, and handbills and so forth at that point for the next week. It probably went on like that for about a year.

RUSTY "PROFESSOR POSTER" GOLDMAN: Now, you asked me, did the artist make anything? They sold their images for $100 a week per poster. Nobody knew they were going to be big-selling. Nobody knew the money thing was going to happen. And, later on, in the early 80s the artists got together and there was a big lawsuit. ARTS: Artists' Rights Today. And they wanted their money. They wanted something. It was a big legal thing, and they lost. Yes. When the poster artists did a poster, they were paid as contract artists. They sold their rights to the artwork when they took the check for the piece.

Light shows

The most effective light shows avoid the static, "hard edge" image and use the sound of the music and the pulse of its rhythm as the skeleton on which to hang the flowing light effects. When this works—and like all improvised art it sometimes does not work—the result can be spectacular. A good show . . . in which the light artists are in sympathy with the music, understand it and, even better, are familiar with it, can add an entirely new dimension to the experience. One can be transported out of the room into a new world entirely, with the huge blobs of color floating on the wall, lines of contrast dashing across it in time to the music and all the while, little inserts of film loops to intrigue the eye.[58]

MARC ARNO: It was an art form to me that was connected directly to the music. A visual interpretation. But the media insisted it was all drug based.

ART ROGERS: I always just loved the light shows. That was my favorite part of a concert, to watch this throbbing color sloshing around, which I knew was oil and water and plates, and then some film clip of Tarzan screaming through the woods, or Laurel and Hardy, a Model T falling apart—I mean, it was just visual candy for me. God, it was so much fun. It was just a zoo.

MARC ARNO: February 11th 1966 I turned pro, doing light shows at the Fillmore. It was being one with the music. Translating music visually, which was a very emotional experience for me. Three bands, two sets each, two bucks.

BANANA: When you're onstage, and there's three light shows going, and there's strobelights going, and you're trying to put this wimpy stuff across after Blue Cheer has just played, you're really concentrating a lot more on trying to play this shit good than you are on who the hell is in the audience or whatever is going on. Even if you tried, you know, you'd just get dizzy and slightly nauseous, so you're better off sticking with the music.

We had to work some things out—how to relate to the music. How to relate to the time. How to relate to 160 degrees or whatever of wall space. I had this rare opportunity to start from scratch. There was no stage lighting at the Avalon. Had there been, it would have been much harder to take these projections and fit them all in, partly because the equipment we had was so limited. We were using classroom overhead projectors and army-surplus things. I was doing purely liquids. I would work spontaneously for an hour, making an abstract image to the music.[59]

MARC ARNO: The very best, most artistic and unique light show there ever was, was a couple of girls. Their light show was called Heavy Water. What made them exceptional was that they hand-painted their own slides. They'd take a picture out of a comic book and hand paint the slide so it was just the character floating in air. They studied chemistry, so their liquids were very volatile, just sitting there and bubbling chemically, instead of the squishy blobby stuff which most light shows were most of the time. They were there in the thick of it; it was just very hard for women to be acknowledged as anything but "my old lady." The hippie movement was so misogynist that women were never given the credit due for what they contributed.

The Fillmore

It's an old joint, built in the year One and used for decades as a dancehall. It's an upstairs loft at Fillmore and Geary with several small balconies and a cafe or lounge. There's no booze, only soft drinks, near beer and food. And it has become, in recent months, the general headquarters for the artistic revolution that is taking place here.[60]

The view from the galleries would make a fundamentalist think of hell. Led by Tony Martin's light show, which fills the huge wall behind the bands and their 30-foot row of amplifiers and electronics with red shapes shifting in time to the music, the hall is filled with swaying, writhing people. A couple of hundred sit or stand near the stage absorbed in watching the bands, keeping rhythm with their bodies, and the rest are dancing. A few do awkward modern dances, but many have given themselves over to the music and are doing beautiful free form motions. . . . The totality of the experience now leaves you catharticized and calm. [The] crowd here is friendly and calm, and most of them seem to understand the music.[61]

LiAnne Graves: It was the music for sure. The variety that came through the Fillmore—you know, the mix was fabulous. I saw Otis Redding there and that changed my life. And God, all the San Francisco bands. It was just the nature of the building too. She was just a grand old music hall. And the floor was beautiful, you could just run around, dance and be free or find a corner to sit in, and everybody was there.

Charles Johnson: Bill Graham did some things that were just extraordinary. I mean, some of the people that he'd have on a bill, he'd have Miles Davis and the Grateful Dead on the same bill. So he was, in his own way, introducing people not to just one style or type of music, he was introducing people to *music*.

Mark Arno: Eventually there was a night when I wasn't part of the light show and felt entitlement to show up for the concert. At which point Bill Graham said, "Who the fuck do you think you are?" And chased me down the street yelling at me. That is when I knew I was part of it. Because until Bill Graham cursed you out you were not really an insider.

San Francisco and the Long 60s

WAVY GRAVY: And Bill Graham realized "there's gold in them thar hills," as far as being a rock promoter, there's money in rock 'n' roll and rock 'n' roll concerts, and he took it from there, as far as the money aspect. But also put on public assemblages that were safe, the sound was good, and didn't cost an arm and a leg.

MARC ARNO: There was no Beatles versus Stones, Fillmore versus Avalon. Inevitably there was a full house every weekend in both places. There were exceptions but not many. There was more than enough people that wanted to hear the music to fill both places.

The Avalon

[The Avalon] had an L-shaped balcony, gilded booths, and columns. Red flocked wallpaper and a lot of mirrors, with the stage in the far diagonal from the door. Like a music hall with a sprung wooden dance floor. The best dance floor *ever*. Better than the old Fillmore. When seven or eight hundred people got dancing on it, the floor moved in sync. . . . I went toe-to-toe with Graham with a smaller hall, no financial backing, and no real business experience. I worked eighteen-hour days, supported twenty to forty employees, and produced over five hundred evenings of entertainment at the Avalon. My lack of ultimate financial success was not the result of sloth or a compassionate admission policy. I was simply undercapitalized.[62]

I would sometimes go for social reasons to the Avalon. To see a band like Sopwith Camel. The original Avalon was run much looser than the Fillmore. Chet's door policy was if you met him once or you could convince him that you met him, he would let you in. Then the band couldn't be paid and they couldn't get home. People loved Chet and he was a very nice man, but he didn't have a sense of responsibility. In that era, that fit. I didn't fit in their eyes. So the Avalon was looked upon with great favor by the Golden Gate Park crowd and the Haight-Ashbury crowd. Chet was in it for *righteous* reasons. Bill does a good job. But he's a *businessman*. The pure hippie of the day thought of the Avalon as the *real* church. Mine was the commercial church.[63]

MARC ARNO: The single biggest problem was that Chet ran his business like a religion and Graham ran his like a business.

KURT "CROWBAR" KANGAS: What turned Graham into that so-called asshole that they called him? Well, I don't blame him. I know why he became what he did. Chet on the other hand was very loose. He was not necessarily concerned about making a profit, and he lost a lot, but I think on Chet's mind, his whole idea was to not lose money. Not necessarily *make* any but definitely not *lose* it. And that's not where Bill wanted to be. Totally different thing.

Albert Neiman: Another thing I think is very important was, before Chet Helms came along, in the 50s and early 60s, when bands played, the owner of the club would hand them a list and say, this is what you guys are playing tonight. Chet Helms, very early in the game, would say to a band, well, whatever you guys really feel you should play, that's what you should play. And let the bands decide. It was a whole different creative experience. And a lot of times the bands played off the audience. Because at the beginning, the bands were the least important element. The most important element was the audience and the light show. Right?

Marc Arno: The sound man stood right behind the speaker stack on the stage with the group. So I could step out and adjust microphones and set up for the next band. Eventually we had a little two track recorder and then a four track—no, I don't know if we ever got to four. But we would also record the PA feed. Eventually I moved about 25, 30 feet down the side wall, but to start with you were right there. You were also the stage hand, stage manager/sound manager. After a while, working at the Avalon, I stopped accepting drinks that were handed to me in the middle of my job and started bringing a bag lunch, a bag dinner and bottles that I opened myself. And lo and behold, one night somebody hypo'd the orange in my lunch bag. So I would say out of all the acid trips I had, which I couldn't begin to count, fewer than half of them were voluntary. What's my overriding memory of working at the Avalon? Bliss. Basically bliss.

One of Ralph Gleason's running themes in the first half of 1966 was the tension between the new youth culture and the old guard, and it extended beyond dance-hall permits. There had been a general tendency toward "rousting the beards and sandals" from the streets of the major metropolitan centers of the United States, dating back to the Beat heyday—but now it intensified in the crusade against LSD. To address this issue, over 150 San Franciscan artists formed a committee "for mutual aid and assistance."[64] In "one of the most important events in SF's cultural history," the committee met to discuss the divide between the arts, and the belief that the important cultural events in the Bay Area were now being held in venues like the Both/And, the Jazz Workshop, and the Fillmore, not at established halls of high culture such as the Opera House:

> We may someday come to realize that what this city is really famed for, culturally, is the life of its artists, the creativity of its artists and its musicians and not for its ability to produce great performances of great examples of other cultures.[65]

Related to this was the Artists Liberation Front, a group of actors, painters, and musicians who offered their services to community groups, churches, anyone who needed them. Not expecting financial help from the city, they raised $5,000 in a benefit to kick-start plans for a five-day festival in September, with hundreds of painters, poets, actors promising to encourage people around the city to watch them work or help them create.[66] This critical artistic mass was the impetus for poet Kenneth Rexroth's editorial that same week in the *Berkeley Barb*:

> There is a cultural revolution, and it is subversive. . . . What is happening today is . . . a mass movement, confined largely to people under 35, recruited from all levels of education and economic class. It is self sustaining where it is not persecuted out of existence, and its creative expression is diffused—democratized. . . . It is a fundamental change in life attitude.
>
> All you have to do is look at them—these people live differently. Art is a kind of life. . . . This is essentially a religious movement, a demand that we as humans live up to our spiritual responsibilities.[67]

Yet the fear-mongering continued. The *Chronicle* ran a front-page story connecting the suicide of a young Berkeley student to an "LSD party" at a Telegraph Avenue apartment.[68] That same young man was eulogized on the *Barb*'s front page: he was a poet who was merely trying to take that trip to Europe.[69] Shortly thereafter, the *Chronicle* published a lurid depiction of a "Berkeley drug party" held in a young single mother's squalid apartment near the corner of Bancroft and Telegraph avenues: marijuana, methedrine, and children eating candy bars.[70]

There was a glamorous side to the hippies, of course. The Mod Hatter Shop in Mill Valley hosted a Psychedelic Fashion Show at the Fillmore in between musical sets. Among the featured items were "optical gearrings," a special earring which "by a light refraction process upon layers of plastic [give] an illusion of internal motion of the red, green, blue and yellow design,"[71] which were already on sale at the department stores in Union Square. Even the *Berkeley Barb* did a little bit of shopping:

> Hippy and hippy-related business grows apace. The Haight-Ashbury is amazing, especially the ecstatic clothing shops, which are the best I've seen in the area, altho [sic] I've not been to Oakland yet. . . . But growing even more is the local rock scene. The goldseekers have hit, with their recording contracts, the Airplane's LP . . . is selling well, there are reputed to be 700 rock bands in Northern Calif [sic], of which at least 10% seem to be hippy bands.[72]

A few months later the hippie fashion show at the new local North Face Ski Shop found Pigpen chatting with postdebs, North Beach bearded types, and Hell's Angels watching Mimi Fariña and Joan Baez modeling the latest. The *Chronicle*'s fashion editor was there and suggested that "maybe it's only the young who have this kind of flexibility. . . . [But] this kind of melange of people is the most interesting social phenomenon of the 1960s."[73]

Not all social phenomena were so warmly welcomed. Police began pursuing minor traffic infractions as a means of busting up communal houses in the Haight. Eventually, about fifty protesters marched from the 1500 block of Haight Street to the Park Police Station to protest "blue fascism": the rise in illegal arrests of local residents and the invasion of citizens' rights—searching without warrants and without consent.[74] The reality of communal living was often less colorful than the paper would have its readers believe, but sometimes more so:

> DICKIE PETERSON: You probably would have seen a few Hell's Angels hanging around our place. You would have seen bales of weed the size of cotton bales. On our kitchen table we had a big fruit bowl that was full of grass and various kinds of pills. You would have seen lofts in every room, these tall Victorian rooms. We had 21 people living in our commune. Lots of posters, wall-to-wall, ceiling-to-floor posters. You would see musical equipment. You would definitely see girls. Probably a motorcycle or two laying around in some living room. That's what our flat was like. It was a very busy place.

For all its focus on the Haight, still the *Chronicle* did not notice the neighborhood's new underground newspaper, or the underground scrummage over its name. As the *Barb* reported, two papers were now printed under the name "P.O. Frisco": the first an effort by Dan Elliott and Richard Sasson, the other by John Bronson, Gary Goldhill, and Ron Thelin, proprietor of the Psychedelic Shop. Thelin had paid the printing bill for the first issue, edited by Elliott, but felt it was "too political—not what we wanted. . . . We think there's a new community happening—we want to encourage it and be a voice for it." As Thelin had published the first issue of what was called the *Psychedelic Oracle*, he felt he owned the name. But the new *Oracle* "is not going to be an acid-head paper. LSD is just another chemical. Hell, I had attained the same state I got with acid much earlier on Yoga meditation."[75]

The Oracle

> The hippies have their own newspaper called The Oracle, and the illustrations took me by surprise. In large part they were religious. The religion that they were seeking to convey was obviously quite unorthodox. So is mine. They seemed to be groping their way toward new expressions of man's relation to the ultimate spiritual reality behind the universe, in order to find new ways of living and acting in harmony with it.[76]

From August 1965 the *Berkeley Barb* delivered a weekly newspaper with a progressive political viewpoint. A year later, the *Oracle* began its brief career publishing content concerned with the new psychedelic sensibility. It marked the difference between outer reality and inner space.[77] Where the *Barb* was functional and visually rudimentary, the *Oracle* proved that an underground newspaper could be at once relevant to its readership and artistically beautiful.[78] As an aggregate, the twelve individual issues of the *Oracle* crystallize an important historical moment, the psychedelic revolution in the "short 60s."

An oracular voice can be optimistic or foreboding, and the pages of the *Oracle* naturally reveal fluidity, affirmation, inconsistencies, tensions; an increasing sense of purpose, of charity, of self-importance, of community. Primarily the *Oracle* reveals the gulf between the head and straight cultures. If the *Chronicle* presented a linear account of the day's events from a particular ideological standpoint, and the *Barb* those same events from the opposite pole, the *Oracle* presented "the artists' vision of the present and the future." These visions were rarely confined to columns; they leaped across pages, dripped over borders, challenged the color-blind, and disrupted the reader's very sense of time and narrative.

Allen Cohen saw the *Oracle* as primarily "interested in the revolution of relations of the Man to Man, man to nature, man to woman. Ours is the politics of the life force."[79] Although some in the overground media saw the *Oracle* as revolutionary, not all found immediate access to its message:

> At first glance, it seems to be 30 pages of hideously designed wallpaper. Its pages are lavishly embroidered with marginal illustration, that take hours to contemplate, and its landscaped layout explodes with color. Although the *Oracle* seems unlikely to win a Pulitzer Prize, it may well influence the "straight" newspaper of the future.[80]

Taking hours to contemplate a newspaper was a new concept, but the concept of "time" for the psychedelic community was always more mutable than it was for the straight. Contemplation, meditation, dialogue: allowing ideas to unfold was a central tenet of artistic expression in the Haight, from musical improvisation to light shows, to poster art, to the *Oracle*.

The *Oracle* provided news content for the psychedelic community, but it also provided the livelihood for many hippies living in the Haight at the time. Between the third and twelfth issues the paper's circulation rose from around 3,000 to over 120,000. The various people stationed in hip neighborhoods around the Bay Area holding copies of the *Oracle* for sale would have splashed a bit of color in the sightlines of straight passersby. Even those unfamiliar with the sight of rock dance posters, or the page layouts of the *Oracle*, would soon have seen psychedelic lettering in the advertising pages of the *Chronicle* and *Examiner*. The *Oracle* may not have influenced the news content of its "straight" counterparts, but it asserted the artistic sensibilities central to a new hip lifestyle that was otherwise so derided in the mainstream press.

The derision heaped on the *Oracle* by other agents in the counterculture is therefore slightly surprising:

> The *Oracle*, I admit, *has* done something to ease life on Haight Street; it's hired street kids to peddle the paper. Having with brilliant graphics and sophomoric prose urged millions of kids to Drop Out of school and jobs, it now offers its dropouts menial jobs. That's hypocritical and shitty, but it's something. It means that a few dozen kids who can meet the Oracle's requirements can avert starvation whenever the Oracle comes out.
>
> Groovy.[81]

This lays bare the growing chasm between the psychedelic "inner" and the countercultural "outer," the desire to affect a more lasting political change from the basis of a new consciousness—because the *Oracle* operated on a level removed from that of direct political engagement. In this sense, the *Oracle* represents only one vision of a multihued community, though the tension between the "short 60s" (meditations on spirituality, on domestic rhythms, on expanded consciousness; artistic expression anchored in psychedelic sensibility) and the "long 60s" (whole food diet, yoga, mindfulness) are all evident in the pages of the *Oracle*.

In late summer, a mysterious collective calling themselves the Diggers, after the seventeenth-century English radicals, had begun offering free food and "Digger bread" to people in the park. The Diggers emerged from the Mime Troupe, and their "free" philosophy was less altruistic, more political street theater. They sought to create an environment free from the constraints of capitalist society, which chimed in principle with the Haight ethos. But their presence in the Haight throughout the short 60s was often confrontational, which created a certain tension with the less politically inclined hippies:

> The Diggers were saying that anybody who used money was a fucking fascist pig. Everybody seems to have misunderstood the Diggers as a Salvation Army group. You know, be nice to people. It was far more dangerous than that. It was a radical anarchist group that was really about authenticity and autonomy. If you had an idea, you took responsibility for it and got it done. There was no sense waiting for tomorrow. . . . Everything was designed to jog consciousness. To break addiction to identity, to money, to job, to whatever. Because we knew that the real problem was the culture. The

5.3 Diggers in the Panhandle.

problem wasn't capitalism. The problem wasn't Communism. The problem was the *culture*.[82]

The city's Board of Permit Appeals was generally not keen to encourage cultural development. Morris "Moe" Moskowitz had applied for a permit to open a branch of his popular Berkeley used bookstore at 1542 Haight Street, but some of the neighborhood merchants objected. Owners of other neighboring shops disagreed— Peggy Caserta of Mnasidika (1510 Haight), Harry Struch of In Gear (1580 Haight), David Rathkop of I/Thou (1736 Haight) all noted the importance of a quality book store to the growing young population of the neighborhood.[83] Though none of the opposing merchants attended the hearing, Moe's appeal lost by one vote. And in other literary news, the Associated Press reported that "junky" words were creeping into pop music.[84]

Could it be that the hippies were being exploited? Amid a regular "happening" in the Panhandle one late September afternoon, someone named Peter could be seen trying to direct hippies in "freaky" behavior, trailed by a crew of cameramen. Some hippies started grumbling about being "free extras" in a film, but hadn't heard one crew member mention the word "documentary."[85]

LSD was made illegal on October 6. To commemorate the event, members of the Haight staged a Love Pageant Rally in the Panhandle with the Dead and Big Brother and the Holding Company providing the music. And then came the banner headline: "Strange Success Story: The LSD Millionaire."

5.4 *Oracle* issue 7 on sale.

Although he is known to thousands, even Owsley's close friends and associates do not know his complete name, or his origins. But information has begun to trickle out.

On a new Capitol Records documentary LP entitled *LSD*, his name . . . appears on the record jacket as the sponsor of The Grateful Dead, a way-out rock 'n roll group supplying the background music. . . .

With the lysergic acid he bought, Stanley had the potential to manufacture at least 1.5 million and perhaps many more doses of LSD, which was selling on the streets at around $5 a dose.

Some of Stanley's acquaintances say he turned out ten million blue, aspirin-sized tablets which later became his trademark.[86]

Just underneath, a promise by Berkeley police to seek indictments against four "fringe drug peddlers" responsible for LSD trade along Telegraph Avenue. According to the report, "Berkeley's source of drugs appears to be San Francisco's Haight-Ashbury district, where enterprising kitchen chemists are able to manufacture [LSD, amphetamine, and methedrine] in small quantities."[87]

San Francisco and the Long 60s

Ken Kesey made a "bold return" to the Bay Area, just in time to stage an acid "graduation," a "super 'trips festival'" at San Francisco State.[88] His trips to various courthouses and jail cells were recounted with a particular attention to detail and a certain sense of fizzling momentum throughout the end of October. By this point, Kesey was no longer a critically acclaimed young novelist; he was "the fugitive novelist and LSD exponent."[89] Caught by FBI agents and freed on $5,000 bail, Kesey insisted that he only returned to the Bay Area from Mexico "to carry out a mission of persuading the Bay Area's 'acid heads' to break their habits of using the powerful, hallucinogenic LSD." The acid graduation, scheduled for Halloween, was intended to lead these wayward acid heads toward "some other way of life."

No one really knew what to expect of Ken Kesey's Halloween party at Winterland. Was he really going to try to convince young people not to take LSD? When he called it a "trip-or-treat" festival, just what kind of "treat" did he promise to replace the "trip"?[90] Momentum stalled. Bill Graham had rented Winterland for Kesey, but when told by two of Kesey's "ex-associates" and two representatives of local rock bands that Kesey planned to dose the hall's water, Graham withdrew from the dance. He did not need to risk losing his business for the Pranksters. So the public graduation of thousands was "replaced by private ceremonies," and the real entertainment that evening was "the Quick and the Dead" at the California Hall.[91]

In other front-page news: the convergence at City Hall of delegates from the Love Pageant Rally and a Black Power press conference.[92] This mix of "love and anger" was certainly new and circled around the image of Jerry Rubin, "a white non-student with the Students for Democratic Action," there to announce

5.5 Chet Helms (2nd left) conferring with Ken Kesey (on the bus) before the acid graduation.

an officially unsanctioned fundraising rally to be held on the Berkeley campus. The hippies were there to bestow a psychedelic gift on San Francisco's Mayor Shelley—morning glory seeds and magic mushrooms—before fluttering back to the Panhandle for "a sort of Fillmore Auditorium happening under the eucalyptus trees." Of course, the hippies were clever enough to realize that they were attracting a lot of attention: a bail and defense fund was set up in the expectation of further arrests in the Haight.[93]

An unusually soul-searching "Folk Scene" column wondered why "Berkeley has a problem when it comes to entertainment and electric art." Oakland occasionally hosted a rock dance, but surely Berkeley had the critical mass of students and young people to sustain its own scene? The problem was infrastructure: the most suitable venues were owned or run by the University.

> So not only does the University withhold part of the community from itself by allowing only certain groups to use the facilities, but it censors what does go on there. Currently a promoter can pay blackmail to a student group and get them to stensibly [sic] put on the event, which is a drag, but you can choose who gets the money.... But even this alternative may not be possible too much longer. If this chink in the College Wall is bricked up, we are primarily at the mercy of the students themselves.[94]

This came a long seven months after Ralph Gleason's account of his own evening *en famille* at a rock dance in the Harmon Gym at UC Berkeley, during which his teenage son and daughter and three of their friends were taken from the dance floor by campus police and put in a locked room, charged with violating the contract stating that "all teenagers under 16 not 'in the custody of their parents' had to be out of the building and en route home by 11 p.m." Bill Graham, the promoter of the evening's concert, was brought to the office, contract in hand, and proved that no such stipulation existed. Gleason's party were released, and duly featured in his next column.[95]

The Police Committee of the SF Board of Supervisors reached a compromise in the amendment to the dancehall ordinance of 1909: teenagers fifteen to eighteen years old would be allowed in public dancehalls until midnight, but only at dances not attended by older people—that is, teenagers older than eighteen, or even their own parents. Bill Graham argued against it, naturally, and even noted that he held Sunday-afternoon dances for the joint enjoyment of young teenagers and their parents. Arguments for and against segregated dances continued through the end of the year.[96]

Merla Zellerbach decided to ask people in the know what the difference was between "a North Beach beatnik and a Haight Street hipster." Besides the obvious distinctions between stimulants and psychedelics, she discovered from Ron Thelin that

> We aren't really that different from the beats. . . . We're merely continuing what they started. The Revolution of the Soul is on! I want us to have our own identity, to be a community known for love, goodness, vision. We will give the world our joy that they can witness. This will be our contribution.[97]

The problem with that "revolution of the soul," however, was apparently all the obscenity. The police raided The Psychedelic Shop (1535 Haight Street) and arrested Allen Cohen for selling Lenore Kandel's slim volume of poetry, *The Love Book*, and another youth for allegedly "striking a police officer." While the statements of the dozen patrons in the shop at the time of this arrest differ from the official version, it is fair to assume that detaining, frisking, and searching customers, and logging their

5.6 Hippies picketing.

personal information, were slightly excessive in the circumstances. Within an hour of the raid, hippies had convened outside the Psychedelic Shop carrying picket signs emblazoned with slogans: "Cops Go Home," "Police Illegal," "Ban the Bible."[98]

When Jay Thelin, co-owner of the Psychedelic Shop, arrived at the Hall of Justice for Allen Cohen's arraignment, he was summarily arrested in the corridor. Cohen told reporters that the reason for his arrest was clear: the Haight-Ashbury District Merchants' Association wanted to keep new merchants and their patrons out of the neighborhood. There followed a similar arrest in North Beach the following day. This prompted four English professors from San Francisco State to stage public readings from *The Love Book* and Michael McClure's play *The Beard*, itself the target of accusations of "lewd conduct in a public place" when staged by The Committee in August 1965. One academic called *The Love Book* "a bad poem—but it is a sincere literary effort and should be judged on that ground alone."[99] For those readers of the *Chronicle* unwilling to risk arrest in order to read the obscene book in question, the paper offered a beautifully euphemistic summary:

> The poems employ many of the underground Anglo-Saxon words for parts of the human anatomy and their interaction. They portray the ecstasies of lovemaking as valuable in themselves and as a means to religious ecstasy.[100]

The censorship of *The Love Book* and the refusal of the Haight-Ashbury District Merchants' Association to allow membership to some of the area's new merchants prompted a press conference at the home of "non-psychedelic friends of the cosmic consciousness community." Members of the psychedelic community defended *The Love Book* and announced the creation of a new neighborhood association, the Haight Independent Proprietors (HIP).[101] As for the public reading of *The Love Book* and *The Beard*, the event was attended by roughly 300 people and no police.[102]

Ralph Gleason was amazed by the Thanksgiving dinner hosted at the Fillmore by Bill Graham for his patrons, staff, local bands and their families. Nowhere else could something like that have happened—nowhere else would an audience actually *applaud* the police when they were brought onstage for an official thanks:

> There's something fundamental changing here. A Los Angeles promoter is going to open a dance hall with "total environment" and "psychedistic dancer" i.e. go-go girls. There will be many such attempts to exploit and/or capitalize on the new Youth but I predict they won't work.
>
> This is a generation which is producing the Diggers at Ashbury and Oak and at Civic Center Park in Berkeley every afternoon with their free food. This is the generation which is making distillery stock a losing proposition for long range investment and this is the generation which says it believes in love and acts on it.

> [S.F. Police Chief] Tom Cahill's blue nosed bluecoats may bust book stores but this thing can't be stopped. In the war between the generations, the kids are right and they will win.[103]

Gleason also suggested, persuasively, that the split between the Old and the New was much deeper than a mere clash of generations:

> The New Youth is finding its poets on juke boxes and its religion in rock 'n roll, its preachers in night clubs and its philosophers with long hair and guitars. They are bound to come into conflict with authority, just as every religious movement always has. When we next see the pictures of the armed and helmeted police rousting the kids on Sunset Strip or, let's hope never, on Haight Street or Telegraph Avenue, let's remember that Jesus Christ was busted by the Roman fuzz for preaching without a police permit. Very little has changed fundamentally.[104]

In December, the Diggers announced the Free Frame of Reference at 1762 Page Street:

> A sort of a permanent happening in itself . . . open 24 hours with hot coffee always available. There will be a free washing machine and dryer. Anyone is welcome to come there for free food, free clothes, free books, free art forms, and free total.[105]

The Free Frame of Reference was soon targeted by the city's Health Commission, who ordered the installation of a toilet for public use, as the six toilets in the converted garage were there as seating for "the performance." To avert any further attention, the Diggers posted a sign inside the Frame stating "Only 50 Friends at a time." On the outside of the Frame, the sign read "Private."[106]

LSD Rescue, staffed by pharmacologists, a doctor, a clinical psychologist, and clergymen, were fielding 400 calls a week from San Francisco citizens experiencing bad LSD trips. In extreme cases trippers were sent to "sympathetic hospitals."[107] On another stage was the peaceful meeting of the hippies and the Hell's Angels. Seven Hell's Angels were riding west on Haight Street one evening, while a parade of 200 hippies were moving eastward by candlelight "to celebrate the death and re-birth of the Haight-Ashbury district and the death of money."[108] The Angels joined the parade, and within minutes two were arrested: Henry "Hairy Henry" Kot and Charles "Chocolate George" Hendricks, the former for permitting a passenger to ride illegally on his motorcycle, the latter for interfering with an arrest. They were taken to the local Park Station, where the hippies descended in an effort to secure their release. When the Angels were taken to the Hall of Justice, the hippies paraded again through the

Haight to collect funds. Within an hour hippies shifted direction downtown to post bail. Their job done, the hippies lit their candles, sang a Christmas carol, and returned whence they came. The Angels then announced a thank you party to be cohosted with the Diggers on New Year's Day, featuring music by the Grateful Dead.[109]

Toward the end of 1966 there were signs that the countercultural aesthetic was seeping into the mainstream:

> Bill Graham . . . said he's stopped putting posters out on light poles—because they just don't last.
>
> Graham said last summer he put up 150 posters along Telegraph avenue in Berkeley, had a cup of coffee and drove back down the street. Of the 150 posters, three were left.
>
> And, at San Francisco State College, the posters are taken down almost as fast as they can be stapled up. . . . In fact, the demand for posters at S.F. State is so great that, early this month, the advertising office of the student newspaper was broken into and the entire collection of posters—nothing else—was stolen. . . .
>
> The Oakland Art Commission has [a] complete collection, acquired from Graham two months ago. "The posters are very exciting works that reflect the spirit of the dances," Theresa Heyman, assistant curator for the Oakland museum, explained.

There were other signs that the new visual arts were being welcomed into "official culture" when Bill Ham performed his light show at the Museum of Art in collaboration with improvisatory musicians Fred Marshall and Jerry Granelli, from the Vince Guaraldi combo. As would be expected, Gleason waxed rhapsodic on the aesthetic experience:

> The complete environment . . . really locks one up in a time capsule and removes all impediments of the outside world. "We're working in space," Bill Ham says, "putting you and me both in the same time as musicians have been doing."[110]

In the last weeks of the year a man called Superspade made a brief appearance in the daily papers. Along with two teenagers from "socially prominent Hillsborough families" and three others, he was called to answer to narcotics charges stemming from raids in the city earlier in the month. One of his party, the young son of a prominent attorney, pleaded not guilty by reason of insanity, and was committed to the psychiatric center at St Mary's Hospital. William Thomas, "who usually wears a button proclaiming himself as 'Superspade, faster than a speeding mind,'" was given his nickname by "a chick," and it stuck.[111] This was unfortunately not to be Superspade's only appearance in the pages of the *Chronicle*.

As the year drew to a close, members of the Mime Troupe were arrested in North Beach for singing Christmas carols outside the Condor Club.[112] Topless bars were safe, but street theatre was not.

Notes

1. RJG, "There's Something Wrong Somewhere," *Chronicle*, October 17, 1966, p. 49.
2. Larry Coffey, "24-year-old hairdresser," quoted in Merla Zellerbach, "In Is Out with the Mods," *Chronicle*, July 1, 1966, p. 43.
3. Donovan Bess, "A Little Parade: Far-Out Voices in the Debris," *Chronicle*, January 1, 1966, p. 2.
4. Brand, Sender, and Jacopetti were interviewed about the Trips Festival by Lou Gottlieb, a former member of the folk trio the Limeliters, then a new *Chronicle* reporter. The resulting article pronounced the Trips Festival "an event of major significance in the history of religion" and "an event of major significance in the history of art." *Chronicle*, January 18, 1966. As Sender recalled, "It definitely was the first time I had smoked a pot pipe with a reporter. And it was his pot." Gottlieb told Sender about his plans to move to rural Sonoma County, offering haven there, should Sender ever wish to try communal living. Gottlieb and Morning Star Ranch return in later chapters. For this recollection, see Bernstein, *The San Francisco Tape Music Center* (Berkeley: University of California Press, 2008), p. 77.
5. George Dusheck, "Baby It Will Be Cool," *Examiner*, January 9, 1966, p. B4.
6. Charles McCabe, "Our Fearless Correspondent: The Dread Drug Habit," *Chronicle*, January 6, 1966.
7. "Marijuana Case: Kesey Sentence—A Jail Term," *Chronicle*, January 18, 1966, p. 3.
8. See Bob Robertson, "Cops Find Kesey—Rooftop Drama," *Chronicle*, January 20, 1966, p. 3.
9. See Bob Robertson, "Writer in Court: Kesey Wears Tie—For a Few Hours," *Chronicle*, January 21, 1966, p. 3.
10. Bob Graham, "Happening Almost Happens," *Chronicle*, January 22, 1966, p. 4.
11. Lenny Lipton, "Trips Festival Hits You High—or Low?" *Barb*, January 28, 1966, p. 4.
12. Tom Wolfe, *The Electric Kool-Aid Acid Test*, (New York: Farrar, 1968), p. 234.
13. RJG, "One Wild Night—A Trips Festival," *Chronicle*, January 24, 1966, p. 49.
14. Bill Graham, quoted in Bill Graham and Robert Greenfield, *Bill Graham Presents* (New York: McGraw Hill, 2003), p. 136.
15. Graham's personal relationship with drugs was rather more nuanced:

   > KURT "CROWBAR" KANGAS: Bill did not pull punches. He would slap a joint hard, right out of your hand, or he would fucking slap it out of your mouth. I mean he had no problem with that. He sent a message straight. And so he became known as anti-drugs, which wasn't true, because he loved drugs just as much as anybody else. I know because I gave him mushrooms every year. What he did is—I never talked about this while he was alive—he took off for the Grand Canyon every year

to do a week or ten days or a two week trip, that he called his cleansing trip. Killer [Steve Kahn] was the one that flew him down there, and Killer was one of my best friends. So Killer would come up to me and I would give him some of the best mushrooms that money can buy and I'd give him about an ounce of mushrooms. I was always surprised: an ounce. Holy smokes! That'll get a herd of horses high, you know, let alone two guys. So I would procure the mushrooms for Bill, and then he would go and cleanse his whole year out.

16. As noted in the previous chapter, Wavy Gravy disagreed with dosing unsuspecting people. This is not to suggest that he was a strict advocate of Timothy Leary's prepared environment, however. When I asked Wavy Gravy how he would compare the approaches of Kesey and Leary, he said that "one was Merlin and one was Flash Gordon." Asked whether he meant that one advocated LSD toward spiritual awakening and the other advocated LSD as inner fun, he replied, "It was all spiritual awakening; it's just that one was more fun than others."

17. See *The Trips Festival Movie* (dir. Eric Christensen, 2007).

18. Jerry Garcia, quoted in Graham and Greenfield, *Bill Graham Presents*, p. 140.

19. Ramon mentions the Buchla Box, the 100 Series Modular Electronic Music System that Don Buchla invented for the Tape Music Center in 1963. For details on the Buchla Box construction and influence, see Bernstein, *Tape Music Center* and Trevor Pinch and Frank Trocco, *Analog Days* (Cambridge, MA: Harvard University Press, 2002).

20. Ramon was one of those "Sicilians" taking part in the New Year's Day parade. He recalls commissioning a friend to sew a banner with the word "NOW," releasing weather balloons into the sky at Union Square, and riding on Further into the Financial District; but between Ramon and Bill Maginnis it was unclear what else happened:

    R: There was a guy used to play piano on a flatbed truck.

    B: I know I was on the flatbed truck.

    R: Oh you were, okay. Was there a piano on it or not?

    B: You're asking me? I mean, I was there; I don't remember.

21. There is some dispute over the details of this arrangement. See *Bill Graham Presents*, pp. 142–49.

22. Jack Viets, "Inside S.F. Pad—The New Beatnik Life," *Chronicle*, March 15, 1966, p. 1.

23. Maitland Zane, "Trouble in the City's New Bohemia," *Chronicle*, March 15, 1966, p. 1.

24. Adam Hochschild, "A Bay Area 'Game': Inside a Nude Party," *Chronicle*, March 1, 1966, p. 1.

25. ED Denson, "The Folk Scene: Rock 'n' Roll is Dead," *Barb*, March 11, 1966, p. 5. One short month later Denson was declaring "Folk is Dead, Long Live . . ." Denson argued that "traditional folk music is dying out among revivalists," that the coffee houses could not sustain a professional network of musicians, and that the local dancehalls require immediate audiences and a lot of money. He cited Country Joe and the Fish as an example of the future of folk music: self-penned songs combining political relevance with "the new guitar music," with less reliance on the standard repertoire of Child ballads and the like. See *Barb*, April 15, 1966, p. 6. It is no secret that Denson was Country Joe and the Fish's manager.

26. Bill Graham recounts his personal visits with each business owner in the Fillmore neighborhood in the wake of these complaints, and his account of his conversation with Rabbi Burstein is particularly colorful. See *Bill Graham Presents*, pp. 149–52.

27. Maitland Zane, "No Batman to Rescue: Police Ban on Fillmore Dance," *Chronicle*, March 16, 1966, p. 6.
28. "Crackdown on LSD by State Urged," *Chronicle*, March 16, 1966, p. 19.
29. Associated Press, "Lynch Calls State Meeting on LSD," *Chronicle*, April 13, 1966, p. 2.
30. Associated Press, "No More Legal LSD," *Chronicle*, April 14, 1966, p. 2. Some of those "highly qualified clinical investigators" were of course CIA agents. See *Acid Dreams* for a full historical overview.
31. "UC Won't Report Its LSD Users," *Chronicle*, April 16, 1966, p. 3.
32. "Stanford Balks at 'Tattling' on LSD Users," *Chronicle*, April 19, 1966, p. 38.
33. Donald Perlman, "Blaze of Creative Action in Psychedelic Drug Test," *Chronicle*, April 20, 1966, p. 1.
34. See "Acid-Head Special," *Barb*, April 22, 1966, p. 6.
35. Editorial: Controls for LSD, *Chronicle*, May 2, 1966, p 36.
36. Jackson Doyle, "Assembly Oks Bill to End the Private Use of LSD," *Chronicle*, May 12, 1966, p. 8.
37. Times-Post Service, "FDA Order Curbs 'Do-It-Yourself' LSD," *Chronicle*, May 18, 1966, p. 6.
38. "The Facts on the LSD World," *Chronicle*, May 30, 1966 p. 1; "Inside Report: Young Mother on LSD—While the Kids Play," May 31, p. 1. "The Acid Users: A Teacher's Weird Trip," June 1, p. 1; "An LSD 'Rebirth': The Trip Back to Religion," June 2, p. 1.
39. "An LSD 'Rebirth,'" p. 23.
40. See David Perlman, "Probing Look at LSD and Our Society," *Chronicle*, June 14, 1966, p. 1.
41. Donovan Bess, "Experts Fear an 'Underground': Danger in LSD Ban," *Chronicle*, June 15, 1966, p. 4.
42. "All Kinds of Things: Psychedelic Theater," *Chronicle*, June 16, 1966, p. 18.
43. Donovan Bess, "Praise for Drug: The High Priest of LDS [*sic*] Tells His Creed Here," *Chronicle*, June 17, 1966, p. 4.
44. David Perlman, "Psychologist's Report: LSD Seen in the Light of Our 'Drug Culture,'" *Chronicle*, June 16, 1966, p. 2.
45. Donovan Bess, "Doubts on LSD and 'Revived' Religion," *Chronicle*, June 6, 1966, p. 2.
46. "LSD: A Curse or . . ." *Chronicle*, June 19, 1966, p. 5.
47. Editorial: The Fillmore Auditorium Case, *Chronicle*, April 21, 1966.
48. RJG, "S.F. Cops' Strange Raid on Dance Hall," *Chronicle*, April 25, 1966, p. 51.
49. Maitland Zane, "The Cops Bust Kids for Dancing," *Chronicle*, April 23, 1966, p. 1.
50. Michael Grieg, "A Shocking Night for Teen Dancers," *Chronicle*, April 26, 1966, p. 1.
51. "Request for a Dance: Teen-Agers Call on Mayor," *Chronicle*, May 4, 1966, p. 6.
52. "The Mayor Speaks Up: Dancehall Law 'Outdated,'" *Chronicle*, May 5, 1966, p. 5.
53. "Fillmore Promoter in the Clear," *Chronicle*, May 25, 1966, p. 1. As for Andy Warhol's Exploding Plastic Inevitable, Gleason was unforgiving, calling it "nothing more than a bad condensation of all the bum trips of the Trips Festival," with local hippies "continually walking out shaking their heads and saying 'Wow!' in wonder that such a

bore could be." He pronounced the Velvet Underground "a dull group, behind at least a half dozen local groups in interest," "really pretty lame," and the entire evening "non-creative and hence non-artistic . . ., not new at all" because "everything . . . has been done better" by local bands. See RJG, "The Sizzle that Fizzled," *Chronicle*, May 30, 1966, p. 47.

54. ED Denson, "The Folk Scene: Funking at the Fillmore," *Barb*, September 9, 1966, p. 2.
55. Richard Alpert, transcript of the Leary Conference, Fairmont Hotel, December 12, 1966, reprinted in *The Oracle* 4 (December 16, 1966), p. 16.
56. R.B. Read, "These Are the Boys . . .," *Examiner*, November 20, 1966, California Living p. 3.
57. Richard Goldstein, Times-Post Service, "A Reason for Hippies," *Chronicle*, June 5, 1967, p. 1.
58. RJG, "Liquid Lights: New Art Form," *Chronicle*, November 12, 1967, Datebook, p. 31.
59. Bill Ham, quoted in Michael Goldberg, "The San Francisco Sound," *Rolling Stone* 585, August 23, 1990, p. 95.
60. RJG, "An Old Joint That's Really Jumpin'," *Chronicle*, July 20, 1966, p. 39.
61. ED Denson, "The Folk Scene: Up Tight and Comfy, a Trip with the Blues," *Barb*, April 1, 1966, p. 4.
62. Chet Helms, quoted in *Bill Graham Presents*, p. 148.
63. Bill Graham, quoted in Ibid., pp. 148–49.
64. RJG, "Law Moves In On Culture," *Chronicle*, May 13, 1966, p. 51.
65. RJG, "Several Sides of the Cultural Coin," *Chronicle*, May 16, 1966, p. 51.
66. "Big Plans for Festival: Artistic Freedom Cry," *Chronicle*, July 21, 1966, p. 2.
67. Kenneth Rexroth, "Subversive Nature of Culture Revolution," *Examiner* July 24, 1966, II. 4
68. "An LSD Link to Suicide in Berkeley," *Chronicle*, August 1, 1966, p. 1.
69. Peter Liptak, "Vernon P. Cox: an Elegy. He Didn't Quite Make It," *Barb*, August 5, 1966, p. 1. A short while later the *Barb* printed a letter from Vernon's mother, explaining in detail the spirit behind Vernon's poetry, some of which the *Barb* printed. See "Letter from the Mother of the Poet," November 25, 1966, p. 6.
70. Nicholas von Hoffman, Times-Post Service, "Inside a Berkeley Drug Party," *Chronicle*, August 24, 1966, p. 1.
71. Blake Green, "Now—Psychedelic Styles?" *Chronicle*, August 19, 1966, p. 22. The idea of mainstream co-optation of hippie style is a running theme in 1960s historiography, and certainly part of the daily tension in the Haight. For a closer look at this issue, see Thomas Frank, *The Conquest of Cool* (Chicago and London: University of Chicago Press, 1997).
72. ED Denson, "The Folk Scene: Shards fm Unkie's Pot [sic]," *Barb*, September 2, 1966, p. 4.
73. Joan Chatfield-Taylor, "Hippy Scene—Social Scene Merge With Style," *Chronicle*, October 31, 1966, p. 22.
74. Bob Bartlett, "A Tea, Pot Tempest on Haight St," *Chronicle*, September 17, 1966, p. 9.
75. "Double P.O. Set to Go in Haight," *Barb*, September 16, 1966, p. 5.
76. Arnold Toynbee, "Toynbee Tours Hippieland," *Chronicle*, May 17, 1967, p. 1.

77. In a survey of the underground press Jerry Belcher remarked that the *Oracle* is "less concerned with 'hard news', with outward events than what might be called inward events." See "Underground Press . . . Who, What, Why," *Chronicle*, July 30, 1967, p. 3.
78. *The Oracle* facsimile edition is available on CD-ROM and DVD (Regent Press, 2005). For more on the history and aesthetics of the underground and psychedelic presses, see Abe Peck, *Uncovering the Sixties: The Life & Times of the Underground Press* (New York: Pantheon Books, 1985) and Geoff Kaplan, ed., *Power to the People: The Graphic Design of the Radical Press and the Rise of the Counter-Culutre, 1964-1974* (Chicago and London: University of Chicago Press, 2013).
79. Quoted in Belcher, "Who, What, Why."
80. Richard Goldstein, Times-Post Service, "A Reason for Hippies," *Chronicle*, June 5, 1967, p. 1.
81. "Uncle Tim's Children," Communications Company, April 1967, Chester Anderson papers, folder 4. The ComCo features more prominently in the next chapter.
82. Peter Coyote, quoted in *Bill Graham Presents*, p. 184.
83. "Hippiness is Moe Books," *Chronicle*, September 27, 1966, p. 4.
84. A.P. "Songs That Have a Double Meaning," *Examiner*, September 25, 1966 p. 13.
85. Lionel Rolfe, "Peter Straight with Haight at the Gate," *Barb*, September 30, 1966, p. 3.
86. George Reasons, Times-Post Service, "Homemade Drugs: Strange Story of Bay Area's LSD Millionaire," *Chronicle*, October 5, 1966, p. 1.
87. "Berkeley Seeks LSD Indictments," *Chronicle*, October 5, 1966, p. 1.
88. Donovan Bess, "LSD Fugitive Challenges Law in Bold Return," *Chronicle*, October 6, 1966, p. 1 and "Fun-Loving Fugitive: Ken Kesey's Mexico," *Chronicle*, October 7, 1966, p. 3.
89. Donovan Bess, "The TV Pimpernel: LSD Novelist Held After FBI Chase," *Chronicle*, October 21, 1966, p. 1. The *Chronicle* never did believe Kesey's "suicide." Jerry Belcher, "Kesey Hoax or Suicide?," *Chronicle*, February 13, 1966, p. 1, though his "suicide note" was reprinted in full in the *Barb*, February 18, 1966, p. 2.
90. Donovan Bess, "Kesey's Baby: Trip-or-Treat Festival Monday," *Chronicle*, October 28, 1966, p. 3.
91. "Bill Graham Tells—How Turn-On Threat Closed Kesey Ball," *Barb*, November 25, 1966, p. 1; "Ken Kesey Cansels LSD 'Graduation,'" *Chronicle*, October 31, 1966, p. 1; RJG, "The Acid Test That Never Was," November 2, 1966, p. 49. Gleason is referring to Quicksilver Messenger Service and the Grateful Dead, who "filled the hall with the wailing of guitars and the beat of the drums all night long."
92. Michael Grieg, "Mixed Emotions: The Scene at City Hall," *Chronicle*, October 7, 1966, p. 1.
93. See "March Minus Hate from the Haight," *Barb*, October 7, 1966, p. 3.
94. ED Denson, "The Folk Scene," *Barb*, October 7, 1966, p. 4.
95. RJG, "What's Going On In This Place?" *Chronicle*, April 24, 1966, Datebook, p. 23.
96. "Teens and Oldies: A New Move in Dance Flap," *Chronicle*, October 14, 1966, p. 4; Mel Wax, "Teen Dance Plan—Pros and Cons," *Chronicle*, December 9, 1966, p. 2.
97. Merla Zellerbach, "Beatnik, Tripster—There's a Difference," *Chronicle*, November 4, 1966, p. 31.
98. See "'Obscene' Poetry and a Big Fuss," *Chronicle*, November 16, 1966, p. 1.

99. "Teachers to Defy 'Love Book' Ban," *Chronicle*, November 22, 1966, p. 1. Transcripts of the event were published in full in *The Oracle* 4, December 16, 1966.
100. Donovan Bess, "Another 'Love Book' Arrest Here," *Chronicle*, November 17, 1966, p. 1.
101. L. Campbell Bruce, "The Psychedelic Press Conference," *Chronicle*, November 23, 1966, p. 2.
102. Donovan Bess, "Eager Audience for 'Love Book'—But No Cops," *Chronicle*, November 24, 1966, p. 24.
103. RJG, "The Fillmore Gives Thanks," *Chronicle*, November 28, 1966, p. 49. The Thanksgiving dinner was a regular event in Bill Graham's ballrooms, notably the epic evening at Winterland that resulted in *The Last Waltz* (dir. Martin Scorsese, 1978).
104. RJG, "The Great War Between the Kids and Society," *Examiner*, December 4, 1966, p. 44.
105. "All for Free in Diggers' Free For All," *Barb*, December 2, 1966, p. 5.
106. "Diggers Not Sweating Bureau's Cry for Potty," *Barb*, December 16, 1966, p. 8.
107. "LSD Rescue Ready to Ride Along," *Barb*, December 9, 1966, p. 6.
108. "Candlelight and Cops: Haight Angels Jailed," *Examiner*, December 18, 1966, p. 1.
109. Silenus, "New Year's Whale Set to Top Diggers' Noel," *Barb*, December 30, 1966, p. 3.
110. RJG, "Show May Put Museum in Orbit," *Chronicle*, December 21, 1966, p. 41.
111. "'Superspade' and Friends in Court," *Chronicle*, December 21, 1966, p. 3.
112. On the latter, see Jonathan Root, "Retreat to Hip Junction," *Chronicle*, December 27, 1966, p. 6.

SONS OF CHAMPLIN, "SING ME A RAINBOW"

(Estelle Levitt/Lou Stallman)
Produced by Randy Steirling
7" single released on Verve Records (10500, 1966)
Recorded in Trident Studios

Bill Champlin: lead vocals, organ
Terry Haggerty: lead guitar, backing vocals
John Prosser: bass, backing vocals
Tim Cain: saxophone, backing vocals
Jim Meyers: drums

> CHARLES JOHNSON: All these groups at that time, when all this music was going on, they all had the same fans. The same people that were crazy about the Dead, crazy about Jefferson Airplane, were also crazy about the best unknown group in the Bay Area in my mind, the Sons of Champlin, from Marin County. They never got the fame they deserved.
>
> "Sing Me a Rainbow" was a small hit in San Francisco, but never reached the Top 20. It received good initial airplay in several major markets and sold better outside the Bay Area. [Trident management] put on the most strenuous promotion campaign possible with [their] resources, literally working the record until the end. The Sons of Champlain [sic] never released a second record and are now privately managed, but Trident, as with all their other artists, still holds their recording and publishing contracts and a completed album.[1]
>
> TERRY HAGGERTY: You know, the Sons had been around just as long as everyone else, but we were kind of aloof. Being from Marin County and playing R&B—I don't think we were better musicians in the sense of what our music accomplished, but we were different from the San Francisco sound. And there was just not a real desire to connect with it, cause it all seemed a bit raggy-ass loose to us, you know?

The Sons of Champlin formed in Marin County in 1965. They were not the only Marin-based band to circulate around the dancehalls of San Francisco,[2] but they were one of the few bands not to have sprung from the folk scene: their repertoire was primarily rhythm and blues. Unlike many recordings of Bay Area bands from this period, "Sing Me a Rainbow" captures the band's energy and offers a sense of the power a straightforward dance number could generate at the end of 1966.

The owner of Trident Studios was Frank Werber, the manager of the Kingston Trio. The Kingston Trio had had enormous success following the release of their debut album in 1958,[3] and in 1960 Werber and the Trio were able to invest strategically in properties around the Bay Area: a few places in Marin County, the Flatiron Building in North Beach, and the Trident Restaurant in Sausalito. The Trident Restaurant had been a jazz club, but by the late 1960s Werber had turned it into a hippie haven, a favorite hangout of musicians from Janis Joplin to the Rolling Stones. Meanwhile, over in North Beach, Werber and the Kingston Trio installed a recording facility in the basement of the Flatiron Building and called it Trident Studios.

Among the early bands to record at Trident were the folk-rock combo We Five,[4] Blackburn & Snow,[5] Mystery Trend,[6] and the Sons of Champlin. The recordings made by these very different groups have one common attribute: the quality of the production. In comparing the Trident singles with the Autumn Records singles the difference in levels of professionalism is clear. Despite Sly Stone's formidable musicianship, as a producer he was not able to elicit uniformly polished performances from the bands coming through the Autumn studios. The early Trident recordings have a brightness and clarity that captured an essence of these early San Francisco bands, a radio-ready quality that remains fresh half a century later. But as with Autumn, the problem with Trident was often distribution and promotion, and in the case of the Sons of Champlin, this amounted to an enormous missed opportunity.

"Sing Me a Rainbow" is a song about unrequited love and musical escapism: the singer's heart is broken and he wants to channel a little happiness through his guitar. The phrase "sing me a rainbow" might sound like an attempt to tap into the blooming flower power *zeitgeist*, but the song's message is really, simply, "don't bum me out." Supporting that message is a soaring, exuberant tune sparkling with color.

There are three main musical components to "Sing Me a Rainbow": verse, chorus, and refrain.[7] The song follows a verse-chorus structure, extended in the last third through repeating and developing the refrain material:

0:00	Intro (keyboards, guitars, drums)	4 bars
0:08	Verse ("Mister guitar, I want so much . . .")	9 bars
0:25	Chorus ("Sing me a breeze . . .")	6 bars
0:37	Refrain ("Don't sing of love")	4 bars
0:44	Verse ("Don't play those blues . . .")	9 bars
1:02	Chorus ("Sing me a tree . . .")	6 bars
1:13	Refrain ("Don't sing of love")	4 bars
1:21	Refrain + countermelody ("you can sing a rainbow . . .")	6 bars
1:33	Verse (piano)	9 bars
1:51	Chorus ("Sing me a tree . . .")	6 bars
2:03	Refrain ("Don't sing of love")	4 bars
2:11	Refrain + countermelody + upper harmony	6 bars

2:23	Intro figure (Hammond organ)	4 bars
2:36	Refrain + countermelody + upper harmony	22 bars to fade-out

The verse and chorus are fairly open-ended: lyrically, the verses capture the singer's inner turmoil in two lines (v.1: "Mister guitar, I want so much to have a good time/to try to forget that that girl will never be mine"), while the chorus looks outward toward objective beauty ("sing me a breeze/sing me a sky/sing me a rainbow"). Musically, they share a sense of urgency, supported by the repetitive guitar line and heavy backbeat. At the final line of the chorus ("sing me a rainbow") that momentum has shifted, and the refrain ("don't sing of love") becomes placid, unhurried. This shift is clear texturally as well: the guitar figure in the verse and chorus was steady and rhythmically unvaried; at the reprise we hear an almost pastoral, arpeggiated figure. The distinction between the two textures reflects the lyrical shift from internal to external worlds.

In the second verse (from about 1:00) there is an additional voice that emerges in the texture to emphasize the song's celestial gaze. This is a counterbalance to Bill Champlin's powerful baritone, but it also allows the direction of the song to shift in its final minute. When the Hammond organ returns at 2:23, its upper note grabs the line from the celestial voice and volleys it back at the return of the refrain, now with three different vocal lines painting rainbows and singing about love into the fade-out.

"Sing Me a Rainbow" could have been one of those ubiquitous hits in the short 60s. It had everything that might have snagged the listener—a great vocal delivery, a good beat, some moments of real beauty—and even now suggests what was possible in a San Francisco dancehall when a band aimed for solid rhythm and blues.[8] Part of the song's appeal now is in its difference: the Sons of Champlin did not live in the city, they were not part of daily life in the Haight, and their musical aesthetic in 1966 was not aligned with what was developing into "acid rock." The Sons enjoyed many of the same recreational pursuits as their Haight colleagues, but as their guitarist once explained to me, their geographical separation fed into their music:

> TERRY HAGGERTY: My normal routine in the Sons was, I would wake up in the morning and I would be in the woods. And I would fish, I'd do something, but I'd just be out where it's really, really quiet. And I think my mantra has always been: I want to be the last to know.

The band's "mission plan" was perhaps their deepest message.

> TERRY HAGGERTY: To really promote love, to live simple lives, to live with less. It was always about living with less, to define ourselves from the things that basically seduced everybody else.

The exuberance of "Sing Me a Rainbow" can be distilled to that essence: nature, beauty, love.

THE GREAT!! SOCIETY!!, "SOMEONE TO LOVE"

(Darby Slick)

Grace Slick: lead vocals
Darby Slick: lead guitar, backing vocals
David Miner: rhythm guitar, backing vocals
Peter Van Gelder: bass
Jerry Slick: drums

Single version:
Produced by Sylvester Stewart
Recorded at Golden State Recorders, San Francisco
Released as Northbeach Records #1001 (2/66); also included on *Born to Be Burned* (Sundazed Music, 1996)

Live version:
Produced by Peter Abrams
Recorded at the Matrix (6/66)
From the album *Conspicuous Only In Its Absence*, Columbia 9624 (4/68).

> [The Great Society] has just started to work and are obviously going to amount to something. Any group which produces original material good enough to make up an entire program has what it takes. This one has several numbers. . . . There's a record due out shortly and the group is learning the only way such a group can learn—on the job. Mark their name—the Great Society. I have a strong feeling they will make a reputation for themselves.[9]

> I have never said much about the Frisco rock bands because I have found them almost uniformly uninteresting. . . . Some seem to be worse than others, but I have not formed any value judgments about any of them because I have had this persistent feeling that there must be something going on in their music that I didn't see. Every couple of weeks I get over and listen some more, but until last week the only band that was more interesting than the light shows was the Great Society and they broke up.[10]

In May 1964, President Lyndon B. Johnson delivered the commencement address at the University of Michigan in which he launched a domestic program that he called "the Great Society": economic equality, education reform, urban renewal, conservation, consumer protection, Medicare, the National Endowment for the Arts. It was the furthest-reaching government legislation since Roosevelt's New Deal. Some new laws failed, some succeeded, some promised more than they could deliver, but in retrospect the Great Society was perhaps his greatest legacy.[11]

Johnson's decision to launch the Great Society at a university graduation was an attempt to enlist the younger generation in these transformations to American life "so that in future men will look back and say, 'it was then after a long and weary way that man turned the exploits of his genius to the full enrichment of his life.'"[12] But in the mid-1960s American youth had other transformations, other exploits, on their minds. Adopting the moniker of sweeping legislative change for a fledgling rock band—with ironic!! exclamation marks!!—was one such exploit.[13] It was also a clear way of distancing the hip community of San Francisco from mainstream American culture, for Johnson's idea of the "full enrichment" of life was no doubt interpreted rather differently in the Haight than it was in the rest of the country.

The Great!! Society!! formed around the nucleus of guitarist Darby Slick, his brother Jerry, and Jerry's wife, Grace. Possessed perhaps of more enthusiasm than raw talent, the band were nonetheless fixtures in the early dancehall scene, and honed their material playing regular sets at Mother's, Tom Donahue's short-lived North Beach club. The Great Society was not the only local band with a female vocalist: Signe Anderson featured on Jefferson Airplane's debut album, *Takes Off* (1966), and when Anderson decided to leave the Airplane in August 1966, Grace Slick was invited to take her place. Slick was bought out of her contract with the Great Society and left the band with two songs from their repertoire: her own "White Rabbit" and Darby Slick's "Somebody to Love."[14]

There are two 1966 recordings by the Great Society of "Someone to Love": the single version, released on the Autumn Records subsidiary, Northbeach, and the live version recorded at the Matrix. By all accounts, the Great Society were not easy to record, and Sly Stewart's demands in the studio resulted in a "flimsy" single.[15] While it is true that the Autumn single lacks a certain spark, the trajectory of the song, from the studio recording to the live recording to the more familiar Jefferson Airplane release (*Surrealistic Pillow*, 1967), reveals a great deal about the development of psychedelic rock in San Francisco over one very brief, but crucial, year.

"Someone to Love" is in simple verse-chorus form: eight bars of verse, followed by eight bars of chorus. The number of repetitions, and the interspersal (or not) of guitar solos, depends on the version: the Great Society's single has a four-bar instrumental break between verse-chorus patterns, and a guitar solo in place of a third verse; their live version follows the same pattern, with an additional verse+chorus, guitar solo+chorus tacked on the end; the Jefferson Airplane's single version has no introduction, no instrumental breaks, four verse-chorus patterns with two guitar transitions, lead guitar *obbligato* from the second verse onward, and guitar solo for most of the song's final minute.

The lyric is surprisingly short on content: each verse contains just two lines of text (v. 1: "When the truth is found to be lies/and all the joy within you dies"), which are generally dependent on the final statement repeated four times in the chorus ("Don't you want . . . /Don't you need . . . /Wouldn't you love . . . /You'd better find somebody to love"), to make any meaningful sense. The narrative thrust suggests a generational "love" revolution, a paradigm shift to replace Johnson's legislative one.[16]

The first distinction between the Great Society's and the Jefferson Airplane's versions of the song is the placement of the lyrics. In the Great Society's single version, the opening line, "when the truth is found to be lies," is sung in one breath, elongating "truth" (3 beats), "is" (3 beats) and "be" (4 beats). The effect of this almost unbroken string of vowels ("ooooo—iiiiih—eeeeee") is that the song drags artificially, and the "wrong" words in the line are emphasized. Whatever "the truth" is "found to be" in this performance, it is swallowed at the end of the musical phrase, and the dreaded "lies" lose all their power. In the live version, Slick changes the emphasis slightly—"truth" (3 beats), "is" (3 beats) and "lies" (4 beats)—but as in the single version, the final point, that "all the joy within you *dies*," loses its sting. In Jefferson Airplane's version Grace Slick launches directly into the verse, dropping "truth" on the downbeat, then swiftly moving on. The words she elongates—"be" (5 beats), "joy" (3 beats), "you" (5 beats)—shift the emphasis dramatically to those sounds that could be easily heard through the filter of local ideology: "be joy"; "be you."

The transformation of the song from one version to the next is also apparent in the backing. The Great Society's single relies on a workaday rhythm guitar figure, a simple drum pattern, and a short but arresting guitar solo. In the live version, the rhythm section is more subtle; the first guitar solo is more melodious, while the second guitar solo begins as though entering into a different song—there's a momentary change in groove (3:36), before the guitar interacts more insistently with Slick's vocal. The lead vocals on both versions are still the most significant textural element. The melody is restricted in range, but Slick manages to maintain the listener's interest by increasing ornamentation and vocal filigree. The backing vocals are worth noting as well: in the studio single's chorus the open intervals between Slick and Miner sound too harsh for the rudimentary melody line; the backing vocals are less prominent in the mix in the live recording. All of these aspects change in the Jefferson Airplane recording: there Slick bends rather than embellishes notes, plays with her vibrato, and the melody is more richly supported by the backing vocals. The whole is part of a much richer musical tapestry, a more fulsome collaboration between musicians. The extensive guitar work throughout the Jefferson Airplane version suggests that the band were comfortable working in the studio environment. Even when the Great Society were captured live at the Matrix the band itself didn't "take off"; the ease with which Jefferson Airplane fly through their three-minute version of "Somebody to Love" is testament to confident musicianship, but also to the maturity of the scene that nurtured their sound.

The Great Society were over almost before they began. With Grace Slick now singing with Jefferson Airplane, David Miner left for Texas, Jerry Slick joined local band Final Solution before pursuing a career in film, and Darby Slick and Peter Van Gelder left for India. Their interest in Indian music was clear on Darby Slick's "Free Advice," the b-side – and musically the more interesting side – of the "Someone to Love" single. After the success of Grace Slick's first album with the Jefferson Airplane Columbia Records began trawling her back catalog:

> A curious piece of San Francisco musical history will be brought to light early this year [1968] when Columbia Records releases an album of tapes made by an early—and now defunct—San Francisco group, the Great Society. The unit, which disbanded over a year ago, was never a very good one, but its members happened to include Grace Slick . . . and her brother-in-law . . . who wrote "Somebody to Love."[17]

The rest of the band did fairly well from the deal—Columbia gave them a $20,000 advance on the recording—but the focus was obviously on Grace Slick, as the full-page advertisement of the recording eventually proclaimed:[18]

> Grace Slick and some others had a group called The Great Society.
> They played Longshoremen's Hall, the Fillmore, Mother's, the Avalon, the Matrix.
> The Great Society disbanded. But it lives in Grace Slick.
> In the San Francisco Sound. In "White Rabbit." In "Somebody to Love."
>
> Grace Slick and
> San Francisco rock when they were younger.
> On Columbia Records.

Notes

1. "Rock and Roll a Bust for Kingston Trio Man," *Rolling Stone* 3, December 14, 1967, p. 8.
2. Indeed, within a year many San Francisco bands were based in Marin County and traveling to the city for performances: in the summer of 1966 the Grateful Dead lived at Rancho Olompali; Quicksilver Messenger Service lived nearby. Big Brother and the Holding Company lived in Lagunitas, and Janis Joplin eventually bought a house on the border between Corte Madera and Larkspur. When the Youngbloods moved to San Francisco from New York in 1967 they settled in Inverness. And Moby Grape began their career practising at the Ark in Sausalito.
3. *The Kingston Trio* (Capitol, 1958) featured the chart-topping single "Tom Dooley," as well as the perennial favorite, "Scotch and Soda."
4. An early folk-rock band, the title track from their debut album, *You Were On My Mind* (A&M, 1965) was a Top 5 hit.

5. Jeff Blackburn and Sherry Snow were an electric folk-rock duo whose single "Stranger in a Strange Land" (1966), which adheres perfectly to the mid-1960s San Francisco rock aesthetic, never met its potential, partially due to complicated business arrangements between Trident and its distributor, Verve. Blackburn continued to be an active musician around the Bay Area and earned a writing credit with Neil Young for the song "My My, Hey Hey (Out of the Blue)," from *Rust Never Sleeps* (Reprise, 1979).
6. The Mystery Trend played at the first Mime Troupe benefit and around the dancehalls until 1967, shortly after the release of their one and only single, "Johnny Was a Good Boy."
7. Aurally, the chorus is heard as one continuous musical thought. I have divided it artificially to delineate the development of the final line, which I have termed "refrain" due to its repetition over the final third of the song.
8. The fact that "Sing Me a Rainbow" was not written by the band is interesting in retrospect, given the trajectory that Bill Champlin's career eventually took: he had writing credits for bands as diverse as Earth, Wind and Fire ("After the Love Is Gone"), Manhattan Transfer ("Smile Again"), and George Benson ("Turn Your Love Around"), sang backing vocals for a range of artists including Barbra Streisand, Donna Summer, and the Tubes, and has been a member of the band Chicago since 1981.
9. RJG, "Great Society A Name to Watch," *Chronicle*, November 8, 1965, p. 49.
10. ED Denson, "The Folk Scene: All Aboard and Turn On A-Holding," *Barb*, October 14, 1966, p. 6.
11. It is also true, however, that the legacy of the Great Society is often complicated by the US military involvement in Vietnam during Johnson's presidency.
12. A full transcript of Johnson's speech may be found at the LBJ Library and Museum webpage: http://www.lbjlib.utexas.edu/johnson/lbjforkids/gsociety_read.shtm (Accessed March 29, 2015).
13. The double exclamation marks appear on the label for the single version of "Someone to Love," though most references to the band leave them out.
14. The slight pronoun shift in the title was a surface detail to accompany the shift in musical context.
15. See Joel Selvin, *Summer of Love* (New York: Cooper Square Press, 1994), p. 88.
16. Darby Slick is reported to have written the lyrics while waiting for his girlfriend to come back home one morning. See his *Don't You Want Somebody to Love: Reflections on the San Francisco Sound* (Berkeley: SLG Books, 1991) for background.
17. "Conspicuous Only In Its Absence," *Rolling Stone* 6, February 24, 1967, p. 8.
18. Published in *Rolling Stone* 12, June 22, 1968, p. 7.

6. 1967

As the evidence mounts up, it becomes more and more obvious that the music of San Francisco, as well as the Hippie Way of Life, is going to attract thousands of young people this summer from all over the country.

Some provision must be made to house and to feed them. Several groups are now working on a Free Food Locker plan, on a soup kitchen and other devices, and a committee is being organized to deal with the housing problem.

The attraction of the music is one of the outstanding facts about the whole new youth attitudes.

Nothing like it has existed in this country before, not even during the Swing Era. The Bay Area with dozens of bands playing for dancing, with free rock concerts in the Panhandle and in Provo Park in Berkeley each weekend, with dozens of other bands appearing everywhere from the Print Mint to Moe's Bookstore to the New Orleans House to coffee houses and clubs on the Peninsula and in Marin, is the center of the whole New Movement of the country.[1]

Summer Invasion Note: Bill Board was sunning nearby and saw it all—two handsome young blonde couples, wearing "straight" clothes, driving their car (Washington plates) into a Marina motel. A few minutes later, they emerged from their adjoining rooms in full hippie regalia, including beads and bells. In the warm afternoon sunlight, they trudged up the Steiner St. hill, looking this way and that. At Green, they stopped an elderly, distinguished-looking man and asked: "Pardon, sir, but how far is it to the Haight-Ashbury District?" After examining them warily, he replied: "Philosophically or geographically?" Very San Francisco indeed.[2]

In its New Year's Day edition the Sunday *Examiner* featured a photo exposé of the Haight-Ashbury.[3] In an attempt "to show some of this hippie scene to those who may be timid about venturing behind the Long-Hair Curtain," photos included local residents moving furniture down the street, the interior of a communal flat, and straights and hippies sharing an orbit. The subtitle, "Affectionate little touches of Paris," may not have convinced the general readership of the neighborhood's charms, however: that day's front-page headline—"'Beat' Runaways: A Fugitive Army"— was but one in a seemingly endless stream of stories about middle-class runaways that filled the paper throughout the year.[4] The larger issues, of choice, lifestyle and sustenance in "beat" enclaves such as Telegraph Avenue and the Haight, were rarely

6.1 Stopping traffic.

explored; the recurring message was that everyone who opted out of safe, suburban existence would of necessity turn to drugs, panhandling, or worse.

The New Year's Wail, the party thrown by the Hell's Angels and the Diggers, "a sort of hippie philanthropic organization based in the Haight-Ashbury district," was attended by two thousand people in the Panhandle.[5] Unfortunately for the *Chronicle*, the event caused no trouble. But on Haight Street a different kind of peaceful pastime was piquing the paper's interest: hippies "lying down in front of cars to see how close the drivers will come to them."[6]

Around this time a new street sheet was being circulated by the Communications Company (ComCo). Printed with incessant regularity on a Gestetner silk-screen stencil duplicator, ComCo broadsides were the work of Chester Anderson and Claude Hayward. Anderson had moved to the city in January, where he discovered "a drug-oriented social revolution" where "everyone wears long hair and odd clothes & strange jewelry." With the founding of the ComCo, Anderson saw himself as "a community leader and, since it's a revolutionary community, a political/revolutionary/ultraradical leader as well. It's all enormous fun. "[7] The ComCo, printed "anything the Diggers want printed,"[8] along with Anderson's own philosophy of hippie life.

The tone of ComCo bulletins throughout 1967 provides an interesting counterpoint to the voices in the daily papers, the *Barb*, and the *Oracle*. Anderson's messages were often parlayed with the best intentions, though his proselytizing, from this distance, can appear rather unsafe:

> You can't explain it to them. DO IT TO THEM.
> Sneak up on them. Surprise them.
> The art of our thing is Total Experience, Assault, Outrage. Be an artist.

Rape every mind and body you can reach.
Put it in their coffee & booze & water. Put it in their cunts.
Have faith. Do what you believe. Share your truth. Do it now. . . .
In our time, not theirs. On our terms, not theirs. Choosing our own weapons. Do it our way & do it now.
Without organization or plans or leaders or any of the rest of their dead weight shit.
And do it because it's fun. Play it for laughs. Save the world for kicks. A practical joke.[9]

Aside from his call to dose the masses freely, it was Anderson's use of "us" and "them" that became ultimately problematic.

The Board of Supervisors' Police Committee heard responses to the proposed new dancehall law, and views about minors attending, with or without their parents, before or after 8.00 p.m., were reported in tedious detail. Still the dancehall promoters had to remind the assemblage that weekend dances drew more people than football games, and even with the Fillmore and Avalon attracting more than 400,000 people over the past twelve months, the police had been called only once to quell a disturbance.

Ralph Gleason had other matters to publicize:

Tomorrow beginning at 1p.m. on the Polo Field in Golden Gate Park, there will be a "Gathering of the Tribes" for a Human Be-In. It marks the first conscious get-together of all the elements in the Brave New World.
Berkeley politicos who have been notorious for their squareness will join the Hashberry hippies uninterested in politics to make an affirmation for life. . . . It ought to be a magnificent and inspiring afternoon. The non-organizers (an anti-organization stance is characteristic of the movement) invited the public to bring "costumes, blankets, bells, flags, symbols, drums, beads, feathers and flowers."
If you want to know what is really happening, you will not miss this. And if you want a glimpse of the future as it will be (poetically if not practically), dig it.[10]

As did the *Barb*:

It's happening.
Berkeley political activists are going to join San Francisco's hippies in a love feast that will, hopefully, wipe out the last remnants of mutual skepticism and suspicion. . . . The two radical scenes are for the first time beginning to look at each other more closely. What both see is that both are under a big impersonal stick called The Establishment. So they're going to stand up together in what both hope to be a new and strong harmony.[11]

San Francisco and the Long 60s

A union of love and activism previously separated by categorical dogma and label mongering will finally occur ecstatically when Berkeley political activists and hip community and San Francisco's spiritual generation and contingents from the emerging revolutionary generation all over California meet for a Gathering of the Tribes for a Human Be-In at the Polo Field in Golden Gate Park on Saturday, January 14, 1967, from 1 to 5 p.m.

Twenty to fifty thousand people are expected to gather for a joyful Pow-Wow and Peace Dance to be celebrated with leaders, guides, and heroes of our generation: Timothy Leary will make his first Bay Area public appearance; Allen Ginsberg will chant and read with Gary Snyder, Michael McClure, and Lenore Kandel; Dick Alpert, Jerry Rubin, Dick Gregory, and Jack Weinberg will speak. Music will be played by all the Bay Area rock bands, including the Grateful Dead, Big Brother and the Holding Co., Quicksilver Messenger Service, and many others. Everyone is invited to bring costumes, blankets, bells, flags, symbols, cymbals, drums, beads, feathers, flowers.

Now in the evolving generation of America's young the humanization of the American man and woman can begin in joy and embrace without fear, dogma, suspicion, or dialectical righteousness. A new concert of human relations being developed within the youthful underground must emerge, become conscious, and be shared so that a revolution of form can be filled with a Renaissance of compassion, awareness, and love in the Revelation of the unity of all mankind. The Human Be-In is the joyful, face-to-face beginning of the new epoch.

A gathering of the tribes for the Human Be-In can be reached by taking the Fell St. exit of the Bay Shore Freeway to the main drive in Golden Gate Park.

6.2 A gathering of the tribes.

The motivation behind the Be-In was optimistic and heartfelt:

> The spiritual revolution will be manifest and proven. In unity we shall shower the country with waves of ecstasy and purification. Fear will be washed away; ignorance will be exposed to sunlight; profits and empire will lie drying on deserted beaches; violence will be submerged and transmuted in rhythm and dancing; racism will be purified by the salt of forgiveness. Spiritual revolution to transform the materialistic bruted body and mind of America is NOW here with the young budding.[12]

The "revolution" that the *Barb* foretold was not a political one, however: "nothing happened at the Be-In, and the opportunity to gather all of those people was wasted."[13] For the *Oracle* it was a peaceful revolution:

> And with the sun setting, Allen Ginsberg and Gary Snyder chant the night with the Om Sri Maitreya mantrum, turned toward the sun, double disks revolving in the red-gold glare, small groupings arms linked moving gently from side to side. She a beautiful Nubian princess, he a motorcycle wizard and warlock, and I poet and participant, swaying, good people, Om Sri Maitreya. The sun . . . heading for the Pacific Ocean just beyond the grove of trees on the horizon, Om Sri Maitreya. The sun coalescing in the trees, gently moving from side to side, the sun nearly gone, thickening and converging into itself, mandala-fire, Om Sri Maitreya Om.
>
> And the day is over, and the last voice from the stage, Allen Ginsberg, "Now that you have looked up at the sun, look down at your feet and practice a little Kitchen Yoga after this first American Mehla. Please pick up any refuse you might see about you."
>
> "Shanti."[14]

The Communication Company saw it as affirmation of purpose:

> Politically speaking, it was an impressive demonstration. There we were: the Berkeley thunderbolts, the Haight elven, the blessed Angels, the awesome lovelies of Marin, unaffiliated strays from everywhere, . . . all the low men on all the totem poles—30,000 of us!—all together on that glowing field in unity. . . .
>
> For five hours yesterday, in that safety of numbers, we were free. Some of us had never been free before. . . .
>
> A parachutist floated down during The Dead's set. We all watched in ecstatic awe, somehow expecting miracles to happen when he landed. But he made a beautiful landing, folded up his 'chute & walked away, & no one even learned his name. . . .

> We walked slowly into the sunset, most of us, to the beach.
>
> There was a fog & everything was opalescent. We stood there, overwhelmed, thousands of hippies on the glistening sand. Flutes piped, a harmonica wailed, the ocean chanted its own mantra. . . .
>
> It got dark & cold. We wandered south along the beach, free & unafraid, & then turned eastward, back into America.[15]

Ultimately it was a tale of two happenings. The Sunday *Examiner*'s page three report, featuring a three-column photograph of "obscene" poet Lenore Kandel, was a cynical description of "the first annual Feast of the Incongruous."[16] The front-page headline, "Hippies Run Wild—Jailed," recounted none of the peace and love of the Be-In and only the "breakout"—hippies pushing citizens off the sidewalk back on Haight Street, "high on LSD," obstructing buses, throwing bottles at police cars, forty piled into police vans, twenty-five arrested and locked up in Park Station, charged with "creating a nuisance." It was a brief report, but ended, tellingly, with "a nonrelated incident," in which "a young man . . . walked through a plate glass window . . . naked and apparently under the influence of LSD."[17]

Gleason's report the following day, however, was clear and measured:

> And so it ended, the first of the great gatherings. No fights. No drunks. No troubles. Two policemen on horseback and 20,000 people. The perfect sunshine, the beautiful birds in the air, the parachutist descending as the Grateful Dead ended a song. . . .
>
> Saturday's gathering was an affirmation, not a protest. A statement of life, not of death, and a promise of good, not of evil. . . .
>
> On Saturday afternoon the Hell's Angels were the peace officers; it took a new force to accomplish that.[18]

Allen Ginsberg was given space in the *Examiner* the following week to reflect on the Be-In, and made a point of differentiating between what the media called "hippies" and what he insisted were "seekers." He also explained the extent of the hippie-Hell's Angels relationship, the measures taken to reach a level of peace and friendship between them, and the augurs for a similar relationship to extend to all Americans. This point would have been well placed, were it not for the "dramatic photo" in the adjoining columns showing "one of three or four minor skirmishes occurring during the Human Be-In," featuring one of the Hell's Angels, restrained by the hand of a nearby hippie.[19] Nonetheless, the *Oracle* managed a gentle warning not to overstate the hippies' purpose:

> To every facet of hate we must reflect love and to know this we must practice it unceasingly in all directions.

Guard carefully against feeling that we are a special, new or unique tribe. We are the ancient tribal consciousness of man in harmonious relationship with nature. The distended machine is the mutant.[20]

Fifty years later, reflections on the Be-In still summon all of the joy, and none of the portents.

The Human Be-In

ALBERT NEIMAN: I think they thought it was going to be a few hundred people. There were about four major posters for that event, and they all just say the same thing: "All San Francisco bands." Cause it was just a big jam. I mean, the Dead played with Big Brother, Quicksilver Messenger Service, and Jefferson Airplane, all the bands played, and they played all day. And there was at least 50,000 people there.

CHARLIE MORGAN: I just sort of stumbled into the Polo Field in Golden Gate Park, with my collared shirt and my kinda white, liberal, middle-class ideas. And I really didn't know where I was, but I knew that where I was, I really liked it. I was just kind of realizing that this was for me.

ERIC CHRISTENSEN: Well, it was a gathering of the tribes, and that was exactly it. Ginsberg was there reading his poetry and it was another one of these seminal transitional events that ushered in the hippie era. The elders were the beatniks and us young pups were kinda looking up to them but also doing our own thing and becoming our own movement. These were the first times you saw people openly doing things that were illegal, but just by sheer numbers were ok to do. So those kinds of gatherings were very reassuring and you saw that there was a change going on.

JHIANI FANON: We were all stoned on acid. And it was incredible. We got to a point where we were passing a generator, and the rhythm of the generator stopped us in our tracks. We must have been there for half an hour, because we couldn't move. There was something about the vibration of the generator that kept us—we didn't realize that we had just stopped there because of this vibration.

VICKI LEEDS: I can vaguely picture it. I remember sun and dancing and music and food, and people sharing everything. It was just a beautiful day at the park. People shared themselves, shared their food and shared their pot, and danced and walked around and were social again. You just kind of wove through the people, danced and chatted, hung out and flirted, and just kept moving and kept going.

LiAnne Graves: I had gone to the beach and there was this migration into the park. Walking up with this throng of people was such a trip. They're just all migrating into the park from everywhere. There's a surfer buddy, old boyfriend of mine, standing on a corner in the park with a blue vial of Owsley liquid acid and a straw. And he was dosing people and "Hey, what's happening." And so I got a good dose of Owsley acid, liquid blue, went to the park, went to the front of the stage and that's about all I remember. I remember hearing Allen Ginsberg give his "This Is Really It" poem and then it's just kind of a blur until I crawled back through people's legs to some friends, saw this guy parachute from the sky with no airplane, and made it home. It was great fun, I think. I can't remember it all but I know that I survived it.

The Human Be-In was a pivotal moment in countercultural history, but it also galvanized HIP merchants and concerned local residents into community action and open dialogue with the police. In the wake of the post-Be-In arrests a town meeting was called to discuss the fractious relationship between the police and residents of the Haight. The committee, comprised of lawyers, merchants, educators, ministers, and hippies, would suggest to the mayor and chief of police ways of resolving local tensions.[21] Some of the suggestions offered at the first meeting were proactive: distributing whistles to hippies for attracting witnesses to police harassment, borrowing city brooms and mops for street-cleaning parties. Some were less tangible: hippies would be courteous to policemen and recognize them as human beings, thereby subverting any intended aggression on their part.[22]

Following a meeting with Police Chief Cahill, Ron Thelin offered to "arrange, with the help of Allen Ginsberg, a finger signal and a mantra chant that, when heard by a crowd in the Haight-Ashbury, would mean they are to disperse."[23] It would need to have been a fairly loud chant, for the sounds of the Haight crowds were by this point increasing in volume at a magnificent rate.

Dickie Peterson: Haight Street was just packed. I mean, just wall-to-wall people, you know. And you would hear the drums coming from the Panhandle, up through the city. You would hear the drums. And this was, like, the call, and people would start filtering down to the Panhandle, and within two hours you'd have a full-blown concert going on, with bands coming up in trucks—all impromptu, no plan whatsoever. They were calling everybody to come, join together, be one with the music, man. Be one with everything, man. That was an experience. You could be down there, you didn't have to know people. I didn't have to know your name. You didn't have to know my name for us to enjoy being around each other. To enjoy the music, to enjoy the environment. It was very gentle.

The Anonymous Artists of America (AAA) landed on the front page of the *Chronicle* as a new breed of band, one that bonded over a lack of musical knowledge, a desire to depart from the university trajectory, and to cohabit in a Mediterranean mansion on the Peninsula.[24] What is notable about this rather extensive feature is the mention of their distinctive element: a Modular Electronic Music System, otherwise known as the Buchla Box, the prototypical synthesizer designed and constructed by Don Buchla in 1963 for the San Francisco Tape Music Center. The AAA had gained some notice for their improvisational explorations at the Avalon and Ken Kesey's Acid Graduation, but ultimately left the Bay Area to live communally in the Huerfano Valley in Colorado.[25] One member of the AAA identified by name in this article was Bobby Beausoleil, known in the Haight as "Bummer Bob," who reemerges later in the decade as a member of the Manson Family.[26]

In one week there were three very different reports on the hippie lifestyle. First, that Swami A.C. Bhaktivedanta was to open a temple at 518 Frederick Street. His friend, Allen Ginsberg, described him as very conservative, and intolerant of the use of LSD, marijuana, alcohol, tea, coffee, and cigarettes; he also forbade "sexual improprieties." He would expect his students to bathe daily and to follow a strict vegetarian diet, all in the name of Krishna Consciousness.[27] Second was a fair review by John Wasserman of the hippie exploitation film, *Hallucination Generation*, with every indication of more to come.[28] And third, a peek inside the psychiatric ward of San Francisco General Hospital for a chat with staff doctors about the incidents of LSD use and psychotic breaks.[29] The doctors explained that many people admitted to the hospital while experiencing a "bad trip" were easily cured with a tranquilizer and eight hours' sleep, though the *Chronicle* was quick to point out that the majority of such cases were young teenagers: a generic message that filtered through to most parents in the Bay Area, to alarming effect.[30] LSD still had a figurehead, of course, but local appreciation of him seemed to be waning:

> Tim Leary's "Death of the Mind" show at the Berkeley Community Theater Friday was the biggest bore since Andy Warhol was here last year. If the mind really died, it was suffocated by monotony, stifled by unimaginative lights and traumatized by the whole bum trip. . . .
> Dr. Leary . . . [delivered] the same speech we have been hearing the past couple of weeks bit by bit in interviews. This time he gave it all at once, in a monotone, holding the mike in his right hand and waving with his left. . . .
> [Leary] ought to disassociate himself from this entire adventure. It stinks of . . . commercialism . . . and if he is serious about his religious trip, he's doing himself and his cause more harm than good.
> It was a small house by the way. About half full.[31]

In February there were four border-crossings to report, from low to high culture, straight to hip, United States to United Kingdom, and secular to sacred. First was the Light Sound Dimension program at the Museum of Art, featuring Bill Ham, Jerry Granelli (percussion), and Fred Marshall (stringed instruments).[32] According to classical music critic Alfred Frankenstein, the weekend ticket sales broke all box office records:

> The over-all form was one of crescendo in pace and brilliance to a climax and a return to the mood and style of the beginning.
>
> Variation, paraphrase, allusion, counterpoint of theme and of tempo—in short, all the time-honored devices of development in time and space—were effectively marshalled, and, as always, the visual effect accommodated itself most obligingly to the rhythms of the music. . . . No obvious effort was made to synchronize visual and aural effect but no such effort was needed. The two always go together no matter what.[33]

This shows the critic's open-minded immersion in an unfamiliar art form: a successful crossover between artistic worlds, and a glimpse of the rich multisensory concert environment that this event was showcasing.

The second crossover saw Herb Caen embark on a trip with Kesey and Babbs on the Prankster bus, from Fifth and Mission, up Market Street to the Haight, through the Park, and back to Pacific and Fillmore:[34] an easy meeting of the minds. A less easy meeting of the minds occurred in London, when Chet Helms and Suzy Creamcheese of the Family Dog attempted a San Francisco "happening" at the Roundhouse, to the bewilderment of the British press.[35] And then there was the Invisible Circus: The Right of Spring. Held at the Glide Memorial Foundation Church, it was a seventy-two-hour, nonstop "complete environmental community," featuring poets, musicians, painters, artists. Novelist Richard Brautigan, one of its driving forces, said that "all are invited to come and 'occur.'"[36] There would be poets, Big Brother playing "Amazing Grace," Pigpen playing the chapel's organ for Sunday service, Stanley Mouse painting t-shirts; belly dancers, panel discussions, open dialogue with civic leaders and citizens—all with the intention of creating "a gigantic new energy force."[37] Of course, in the main section of the paper, the three-day event was announced with a pithy summary: "A group of dancers is scheduled to flit around the church altar as lights flash on the screen while droppers-in sit in pews holding sticks of incense."[38] The *Barb* recounted the events, with photographs:

> A procession started around the banks of pews, each participant holding a candle and moving slowly in the undulating line. Soon there were two lines moving in opposite directions. . . . In another downstairs room "the communication company" mimeographed bulletins about the happening as it evolved, posting copies outside the door. . . .

Several African drums started their pulsing beat in one corner. Soon many were dancing to the insistent throb, some of the belly dancers among them. Around the altar, loud voices projected selections from holy books, while couples kissed and caressed under the cross of Jesus. . . .

In a room downstairs a sex film was shown. . . . On the improvised beds in other rooms, couples were seen sleeping, talking, loving freely. Still other rooms had discussions, recording sessions, improvised folk and rock music. . . .

The church leaders did call a halt to the proceedings at dawn Saturday, well before the Happening had been scheduled to end. . . . Nobody was sure why.[39]

Chester Anderson broadcast his desire to host a Feast of Brothers in March, because "Freedom Power is Soul Power is an Army of Brothers. Let us love each other and be free."[40] He felt that the freedom the hippies and the black community sought was the same: "freedom to be, to be what we are, to do our own thing. . . . Freedom from exploitation. Freedom from being used against our will. Freedom from hate and fear." This was prefaced by Anderson's extended riff on "SpAdEs" [sic]:

In [Greenwich] Village I could hang out with spades, pal around with spades, turn on with spades, sleep with spades, live with spades, BE with spades, because they were really just as people as I was. . . .

The spades, dear my brothers, are our spiritual fathers. They turned us on. They gave us jazz & grass & rock & roll, in the early best days they provided a community for us, from the beginning they were our brothers deeper than blood, & now we & they don't like each other. If it weren't for the spades, we would all have short hair, neat suits, glazed eyes, steady jobs & gastric ulcers, all be dying of unnameable frustration.

Now we are estranged. Why? What happened?[41]

This elicited a number of thoughtful responses via letters to the *Barb*, primarily informing Anderson that "the fact that both the hippies and the spades find themselves to be oppressed minorities with a common enemy is not sufficient to make us a community." More pointedly, one writer urged Anderson to recognize that "Stokely Carmichael understands the problem much better. He tells us to stay out of the ghetto and let black people create their own manhood. Our job, he says, is to save the white community."[42] More pertinently, perhaps:

One of the most notable things of the old North Beach and Greenwich scenes was the liberal amount of soul atmosphere. Soul music, soul humor, soul love and soul, soul, soul. In the new bohemia soul is out. The thing is folk atmosphere. And this is really white folk music, white folk humor, and white folk love. . . . There is nothing new or experimental about the "folk" music of the hippie scene. It is as old as the Tennessee hills.[43]

A subsequent letter to the editor focused on semantics:

> In one sense [Anderson] uses the words "spade" and "nigger," this being the slang for Negro. With no malice meant, these are deterring factors to the Negro himself. The hippie or hipster uses these facets of speech as "cool" pronouns, when the words are, in fact, resented by every Negro, hippie or not. So how does he expect to go into Fillmore saying "Hey, spade (or nigger)! I'm on your side" or "I groove with your plea for freedom."
>
> Freedom is also to unshackle the word. The word is a drag within itself. . . . But in essence, in all that prevails, the only way for a person to understand a Negro is to be one. This is the only way.[44]

After these exchanges, one might infer that all hippies were white.[45]

> JHIANI FANON: No, that was not the case at all. The media did this. I mean, most of the kids were white, but most of the kids in America are white. There was an equal representation from just about every group—Mexicans, Indians, Chinese, Japanese, we were all there. And it wasn't a big deal. I got to be called Spade Johnny, and there was a guy, Curly Jim, he was quite a big part of the scene. He was from Texas, and he was Jewish. And rather than have people think about him being different as Jewish, he could point out that I was a spade, or I was black, right? So that got to be a tag that I carried around for a while. And in fact I started calling him Jew Jim sometimes. But we were buddies, and it didn't mean anything, you know.

There were tensions between hippie factions, and by Spring they were beginning to intensify. The Diggers were always averse to any whiff of capitalism, so when something called the Love Conspiracy Commune held the First Annual Love Circus at Winterland, the Diggers picketed the venue and volleyed accusations of an "exploitation of love." Again, the problem was semantics: "Love Circus" was too close to the Diggers' "Invisible Circus." Plus, tickets were being sold for $3.50, and "if it's really love it would be free." The Diggers suspected the Commune was a front for a late-night club syndicate; the Commune, compelled to document their $3,000 net loss, complained that "Haight Street has become a source of ugliness, characterized by petty politicking and back-stabbing and power plays. If I want THAT kind of living . . . I can join the straights."[46]

At this point, the straights were worrying about a new narcotic threat: Mellow Yellow, sourced by the unexpectedly psychedelic banana.[47] After a protracted period of speculation, the United Fruit Company finally sponsored experiments into the hallucinogenic properties of their most commonly imported product, only to discover that "the fruit does not induce the euphoria, the mental changes or the perceptual variations associated with marijuana," pending formal chemical analysis at the Veterans Administration Neurobiochemistry Laboratory.[48]

At least there was acknowledgment that the psychedelic counterculture was impacting on the mainstream, though one syndicated item curiously pinpointed the psychedelic nexus on the East Village of New York:

> [There] is no denying that the symbols, the sights and sounds—the ambience, if you will—of the so-called drug culture are being rapidly appropriated by the taste-maker establishment—the publicists, press agents, ad agencies and fashion designers who mold the tastes of New Yorkers, and by extension, the nation.[49]

The "taste-maker establishment" was now embracing those "multimedia technique" artists from Timothy Leary's orbit, while the young promoters responsible for exploiting the "almost unlimited commercial possibilities in the psychedelic movement" and ad agency executives tuned into the youth market. The result was soundtracked by "the emergence of raga rock, a hybrid of rock and roll and oriental music which is a clear off-shoot of the drug-takers' preoccupation with Eastern mysticism." This was to be found in the music of "current pop heroes" Bob Dylan, The Byrds, The Rolling Stones, and The Mamas and the Papas.[50] At no point was it suggested that New York's psychedelic "style" had been appropriated from the San Franciscan (not West Coast) template; rather the focus was on LSD "alumni" whose mission was to share the *style*, not the *substance*, of the acid experience, with a view toward commerce.[51] San Francisco did not factor in the narrative: indeed, even the Human Be-In had garnered no attention in the *New York Times*.

Back at the Fillmore, the dancehall drama continued apace, with arguments raging over curfews for the segregated teens. With some foresight, Bill Graham announced that in anticipation of "a flood of four million hippies" into San Francisco in the summer, he was planning to operate the Fillmore six nights a week for the sixteen-plus.[52] Besides the realization that the dancehall scene could sustain that kind of activity, the important point here is the forecasting of a busy summer: the arguments with city officials about a duty of care for these visitors had barely begun. Yet even though reports showed that Park Station was "averaging 50 teletypes a week to look out for runaway juveniles. . . . We're so swamped now we couldn't possibly remember the description of every one of them,"[53] and that runaways were coming from as far afield as Hawaii, Canada, and Mexico, still Graham's idea of a "busy summer" was dismissed as fanciful.

Soon enough the *Chronicle*'s front page screamed "Huge Invasion: Hippies Warn S.F." And what was the Recreation and Park Commission's response? To forbid the use of city parks between sunset and sunrise for "resting, sleeping or other purposes." The Diggers had already been housing 300 people a night, and saw the numbers of incomers to the neighborhood steadily increasing toward "a world-wide pilgrimage—people are coming here out of a sense of hopelessness and despair." Even the pastor at Haight's Church of All Saints predicted that the invasion "will be in numbers more than one-fourth of the population of San Francisco."[54] Nevertheless, the following day Police Chief Cahill announced that "law, order and health regulations must prevail" even in a hippie pilgrimage. He gave his staunch support to the Park Commission's resolution, and warned parents "that young people should not be in San Francisco unsupervised and without a proper place to stay," though he insisted that "the police have no reliable intelligence to indicate there will be an influx."[55]

The *Barb* saw a more insidious problem with the daily papers' coverage of Cahill's press conference. The *Chronicle* had ignored contributions made by a "vigorous spokesman" of the Haight, one Roy Ballard, who was dismissed as "a leftist Negro activist and Black Power advocate, wishing to be heard." Ballard had insisted that "if the Diggers do not receive the help they are asking for in advance, as far as the black community is concerned there will be no riot this summer—there will be war!" Ballard established a clear alignment: "Black people need food and clothing and shelter just like everybody else. The Diggers are moving in the right direction. It's time for the black man to do the same, and it's time for the City of San Francisco to help!"[56]

Police Chief Cahill also stated that "hippies are no asset to the community." This dismissed the many and varied ways in which hippie commerce had improved the Haight-Ashbury and injected money into the city: from the payroll at the Avalon and Fillmore (20–30 part-time employees, 6 full-time; 10–20 musicians employed every weekend), to the burgeoning poster art businesses run by Chet Helms and Bill Graham (200,000 lots of every poster for sale and distribution around the world), to the hippie media, retail outlets, the Job Co-Op, "and a host of other gainful and meritorious activities of which the Chief ... ought to make himself aware."[57] Instead, the mayor sought to establish an official declaration of policy stating that a hippie migration was "unwelcome." The headline: "Mayor Acts. War on Hippies."[58]

Such an environment of civic conservatism can foster academic liberalism. Professor Leonard Wolf, one prominent member of "straight" society, imagined a constructive outlet for members of the Haight community: Happening House, "the learning process of the new tribal culture."[59] An embryonic event was the "non-happening" in the Panhandle—no electricity, no music, "just poets reading their poetry, people learning about yoga or how to work a loom."[60] Across the Bay, Mills College in Oakland hosted the first public symposium on popular music, sponsored by the UC Extension. The Rock 'n' Roll Conference featured presentations by Ralph Gleason, composer Pauline Oliveros, disc jockey Tom Donahue, and Bill Graham; contributions by local art historians, criminologists, and anthropologists; industry insiders such as tour managers, producers, and composers; a panel of students

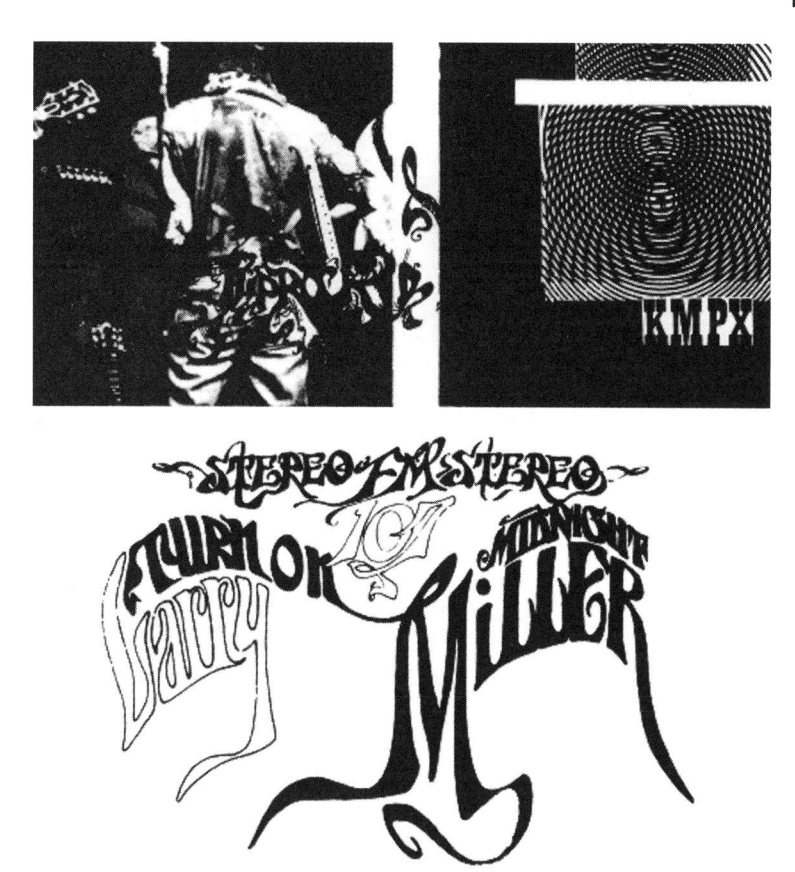

6.3 Listen to Larry Miller.

discussing contemporary pop music; and a special light show performance by Tony Martin, Graham Leath Dancers, and the Jefferson Airplane.[61] High and low, visual and aural, performers and audience: this list of participants showed not only the dimensions of the new musical culture, but also its wider significance. And one important new dimension was the establishment of "underground radio" station KMPX in March 1967.

KMPX

> KMPX was broadcasting in stereo with a power of 80,000 watts, non-directional, in March 1967. Its transmitter was located on top of Mt. Beacon in Marin County at a height of 1,250 feet. Listeners could tune it in at 106.9 on the FM band. The station was operated out of a moderated warehouse building at 50 Green Street . . . close to the base of Telegraph Hill.[62]

CHARLES JOHNSON: I think that one of the greatest things about it is that the people they had at that time playing the DJ role were also interested in discovering new avenues of listening, and new avenues of love music. And love music wasn't just per se the hippie music—love music is all the music there is.

Tom "Big Daddy" Donahue was a popular disc jockey on AM station KYA and the head of Autumn Records. When Autumn folded he had some time on his hands, and the midnight-to-six show on the fairly obscure KMPX gave him the idea for a new musical venture. What he had heard was Larry Miller's show, a catholic mix aimed at the eclectic palate: the head community of the Bay Area, hungry for something more than Top 40 fare, who needed a complement to the dancehall culture. From its inception the idea of free-form radio was greeted as a radical new departure. Soon Donahue had opened a similar station in Pasadena and before long, *Billboard* magazine had taken notice of the growing "underground radio" movement. The hip and radical audiences now had a dedicated space on the local airwaves.

When Nicholas von Hoffman came to San Francisco on an extended investigative visit for a nationally syndicated report on the Haight, he began at the offices of KMPX. This was the radio station for "institutionalized dope music" and the only station

> in the world where you'll see hips, frozen in the lotus position in the lobby. The Haight comes there every evening to chat, to ask for announcements to be put on the air, or listen to the music and use the crayons and paper supplied by the management for itinerant speed freaks who have nothing to do with their hands.[63]

Tom Donahue felt that this belittled the station's work, but KMPX soon garnered better national publicity, when *Billboard* labeled its new format: "progressive rock." That term, "progressive," might have different connotations now, but the idea then was simple: it was "taste, not sales" that directed the playlist:

> Listening to KMPX for an hour you are likely to hear tracks from the Decca album by Frankenstein, English albums not generally available in the U.S., advance dubs of U.S. groups, 20 minutes of Ravi Shankar, tapes by local rock bands, and other fascinating things. The Mainstream discs by Big Brother & the Holding Co. were introduced to the radio audience by KMPX and a whole new market for English LPs has developed out of the station's plugging of . . . Jimi Hendrix, Cream, Procol Harum and other packages.[64]

It may have been Larry Miller's midnight-to-six show that formulated what became "underground" radio, but it was Tom Donahue who made it a success. The salespeople Donahue hired to sell commercial airtime were hip, and knew hip proprietors; the public service announcements publicized community projects such as the Free Clinic, the Job Co-Op, and the Switchboard;[65] the disc jockeys shared a broad and intriguing taste in music that reflected the listening habits of its hip listeners.[66] Then there was Donahue's "female engineer policy," clearly in line with the Haight's dubious approach to gender equality: "I got tired of looking at all those old men through the glass who didn't like the music . . . so I decided to hire chicks. They're prettier."[67]

Donahue's plan was for KMPX to act as a community service, but eventually expansion and operating costs demanded a certain gesture toward commerce:

> There will always be a segment of your audience that considers any kind of advertising that goes beyond head shops and boutiques as a form of sellout. If this is the guideline then we have indeed sold out. . . . I do not believe the commercial per se is evil.[68]

Running deep in the story of KMPX is this fear of "selling out," of allowing the establishment to co-opt "underground" sensibilities for corporate gain. The station had established its direction in line with the underground news aesthetic and community focus of the hip community. But the imposition of managerial control, the competition from other stations, the desire to maintain a sense of authenticity within the corporate system, and attempts at reviving the lost magic, were a natural and unavoidable cyclical pattern.[69]

KMPX was an experiment in taste that infiltrated radio markets across the country, a virtual representation of an aesthetic that was nurtured in a new kind of experiential freedom: freedom to create, explore, connect. Though the story of this particular radio station echoed the stories of many earnest hip enterprises in the short 60s—a brief spark of "authenticity" within the establishment—the KMPX effect is still palpable on Bay Area radio in the long 60s.

In the climate of concern over the influx of travelers to the Haight, the city's health department decided to issue an ultimatum to the hippies: "clean up or move out." Health Director Ellis D. Sox announced his intention to tighten up on sanitation in the neighborhood,[70] citing slum conditions that were endangering the health of the city at large:

> When water is shut off for failure to pay the bill, toilets are not being used. . . . Garbage is thrown around, and this attracts flies and rats. Bubonic plague is carried by rats on fleas [sic], and it is not impossible there might be an outbreak of epidemic meningitis.[71]

As if that weren't enough, venereal disease and infectious hepatitis were on the rise. Clearly this was no place for those estimated 100,000 hippies to invade. An *Examiner* columnist figured that the underlying problem might rest with the Convention and Visitors Bureau:

> We are being selectively moral about the rumored hippie invasion. If the hippies did whatever they do in properly expensive hotel rooms and saloons, with big tips all around and everything, there would not be so much as a murmur from officialdom.
> Such hypocrisy is for spitting upon.[72]

The city soon toned down its rhetoric and extended a welcome to hippies, provided they were lawful.[73] The hippies responded with a "sleep-in" in Golden Gate Park, and an Easter Sunday "mill-in" on Haight Street, which resulted inevitably in arrests and local disturbance.[74] In response, a *Chronicle* editorial opined that local hippies should act on the tenets of their own peaceful ethos and not force police to take action against them, especially in "the salubrious and generally tolerant atmosphere of San Francisco."[75]

The health inspectors stayed busy though Sox soon admitted that the area's sanitation situation "is not as bad as we had thought."[76] Despite this change of heart, members of the Public Utilities Commission sought a way of "protecting" people living in the neighboring Sunset district from passing through the "Sodom" of the Haight: rerouting bus lines 71 and 72 off Haight Street on weekends and holidays, for at least six months, or "until the Hippie era ends."[77] Ralph Gleason had a few things to say about this, reporting that the Family Dog had organized a Spring Clean-In in the Haight, and urging sense to prevail:

> To reroute the buses and to order mass inspections is to discriminate against a part of the San Francisco community. Neither the Mayor, the Chief of Police, nor the Health Commissioner has a right to do this.... In fact, since the Hashberry is a tourist attraction now, it has every reason to ask for Convention A Tourist Bureau hotel tax funds.[78]

Poet Lew Welch urged a rerouting of a different kind:

> When 200,000 folks... suddenly descend, as they will, on the haight-ashbury, the scene will be burnt down. Some will stay and fight. Some will prefer to leave. My brief remarks are for the latter. I will stay. At some distance. Available. But my advice for those who have a way or ways similar to mine: *disperse*....
> Disperse. Gather into smaller tribes. Use the beautiful public land your state and national governments have already set up for you, free. If you want to.
> Most Indians are nomads. The haight-ashbury is not where it's at—it's in your heads and hands. Take it anywhere.[79]

The Public Utilities Commission finally voted in favor of rerouting the buses off Haight Street. Concerned citizens could now avoid unwanted exposure to the "exhibition of nude broads and nude fellows," begging the question: was public nudity the purview of the Police Commission or Muni?[80]

The *Barb* reported the arrest of Chet Helms and his wife Lori near the corner of Fillmore and Geary. A plainclothes policeman was in pursuit of an alleged shoplifter, who he proceeded to club to the ground. Helms requested to see the officer's badge, was ignored, and then beaten. Both Helmses were arrested and taken downtown to be charged with battery and disturbing the peace. That night at the Avalon, Chet Helms stood on stage and bared his back to the crowd of 3,000 people.[81]

It was within this climate that the Digger Intelligence Agency (DIA) announced the Digger Early Warning System (DEW):

Working in conjunction with Radio KDIG and the Communication Company the DEW . . .

I. will keep you well informed of impending police activity & warn you in time to take such steps as you feel safety calls for.

II. The Digger Press Service, working in conjunction with The Communication Company, will put the news on the street in psychedelic black & white, as well as informing the Underground Press Syndicate.

WARNING!

III. The narcs are out in force. There has been a sudden strong increase in narc activity on the street, & the number of agents working in this area has also increased. So be careful. IF YOU SEE MORE STRAIGHT MEN THAN WOMEN IN A GROUP, IT'S MOST LIKELY A BAND OF NARCS. BE ADVISED.[82]

The threat of hepatitis and bubonic plague was not enough to deter Gray Line Tours from launching in April a daily "Hippie Hop" tour through the "Sodom" of the Haight. Bus drivers would be "specially trained in the sociological significance of the Hippie world" and would follow a route down Haight Street without stopping, due to the "'hostile shyness' of the natives" and, naturally, health department recommendations. Lest the *Chronicle* readership believe this was purely an urban safari adventure, the president of Gray Line tours said that it was designed to offer tourists "some insight into what they might expect in their own communities some day."[83] *Chronicle* stalwart Herb Caen saw it differently:

I really can't explain why I feel this way, but I think Gray Lines' daily sightseeing tour of the Haight-Ashbury is a creepy-crawly thing, reeking of fast-buckism. Jack Cohen, Pres. of Gray Lines, doesn't make it any better with his tongue-in-cheek quote (at least, I assume that's where his tongue is) that "these tours will allow the Hippies to see what the outside world is like." The outside world is a bunch of tourists with their noses pressed to the windows, staring out at the hippies staring at them? The question that comes to mind is: "Who's in the cage?"[84]

And the hippies responded accordingly: some sold tourist maps of the Haight listing the names of every business and charity in the neighborhood; others held up mirrors to the bus windows so the tourists would see nothing but their own reflections.[85]

Amid the hysteria, the *Chronicle* announced that "a group of the good hippies"— those who "wear quaint and enchanting costumes, hold peaceful rock 'n' roll concerts, and draw pretty pictures (legally) on the sidewalk, their eyes aglow all the time with the poetry of love"—had formed The Council for a Summer of Love. Including members of the Family Dog, the Diggers, the Straight Theatre, the *Oracle*, the Church of One, and the Kiva, the Council intended to act as "a central clearing house for theatrical, musical, and artistic events, dances, concerts and happenings" in the Haight.[86] This was followed the next day by Gleason's announcement of another peaceful event, the First Monterey International Music Festival, to be held on June 16–18 at the Monterey Fairgrounds.[87]

But the *Chronicle* continued to notice the "bad" hippies, reporting LSD-related deaths of promising young persons from well-respected middle-class families, photo essays on the hippie lifestyle, extended ruminations on the original Diggers, and brief reports of hippie crack-downs in unexpected places like Big Sur, where anti-hippie forces took to razing abandoned cabins in an effort to rid the area of hippies, their

6.4 Gray Line tourists on an urban safari.

"infectious hepatitis . . . body lice, scabies and external and internal parasites."[88] Even in the Santa Cruz mountains, residents in the small hamlet of Ben Lomond viewed the application by one resident for a local service center as a sure sign of a hippie invasion.[89] In an effort at reversing this sinful coastal demise, a group of twenty-five fundamentalist ministers undertook missionary work with the hippies, but to little success.[90]

The hype in the daily papers was as nothing to Chester Anderson's April 16 communiqué. In one of the more infamous ComCo sheets, running to four pages of diatribe and bile directed at Timothy Leary, the *Oracle*, HIP merchants, the Council for a Summer of Love, and anyone not involved with the Diggers, Anderson painted a picture of "Uncle Tim's Children":

> Pretty little 16-year-old middle-class chick comes to the Haight to see what it's all about and gets picked up by a 17-year-old street dealer who spends all day shooting her full of speed again and again, then feeds her 3000 mikes and raffles her temporarily unemployed body for the biggest Haight Street gang bang since the night before last.
>
> The politics and ethics of ecstasy.
>
> Rape is as common as bullshit on Haight Street.
>
> The Love Generation never sleeps.
>
> The Oracle continues to recruit for this summer's Human Shit-In, but the psychedelic plastic flower and god's eye merchants, shocked by the discovery that increased population doesn't necessarily guarantee increased profits at all, have invented the Council for a Summer of Love to keep us all from interfering with commerce.
>
> Kids are starving on The Street. Minds and bodies are being maimed as we watch, a scale model of Vietnam. . . .
>
> Why doesn't Doctor Timothy Leary help the Diggers? He's now at work on yet another Psychedelic Circus at $3.50 a head . . . and there isn't even a rumor that he's contributed any of [his fortune] toward alleviating the misery of the psychedelphia he created. . . .
>
> For all their messy imperfections, the Diggers are the only human beings in the psychedelic ghetto. They're the only people here who aren't out to pick your pockets. They're the only people here who aren't so full of oldy bullshit that they have to wear perfume to mask the stench. The Diggers & the Radha Krishna Temple, & the Diggers don't even require you to believe in anything.[91]

When he was interviewed early in the 1970s about the "end" of the Haight, Jerry Garcia placed the blame almost directly on this bulletin:

> Do you want me to tell you the incident where I thought it started to get weird? I was walking down Haight Street, and all of a sudden in a window was a little notice. It said "Communications Company." And it was this horrible bummer of a depressing story about some 13-year-old meth freak getting raped by nine spades and smack heads. It was just a bummer. Bad news. This guy took it upon himself to print up bad news and put it up.
>
> Then he started putting out the whole "Free the Street" trip and he just brought in all this political, heavy-handed, East Coast, hard-edge shit, and painted it on Haight Street, where none of it was happening like that. It was still groovy. And that was the point where I thought, this scene cannot survive with that idea in there. It just goes all wrong.[92]

The scene had enough trouble surviving as it was. Roy Ballard, the "Negro spokesman" previously ignored by the *Chronicle*, tried to warn the Board of Supervisors that "it's going to be hell in San Francisco this summer," but was removed from the meeting by a policeman. Ballard had recommended that the city stock a warehouse with food which would be available to the hippies entering the city as well as to the city's poor population, but civic officials merely reiterated that an influx of hippies would aggravate the city's present problems. Despite other participants' insistence that there could be a "creative approach" to the summer onslaught, the committee voted to endorse the mayor's request for a policy declaration that

> a summer migration into the city of indigent young people is unwelcome; that existing ordinances will be strictly enforced; and that such migratory persons will not [be] permitted to sleep in public parks, or otherwise violate laws involving public health and the general peace and well-being of this community.[93]

Letters to the editor, editorials, and columns fancifully imagining a "tourist pogrom" duly followed.[94] Assemblyman (later Mayor) Willie Brown wrote that

> whether we like or dislike, agree or disagree, with the "hip" community is not the issue here. The issue is whether you can by fiat declare a minority "unwelcome" in our community. If you declare against these young people today, what minority is going to bear the brunt of your discrimination tomorrow?[95]

The supervisors' motion passed, in language allowing for the "right of all Americans to move freely in our country, and without derogating from San Francisco's proud tradition of extending a warm welcome to visitors." Yet the city "does not have the facilities to insure [sic] the safety and welfare of any large influx of such persons who, unable to provide for themselves for basic necessities, would therefore be dependent upon public facilities," thus necessitating "a fair and firm enforcement of applicable laws to the end that public peace and welfare will be maintained."[96] The *Barb* made the point clearly: not only were the hip communities of the Bay Area already crowded, the Haight

> looks like the Bowery, panhandlers stop you a couple of times each block, and lots of the people on the street look exhausted—not high, not turned on, not really digging a new experience. . . . Another thousand will make the scene very much the Bowery, 30,000 will make it look like India with starving beggars sitting on the streets. . . . There is no chance of solving the problem by ignoring it, and I can't think of any way to discourage those people from coming.[97]

The *Barb* highlighted some of the changes in place in the Haight for the expected influx, both hippie and tourist, and did not like what they saw. "There's nothing like a little love, and most Haight-Ashbury merchants are shucking it out by the truckload." Up and down Haight Street the *Barb* noted shops changing names, offering "love burgers" and "love dogs," offering "happiness unlimited," all in an effort to chase the tourist dollar.[98] But the *Examiner* wondered at the appearance of a revolutionary new organization called The Black Panthers. One intrepid reporter sought information from members Bobby Seale and Huey Newton, and outlined their basic beliefs: that "the black community is oppressed by the 'white power structure'; . . . that The Black Panthers oppose Negroes fighting the 'white man's war in Vietnam' . . .; Unless private enterprise provides jobs for Negroes, all big businesses should be nationalized." The reporter offered information on Newton's and Seale's arrest record, and noted that "law enforcement agencies are deeply concerned, but feel they are handcuffed."[99]

The *Chronicle* did eventually try to affect a hipness when they launched a new column, "Astronauts of Inner Space." Written by Jeff Berner, "minstrel, traveler and educator," the column promised to take readers "far out into the future of the past and the now." Any hip credentials the paper gained were soon revoked, however, when it sent a straight, 34-year-old reporter named George Gilbert into the Haight for one month's field research. The resulting series, "I Was a Hippie," purported to be an insight into "what the High Life is like" and "what the summer invasion of 'flower children'— and tourists—can expect."[100] The information that Gilbert procured during his month as a hippie was framed by decidedly un-hip language ("Why do you live in a slum?" "Why did you come to the Haight?"). The *Barb* soon called Gilbert's bluff: much of the material had been lifted directly from the *Barb* itself.[101]

As an antidote to any positive reportage, the *Chronicle* duly painted a picture of the "most pathetic sight in Hippieville": parents from across the country traveling

> If you dig your lovers enough to ball them you dig them enough to avoid giving them the clap.
> Help keep our neighborhood clean....
> FREE CHECK UP AND TREATMENT AT 33 HUNT ST.
> Hours: Mon. and Thurs. 9:30 - 5:30
> Tues., Wed., Fri. 8:30 - 4:00
> Phone: KL 84839 for information regarding V.D.

PHOTO: PAUL KAGAN

6.5 Free love needs care.

to San Francisco to scour the Haight-Ashbury in search of their missing children, "peering into bearded faces hopefully."[102] The *Barb*, and later the *Oracle*, took a proactive approach direct to potential runaways, itemizing equipment necessary for living on the streets, appropriate modes of behavior to avoid disease and arrest, and simple words to live by: "Dress warm, keep clean and healthy, eat a balanced diet, live indoors, and avoid crime."[103] And avoid poetry: a jury of ten women and two men found Lenore Kandel's *Love Book* not to possess any redeeming social importance, and to appeal only to "a shameful and morbid interest in sex." Jay Thelin and Allen Cohen of The Psychedelic Shop and Ronald Muszalski of City Lights were found guilty of possessing obscene matter with an intention to sell it.[104] The "shameful and morbid" interest in sex no doubt derived from the rise of what became known as "free love"—a breaking down of the traditional moral structures of monogamous, heterosexual union.

Free love

> ART ROGERS: What really happened? Like everything else, it depends who you talk to. Some people just slept around a lot, male and female. There was probably a lot of experimental sex. Some people were looking for longer relationships. And you were free to sleep with somebody, and you were free to live with somebody and not marry them. And I'm sure men got their hearts broken and women got their hearts broken. You know, to me it's all about

coming home. Where is home for you? And the same things just keep coming up: family, community, peace. You know, being nice to people makes you feel good. Do something nice to somebody for free, for no reason at all. Be happy for no reason at all. Just to make somebody feel good and smile.

Vicki Leeds: You could basically have sex as much as you wanted to or as little as you wanted to. Date rape wasn't something that existed as a concept then, but it happened. There were people I slept with that I didn't really want to sleep with, I was kind of coerced into it and it wasn't really fun; it didn't make me like myself or like the other person for it. And then there was other times when it was really fun. So it just depended.

LiAnne Graves: Free love? Well you love, you give it freely. There were none of those attitudes toward women who give it up easily. It was like—if you'll pardon my French—fuck freely, love the one you're with. And a lot of males took dark advantage of it.

Suzi Young: In the 50s, when I was growing up in high school, there was a lot of competition among women. I grew up with the thing of, you had to protect your boyfriend cause some other girl was going to come and steal him. In the 60s things were a lot looser. But when you were married, it was all about groupies. And it was all about protecting your relationship from that. Most of us could not do it. It was just like a kid in a candy store. And like everything else the sexual revolution had its bright side and its dark side. I don't know many relationships that survived it.

Vicki Leeds: For us as women, we were exploring our sexuality on unknown turf, trying to figure out what we wanted, and how we could play this game, or not. There was no history to look at. We had to figure it out on our own. But we had each other to talk to. I know some people that were very virtuous through all this and hardly slept with anybody, and I know other people that slept with hundreds of people, and they had a great time doing it. So in one respect I don't know that it's any different to how people struggle with their sexuality now; it was just more up front and there were a lot of us going through it at the same time.

Teresa Tudury: What was going on was a sexual revolution in terms of the relatedness of men and women. We were really struggling to pull things out of what had been a runaway patriarchy in the 50s, to a more equitable one—and really succeeding in many ways. So it was a huge shift. Huge.

Marc Arno: I had more than my fair share. And it was always "That was wonderful, what's your name." But it was always sincere and heartfelt and loving. And totally inept. None of us knew what we were doing sexually. It was amateur time at the orgy.

Despite the hippies' bad press, there was an awful lot of bandwagon-jumping to report: psychedelic artwork tagged onto the opera, airlines, and department stores; an influx not of flower children, but record talent scouts; bands being recorded at the Avalon; quick-release movies of the B and blue variety, capitalizing on free love; the "Liverpool of the US" label being misattributed everywhere; so much so that

> if the hippies and the current exciting, creative, provocative music of San Francisco survives all the Love Bagels, Flower Ice Cream, Psychedelic hats, dresses, ties, do-it-yourself kits and "I Was a Hippie" games that the future holds, it will be a miracle.[105]

And now neighbors were complaining that the Sunday concerts on the Panhandle were too noisy. Officials admitted that they had recommended alternative locations for the weekly gatherings, but no one would provide details. It was not entirely inconceivable that this was an attempt at dissuading summertime hippie incomers,[106] but the Council for a Summer of Love had already recognized the effect of amplified music on the neighborhood residents, and the better acoustic environment available in wider, more open, less trafficked, spaces. The Haight-Ashbury Neighborhood Council endorsed the views in the spirit of mutual cooperation and sensitivity.[107]

Gleason chimed in with his support of the right of all persons to move rhythmically to organized sound:

> The magic of music, when played free, sublimating the hostility in masses of people, has been proven in this city over and over this year. There is, in the act of giving, something mystical and purifying which works much better than the policeman's club.

The fact that the dancehalls charged admission did not lessen the importance of their contribution to local culture; indeed the business of rock dances had grossed over $700,000 in just sixteen months. The Fillmore was now open six nights a week, the Avalon four. Regular dance concerts were held in other venues in the city and all around the Bay Area, every one serving as "a positive good, a harmless outlet for the frustrated energies of everyone and they should be encouraged rather than attacked."[108]

Impure LSD was beginning to reach the streets, and no one knew what the additives to the drug might be. Medical research suggested that people were developing a tolerance to LSD, requiring larger doses to be effective.[109] Perhaps coincidentally, venereal disease was reported to be spreading through San Francisco with greater swiftness than before. As of May 1967 the number of reported cases of gonorrhea was already 50 percent more than the total for the entire previous year and now

6.6 Worlds collide at the Panhandle.

spreading to upper-income, professional classes, the under-25s more particularly. The emergence of strains of gonorrhea resistant to penicillin was particularly worrying.[110]

Then an untested new drug known as STP appeared on the streets. Believed to have been developed by the Army Chemical Warfare Service, the drug mimicked an LSD trip, albeit with a slower progression (four hours) and a much longer effect (seventy-two hours). According to Dr. David Smith, director of the Alcohol and Drug Abuse Screening Unit of San Francisco General Hospital—and soon founder of the Haight Free Clinic—the drug

> is extremely disturbing because it has simply not been tested adequately to determine what its effects may be. And worse yet, there is no known antagonist to it. . . . It could be extremely hazardous, and all I can say right now to anyone is: For God's sake, don't try STP![111]

Within days, the FDA had sent samples of STP back to Washington for analysis, still uncertain how the drug got from the manufacturer to the black market. The *Chronicle* was quick to point fingers, however, citing "sources" in the Haight who were certain that "the drug is being made and wholesaled somewhere in the East by Augustus Owsley Stanley III, . . . best known as a wealthy undercover manufacturer of LSD."[112] Before the summer's end, the FDA had traced the drug back to the Dow Chemical plant in Walnut Creek, with neither organization able to say how samples of the drug had found their way to the black market.[113]

In more mundane drug news, marijuana possession landed three members of local band Moby Grape in the papers,[114] just one step in their remarkable journey.

Moby Grape

> Moby Grape is a group which was afflicted by the curse of a perfect first album. There was a stylistic consistency to that album which belied the diversity of sources it drew upon. What resulted was an American *Rubber Soul*.[115]
>
> MARC ARNO: So there was a big commercial push behind them. But when they played? The best comparison I make is: Creedence Clearwater *wished* they sounded that good. Performing live, Moby Grape had all that raw, deep flowing energy that was hard to compare. There wasn't anybody else quite that strong.

Of all the San Francisco bands in the short 60s, Moby Grape promised the most: five songwriters, five distinct voices combining in effortless harmony, the biggest record deal, and the biggest promotional machinery behind them.[116] There was no reason for them not to succeed. Like other local bands, Moby Grape boasted a roster of uncommonly talented musicians—Jerry Miller, Don Stevenson, Bob Mosley, Peter Lewis, Alexander "Skip" Spence, all incomers to San Francisco, brought together in 1966 by the litigious entrepreneur Matthew Katz. Their eponymous debut album is a defining recording of the short 60s, a "perfect first album," and stands as supreme testament to the unmatched potential of an extraordinary group of musicians and their vibrant musical community.

Moby Grape is an eclectic record, a rare studio insight into the many musical facets that contributed to a "San Francisco sound":[117] compared with other releases from 1967, it is more eclectic than Jefferson Airplane's *Surrealistic Pillow*, more disciplined than *The Grateful Dead*, and less lysergic than Country Joe and the Fish's *Electric Music for the Mind and Body*. Every track on the album exploits their unique group sound and optimizes the musical strengths of each individual member.

The Moby Grape sound, particularly on the gentler acoustic tracks, is worth exploring a bit further. If there were a shift in pop music aesthetics around 1968 toward country rock,[118] songs such as "8:05" had already ventured in that direction. The gentleness of the song foreshadows songs such as "Ripple" in effect, if not in message: "8:05" is a lyric of love and loss, the melody almost secondary to the increasingly prominent background textures. The lyrics breathe in "8:05," as in "Ripple," but the progressively intricate vocal harmonies amplify certain lines and act not as an external chorus but rather as an internal dialogue. The ways in which the vocal lines meander and meld are supported by the acoustic guitar interplay, a musical construct that could exist independently, similar to the complementary strengths of the musical and lyrical elements in "Ripple": a display of effortless musicality, sensitivity, and subtlety.

Drummer Don Stevenson explained how those attributes were refined in the Moby Grape sound:

> I always liked playing funky shuffles. But when you have one guy [Lewis] who is a finger picker, Skippy, who would float in and out, and Jerry, who could tear it up, you had this situation where you don't want to get in the way of all that. And I kind of learned where you really have to consider the space rather than fill in the space. What I loved about Skip was that he would play guitar like a drummer . . . just play rhythms, and not on two and four, but rhythms that played around inside the patterns. And he was very ethereal. You would think it would be very difficult to have three guitars, but Skip always wound his way in and out of the picking and lead guitar parts, winding his way inside of everything that created this great tapestry.[119]

Their mix of psychedelia, close-harmony singing, gentle ballads, heavy rockers, pure pop, had something for everyone, and there was an undoubted excitement building to the album's release, with Columbia Records investing "thousands—more than on any other artist in memory."[120] At the center of Columbia's publicity campaign was the simultaneous release of five singles from the album.[121] It was an audacious and unprecedented marketing strategy, and needless to say, it backfired: "Omaha," the only single to get any kind of airplay, barely scratched the Top 100.

The release party was by all accounts an odd evening: stilted and overproduced, nothing like a regular night at the Avalon. Then there was the event *after* the release party, which shifted the band's momentum in the wrong direction: in the early hours, Miller, Lewis, and Spence were arrested while in the company of three minors in a car parked on a fire trail above Marin City. Miller was also found to be in possession of marijuana.[122] The band posted bail and left for promotional engagements on the East Coast, but they were not cleared of charges until early 1968. Eight months later *Rolling Stone* ran a brief piece that divulged a few lesser known details about the arrest:

> The musicians' court defense claimed that the girls were high school students interviewing the three members of Moby Grape for their school newspaper. The reason, the defense said, that Skip Spence was discovered by officers with his belt unbuckled was that he had worn a belt with a large buckle to the press party and although it was comfortable when he was standing, it cut into his skin while seated; hence Skip unbuckled. The narcotics charges were dropped before the actual trial began.[123]

There were other troubles as well. Gleason's announcement of the record release party included a veiled reference to Katz's nefarious management style:

> Meanwhile the Grape's manager, Matthew Katz (pronounced Cates) is suing the Jefferson Airplane and Bill Graham for $2,500,000 over the Airplane's contract and the scuttlebutt has it that Columbia is trying to buy Katz out of his contract with Moby Grape.[124]

While it is unfortunate that any mention of Moby Grape must include Katz, it is also true that Katz can be blamed for most of Moby Grape's troubles.[125] Less than a year after the *Moby Grape* launch, it was reported, with some confusion, that there were now two Moby Grapes: the local one, and another one playing society parties and working out of the Seattle area. Katz claimed to "own" the name; the band members claimed they did.[126] Columbia pushed ahead with the release of a second Moby Grape album, but the augurs were bad, and "as it must to all managers and groups, it will end in court."[127] And so it did.

Hard drugs and mental instability also shaped the ensuing trajectory of spiral and decay: the "difficult second album" syndrome hit Moby Grape hard, and Skip Spence's increasingly fractured mental state led him ultimately to an extended stay at New York's Bellevue Hospital. Spence never fully recovered, and neither did Moby Grape. In 1969 Ben Fong-Torres considered Columbia Records' failed marketing strategy: the cost of promoting the album, and the fact that "Omaha" was the band's only minor hit, left "each Grape with royalties of something like $180."[128] This, compounded by the failure of their subsequent albums and the million-dollar lawsuit over the use of their own name, accelerated the band's demise. Though various members of Moby Grape reassembled, toured, recorded, and disbanded with regularity following their official breakup in 1969, their protracted battles with Katz prevented them from performing under the name Moby Grape until the turn of the millennium. These legal woes, the death of Skip Spence in 1999, and the indigent lifestyle of Bob Mosley, scuppered any attempt at benefiting from the renewed interest in the band among newer generations of musicians and listeners. Moby Grape's appearance at the fortieth anniversary celebration of the Summer of Love, in Golden Gate Park in September 2007, was a bittersweet homecoming and proof of their enduring appeal.

Back in the short 60s, the hip community was still struggling with its mainstream representation. A March *Ramparts* feature article on the hippies was particularly ill received. Though possibly an illuminating read for its "straight" audience, the Thelin brothers and Bill Graham railed at the author's ignorance, and Ralph Gleason resigned from the magazine's board in disgust.[129] It certainly contained some surprising passages: "Drug song lyrics may, in fact, be the entire literary output of the hippie generation"; "Hippies do not share our written, linear society—they like textures better than surfaces, prefer the electronic to the mechanical"; Bill Graham was a "robber baron,"

Chet Helms was part of "the pioneer, non-profit rock group called The Family Dog"; Digger Emmett Grogan was "the closest thing the hippies in the Haight-Ashbury have to a real life hero"; and "if more and more youngsters begin to share the hippie political posture of unrelenting quietism, the future of activist, serious politics is bound to be affected." When Gleason's angry letter of resignation was not reprinted in *Ramparts* or acknowledged publicly, he refused to set foot in the magazine's office ever again.

In a letter to the *Barb*, Chester Anderson, never a fan of concision, explained that he had once offered *Ramparts* "the outline of an enormous essay" on "The Psychedelic Conspiracy." That basic idea was bought and a new article was commissioned with a ten-day turnaround. The research was conducted by Anderson, Claude Hayward and Jann Wenner, "Ralph Gleason's right-hand teenybopper," who provided background detail on local music, rock dances, the Hell's Angels; Hayward and Anderson conducted interviews and "a detailed socio-political study of the hip community." All of this material they presented to *Ramparts* editor Warren Hinckle, who was tasked with the job of condensing it all. The result, Anderson claimed, was that Hinckle perverted facts, ignored evidence, and falsified information.[130] Chet Helms' response was rather more succinct.

```
                    Family Dog Productions
                    639 Gough Street
                    San Francisco, California
                         94102

                    February 23rd, 1967

          Mr. Warren Hinckle
          c/o Ramparts
          301 Broadway
          San Francisco - 94133

          Re:  Rampart's March Issue

          Sir:

          "May the Baby Jesus Shut Your Mouth and
          Open Your Mind."

                         Sincerely,

                         Chester Helms
                         FAMILY DOG PRODUCTIONS
          CH/hs

          cc: Editor, San Francisco Chronicle
              Editor, San Francisco Examiner
              Ralph Gleason
              John Wasserman
              Phil Elwood
              Editor, Berkeley Barb
              Editor, San Francisco Magazine
              Editor, San Francisco Oracle
              Doyle Phillips, I. D. Magazine
              Jann Wenner, Sunday Ramparts
              Bay Guardian
```

6.7 A letter to the editor.

There were soon reasons for the hippies to revel in their good press. In early June, the two-day Fantasy Fair and Magic Mountain Festival was held at the top of Mount Tamalpais. AM station KFRC sponsored the event, featuring eleven bands of various stripes. Proceeds from ticket sales—nearly $60,000—went to Hunters Point Child Care Centers. The crowd numbered in the tens of thousands and there were no disturbances from the audience, the Hell's Angels or the forest rangers.[131] There was little criticism in the papers' summation of the weekend, "very like transplanting the Fillmore Auditorium and the Panhandle and Haight street to the top of Marin's Mt. Tamalpais."[132] Yet despite its success, the Magic Mountain Festival inevitably got less press than a festival that took place down the coast the following weekend.

Monterey Pop

The rapturous reception of the Monterey Pop Festival is not surprising. Its success was obviously unprecedented, but as a collective experience, and as a showcase for Bay Area talent, Monterey represented a utopian vision of "music, love and flowers" that was never equaled.[133]

After the festival, it was pronounced "one of the most remarkable scenes in contemporary American history, a gigantic musical love-in which set a standard of peacefulness and sobriety for the entire country."[134] Excessive? Perhaps. But in itemizing the highlights of the weekend, Ralph Gleason set the tone for much of the festival's ensuing mythology:

> The police wearing flowers on their helmets . . . the constant sound of bells . . . the cameraman holding his ears when Janis Joplin screamed . . . Chet Helms dancing backstage . . . Steve Miller's use of a pre-recorded tape in one number . . . the Volkswagens [sic] parked in line with kids sleeping in them Monday morning . . . the girl drawing a flower on a cop's helmet . . . the absence of trouble . . . the sobriety of the audience . . . the inclement weather . . . the splendid time.[135]

Even in the moment, it was difficult to process it all. Michael Lydon's notes on the Dead's performance were typically impressionistic:

> accumulated sound like wild honey on a moving plate in gobs . . . three guitars together, music, music, pure, high and fancy . . . the total in all parts . . . loud quiets as they go on and on and on . . . sounds get there then hold while new ones float up, Jerry to Pig Pen, then to drums, then to Lesh, talking, playing, laughing, exulting.[136]

The documentary evidence of the Dead's performance does not reveal such subtleties, however. One problem with the Monterey Pop Festival was the filming of it: while the Los Angeles producers had arranged for D. A. Pennebaker to document the weekend, not all the bands agreed to have their performances filmed. Big Brother were one, the Dead were another. The Dead always blew their biggest chances, which is part of their mythology. But because Big Brother were counseled not to sign the release form, their rapturous Saturday afternoon performance went undocumented: a catastrophic career move. So they pleaded for another chance to perform, specifically for filming. That performance of "Ball and Chain," included in the documentary, captures a moment in their career, between local and national success.[137]

The festival's administration was a different matter. On the front page of *Rolling Stone*'s first issue was an article posing the question: "Where's the money from Monterey?" The festival's expenses, the "amateurish good will" and "lavish generosity" of the festival's administrators, showed the "uneasy wedding" of the hip San Francisco culture and its more commercial Los Angeles counterpart. The festival did not hire a bookkeeper until well after the festival, when the bills and receipts were in a state of chaos.[138] Yet the festival management continued to negotiate rights over the film. The fact that bands were asked to sign control over to organizers Lou Adler and John Phillips merely added to the unease that some San Francisco musicians felt about the commercialization of their local scene.[139]

Commercialization was perhaps inevitable, but in retrospect, so was the extended debate about the festival's profits. Throughout the rest of the year, and well into 1968, the organizers' reputations were called into question in Gleason's column, in *Rolling Stone*, and in the underground press:

> Expenses were wild: over $50,000 for transportation; almost $35,000 for hotels and motels and $20,000 for police. . . . Charges and counter charges are rife; Lou Adler . . . is accused by some of getting his own acts on the show when the money would better have been spent for more recognized people. . . . The SF contingent apparently sees every Festival move as a malevolent conspiracy by Hollywood millionaires, while Adler and Phillips appear mystified as to why their good intentions should be misread.[140]

> Lots of love and beautiful music and a pitch about how the money made from the festival would not be used for any crass commercial purposes, but rather would be spread about in the hip community, or some community, for elimosinary purposes or some other such happy horseshit. . . . To this day the money has not been disbursed and the story is beginning to change, the sure sign of a con-trip. . . . Dig it and dig yourself when you think of the Pop Festival. It was a gas, wasn't it baby?[141]

The fact that most of the San Francisco bands were now signing major-label contracts and recording in Los Angeles is rife with complications: purists may still believe that the "authentic" musical product of the San Francisco dance renaissance was the live event; others may appreciate the lengths to which some San Francisco bands went to preserve a sense of their individuality on record. Either way, the Monterey Pop documentary reveals the ideological differences between the southern and northern California pop sensibilities, and the film's initial reception echoed some of those distinctions: *Rolling Stone*'s extended review included references to the Mamas and the Papas' appearances "cut in as if they paid for the film," and the "curious" fact that "their sound tracks are impeccable and their musicians are too incredibly tight."[142]

When the Monterey officials demanded more provisos on a second festival than the organizers could reasonably meet, it was clear that the first Monterey International Pop Festival would be the last. Amid the missing money, the film, and the failed negotiations, Gleason's *Rolling Stone* column argued that Monterey "showed the difference between Los Angeles and its lotus land dream and San Francisco and its rejection of that as well as the orthodox American dream."[143] But when the film was finally released, Gleason raved about it and encouraged everyone—those who were at the festival and those who weren't—to experience it (again) for themselves.[144]

But there was another problem: Scott McKenzie's single, "San Francisco (Be Sure to Wear Flowers in Your Hair)," written by John Phillips as the "theme song" to Monterey. It had climbed into the Top Five by July 1967, and into the Top Ten in the United Kingdom and Europe. If the subtext to any discussion of Monterey is the commercialism of Los Angeles versus the "authenticity" of San Francisco, nowhere is it more apparent than in discussions of this particular single.[145] ComCo distributed a subtle yet scathing commentary on the song, which is unsurprising, given their mistrust of any commercialization of the Haight;[146] but criticism of the song is still widely shared in the long 60s:

> SAM ANDREW: John Phillips made all that money from that song, the theme of Monterey, and it didn't have anything to do with us. You know, we thought it was just so childish, but we're gonna go along with the Festival because it's really great, it's big and everything, even though it was hokey and typical LA. And they hadn't seen us yet, that was the funny thing: they were gonna sell us, but they hadn't really experienced us—I mean the whole San Francisco thing, not just Big Brother. They didn't know what it was, and they were there to sell it. And they were very patronising about it, but you could see, they went, "these guys are light years beyond us! How did this happen?!" You know, that was their revelation.

If the underlying message of the single was that "summertime will be a love-in there/ . . . in the streets of San Francisco/gentle people with flowers in their hair,"

> **MESSAGE FROM THE SAN FRANCISCO ORACLE**
>
> The Haight Ashbury has been practicing the warless way of living and loving and creating and exchanging for a new age. New forms, successes and failures and dreams have drawn great attention to the Haight Ashbury.
>
> While America nightmares its military hells of the mind, Americans loving love and hoping peace and seeking wisdom and guidance have turned toward the Haight Ashbury and are journeying here. Our best efforts have so far failed to gather civic support and material resources for the many thousands expected.
>
> We feel that every community in America must practice the warless way and communicate among its races and between young and old; CELEBRATE, COMMUNE TOGETHER, PRACTICE FREE GIVING AND RECEIVING IN YOUR OWN CITIES AND COUNTRY-SIDES.
>
> If you want to journey to San Francisco you should bring in addition to flowers and bananas: 1) Money for rents and food. 2) Sleeping bags and rucksacks (or packframes) 3) Extra food (brown rice and soysauce - 100 lb. bags at rice mills for $12 4) Camping equipment for living in wilderness and national parks 5) Warm clothing for very cold foggy San Francisco summer climate 6) Proper identification.
>
> SHANTI SHANTI
>
> I often wonder if Sir Galahad, the perfect knight
> Had often wished his armour not so bright.
> — john monahan
>
> **SUMMER SOLSTICE CELEBRATION**
>
> Sunrise ceremony 4-5 a.m., Twin Peaks
>
> Pilgrimage to Park down Haight Street 8-9 a.m.
>
> Day-long festivities throughout Park
>
> Bar-b-cue picnic Polo Fields
>
> June 21
>
> Sunset pilgrimage to beach
>
> Rising moon ceremonies on beach.
>
> BRING
>
> costumes, gongs, cymbals, bells, horns, chants, beauty, peace, harmony, flowers

6.8 *The Oracle's* summer announcement.

the LA musicians who recorded it were certainly not responsible for the inevitable outcome.

>   ALBERT NEIMAN: And so there was a group of us who said, you know, there's going to be a couple hundred thousand kids coming out here this summer. And this is every kid who's a little creative, or a little psychotic, or a little misfit,

from every little town, you know, all over the country, is gonna hitchike to San Francisco with a flower in his hair after hearing that song, right? And we are totally unprepared to deal with this. You know, these kids are going to come out here, and they're gonna get in trouble. And they did.

Just before the Monterey Pop Festival and the expected summer onslaught, the *Chronicle* ran a thoughtful profile of Happening House's new venture: a free clinic treating hippies in a safe and nonjudgmental environment, located in a former dentist's office at 558 Clayton, near the corner of Haight. Dr. David Smith was volunteering three hours of his time every night as medical director, coordinating a staff of eight other volunteer doctors and ten registered nurses. Within a week of opening, the clinic physicians were treating thirty patients per night, with more arriving constantly:

> The night-time scene outside is full of sound and potential violence: a barefoot girl is questioned by police for panhandling; hunting for sex, three sailors gawk at the hippies; a trio of tribal types walk by, beads dangling, ankle bells tinkling; one whacks a tambourine and the rhythm penetrates into the clinic.[147]

Clinic staff treated problems ranging from bad trips to pneumonia, referring patients to other local hospitals for further treatment as necessary. There was no mention here of the Summer of Love or the hippie invasion; just a clear statement that the clinic operated a twenty-four-hour emergency hotline, and that they needed medical equipment and more volunteers to maintain the type of services so desperately needed in the community.

It was soon announced that the Health Department had proposed a $200,000, city-sponsored program calling for the establishment of a Haight clinic by the end of July, in the hope that this would reduce the number of cases of venereal disease, infectious hepatitis and serum hepatitis, prevent epidemics of typhoid fever and meningitis, educate neighborhood young women in matters of birth control and prenatal care, assist the "borderline psychotics" in the area experiencing bad reactions to LSD and STP, and provide bandages and mercurochrome to the many barefoot flower children suffering cuts to their feet. The Haight would be faced with a crisis in the warmer late summer and early autumn months, with the easy spread of communicable diseases throughout the hippie community. Most important to the success of this proposal was the fostering of trust between hippies and the medical professionals. A punitive approach, such as normally taken by the city government, would be antithetical to this mission.[148]

The proposal of $200,000 was never pushed forward to the Board of Supervisors, however, and at the end of the summer the Haight-Ashbury Medical Clinic was forced to close. Although they had helped roughly 200 patients a day since June, the

Clinic had received no support from any San Francisco agency, and the city's health director stated, "I don't believe the closing of the clinic is an acute emergency, and if I went to the Supervisors for money I would have to ask for funds to set up a clinic [in other neighborhoods] too."[149] The inevitable benefit concert for the Clinic was to be held in San Jose, the irony of which was not lost on Ralph Gleason: "It is a strange world indeed when such a valuable public service as this should have to go to an adjacent city to, almost literally, beg for funds."[150] Within days more benefits were announced at local venues, and the *Chronicle* printed an editorial declaring "that the Haight-Ashbury health problem is a city health problem," urging city supervisors to "move vigorously, as the situation requires," to ensure income to the clinic.[151]

Throughout the hippie emergence there was a question about how they collectively saw themselves: were they a "scene"? A "culture"? Or as some suggested, a "tribe"? According to Timothy Leary, the seekers at his center in New York were "a tribal community . . . and we have to come to terms with the white men around us."[152] Astronauts of Inner Space declared that "hippies are American Indians," the kind of statement carried lightly by the *Oracle*. Richard Alpert claimed that he

> was reading an account about an Indian tribe the other day and thinking about the Haight Ashbury district and I'm going to do a kind of a cut-up of those two things together because they are so beautiful, . . . because they are both the same.[153]

It is easy to itemize the similarities between the two groups:

> Living together, taking care of each other's children, sitting in circles to smoke holy grass as the Cosmic Peace-pipe is passed from hand to hand . . . the tribal spirit has arisen from the living. Hip tribesmen believe in magic; not the white man's magic which does card-tricks, fools the eye and hides things, but Indian magic that reveals things.[154]

The ritual ingestion of peyote, the adopting of Indian dress, plans to construct a Kiva (a Hopi temple) in San Francisco, seeing spirit all around them; an interest in the "other" was a natural extension of the hippies' exploration of inner space.

> There has never been a tribe of young people in history which took so much interest in life and its kaleidoscope of forms: Zuni culture, Oriental music, Zen, Nineteenth [sic] Century British Digger Socialism, jazz, electronic composition, magics and religions from everywhere. Even some of the new psych/art resembles American Indian sand-painting.[155]

But there was a problem in the hippies' desire to form a tribe: "the new seekers tend to be superficial in their studies," and "from the drab middle-classes come kids hungry to borrow a really interesting culture from somewhere, but [bringing] with them the once-over-lightly dilettantism of their parents even when it comes to religious exploration." A further problem? "It's weird that the simplest young braves are being treated by white men of the Establishment a lot like the ancient Red Men were."[156]

The President of the American Indian Historical Society of San Francisco offered a public reply:

> We remain . . . largely unrecognized in this city, where we were founded by four authentic tribal chiefs, and eleven other Indian leaders of respectable reputation and great pride in themselves and their heritage. . . .
>
> Indian life, even in aboriginal times, was highly ordered. Every one worked. To beg is the greatest sin a man can be guilty of. To use drugs in order to induce hallucinatory experiences for their own sake is a crime against God, and foreign to our religions. . . .
>
> The way of the hippie is completely at variance to that of the Indian. It is disgusting. It is demeaning. It is the Way of the Bum. And we are not now, nor were we in the beginning—Bums! . . .
>
> We Indians have borne massacre, destruction, genocide, exploitation. But in the last years there has been a certain insidious and subtle exploitation of the Indian which is the worst of all. We are for real. We . . . despise fraud and hypocrisy. The Hippies exemplify both.[157]

At the same time, the *Oracle* devoted an issue to the American Indian, which included ruminations on myth, metaphysics, yoga, and the Haight community itself. Largely a reaction to the Omnibus Bill (The Indian Resources and Development Act of 1967), it ended with the following observation:

> Many young people look towards the Indian for some spiritual guidance and for communal and ecological guidelines. This is not a free ride! If it is, then we are simply Ugly Americans stepping over poor dark foreigners. Americans are not Indians, cannot form a traditional Indian Tribe, but we can help each other and work toward a proper development of our respective Karmas.[158]

The dialogue between the hippies and the Indians was not yet over.

The Sociology Department of San Francisco State College provided an interesting demographic snapshot of the Haight, drawn from fifty personal interviews and 200 questionnaires completed by neighborhood hippies:[159]

30% were born in California

75% have been in the district less than two years

- 52% have been in the district less than one year
- 90% come from middle-class, upper-middle-class, or upper-class homes
- 4% identify as Buddhist
- 22% identify as Christian
- 2% were over the age of 30
- 100% of subjects of voting age vote in all elections
- 96% have smoked marijuana
- 90% have ingested LSD
- 50% have tried DMT
- 42% of males have had same-sex relations
- 24% of females have had same-sex relations

No wonder so many people were drawn to San Francisco in the summer of 1967—not only was the local demographic open-minded and accepting, their Solstice celebrations made their lifestyle sound fairly idyllic, "a big, colorful, friendly affair," reason enough for continued free music in the park.[160] But the waves of incomers to the Haight spelled a decisive shift: "Some of the old-timers, the hard core of the district, are moving out in disgust over the appearance of what they call the plastic hippies and the tourists."[161]

Doctors David Smith and Frederick Meyers were still urgently warning hippies, real and plastic, against consumption of STP. Because the drug was often spiked with cocaine or strychnine "to give an added kick," it closely resembled the army combat weapon BZ. If that weren't enough, the doctors stressed that chlorpromazine, the antidote commonly used to counteract LSD's adverse effects, if used to counteract STP, could cause respiratory paralysis and death. Dr. Smith warned that "the best we can do . . . is to give supportive care during the maniacal period which sometimes lasts three days or more." STP had been given away as "free pills, some pale peach, some aquamarine blue" in their thousands at the Summer Solstice celebration, and now sold for up to $5 each. The amount still available created a critical situation for the area, and the doctors were anxious to "kill the market immediately."[162]

Lou Gottlieb, former folk singer with The Limeliters, was arrested at his Morning Star Ranch for running an "unsanitary camp for hippies." County health officials had visited the ranch in Sonoma and found conditions unsuitable for the forty to one hundred people who stayed there in any given week. Gottlieb—"who holds a PhD in musicology from the University of California, and who now sports a full beard"—insisted that they were "personal guests," and that Morning Star, one of several ranches in Sonoma popular with hippies, "is far cleaner than most."[163]

When Gleason trekked out to Morning Star to see what all the fuss was about he saw a combination of hippies and tourists, drawn there by stories on television and in *Time* magazine, a variety of sleeping areas, clothed and unclothed persons wandering the land, and more importantly, signs that the "pilot study" of Morning Star Ranch was being replicated elsewhere in intentional communities across the country.[164] The press continued to take a prurient interest in Morning Star and the tendency of some of its residents to "show 'private parts' of the body" in full view of neighboring properties. Compounded by violations of health and sanitation laws, Morning Star attracted the attention of the FBI, local law enforcement, the chief probation officer, a municipal court judge, and border patrolmen who arrived "in search of Canadians."[165]

Back in the city, Herb Caen noted briefly that The Grateful Dead, "one of our very best 'SF Sound' rock groups," were moving out of 710 Ashbury and "heading for an unlikely place—Santa Fe, New Mexico, after a spell in Vancouver. Says a spokesman: 'We want to check out some new faces, new scenes.'"[166] The shift in the Haight was reflected in new ways of living and new forms of spirituality. Some hippies followed Swami Chinmayananda, others Krishna Consciousness, which inspired hippies to work and even bathe occasionally. Plenty of fodder for an evocation of hippiedom's "otherness."[167]

Back on the street, the Switchboard—a new volunteer service providing information on crash pads for hippies and runaways—was profiled in the *Chronicle*

6.9 "Walk in the park . . . to see the young people blossoming there like clusters of butterflies and flowers."

as an example of straight and hip factions in the Haight working together for the community. This emphasized the establishment's ignorance of the real problems: "The kids coming in have no place to stay. They have no money. They're sleeping in the park, in doorways, any place they can find." The situation was so critical that one of the few enlightened organizations in the area, All Saints Episcopal Church, sent 1,000 letters into the straight community, appealing for temporary housing for the incoming young people.[168]

Perhaps it was inevitable that high culture would crash into low culture. Dame Margot Fonteyn and Rudolf Nureyev, in town with the Royal Ballet, were arrested on a rooftop during a raid on a party in the Haight. Neighbors complained about the noise, police followed the sound of people running upstairs to hide, and they discovered Nureyev "dressed typically: red satin-lined, double-breasted blue pea jacket, mod pants, zippered boots and multi-colored shirt." When taken to Park Station, Fonteyn "graciously declined to give her age, but police listed it as 49." The dancers spent four hours in custody, booked for disorderly conduct and being in a place where marijuana was kept, and were eventually released without charge. Descriptions of the scene—Fonteyne "wrapped in a magnificent white mink coat and crouched near a roof parapet. Nureyev, the fey Russian genius who defected to the West six years ago . . . lying flat on a graveled roof"—accompanied an illustrated photo-diagram of the events. The article stretched across several pages, including mug shots of other arrestees, a candid shot of the two ballet dancers "annoyed, and . . . vaguely amused," respectively, and a photograph of the two on stage in a *pas de deux*.[169]

Given the speed with which this episode concluded, it is perhaps surprising that the *Chronicle* devoted so much space to it: the obligatory picture of freaks dancing "a kind of hippie tribute" outside the Opera House,[170] an extended interview with the *maitre d'* at Trader Vic's, recounting every detail of the previous evening's dinner service and the "naughty conversation" between the dancers and "the other boys,"[171] and a fairly florid editorial retelling of the story in balletic metaphor, praising the two dancers for embracing local culture.[172] The following week, columnist Charles McCabe saw the story about "the two jolly jumpers from Covent Garden" as focusing needed attention "on the idiot laws governing the use of marijuana in California, and most other places in the Western world."[173]

Perhaps the biggest news of the late summer was the opening of the Straight Theater, at 1702 Haight Street. Brothers Bill and Hillel Resner headed the team of locals who took over and renovated the abandoned movie house. In the adjacent Masonic Hall was a dance school and a studio for children's craft classes and other events. The intention was to create "a total environmental theater." In its first three weeks the theater hosted poetry readings by Michael McClure, a drama, and a number of rock shows: it was "a magnificent structure for the cultural enhancement of not only the Haight-Ashbury district but the entire city."[174]

6.10 "Thou shalt sing, love, dance."

The Straight's path to dance permit was not so smooth, however. At an initial meeting the Board of Permit Appeals heard—for three hours—testimony from Haight neighbors. The main argument rested on whether the Straight Theater could affect any kind of meaningful change in the area, or whether it was part of the "problem" that faced the community.[175]

A short piece tucked away in the front section of the *Chronicle* announced the discovery near the Point Reyes Lighthouse of a body, tied up in a sleeping bag. It was a man "about 25 . . . bearded and fully dressed in Mod-type clothes. A small puncture wound was found in his left chest." The body was presumed to have been thrown over the cliff, the bag caught on rocks and undergrowth; the man had already been dead for a couple of days.[176] The next day, alongside a photograph of George Harrison and Pattie Boyd walking down Haight Street,[177] came rumors of an Eastern crime syndicate moving into the city to gain control of the drug traffic. The body found in Point Reyes was soon identified as William E. Thomas, "a notorious hippieland narcotics dealer who styled himself Superspade." Friends of Superspade told detectives that he had "recently been told to join 'The Organization' or suffer the consequences." This, compounded with another recent murder of a known "drug pusher," whose body was found *sans* the right arm, inspired attempts at connecting the two incidents.

Rumors of Superspade's last day abounded though the true details were somewhat less colorful:[178]

> KEN IRVING: We think he was killed at Gate 5 in Sausalito, and his body hauled out to Point Reyes and dumped. But it all started out with a dope deal in San Francisco. He heard that there was I think five ounces of pure lysergic acid for sale at Gate 5. Evidently he was set up, because he got the $55,000 together in about an hour and headed over to Sausalito, and was killed there. I think it was just a setup, a come-on to get Superspade to get the $55,000 from his backers and then kill him for it.[179]

The two Haight murders gave Chester Anderson an opportunity to spin the Mafia angle into a conspiracy theory:

> [The police announced they are looking for] Charlie Garcia, 31, sometime rockdance promoter &c and friend of Super's, not as a suspect but for questioning as a material witness. This is interesting. In The Love Circus affair, Garcia was the link between the hippies who produced the dance & the probably "Syndicate" backers . . . who ran it.[180]

The threat of violence was enough to make some hippies arm themselves, while others simply moved to quieter spots in Marin County.[181] And thus began the "hippie exodus." Dr. David Smith told the *Examiner* that "new highly commercial peddlers have appeared who will sell anything from heroin to methedrine to unknown mixtures of allegedly psychedelic drugs." This was in stark contrast to hippie commerce, drugs sold by hippies to hippies. The police, predictably, had another theory: that very little heroin had infiltrated the community, and that some hippies were "running scared because of guilty consciences arising mostly from their use of marijuana or LSD."[182] In the end, the *Oracle* saw the deaths of Superspade and John Carter as cautionary tales, urging readers to "plant dope and give away all you can reap."[183]

San Francisco and the Long 60s

In society news, Merla Zellerbach dined at a hippie restaurant, Good Karma Café in the Mission, wondering at the menu (squid and vegetables for $1.45; raw goat's milk; short grain brown rice), unknowingly highlighting the trend toward natural foods that the hippies were responsible for promulgating into the new century.[184] Though hippies were advancing the cause of macrobiotics, they lost a vital expressive outlet when the Parks and Recreation Commission decided to deny the use of Golden Gate Park to "electric" bands. Calling the move nothing more than discrimination against the new generation, critics devoted entire columns to challenging the "foolish rule."[185] The Commission did lift the ban, subject to the successful application of permits for future concerts,[186] which the *Barb* saw as a victory and Leonard Wolf saw as "more important than just Haight-Ashbury. There is a kind of free speech issue involved. . . . San Francisco has produced a musical sound unique in this country. To have that sound arbitrarily silenced is outrageous."[187]

The way that sound was represented beyond San Francisco's borders was another matter. The trade papers failed to "adequately cover the subject." *Variety*'s pop coverage was "hopelessly obsolete," *Billboard* was rife with misinformation, the British press, *Melody Maker* and *New Musical Express*, were "inadequate to the job any longer."[188] The answer?

Rolling Stone

> VICKI LEEDS: I was at my brother's house and Jann came over really excited one day and said, "I have this idea for this rock and roll magazine. What do you think?" And I said, "oh, I don't think it'll ever catch on." And that was *Rolling Stone*. So obviously I was wrong.

> We hope that we have something here for the artists and the industry, and every person who "believes in the magic that can set you free."
> ROLLING STONE is not just about music, but also about the things and attitudes that the music embraces. We've been working quite hard on it and we hope you can dig it.[189]

Rolling Stone might have been just another relic of the short 60s. Arriving in the wake of the Summer of Love, the first issue of *Rolling Stone* (November 9, 1967) was a decidedly local production: a short piece about the struggle to reopen the Haight Clinic, a two-page photo spread on the Grateful Dead's arrest at 710 Ashbury, a brief note of the narcotics arrest of members of the Electric Flag, a half-page article on Country Joe, and a half-page report on the Death of Hippie ceremony. The cover photo of John Lennon in a still from *How I Won the War* connected the San Francisco scene to the wider pop world, but there was certainly no promise in that first issue that *Rolling Stone* would still be publishing biweekly issues fifty years later.

Rolling Stone arrived at a time when the nature of the pop music industry itself was changing. The Monterey Pop Festival was not just celebrated, but challenged; the "rotting corpse" of Top 40 radio was buried by Tom Donahue;[190] the steady stream of studio recordings by psychedelic forerunners were not just praised, but critiqued. For a West Coast music magazine, this combination of all the "things and attitudes that music embraces" was novel and necessary. There were inevitably tensions—within a year, Ralph Gleason had resigned as contributing editor on the grounds that he could "no longer accept responsibility for an editorial and reportorial policy with which I am not in sympathy and over which I have no control." There had long been rumors of his disagreement with *Rolling Stone*'s early promotional campaigns, one of which included the offer of a free roach clip with every new subscription.[191]

The magazine itself was borne out of the tensions with another local publication, *Ramparts*. At the suggestion of Ralph Gleason, Jann Wenner had been working as the entertainments editor for the *Sunday Ramparts*, a short-lived offshoot of Warren Hinckle's monthly magazine.[192] When *Sunday Ramparts* folded early in 1967, Wenner began amassing the capital necessary to launch his own venture, Straight Arrow Publishers, which would publish his new rock magazine. Wenner based the look of *Rolling Stone* on the *Sunday Ramparts* format, with a logo by local poster artist Rick Griffin. On the skeleton editorial staff were Gleason, *Newsweek* reporter Michael Lydon, and photographer Baron Wolman.

Rolling Stone did not enter an entirely empty field, of course. The East Coast rock magazine *Crawdaddy!* had been circulating since February 1966, and *Mojo-Navigator* began covering the San Francisco scene in the autumn of 1966. Important singular voices were emerging as well: Richard Goldstein at the *Village Voice* (1966–69) and Robert Christgau for *Esquire* (1967–68) and the *Village Voice* (initially 1969–72), while Ellen Willis was the first popular music critic at the *New Yorker* (1968–75).[193] But *Rolling Stone*'s clearest influence was *Ramparts*, and despite its contentious exposé on the hippies Wenner acknowledged the two magazines' "overlapping trajectories";[194] Warren Hinckle, however, remained dismissive of the local culture:

> The attempt to make a serious political stance out of goofing off. . . . One of the leading merchandisers of this counterculture bullshit was *Rolling Stone*, the rock culture tabloid that was started by two disgruntled *Ramparts* types.[195]

Whether or not Jann Wenner was "disgruntled" when he left *Sunday Ramparts*, it is true that he instilled in the new magazine a sense of "wildness," and with the exposé on Monterey Pop a continuation of the "muckraking" tradition established by *Ramparts*.[196]

The stable of critics working for *Rolling Stone* into the 1970s shaped the magazine's voice and sense of aesthetic values. Some of the longer-form articles became cultural touchstones (Hunter S. Thompson's *Fear and Loathing in Las Vegas* (1971) and Tom Wolfe's *The Right Stuff* (1973)); some became the basis for films (*Perfect* (1985), *Almost Famous* (2000)); and some of the magazine's original photography (by Annie Leibovitz, Baron Wolman, and Robert Altman) enjoyed an artistic life of their own:

> VICKI LEEDS: Blue Cheer were doing an album cover shoot with Baron Wolman. Marlene and I went along and Baron asked if he could take our picture. Out of the many, many rolls of film he took, there was one really good picture—and that was it. That picture made it around the world. I met people for at least ten years afterward, especially men, that had that picture. It was in the jail in Marrakesh, it was in the jail anywhere somebody might get busted for hash or pot all over the world. It was really kind of bizarre—and it was fun.

As an embodiment of the "long 60s," *Rolling Stone* occupies interesting journalistic territory. "The things and attitudes that music embraces" in 1967 San Francisco were fairly radical, culturally and politically. In the five decades since, *Rolling Stone*'s political and current events reportage has generally maintained this left-leaning focus, though the music content has by necessity expanded to embrace all genres, from the now "classic rock" to the determinedly mainstream pop of current chart artists.[19/] The progressive approach to politics, music, and popular culture expounded in the pages of *Rolling Stone* in the long 60s relays a decidedly local ethos to an international readership.

In August the *Barb* ran a feature article on Matthew Katz ("a 37-year-old Saggitarius who towers well over six feet in his bare boots)," whose role in the new musical

6.11 Vicki and Marlene in *Rolling Stone*.

culture was not yet fully understood. What Katz called "a national phenomenon, the San Francisco 'Sound,'" was an "outgrowth of rock and folk, a driving, bluesy, sometimes soft, often screaming expression of musical freedom." When asked where it came from Katz replied that "it's brought about by drugs like grass and LSD, which eventually [musicians] get off because it blows their thing. But it's the mind-opener. They get on stage, the audience gets into it, digs it, trips out, and people groove. This is it—the San Francisco Sound!"

He claimed that the poster artists' recent Joint Show should serve as a model for "the kind of cooperation needed in the music scene."[198] It is unclear where cooperation was actually lacking, but the *Barb* remarked that such "lack of unity" resulted in Katz's "multi-thousand dollar breach of contract suit with the Airplane and Fillmore Auditorium owner Bill Graham." No matter; Katz had a formula for putting together successful rock groups: "four or five better than average musicians who can sing—and I mean sing together—and you work like hell." Katz then plugged his newest project, a conversion of the jazz-rock fusion Orkustra into a "musical happening" to be called It's a Beautiful Day: "We've added two chick singers and a new sound."[199] And the lawsuit drags on, fifty years later.

6.12 Chocolate George's funeral cortège.

The happening in Lindley Meadow one late-August morning was a wake for Chocolate George, the Hell's Angel who died in an accident on the corner of Haight and Shrader. The Dead and Big Brother played for the crowd, who sat happily smoking weed and dancing. George was a friend to the hippies, and had been working for the Recreation Center for the Handicapped for over a decade. The *Chronicle* story featured a photo showing a line of motorcycles en route to the funeral, snaking for blocks up Dolores Street: a sensitive reminder of the humanity behind the Harley-Davidsons.[200]

A call went out from the Marin County Undersheriff to the elusive Owsley Stanley for a bit of help with the Superspade case. An intrepid *Examiner* reporter found Owsley's last-known address in Berkeley and spoke to a "barefooted, bare-chested man who answered the door"—a man with a theory that alcohol is a worse drug than acid, whose living room furniture included three microphones and an "army" of stringed instruments—who finally told the reporter go to 710 Ashbury to ask Jerry Garcia or Danny Rifkin where Owsley might be.[201]

The *Barb* marked the end of the Summer of Love with a walk, unencumbered, down Haight Street. No one asked for spare change, no one blocked the sidewalk, and automobile traffic could even reach the speed limit.

> It all goes to prove what every veteran Haightie knew all along. Most of the summer lovers were out for their vacation thrill. They were tourists, plastic hippies, pseudohip, middle and upper class straighties who came down to play the game. . . . But one thing happened that no one can dispute. In one way or another almost all these people were turned on, and while they may never again see San Francisco it's a virtual sure bet that somewhere in the world they'll someday be wearing flowers in their hair.[202]

And what was left in the wake of the hippie exodus? Hippie detritus. According to Golden Gate Park officials, the impact of the hippies was worse than expected: not only did the flower children avail themselves of blossoms, they broke off branches of trees and shrubs for firewood, they cleared several wooded areas for camping and slept on the grass, which had now turned brown. They cooked in the park and failed to clean up, which attracted rats; and there was the increase in vandalism, purse-snatching, holdups, strong-arm robberies, and rapes, not to mention the mountain of "papaya juice cans, cardboard suitcases, iron frying pans, banana peels, orange rinds—all the day-to-day litter of transients," which made parts of the park look "like Vietnam."[203]

And there was the demise of the dancehall scene, predicted not from a lack of permits, but from the overpopularity of the events. Too many people were now crowded into the Avalon and Fillmore—so many that no one could dance—and "unless the bands play music which is impossible NOT to dance to," the scene could be over.[204] At this point, Chet Helms and Bob Cohen were planning to open a second Family Dog operation in Denver, with plans eventually to find a third spot in London. The *Barb* asked Helms "if Family Dog Productions had turned stone capitalistic with the hope of opening many places world-wide," to which Helms responded that "present vision is to have five or six places as showcases for our products" and a Family Dog label for releasing in-house recordings made at each of the Family Dog ballrooms.[205] This idea of "showcasing products" was notably detached from the original dancehall ethos.

Then, with thundering inevitability, the Straight Theater's application for a dance permit was denied.[206] So to abide by the city's decision, and in keeping with their original prospectus, the Straight Theater announced that its School of the Dance would begin holding evening sessions:

> The first dancing class, open to the public, will be held Friday evening. Registration begins at 8 o'clock and instruction begins one hour later.
> There will be a registration fee of $2.50 for dancing students, and "qualified, college-trained" instructors will be on hand. Musical accompaniment to the classes will be provided by the Grateful Dead.[207]

The opening night at the Straight Theater School of Dance was policed by a range of media and law enforcement representatives, and the line for registration extended out the door well past the opening lesson:

> Dance instructor Peter Weiss . . . mounted the podium . . . and faced the dozens of couples standing on the floor. The Grateful Dead held their instruments at the ready. . . .
> "What I would like everyone to do," Weiss, a former dancer with the Anne Halprin troupe said, "is to close your eyes and relax and note how you breathe

6.13 The Straight Theater School of Dance.

6.14 Death of the Hippie . . .

6.15 . . . and the Birth of a Freeman.

and how your heart is pumping. . . ." The Grateful Dead broke into "Dancing in the Street" and the crowd began to dance.[208]

Unsurprisingly, the Grateful Dead's house at 710 Ashbury was finally raided, and Pigpen, Bob Weir, Rock Scully, and Dan Rifkin, along with assorted young persons, were arrested on marijuana charges. The banner headline, "The Grateful Dead: Rock Band Busted," fairly shrieked of retribution, though the story did little to reveal what actually happened, why the Dead's house was targeted, or whether the narcotics agents were aware that they had arrested the two band members who did not habitually partake of marijuana.[209] The *Barb* reported that ten people were also arrested at the Blue Cheer house at 369 Haight Street. Perhaps the police wished to make examples of prominent members of the Haight community, or perhaps this was "retaliation" for the two bands' separate appearances at the Straight Theater School of Dance.[210]

By the autumn of 1967 the hippie had become a casualty of "narcissism and plebian vanity," according to Ron Thelin, and now that the hippie had transcended the boundaries of San Francisco it was time to close the Psychedelic Shop and "concentrate on how it feels to be free every minute of the day." The trappings of hippie life—beads, flowers, copies of the *Barb* and the *Oracle*, the sign from the Psychedelic Shop—would fill a cardboard coffin, and be the focal point of a symbolic funeral march in a "Death of Hippie" celebration. The Psychedelic Shop was $6,000 in debt when it closed its doors for good, but worse was the hippie zoo that the media created solely for the entertainment of straight society.[211]

The Grateful Dead echoed this sentiment at a press conference. In a prepared statement Dan Rifkin said that "the mass media . . . created the so-called hippie scene" as well as the false danger attributed to marijuana use. That lie, and the "hippie" lie,

> prop each other up. Behind all the myths is the reality. The Grateful Dead are people engaged in constructive, creative effort in the musical field and this house is where we work as well as our residence. Because the police fear and misinterpret us, our effort is now being interrupted as we deal with the consequences of an harassing arrest.[212]

The following day, the paper announced the closing of the Matrix. The police cited neighbors' long-standing complaints about the noise, and warned that Big Brother and the Holding Company, who had just begun a three-night residency there, would be arrested for disturbing the peace. The club manager's only option was to close the place indefinitely, as he could not ask other bands to risk arrest or jail.[213]

> ALBERT NEIMAN: By the Death of Hippie the Haight-Ashbury had already ceased to exist as a social center. What happened was we had tourists coming in, we had this influx of kids coming in searching for nirvana. So the Death

of Hippie said, it's over. Because once you get to a point where there are more people needing help rather than giving help, it becomes a whole different thing. Once there's more people to take care of than you have time to take care of them, it became overwhelming. So just about everybody I know moved out of the Haight and abandoned it. And then the alcoholics and the heavy drugs started moving in. The CIA was experimenting with STP and other drugs, and they were doing their evil little experiments in hotel rooms, spreading bad drugs into the Haight.

ART ROGERS: Things really did change. At first you had the feeling that everybody that was a hippie was really your brother and sister. And it was true. And then this horrible thing happened that really made you grow up. That there were these narcs that dressed like hippies. How could anybody do something like that? How could anybody be so deceitful? We were really—what's the word?—idealistic.

The *Chronicle* duly covered the Death of Hippie observances, accompanied by a Bergmanesque image of the funeral cortege.[214] If the Death of Hippie signaled a desire "to be free," its poignant counterpoint was the Morning Star Ranch. Lou Gottlieb was found in contempt of court and fined $500 for failing to bring his "organized camp" to the standards required by state and county health codes, with the threat of $500 more for every day that his "guests" failed to leave.[215]

Closer to home, one *Chronicle* reporter spent a long and mournful day in the company of Leonard Wolf roaming the Haight from the I/Thou Coffee Shop to

6.16 Carrying the casket through Buena Vista Park.

Happening House, past some teenagers selling hits of acid for $3, to the Haight-Ashbury Medical Clinic, to the Straight Theater, to the Diggers' Free Store, talking about the media treatment of the hippies, the state of the street, and the point of The Community.[216] A sense of finality was unmistakable.

The *Chronicle*'s scorn for the Haight Free Clinic elicited a stream of angry letters from readers. One in particular summarized beautifully the city's war between generations:

> The [Straight] Theater, appealing to the city, was helped by the clinic, and now the clinic, abandoned by the city, is being helped by the theater which is being helped by the Grateful Dead and look what happened to them. It's quite a life.
> We have the clinic, theater, diggers, Grateful Dead (and other artists), volunteer street sweepers, a free employment agency, a switchboard, lawyers, social workers, college professors, housewives and even teen-agers working almost around the clock performing services for this community that we pay taxes for but the city fails to provide.[217]

Police Chief Cahill then ordered daytime raids in the Haight because of "a large number of truants moving into the area and because motorcycle gangs are attempting to take the place over." Officers stopped anybody who "looked like a runaway or didn't have identification." The backlash was predictable: hippies claimed that the Haight had seen an increase in crime, from burglary to rape—and indeed that the hippies themselves needed protection from the police.[218]

Even academics were being hounded by police. Prof Leonard Wolf was arrested at the Straight Theater for contributing to the delinquency of a minor—for sponsoring, on behalf of Happening House, a performance by a nude dance troupe. As one lawyer noted, "It's going to be interesting to compare San Francisco's attitude toward nude dancing with the city's view about topless and bottomless dancers in North Beach."[219] Then Huckleberry House, the home for runaways, was raided, nine of its juvenile occupants were taken to the Youth Guidance Center, and three of the House's staff were arrested for contributing to the delinquency of minors. Representatives of various churches held a press conference the following day condemning the arrests. The purpose of Huckleberry House was to enable runaways to return home "with dignity and integrity"; a minor could only stay there with the written or verbal consent of his or her parent, and the House had been a safe refuge for at least 300 teenagers since its opening in June.[220] Herb Caen saw the underlying problem clearly:

> For all their dirt, disease, slovenliness, laziness; for all their hedonism, clannishness, and undoubted egomania; for all the possibility that they might be in their death throes, the hippies have a message, even if few can be bothered to articulate it. As a wise old doctor once observed rather sadly, "They are our consciences, walking around in bare feet." It simply is not enough to flog

them, as Establishment critics do, for dropping out, "for refusing to integrate themselves into a meaningful protest movement" . . ., for using drugs, "for creating an unnecessary burden on the taxpayer" . . ., for leading "lewd and immoral" lives . . .; anyway, most of the foregoing applies equally to Brooks Brothers types living at good addresses.

No, what really bugs the critics is what the hippies are saying without saying a word: "What are YOU doing, brother, that's so damn important?" And this is the question—with its ghostly overtones of Vietnam, taxes, bigotry, hypocrisy, corruption, cancer and all the other ills of established society—this is the question that has no answer except fury.[221]

Though they were still seeking operating funds, the Haight-Ashbury Medical Clinic secured an influential group of local physicians to serve on its advisory committee. These physicians stressed the importance of the service that the Clinic had been providing, encouraged other specialists to volunteer their time, and offered their own institutional resources for referrals and specialist treatment. Ten days later it was announced that the Clinic had raised $15,000, sufficient to reopen for five months.[222]

Then a particularly bloody instance of police brutality was witnessed by two upstanding members of the Haight community. In full view of a crowd of people at the corner of Haight and Cole streets, a young man was beaten unconscious. When asked to clear the sidewalk, one bystander allegedly called the police "fascists"; more police arrived and began beating at the heels of onlookers with their clubs.[223] Herb Caen was there. It was, at first

> unusually quiet. Just a few sons sitting around. . . . Then the police arrived in great numbers and pretty soon night sticks were flying, heads were cracking and blood was flowing. The question, class, is: "Do police start riots or stop them?" I confess I don't know. But I do know it was quiet and peaceful on Haight before they arrived.[224]

Barb staff witnessed it as well and reported on the event's aftermath: the following day a shrine to the young man was erected with a sign reading "On this spot our brother was beaten into unconsciousness by police billy clubs, handcuffed, and thrown into a paddy wagon. How much longer are free men going to allow this to continue?" Over a period of hours the police destroyed the shrine, the "freemen" rebuilt it, the police destroyed it again, and so on, with ever-increasing force.[225]

Charles McCabe wrote a number of *Chronicle* columns in 1967 condemning the categorization of marijuana possession as felonious. He also expressed his support for the hippies, and showed an astute understanding of countercultural nuance. Early in November McCabe wrote about an event in Bakersfield, where a Republican senator essentially equated anti-Vietnam War demonstrators with hippies. When asked what should be done about them, the senator said that he "would call the fire department . . . [to] do two things: Blow them out of their sitting position and give them a bath." McCabe's anger at this comment stemmed from a basic observation:

> [The] hippies and war protesters have little in common. The hippies hate political activities. They pretty much hate politics in any form. The war demonstrators operate from another base altogether. Whether members of either or both groups need a bath is wholly irrelevant. . . . Does [the Senator] know who these hippies and war protesters whom he so ignorantly lumps together, are? They are the daughters and sons of the law-abiding [citizens of Bakersfield] and of Senators of the U.S., and of superbly secure and composed squares anywhere.[226]

In October, the *Chronicle* published Nicholas von Hoffman's serialized account of his time embedded in the Haight during the Summer of Love. Bad timing, really. The *Barb* did a little fact-checking, and discovered that the "Acid King" at the heart of an "acid factory" story was actually a federal agent, making von Hoffman nothing more than "a consort of a high nark."[227]

Demonstrators at the Oakland Induction Center encountered a different kind of police force. Officers asked the pacifist crowd politely to disperse; the demonstrators sang Christmas carols and cooperated with the police when they were arrested.[228] On the other side of the Bay, carol-singing Haight hippies merely amplified the noise of police raids and hostile crowds.[229] In Contra Costa County one raid uncovered the mother lode: Owsley's Orinda processing plant, manufacturing enough concentrated LSD for more than two million hits. The "Acid King" was duly arrested along with three other people just before Christmas.[230]

The year 1967 was a busy one in the Haight, and not always for the right reasons. But stripping the scene down to its music, 1967 was the year that

> San Francisco became the Number One city in rock, with dozens of bands recording for dozens of labels. It was the year the Quicksilver Messenger Service and the Steve Miller Blues Band obtained unprecedented contract terms from Capitol Records—the advances of $50,000 and $60,000 are greater than any unrecorded rock bands or any one else, come to think of it, has ever gotten.[231]

Notes

1. RJG, "The City That Means Love to Everybody," *Chronicle*, May 14, 1967, Datebook, p. 27.
2. Herb Caen, "Have a Weak Nice-End," *Chronicle*, June 30, 1967, p. 25.

3. "The Haight Ashbury Scene," photography by John Gorman and Fran Ortiz, in *California Living*, week of January 1, 1967, pp. 9–12.
4. Jonathan Root, "'Beat' Runaways—A Fugitive Army," *Chronicle*, January 2, 1967. Root reports that "about 200 teen-age boys and girls, ranging in age from 12 to 17 . . . leave their outwardly comfortable homes in the pleasant unincorporated suburbs of Alameda county every year—at the rate of at least one every other day."
5. David Swanston, "Angels Join the Hippies for a Party," *Chronicle*, January 2, 1967, p. 1.
6. "The Hippies' Strange New Game," *Chronicle*, January 12, 1967, p. 1.
7. Letter from Chester Anderson to Thurl [no further details], dated January 27, 1967, typed on the back of a ComCo sheet from the same date. In Chester Anderson papers, Bancroft Library, University of California Berkeley BANC MSS 92/839c, Folder 1. Some ComCo sheets can also be accessed online at http://www.diggers.org/comco/comco.html.
8. ComCo "policy" document [no date]. Stating "Love is communication," the company's goals also included printing services for the hip community, "to supplement The Oracle with a more or less daily paper whenever Haight news justifies one . . . adding perspective to The Chronicle's fantasies, . . . to compete with the Establishment press for public opinion . . . to function as a Haight/Ashbury propaganda ministry . . . to do what we damn well please." As an early instance of a "hyper-local" news source, the ComCo papers offer an important punctuation to much of the weekly and biweekly underground and hip press of the time.
9. ComCo, January 28, 1967. Chester Anderson Papers, Folder 1.
10. RJG, "A Brave New Whirl in the Park," *Chronicle*, January 13, 1967, p. 39.
11. "The Beginning Is the Human Be-In," *Barb*, January 6, 1967, p.1 .
12. *Barb*, January 13, 1967, p. 1.
13. ED Denson, "What Happened at the Hippening," *Barb*, January 20, 1967, p. 1.
14. Steve Levine, "The Be-In," *Oracle* 6 (February 1967), p. 24.
15. ComCo, January 14, 1967. Chester Anderson Papers, Folder 1. On the reverse side of this sheet: "(The mystery sky diver, it turns out, was Owsley Stanley, San Francisco's major manufacturer of black market acid.)" This rumor was repeated as fact; Owsley emphatically denied it, though he did admit to providing 300,000 hits of "White Lightning" acid for the event. See Robert Greenfield's retrospective, "Owsley Stanley: The King of LSD," *Rolling Stone* 1030, July 12, 2007.
16. "Hippies' Love and Activism: They Came . . . Saw . . . Stared," *Examiner*, January 15, 1967, p. 3.
17. "Hippies Run Wild—Jailed," *Examiner*, January 15, 1967, p. 1. The *Barb*'s report on the post-Be-In disturbances provide a good foil. See Silenus, "Police Fury Lashes Blindly in Haight," January 20, 1967, p. 1. Even Merla Zellerbach found it difficult to summon much animosity toward the Be-In: "The Human Be-In was a gentle success. . . . Everywhere, love and goodness air-mingled with the thick, sweet odors of pot and incense. Free, they danced, free, they smiled, free, they embraced. Free they were to respond *sans* enthusiasm to Tim Leary's exhortation to 'drop out of school' and 'turn onto the scene.' . . . The air was warm and the scene was cool." See "S.F. is Beautiful for Allowing It to Happen," *Chronicle*, January 18, 1967, p. 43. Her subsequent column addressed with humor (and pointed criticisms) some of the hostile mail she had received in response to her favorable review of the Be-In. See "Some Reactions to the Gathering," *Chronicle*, January 25, 1967, p. 43.

18. RJG, "The Tribes Gather for a Yea-Saying," *Chronicle*, January 16, 1967, p. 43.
19. George Dushek, "'They're Young Seekers, Not Hippies,' Says Poet Ginsberg" and "An Unscheduled 'Happening,'" in *Examiner*, January 22, 1967, p. 11.
20. Tom Law, "The Community of the Tribe," *Oracle* 6 (February 1967), p. 15.
21. See David Swanton, "Human Be-In's Aftermath," *Chronicle*, January 16, 1967, p. 3.
22. See Michael Mahoney, "A Hippie Plan to Foil the Fuzz," *Chronicle*, January 17, 1967, p. 3.
23. "Hippies and Cops Have a Happening," *Chronicle*, January 25, 1967, p. 4.
24. Jonathan Root, "Rock, Roll 'n' Rumble," *Chronicle*, January 13, 1967, p. 1. It is interesting to note the mention in this article of Matthew Katz, "who was assigned to play the organ," though it is unclear whether this could be the same Matthew Katz whose management of many local bands ended in litigation and financial ruin, about whom more later.
25. For more on this ripple, see Roberta Price, *Huerfano: A Memoir of Life in the Counterculture* (Amherst and Boston: University of Massachusetts Press, 2004). I am grateful to the late Charlotte Greig for the (now permanent) loan of her copy of this book.
26. Bobby Beausoleil was also an acquaintance of David LaFlamme of It's a Beautiful Day. In the wake of Beausoleil's 1969 arrest, he entrusted his material possessions to LaFlamme, who was still wondering what to do with them when we last spoke in 2012.
27. "Swami in Hippie-Land," *Chronicle*, January 18, 1967, p. 2. The International Society for Krishna Consciousness, or Hare Krishnas, was established in New York in 1966, and has retained a presence in the Bay Area ever since.
28. John L. Wasserman, "'Hallucination' Opens," *Chronicle*, January 19, 1967, p. 43. And more did come: *The Trip* (written by Jack Nicholson; dir. Roger Corman, 1967), *Psych-Out* (dir. Richard Rush, 1968) and *Petulia* (dir. Richard Lester, 1968), among others.
29. Maitland Zane, "The LSD 'Freak-Out' Victims," *Chronicle*, January 26, 1967, p. 1.
30. One hippie I spoke to was institutionalized twice: first for four months in 1966 at the Napa Mental Institution, on "a general ward, with some very disturbed people. They thoroughly drugged me. It was truly a *Cuckoo's Nest* experience." Second for three months in 1967 at Agnew: "Well, that was my karma. I would say from that experience, in the longevity of my life to here, it taught me compassion. I probably would not have learned compassion anywhere else but being with people who would never get out of that place."
31. RJG, "Turn On, Tune In and Be Bored," *Chronicle*, January 30, 1967, p. 43.
32. Grace Eaves Prien, "Turning On at the Museum," *Chronicle*, February 3, 1967, p. 21.
33. Alfred Frankenstein, "Exciting Experiment in Light and Sound," *Chronicle*, February 6, 1967, p. 44. Art critic Thomas Albright was slightly less forgiving (see "The Big Sound and Bright Lights," *Chronicle*, February 3, 1967, p. 42), but did include light show pioneers Bill Ham and Elias Romero in his *Art in the San Francisco Bay Area, 1945-1980: An Illustrated History* (Berkeley: University of California Press, 1985).
34. Herb Caen, "A Bus Named 'Further,'" *Chronicle*, February 5, 1967, p. B1.
35. Anne Sharpley, "Freaking Out Without Benefit of Psychedelics," (*London Evening Standard*) *Examiner*, February 12, 1967, p. 25. The psychedelic nexus in London was the UFO club in Tottenham Court Road, with biweekly "happenings" based on the Haight model, soundtracked by Pink Floyd and Soft Machine. See Joe Boyd, *White Bicycles: Making Music in the 1960s* (London: Serpent's Tail, 2006).

36. Richard Brautigan is an intriguing shadow in this story of the Haight counterculture. He struggled for money and recognition through most of the 1960s, but was part of the poetic orbit circling City Lights, and a supporter of the Diggers and the Artists Liberation Front. In 1967 his novel, *Trout Fishing In America* was first published, and he contributed a series of very short pieces for the new *Rolling Stone Magazine*. For an exhaustive survey of his life and works, see William Hjortsberg, *Jubilee Hitchhiker* (Berkeley: Counterpoint, 2012).
37. RJG, "The Carmen McRae Way with a Song," *Chronicle*, February 24, 1967, p. 43.
38. "Hippie Show in the Tenderloin," *Chronicle*, February 25, 1967, p. 2.
39. "Hippy Happy Hour Makes Glide Glow," *Barb*, March 3, 1967, p. 1. For more on the Invisible Circus as "happening," see Bradford D. Martin, *The Theater Is in the Street* (Amherst and Boston: University of Massachusetts Press, 2004), pp. 86–124, and Emmett Grogan, *Ringolevio* (Boston: Little, Brown, 1972). ComCo broadsides from the Invisible Circus are in the Chester Anderson papers, folder 8. These sheets include one-page poems, I Ching readings, cartoons, a half-page note stating simply "Fuck Entropy," and a handwritten blast against the "greedy people dressed in clothes that would buy two weeks food . . . panhandling and trying to bum-trip people who don't pay. WHY? filth greed is this really what a hippy means? I am disgusted by this shit. stop it, please."
40. This was the same message printed on the ComCo bulletin of February 9, 1967, a two-page handwritten "racial rap in memoriam Malcom X," a statement that "HAIGHT/ASHBURY IS THE FIRST SEGREGATED BOHEMIA I'VE EVER SEEN!" Chester Anderson Papers, folder 2.
41. "Trouble in Bohemia," *Barb*, March 3, 1967, p. 7.
42. Stokely Carmichael was chair of the Student Nonviolent Coordinating Committee (SNCC) from 1966 to 1967, during which time he first coined the term "Black Power"; the following year he published *Black Power: The Politics of Liberation* (New York: Vintage, 1967).
43. "Dear Editor: To No More Call a Man a Spade" and "A Spade's View of Hippies," *Barb*, March 10, 1967, p. 6.
44. Walter S. Lacy, "Dear Editor . . .," *Barb*, March 17, 1967, p. 11.
45. In 1968 Stuart Hall wrote that "there are black faces on the Haight Ashbury sidewalks, and organized Black militant groups, like the Panthers, in other parts of California, but by and large the Hippie scene in San Francisco is separated from the largely black slums which surround it by high, though invisible walls." Hall's recognition of the (albeit not comprehensively) diverse Hippie demographic, its distinction from political factions of the youth countercultures, and its separation from neighboring social realities, are particularly notable. Stuart Hall, "The Hippies: An American 'Moment,'" in Julian Nagel, ed., *Student Power* (London: Merlin Press, 1969), pp. 170–202.
46. Jeff Jessen, "Love Community, Conspiracy Clash," *Barb*, March 10, 1967, p. 1.
47. "Kicks for Hippies: The Banana Turn-On," *Chronicle*, March 4, 1967, p. 1. Shortly after this screaming banner headline came a much more considered follow-up, with further details of the recommended oven temperature for drying bananas, some hippies' disagreement with the psychedelic efficacy of bananas, the acknowledgment of a possible connection between the banana "craze" and Donovan's hit single, "Mellow Yellow"—and, naturally, a hippie's closing remark: "I think the whole thing is propaganda put out by United Fruit Co. to sell bananas." See "Bananas Flunk the Hippie Test," *Chronicle*, March 6, 1967, p. 3.

48. Art Seidenbaum (Times-Post Service), "Science Tackles the Banana Cult: Turn-On May Be a Put-On," *Examiner*, June 18, 1967, Punch, p. 5.
49. Leroy F. Aarons, "Psychedelia Goes Mainstream," *Examiner*, March 5, 1967, This World, p. 16.
50. In January the lead article in *Crawdaddy!* was Sandy Pearlman's "Patterns and Sounds: The Uses of Raga in Rock." If the *Times* reporter had read that article, he must not have noticed that a San Francisco band, Jefferson Airplane, was on the issue's cover. See Paul Williams, ed., *The Crawdaddy! Book* (Milwaukee: Hal Leonard, 2002).
51. Frank Thomas, *The Conquest of Cool* (Chicago and London: University of Chicago Press, 1997) covers this in great detail.
52. "New Go-Around on Teen Dances," *Chronicle*, March 10, 1967, p. 2. Gleason later posed some very simple questions:

    > Does [Supervisor Francois] seriously think you can cull the 16 year olds [from a dance] and send them home at midnight? And who, may I ask, has the right to interfere with any parent, you or me, from taking his children to a non-alcoholic public dance no matter what their ages? ... The kids are better off [at the Fillmore] than in the back of a car at a drive-in movie with a bottle. (See "Teen Dances— What Are We Afraid Of?," *Chronicle*, March 13, 1967, p. 47.)

    The Board of Supervisors finally agreed to lower the age limit for public dances, though of course the Fillmore had always welcomed sixteen-year-olds. See Mel Wax, "Supervisors Lower Teen Dance Age," *Chronicle*, April 11, 1967, p. 1.
53. See "Runaways in Hippieland Tire Police," *Chronicle*, April 19, 1967, p. 3.
54. "Warning on Hordes of Hippies," *Chronicle*, March 22, 1967, p. 1.
55. "Blunt Warning by Cahill on Hippie 'Pilgrims,'" *Chronicle*, March 23, 1967, p. 1.
56. Jeff Jassen, "Hippies Warn SF; Police Chief Warns Hippies; Black Warns All," *Barb*, March 24, 1967, p. 1. This echoes the early works of the Black Panther party, whose breakfast program for school children was met not with understanding and public funding, but with suspicion and hyperbole.
57. RJG, "S.F., Love, Easter and the Hippies," *Chronicle*, March 24, 1967, p. 35.
58. See "Official Action: Mayor Warns Hippies to Stay Out of Town," *Chronicle*, March 24, 1967, p. 1.
59. Allen Cohen, quoted in "Hippy U. Cosmic Egg Happening," *Barb*, March 17, 1967, p. 1.
60. Maitland Zane, "A Hippie Non-Happening," *Chronicle*, March 21, p. 3.
61. RJG, "Making the Rock 'n Roll Scene," *Chronicle*, March 12, 1967, p. 41.
62. Susan Krieger, *Hip Capitalism* (Beverly Hills and London: Sage, 1979), p. 30.
63. Ibid., p. 52.
64. RJG, "Something New on Pop Music Scene," *Chronicle*, August 16, 1967, p. 41.
65. These were local Haight ventures launched for the benefit of the local community, all of which return in the following pages.
66. In a *Rolling Stone* retrospective, former KMPX disc jockey Howard Hesseman spoke of the way Donahue's friends "infiltrated the station," gradually taking over time slots like a "freak fungus slowly spreading across the clock face until pretty soon it was a twenty-four hour operation." See Michael Goldberg, "The San Francisco Sound," *Rolling Stone* 585, August 23, 1990, pp. 91–96.

67. Tom Donahue, quoted in RJG, "Something New."
68. Tom Donahue, quoted in Krieger, *Hip Capitalism*, p. 289.
69. This pattern is examined in great detail by Krieger in *Hip Capitalism*.
70. The homophonic coincidence of Ellis D. Sox's name was not lost on the hip community; the daily papers, however, tended to leave out his middle initial.
71. "Disease Threat: Health Crusade to 'Clean Up' the Hippies," *Chronicle*, March 25, 1967, p. 1. In one letter to the editor:

    > It looks to me like a flimsy excuse to further harass a group of young people who have given us a lot of beautiful art and music and who, as far as I have seen or read, have done no harm to anyone. I would also like to remind the health authorities that those "slums" in which the hippies live belong to landlords who are getting much more than they are worth in rent. (See Letters to the Editor: "Look Around," *Chronicle*, April 4, 1967, p. 36)

    In any event, the message "don't come to San Francisco—it's filthy" was not one for the billboards.
72. Dick Nolan, "Rich Hippies Would Be OK," *Examiner*, March 26, 1967, p. 3.
73. "City Toning Down Its 'War' on Hippies," *Examiner*, March 26, 1967, p. 1.
74. "Hippies vs. Police at a Big 'Mill-In,'" *Chronicle*, March 27, 1967, p. 1.
75. Editorial: "The Hippies' Tie-Up," *Chronicle*, March 28, 1967, p. 36.
76. Keith Power, "Hippies Get 'Clean' Bill of Health," *Chronicle*, March 29, 1967, p. 1.
77. Mel Wax, "A Muni Detour to Shun Hippies," *Chronicle*, March 29, 1967, p. 1.
78. RJG, "Spring Clean-In in the Hashberry," *Chronicle*, March 31, 1967, p. 47. On March 26 the Haight-Ashbury Neighborhood Council had produced an official statement, distributed by ComCo, which read, in part:

    > Haight-Ashbury is a state of mind as well as a geographical area. Almost accidentally, the area itself has become a focus of international attention because the neighborhood is to a degree unique in . . . its tolerance of diverse peoples and lifestyles. . . . *Now that our community is a tourist attraction, we would request that the area be serviced by the Convention & Tourist Bureau using available hotel tax revenues. . . . What we who live here see happening is that the area is being singled out for selective law enforcement* . . . because public officials or others object simply to a new life style which is implicitly critical of the hypocrisies of the dominant culture. . . . But we repeat that because Haight-Ashbury is a state of mind . . . we will resist any efforts by city officials or others to persecute or brutalize citizens in the mere act of being themselves. (Chester Anderson papers, folder 3)

79. "A Moving Target Is Hard to Hit," ComCo bulletin, March 29, 1967. Chester Anderson papers, folder 1:3.
80. Mel Wax, "Muni Detour—Hippie Crossing," *Chronicle*, June 14, 1967, p. 1.
81. "Cops Beat Chet Helms, Charge Him," *Barb*, March 24, 1967, p. 1.
82. Notice signed Scot Van Hoy, DEW System, March 18, 1967. Chester Anderson papers, folder 3.
83. "To Deepest Hippieland," *Chronicle*, April 4, 1967, p. 1.
84. Herb Caen, "Just Foolin' Around," *Chronicle*, April 10, 1967, p. 31. Elsewhere in the paper that same day a reader noted that "directly or indirectly, every earner in the city benefits

from the fact that tourists are willing to pay good money to visit hippiedom. The hippie goose is laying golden eggs for San Francisco. Why kill it?" See Letters to the Editor, p. 46.

85. I discuss this map further in Chapter 11.
86. Mike Mahoney, "Nice Happenings: Good Hippies' Summer Plans," *Chronicle*, April 6, 1967, p. 3.
87. RJG, "UC Jazz Festival Switched to Gym," *Chronicle*, April 7, 1967, p. 49.
88. Phiz Mozesson, "What Is a Hippie?," *Examiner*, April 9, 1967, California Living, pp. 6–9; Nancy Griffin, "The Pre-Hippie Diggers," *Examiner*, This World, p. 18; "Big Sur Hippie Pads KO'd," *Examiner*, April 9, 1967, p. 3.
89. See Mary Crawford, "Ben Lomond is Hipped on Hippies," *Examiner*, April 16, 1967, p. 6.
90. "Evangelism Among the Daffodils," *Chronicle*, April 21, 1967, p. 1.
91. Chester Anderson, "Uncle Tim's Children," ComCo, April 16, 1967, Chester Anderson papers, folder 4. This broadside was quoted in Joan Didion's *Slouching Towards Bethlehem* (New York: Farrar, Straus and Giroux, 1968) and Nicholas von Hoffman's *We Are the People Our Parents Warned Us Against* (Chicago: Elephant Paperback, 1989), among others. Didion's description is particularly revealing:

> It is [a] tenet of the official District mythology that the communication company [sic] will print anything anybody has to say, but in fact Chester Anderson prints only what he writes himself, agrees with, or considers harmless or dead matter. His statements, which are left in piles and pasted on windows around Haight Street, are regarded with some apprehension in the District and with considerable interest by outsiders, who study them . . . for subtle shifts in obscure ideologies. (*Slouching Towards Bethlehem*, p. 86)

92. Jerry Garcia, quoted in Garcia, Reich and Wenner, *Garcia: A Signpost to New Space* (Cambridge: Da Capo Press, 2003), p. 38.
93. "Supervisors Back War on Hippies," *Chronicle*, April 29, 1967, p. 2.
94. See Arthur Hoppe, "San Francisco's Tourist Pogrom," and Royce Brier, "Hippy Folk and City Hall Folk," both *Chronicle*, May 4, 1967, pp. 48–49.
95. Mel Wax, "Supervisors to Delay Decision on the Hippies," *Chronicle*, May 2, 1967, p. 2. Willie Brown's letter to the city's Board of Supervisors was reprinted in full in *Oracle* 8 (June 1967), "Love Haight Ashbury Bush," p. 31.
96. William Chapin, "Discouraging Word for The Hippies," *Chronicle*, May 9, 1967, p. 1.
97. ED Denson, "Banana ED's Sure Cure for Summer Hippiness," *Barb*, May 5, 1967, p. 10.
98. Jeff Jassen, "The Year of the Shuck: What Price Love?," *Barb*, May 5, 1967, p. 5. This is an issue to which I return in "Hippies, Inc."
99. Jerry Belcher, "Oakland's Black Panthers Wear Guns, Talk Revolution," *Examiner*, April 30, 1967, p. 1. Another important connection to make here is between the Black Panthers and *Ramparts* magazine. In 1966 *Ramparts* published two works by Eldridge Cleaver: "Notes on a Native Son" (June, pp. 51–57), and "Letters from Prison" (August, pp. 15–26). When he was released from prison Cleaver joined the *Ramparts* staff. He first met the Panthers in February 1967; shortly afterward Huey Newton and other Panthers, fully armed, brought Malcolm X's widow, Betty Shabazz, to the *Ramparts* office for an interview with Cleaver. This attracted the police and media, and increased the celebrity of the Panthers locally and internationally. As the party's

1967

minister of information, Cleaver was instrumental in forging the alliance between the Black Panthers and radical white groups. See Peter Richardson, *A Bomb in Every Issue* (New York: New Press, 2009), chapter 4.

100. The series ran from May 15 to May 20, 1967. It was shadowed, oddly, by Arnold Toynbee's three-part report on "Hippieland," May 16–18, reprinted from the *London Observer*. Satire inevitably ensued: Art Hoppe's "Exclusive: 'I Was a Square' (May 21, 1967, p. ii. 1);" followed an intrepid correspondent "and zither player" from the *Daily Guru News*, who infiltrated straight society for a month: cutting off her hair, wearing high-heeled shoes and a girdle, working 9-to-5 in an insurance company, enduring the unwanted advances of her office manager. "Hippie leaders passed a resolution excoriating the high incidence of cirhossis of the liver, suicides and the lack of mental hygiene among squares and announced that any further influx of square tourists this summer would be highly unwelcome." The *Barb* played that game as well, offering a two-part "lowdown on the uptights." See "I Was a Straightie," May 26, 1967, p. 1.

101. "It would appear that aside from trips, physical not mental, to the Psychedelic Shop to pick up communications company leaflets and a weekly venture on Haight to secure the latest copy of the BARB, Gilbert never left his apartment. Gilbert's true confession is a masterpiece of stereotyped space filler. . . . In his Friday installment . . . 32 of Gilbert's 56 inches of copy were reworded communications company fliers. The following day, no less than seven paragraphs of this reporter's 'Love Shuck' story of several weeks ago were reprinted almost verbatim, without so much as credit to the BARB." (See Jeff Jassen, "'Hippie' Article Hoax?," *Barb*, May 25, 1967, p. 4.)

102. Jack Rosenbaum, "Lost Generation," *Examiner*, May 21, 1967, p. B1.

103. Lovable Ol' Doc Stanley, "How to Survive on the Streets," *Barb*, June 2, 1967, p. 10.

104. Donovan Bess, "Jury Finds 'Love Book' Obscene," *Chronicle*, May 27, 1967, p. 1.

105. RJG, "The Influence of Hippie Art," *Chronicle*, June 4, 1967, Datebook, p. 27.

106. See "Panhandle Hippie Scenes Will Be Banned," *Chronicle*, June 10, 1967, p. 4.

107. James Browne, "Hashberry Rock," Letters to the Editor, *Chronicle*, June 15, 1967, p. 42.

108. RJG, "Musical Refugees from Hostility," *Examiner*, June 18, 1967, Datebook, p. 31.

109. See "Science Tests 'Mellow Yellow,'" *Chronicle*, May 1, 1967, p. 8.

110. "S.F. Surge in VD Cases," *Chronicle*, May 2, 1967, p. 1.

111. David Perlman, "A War Drug on LSD Scene," *Chronicle*, June 7, 1967, p. 1.

112. "Washington to Analyze Hippie Drug," *Chronicle*, June 9, 1967, p. 9.

113. "'STP' Drug—A Stolen Dow Secret," *Chronicle*, August 3, 1967, p. 1. For more on STP and its 1967 contexts, see Lee and Shlain, *Acid Dreams* (New York: Grove Weidenfeld, 1985).

114. "Moby Grape Arrests: Marin Cops Nab 3 Rock Performers," *Chronicle*, June 8, 1967, p. 14.

115. Ben Gerson, Review: Moby Grape, *Truly Fine Citizen*, *Rolling Stone* 44, October 18, 1969, p. 36.

116. Early reviews of Moby Grape are almost uniformly ecstatic: "The Moby Grape is unbelievable. On one end is the lead guitarist who . . . plays in the same creative category as James Gurley of the Holding Company only cleaner. . . . To his left is . . . one of, if not the most, magnetic FLASH! rock characters today. . . . Put them all together it spells groovy." *Oracle* 4 (December 16, 1966), p. 24.

117. The album was released on the San Francisco Sound label. Its back cover featured a disproportionately large reminder of the businessman behind it ("a Matthew Katz production"), and the center label a geographically imprecise rendering of the Bay Bridge, with the sun seeming to set, curiously, over what appears to be Oakland.
118. I suggest this shift in the Introduction as a type of musical division between the "short" and "long" 60s.
119. Don Stevenson, quoted in Harvey Kubernik and Kenneth Kubernik, *A Perfect Haze: The Illustrated History of the Monterey International Pop Festival* (Solano Beach: Santa Monica Press, 2011), pp. 120–21.
120. RJG, "Big Push for Moby Grape," *Chronicle*, June 5, 1967, p. 45.
121. The five singles were "Fall On You"/"Changes," "Sitting By the Window"/"Indifference," "8:05"/"Mister Blues," "Omaha"/"Someday," and "Hey Grandma"/"Come in the Morning."
122. "Moby Grape Arrests," *Chronicle*, June 8, 1967, p. 14.
123. "Moby Grape Cleared in Court," *Rolling Stone* 6, February 6, 1968, p. 8.
124. RJG, "Big Push."
125. Indeed, Katz can be blamed for many other misfortunes. Bill Graham claimed to have sensed a certain doom when he first met Katz: "Bad, *bad* news bear. *Baaad* news. He invented the idea of having two or three groups go out under the same name to different parts of the country." Grace Slick remembered the first time she saw Katz:

   [The members of Jefferson Airplane] pointed to him across the room. He had on a black beard, a black mustache, and a black cape with a red lining, and white lace cuffs. *Okay?* He looked the way Hollywood says, "*Here's the devil.*" The guy was *telling* them who he was. He was not even jacking them around. I looked from across the room and I went, "*That's* going to be your manager? You're *kidding*." (Both quoted in *Bill Graham Presents*, p. 164)

   Though some musicians managed to extract themselves from his grip, Katz's managerial hold wreaked long-term havoc on the careers of other bands, most notably, It's a Beautiful Day.
126. Details of Moby Grape's initial contract, and further insights into the band's fate, may be found in Joel Selvin's *The Summer of Love*, pp. 115–18.
127. RJG, "April Will Be a Crowded Month," *Chronicle*, March 25, 1968, p. 41. See also "Playing the Name Game, or a Tale of Two Grapes," *Rolling Stone* 9, April 27, 1968, p. 19.
128. Ben Fong-Torres, "Moby: the Grape Turns Sour," *Rolling Stone* 36, June 28, 1969, p. 8.
129. Warren Hinckle, "A Social History of the Hippies," *Ramparts*, March 1967, pp. 9–27. For fallout, see "Ramparts 'Hippie' Article Raises Row," *Barb*, June 9, 1967, p. 7.
130. This would explain Anderson's star turn in Hinckle's narrative. See Chester Anderson, "Inside Inside Story on the 'Hippie' Tale," *Barb*, June 16, 1967, p. 4; and Peter Richardson, *A Bomb in Every Issue*, pp. 107–08.
131. "Magic Mountain Festival: Old 'Tam' Rocks and Rolls," *Examiner*, June 11, 1967, p. 3.
132. Maitland Zane, "A Wild Fantasy Fair: Bash on Mt. Tam," *Chronicle*, June 12, 1967, p. 3.
133. This is an issue I explore in greater depth in "When Deep Soul Met the Love Crowd: Otis Redding at the Monterey Pop Festival," in Ian Inglis, ed., *Performance and Popular Music: History, Place and Time* (Aldershot: Ashgate, 2006), pp. 28–40. For a retrospective history of the festival, see Kubernik, *A Perfect Haze*.

1967

134. RJG, "A Warm and Groovy Affair," *Chronicle*, June 19, 1967, p. 43.
135. RJG, "Memories of a Pop Festival," *Chronicle*, June 25, 1967, Datebook, p. 29.
136. Michael Lydon, "The Monterey International Pop Festival," in *Flashbacks: Eyewitness Accounts of the Rock Revolution 1964-1974* (New York and London: Routledge, 2003), p. 34.
137. Although Big Brother's first performance was not filmed, the audience was. It is Mama Cass' reaction to the Saturday performance, mouthing "wow, that's really heavy," that is included in the film.
138. This fact aided the bookkeeper's embezzlement of $52,000, via a check for that amount made payable to her husband: "In the space where it says what the payment is for, she wrote 'Donation to the Mexican Musical Appreciation Society of Utah.'" John J. Rock, *Rolling Stone* 12, June 22, 1968, p. 8. In the Kuberniks' history of Monterey Pop they list the organizations that have since benefited from the Monterey International Pop Festival Foundation: "arts organizations, music therapy programs, health care subsidies for struggling musicians . . . a wall mural to UCLA Children's Hospital . . . scholarships in rock music at . . . NYU . . ." See Kubernik, *A Perfect Haze*, p. 222.
139. Michael Lydon, "The High Cost of Music and Love: Where's the Money from Monterey?" *Rolling Stone* 1, November 9, 1967, p. 1.
140. RJG, "The Two Careers of Rex Stewart," *Chronicle*, September 11, 1967, p. 45.
141. Lovable Ol' Doc Stanley, "Monterey Pop Cop," *Oracle* 10 (October 1967), p. 28.
142. Al Kooper, "Hendrix Bobbed and Weaved; Paul and Art Fugued; and Otis Makes the Rescue," *Rolling Stone* 5, February 10, 1968, p. 17. The version of the film that Kooper reviewed was apparently not the final product.
143. RJG, "Perspectives: What Happened to Whatshisname?," *Rolling Stone* 11, May 25, 1968, p. 10.
144. RJG, "Film Captures Jazz Festival Spirit," *Chronicle*, April 9, 1969, p. 43.
145. The Kubernik brothers' interpretation of the song betrays their cultural position as southern Californians:

    [The song] nagged at your ear with just the right proportion of craft and emotional yearning; not a clarion call, but a gentle nudging that proved irresistible. Unless, of course, you were from San Francisco, and raged yet again at Phillips and Adler . . . for co-opting the Bay Area's self-styled *hauteur* for their own nefarious ends. Like squabbling brothers, the musical poles of the Golden State would continue to accuse each other of buying in and selling out. (See *A Perfect Haze*, p. 201)

    I make no apologies for the northern-centricity of my own interpretation, of contemporary reports in the *Chronicle* and *Rolling Stone*, or more recent reminiscences of Haight hippies, upon whom the term "*hauteur*" would be woefully misplaced.
146. "Rioting in the ghettos/Won't effect [sic] you if you wear/A flower in your hair/ . . . / There'll be gentle people there/In the flowered hair/Raging in the streets." Hand-printed ComCo sheet, no date, 1967.
147. David Perlman, "A Medical Mission in the Haight-Ashbury," *Chronicle*, June 17, 1967, p. 1.
148. Don Wegars, "A City Plan for a Hippie Health Clinic," *Chronicle*, June 21, 1967, p. 1.
149. David Perlman, "Hippie Clinic Folds—'Broke and Exhausted,'" *Chronicle*, September 23, 1967, p. 1.
150. RJG, "A Hippie Clinic and a Benefit," *Chronicle*, October 1, 1967, Datebook, p. 31.

151. Editorial: "The City's Stake in Hippie Clinic," *Chronicle*, October 5, 1967, p. 36.
152. Timothy Leary, quoted in "Changes: The Houseboat Summit," *Oracle* 7 (April 1967), p. 7.
153. Interview: Ees Setisoppo (See Opposites) with Dick Alpert, in *Oracle* 5 (January 1967), p. 10.
154. Jeff Berner, "Astronauts of Inner Space," *Chronicle*, June 18, 1967, Datebook, p. 30.
155. Ibid.
156. Ibid. Certainly the image of Monkee Mickey Dolenz in full tribal headdress at the Monterey Pop Festival is indication of the widespread adoption of Indian signifiers in the hip community outside of the Haight-Ashbury. See *Monterey Pop* (dir. D.A. Pennebaker, 1968) for footage.
157. Rupert Costo, Letter to the Editor: "Hippies Are NOT American Indians," *Examiner*, June 25, 1967, Datebook, p. 26.
158. "Indians for Sale," *Oracle* 8 (June 1967), p. 19.
159. The Diggers had used the ComCo to distribute a handwritten broadside warning hippies against taking part in this very survey, stating that the information gathered would go to advertising agencies for more profit from the hippies: "When are the hippies going to wise up? FUCK these impersonal censuses. FUCK supporting the money system with information that is used to supress FREE. If someone wants to dig the hippies, let him quit his job or school and start DOING ACTS AND PEOPLE AND STREETS AND COUNTRY. FREEDOM NOW." [no date] Chester Anderson papers, folder 3. For results of the census, see Donovan Bess, "What the Hippies Are Really Like," *Chronicle*, June 19, 1967, p. 2
160. Jack Viets, "Hippies Begin Their Summer of Love," *Chronicle*, June 22, 1967, p. 1; RJG, "The Summer Solstice Affair," *Chronicle*, June 23, 1967.
161. Capt. Kiely, quoted in Charles Raudebaugh, "The Ebb and Flow of the Hippie Tide," *Chronicle*, June 23, 1967, p. 1.
162. Carolyn Anspacher, "Hippies in Danger: Dire Warning on Hippies' Latest Drug," *Chronicle*, June 27, 1967 p. 1. A later report noted that the drug had infiltrated several metropolitan areas. "STP Drug Use Spreading Fast," *Chronicle*, June 28, 1967, p. 3. Dr. Meyers was later quoted as saying that "the use of [STP] has fallen off sharply in the last week," thus proving that hippies had heeded his and Dr. Smith's warnings about the drug. George Dusheck, "Doctors Scared Hippies from Using STP Drug," *Examiner*, July 9, 1967, p. 7. The chemist who developed STP for Dow, Alexander Shulgin, was profiled in August, and he denied emphatically that he was responsible for the leak of the drug into the Haight: "There were many persons who could have passed the STP formula into illegal channels and . . . when the truth is known . . . it may well be that the formula leaked out of the East Coast laboratory under contract with Dow to test the drug on humans." See Peter Vogel, "The Creation of STP—Inside Story," *Chronicle*, August 25, 1967, p. 1, and Lee and Shlain, *Acid Dreams*.
163. "Legal Test at Hippie Guest Ranch," *Chronicle*, July 7, 1967, p. 35.
164. RJG, "A Limeliter's New Thing," *Chronicle*, August 14, 1967, p. 41.
165. Rob Haeseler, "A Groovy Life—But the Heat's On," *Chronicle*, September 16, 1967, p. 1.
166. Herb Caen, "Big Wide Wonderful World," *Chronicle*, July 13, 1967, p. 23. The Dead did not officially leave the Haight until early in 1968.
167. Merla Zellerbach, "The Heresy of Post-Hippiedom," *Chronicle*, June 28, 1967, p. 39.

1967

168. George Gilbert, "'Hot Line' Between Hip and Straight," *Chronicle*, July 10, 1967, p. 1.
169. Keith Power, "Dancers' Rooftop Arrest—Charges Are Dropped," *Chronicle*, July 12, 1967, p. 1. The banner headline gleefully read "Dancers' Hippie Spree."
170. "On the Scene," *Chronicle*, July 12, 1967, p. 3.
171. Carolyn Anspacher, "A Campy Prelude to the Escapade," *Chronicle*, July 12, 1967, p. 3.
172. Editorial: "A New, Exciting Rooftop Ballet," *Chronicle*, July 12, 1967, p. 42.
173. Charles McCabe, "The Perils of Pot," *Chronicle*, July 19, 1967, p. 24.
174. RJG, "A Not So Straight Theater," *Chronicle*, August 7, 1967, p. 39.
175. George Gilbert, "A Dancing Debate on Haight," *Chronicle*, August 29, 1967, p. 2.
176. "Pt. Reyes Cliff Yields Body in Bag," *Chronicle*, August 7, 1967, p. 6.
177. The accompanying article notes that Harrison and Boyd wandered Haight Street unnoticed, only "discovered" when Harrison borrowed someone's guitar on Hippie Hill and began playing. Then "hippies clammered [sic] down hills, dropped from trees and sprang from behind bushes. A sizeable crowd formed." When asked what he thought of the Haight-Ashbury, Harrison reportedly replied, "Wow. If it's all like this it's too much." David Swanston, "A Beatle Does His Thing," *Chronicle*, August 8, 1967, p. 3. The next month Harrison painted another picture for English reporters: "Haight/Ashbury reminded me a bit of the Bowery. There were people just sitting around the pavement begging. . . . These are hypocrites. . . . The moment you start dropping out and then start begging off somebody else to help you, then it's no good." RJG, "Present Status of the Beatles," *Chronicle*, September 4, 1967, p. 37. Many years later Harrison recalled "expecting [the Haight] to be a brilliant place, with groovy gypsy people making works of art and paintings and carvings in little workshops. But it was full of horrible spotty drop-out kids on drugs, and it turned me right off the whole scene. . . . That was the turning-point for me—that's when I . . . stopped taking the dreaded lysergic acid." See The Beatles, *Anthology* (London: Cassell & Co, 2000), p. 259.
178. Charles Raudebaugh, "Pot, LSD Sales: Hippie Murders Raise Fears of 'The Syndicate,'" *Chronicle*, August 8, 1967, p. 1.
179. Ultimately the Superspade case was solved, but police were unable to arrest the person(s) responsible as there was not enough evidence to convict.
180. No date, but references to early August. Chester Anderson papers, folder 7. It was at this point that ComCo split into three separate bodies: one run by Claude Hayward for the Diggers, one run by Anderson "in absentia . . . for the community at large (including the diggers), the peripheral underground & the UPS [Underground Press Syndicate]," and "the communication company (ups) in exile, operated between working on two novels & a history by Chester Anderson." Anderson published his first novel, *The Butterfly Kid,* in 1967; included in his papers at the Bancroft Library are manuscripts for two novels, *Fox and Hare* (written 1963–64, published 1980) and *Puppies* (1979), published under the pseudonym John Valentine. In the context of his creative output, *Puppies* is a particularly shocking departure from the Haight-era Anderson, being an explicit chronicle of one man's erotic adventures with adolescents and servicemen in Los Angeles at the turn of the decade.
181. Charles Raudebaugh, "Frightened Hippies are Arming," *Chronicle*, August 10, 1967, p. 1.
182. "Hippie Exodus Forecast," *Examiner*, August 13, 1967, p. 3.

183. Allen Cohen, "In Memoriam for Superspade and John Carter," *Oracle* 9 (August 1967), p. 4. Cohen ends with a benediction: "May their consciousness return to bodies that will not want for anyTHING but the beauty and joy of their part in the great dance."

184. Merla Zellerbach, "Natural Foods and Peaceful Bodies," *Chronicle*, August 11, 1967, p. 43.

185. RJG, "The Decline and Fall of Civilization," *Chronicle*, August 23, 1967, p. 39. The question of what constituted an "electric" band was intriguing, especially in light of the Grateful Dead's "legendary" jam sessions with avant-garde composer Karlheinz Stockhausen, a guest professor of composition at UC Davis for the academic year 1966–67. See Jonathan Kramer, "Karlheinz in California: A Personal Reminiscence," *Perspectives of New Music* 36/1 (Winter 1998): 247–61.

186. Maitland Zane, "Park Music Victories for Hippies," *Chronicle*, August 25, 1967, p. 1.

187. "Rock Fans Win First Round," *Barb*, August 25, 1967, p. 7.

188. RJG, "Are the Trade Papers Failing?," *Chronicle*, August 13, 1967, Datebook, p. 27.

189. Jann Wenner, "A Letter from the Editor," *Rolling Stone* 1, November 9, 1967, p. 2.

190. Tom Donahue, "A Rotting Corpse, Stinking Up the Airways . . .," *Rolling Stone* 2, November 23, 1967, p. 14.

191. "Regrets," *Rolling Stone* 19, October 12, 1968, p. 6. See also Robert Draper, *Rolling Stone Magazine* (New York: Harper Perennial, 1991) and Robert Sam Anson, *Gone Crazy and Back Again: The Rise and Fall of the* Rolling Stone *Generation* (New York: Doubleday, 1981).

192. For more on *Ramparts*, see Richardson, *A Bomb*.

193. For more, see Devon Powers, *Writing the Record: the* Village Voice *and the Birth of Rock Criticism* (Amherst: University of Massachusetts Press, 2013).

194. Quoted in Richardson, *A Bomb*, p. 192.

195. Warren Hinckle, from his memoir *If You Have a Lemon, Make Lemonade: an Essential Memoir of a Lunatic Decade* (New York: Norton, 1974), quoted in Richardson, *A Bomb*, p. 109.

196. Certainly some of the anecdotes in Draper's *Rolling Stone* support this interpretation.

197. "Left" is relative, but the general political viewpoint expressed in *Rolling Stone* over the last half-century can be charted by the presidential candidates the magazine has chosen to support, either implicitly, via exposés on the Nixon administration and the Republican leadership of the 1980s, or explicitly, as with the issues featuring cover photos of presidential candidates: George McGovern, Jimmy Carter, Bill Clinton, Al Gore, John Kerry, and Barack Obama. Coverage of presidential elections are echoed throughout the magazine's history, most notably in support of progressive social issues (the *Whole Earth Catalog*, gun control) and alternative viewpoints of current affairs (the Iran-Contra affair, the Iraq war, the banking crisis). For a more critical view, see Craig Pyes, "Rolling Stone Gathers No Politix," in David Horowitz, Michael P. Lerner, and Craig Pyes, eds., *Counterculture & Revolution* (New York: Random House, 1972), pp. 103–11.

198. The Joint Show was held at the Moore Gallery in July 1967.

199. Jeff Jassen, "This Katz Where It's Happening," *Barb*, August 25, 1967, p. 8.

200. Maitland Zane, "An Angel's Last Blast," *Chronicle*, August 29, 1967, p. 4. A more heartfelt and descriptive account can be found in "A Garland for Chocolate George," *Barb*, September 1, 1967, p. 3.

1967

201. Mary Crawford, "'Acid King's' Help Sought by Marin," *Examiner*, September 3, 1967, p. 1.
202. Jeff Jassen, "Haightians Thrill to Spacious Street," *Barb*, September 15, 1967, p. 5.
203. Mary Crawford, "The Hippie Debris Lingers," *Examiner*, September 17, 1967, p. 3.
204. RJG, "History May Repeat Itself," *Chronicle*, September 3, 1967, Datebook, p. 27.
205. Earl Segal, "Denver Gets a Family Dog," *Barb*, August 25, 1967, p. 5. The further adventures of the Denver Dog are covered in the following chapter.
206. Ron Moskowitz, "Permit Denied: No Dance Hall for Hippieland," *Chronicle*, September 26, 1967, p. 2.
207. "Latest Step in Dance War," *Chronicle*, September 27, 1967, p. 1.
208. RJG, "A Most Unusual Dancing Class," *Chronicle*, October 2, 1967, p. 45.
209. "Haight Roundup: Cops Raid Pad of Grateful Dead," *Chronicle*, October 3, 1967, p. 1.
210. "Not Dead Yet," *Barb*, October 6, 1967, p. 2.
211. Michael Grieg, "Decline and Fall of Hippieland," *Chronicle*, October 5, 1967, p. 1. This was partially borne out the following day, when the Question Man asked, "Have the Hippies Had It?" Some respondents said that the real hippies had moved away; others that "they're just obnoxious now. Hippies used to be interesting. Now they're just publicity hounds. Exhibitionists." See *Chronicle*, October 65, 1967, p. 42.
212. Charles Raudebaugh, "Grateful Dead Hold Lively Wake," *Chronicle*, October 6, 1967, p. 2.
213. Steve Pelletiere, "Rock Club Closes—Police Pressure," *Chronicle*, October 7, 1967, p. 1.
214. Michael Grieg, "Death of the Hippies," *Chronicle*, October 7, 1967, p. 2.
215. "A Costly Ruling for Gottlieb's Hippie Ranch," *Chronicle*, October 7, 1967, p. 2; see also Peter Vogel, "A Showdown at Gottlieb's Hippie Ranch," *Chronicle*, October 9, 1967, p. 1. I am grateful to Ramon Sender for the gift of a copy of *The Morning Star Scrapbook*, which includes a complete collection of newspaper clippings from the life span(s) of the Morning Star Ranch interspersed with contemporary photographs from the Ranch's "tribal family." The juxtaposition of the more aggressive newspaper headlines with pictures of happy young children, of men and women tending gardens, smiling in the sunshine, playing music, practising yoga, is an important reminder of the very basic tensions enacted in the face of "otherness."
216. William Chapin, "A Day on Hippieland Scene," *Chronicle*, October 9, 1967, p. 14.
217. Joanna Arnow, Letter to the Editor: "We're Pretty Busy," *Chronicle*, October 10, 1967, p. 38.
218. "Daylight Raid on Haight Street," *Chronicle*, October 10, 1967, p. 1. The first raid netted Timothy Leary's seventeen-year-old son, John. See also Charles Howe, "Hippies Say They Need Protection from Police," *Chronicle*, October 11, 1967, p. 3.
219. "Arrest Over Hippieland Nude Dance," *Chronicle*, October 21, 1967, p. 1. Wolf was later acquitted. See "Poet Not Guilty in Nude Dance Case," *Chronicle*, February 10, 1968, p. 6.
220. Keith Power, "Runaway Haven: Police Raid Outrages Sponsors," *Chronicle*, October 24, 1967, p. 1.
221. Herb Caen, "Here and Now," *Examiner*, October 15, 1967, p. B1.
222. David Perlman, "S.F. Doctors: Prominent Aid for Haight Clinic," *Chronicle*, October 18, 1967, p. 3; "Hippie Clinic Has $15,000—To Reopen," *Chronicle*, October 28, 1967, p. 2.
223. "A Violent Clash in the Haight," *Chronicle*, October 31, 1967, p. 1.
224. Herb Caen, "A Day in the Life," *Chronicle*, November 1, 1967, p. 27.

225. Jeff Jasssen, "Haight Freemen Seek 'Peace Not Police,'" *Barb*, November 13, 1967, p. 3. Jassen went on a little rant in the following issue around the use of the term "freemen," calling on former "leaders" of the hip community to take responsibility for what they had left behind: "The people who plotted the 'Death of the Hippie' fiasco . . . are the people who called everyone to San Francisco and then decided that it was too much for them to handle. So they thought of a way to get out of it. 'You're all free now!' Or in other words, get outta the way, kid, ya bother me." This he directed at Jay Thelin, Allen Cohen, and Emmett Grogan ("Who's feeding all those starving flower children now that they took everybody's advice and dropped out?"). "'Freemen' Head Miffs Hippie Ed," November 17, 1967, p. 2.

226. Charles McCabe, "Senator, and Hippies," *Chronicle*, November 2, 1967, p. 32.

227. Jeff Jassen, "How Nark Dealt Haight," *Barb*, December 15, 1967, p. 1. This certainly raises interesting issues around von Hoffman's *We Are the People Our Parents Warned Us Against*, one of the central historical tracts in 1960s scholarship.

228. "Why the Protesters Were There," and "Cops Were Ever So Gentle," *Examiner*, December 19, 1967, p. 18.

229. "Hippie Drug Raids—25 Carted Away," *Chronicle*, December 21, 1967, p. 1.

230. Charles Raudebaugh, "Acid King's Huge Supple of 'Trips,'" *Chronicle*, December 23, 1967, p. 1. For more on this arrest and the story behind the Orinda plant, see Rhoney Stanley, *Owsley and Me: My LSD Family* (Rhinebeck, New York: Monkfish, 2013).

231. RJG, "In '67—Be-Ins, Beatles and Bands," *Chronicle*, December 31, 1967, This World, p. 31.

SOPWITH CAMEL, "HELLO HELLO"

(Peter Kraemer/Terry MacNeil)
Produced by Erik Jacobsen
7" single released on Kama Sutra (KA217, 1966).
Also on *Sopwith Camel*, Kama Sutra #8060 (10/67)
Reached #26 on US pop music charts, January 1967
Recorded in New York, NY (1966)

Peter Kraemer: lead vocals
William Sievers: guitar, backing vocals
Terry MacNeil [Nandi Devam]: piano, backing vocals
Martin Beard: bass, backing vocals
Norman Mayell: drums

> The Bay Area continues to make itself heard nationally in popular music. This past week, Moby Grape signed with Columbia and The Family Tree signed with RCA Victor. In addition, the Jefferson Airplane's "My Best Friend" . . . is Number 102 in the Billboard national chart. . . . The Sopwith Camel's disc of "Hello, Hello" . . . is 46 in the Billboard chart and the Airplane's RCA Victor album, Surrealistic Pillow, is listed this week as a "breakout" album, meaning it's beginning to sell nationally.[1]

The Sopwith Camel was a British First World War single-seat biplane fighter. Although its active career was a short four years, its reputation as the most successful Allied aircraft in the war secured its legacy in military history and in popular culture. In 1966 Bay Area cartoonist Charles Schulz depicted his beagle, Snoopy, as the World War I flying ace, fighting the Red Baron atop his Sopwith Camel. This was a recurring subplot and conceivably did more to secure the airplane's legacy than any statistics about (real) historic victories. Whichever version of the airplane, the actual flying contraption or the cartoon doghouse, served as the inspiration for the eponymous band, the Sopwith Camel scored a Top 40 hit when "Hello Hello" reached number 26 in January 1967.[2]

Sopwith Camel are often dismissed for the very song that got them recognized. In the context of the music that other San Francisco bands were playing around town in 1967, "Hello Hello" sounds like an anomaly. How could anything that simple, that *straight*, have come from the same scene as Moby Grape or Jefferson Airplane? One of the criticisms leveled at Sopwith Camel was that they were misrepresenting the

San Francisco "scene" to the wider culture: "Hello Hello" was a strange bit of fluff in the context of the flights of sonic exploration heard most weeknights at the local dancehalls.

Producer Erik Jacobsen had already had a string of hits with the Lovin' Spoonful, and was in the city in 1966 working with the Charlatans when he first heard Sopwith Camel.[3] Sopwith Camel therefore tie into a particular San Francisco lineage: just as the early Autumn Records singles were produced with the sound of the British Invasion in mind, so does "Hello Hello" reference contemporary hits. The honky-tonk sound of "Hello Hello" echoes the Charlatans' own appropriations of "Wild West" signifiers. Any suggestion that Sopwith Camel were not "of" the scene is also somewhat misguided. Singer Peter Kraemer came from Virginia City, and was one of the boarders at 1090 Page Street, further connecting the Red Dog Saloon to the Haight; drummer Norman Mayell was introduced to Ken Kesey and the Merry Pranksters by Denise "Mary Microgram" Kaufman, later a member of the Ace of Cups; and in their early days, Sopwith Camel were regulars at the Matrix. "Hello Hello" may have been a strange bit of fluff, but it emerged from within the scene that tried to deny its inclusion.

Erik Jacobsen saw commercial potential in "Hello Hello" and flew the group to New York in late 1966 to record it for Kama Sutra. Sopwith Camel toured the United States with the Lovin' Spoonful, the Who, and the Rolling Stones, but a series of mishaps between recording "Hello Hello" and completing the follow-up album left the band unable to capitalize on their chart success. By the time *Sopwith Camel* was released, it was festooned with a sticker asking, "Remember 'Hello Hello'?" According to Jacobsen, the pressure the band felt when their debut single hit the charts "just blew their minds," and Sopwith Camel "broke up behind absolute, psychically unsettled waters at all times."[4] They were not the only San Francisco band to earn "one-hit wonder" status, but they are the only "one-hit" San Francisco band to be scorned for it.[5]

"Hello Hello" follows a very simple, symmetrical pattern: Intro–ABABA–Outro. Each A section contains two contrasting eight-bar verses, the first beginning with "Hello, hello," the second with "Would you like some of my tangerine." The B section is a contrasting 8-bar phrase that resolves with the return of the A section. The two sections therefore flow together naturally, and the whole song has a sense of clear and easy balance:

0:00	Intro	piano, wordless vocal flourish	8 bars
0:15	A:	"Hello, hello. I like your smile . . ."	8 bars
0:29		"Would you like some of my tangerine . . ."	8 bars
0:43	B:	"Never knew how I'd need you . . ."	8 bars
0:56	A:	"Hello, hello" once; instrumental break	8+8 bars
1:24	B:	"Always longed to say 'I love you . . .'"	8 bars

1:38	A:	"Hello, hello. You got pretty hair . . ."	8 bars
1:52		"Would you like some of my tangerine . . ."	8 bars
2:09	Outro	descending piano line to full band cadence	8 bars

The breeziness of "Hello Hello" has as much to do with its "sunshiny quality" as with its structure.[6] The upright piano sets the honky-tonk vibe in the opening bars, then is met by a fairly sparse accompaniment on the bass, guitar, and drums. The backing vocals are similarly unobtrusive. There is no beat to inspire dancing, but the song still swings, mostly because of the lazy, lilting lead vocal. Each line of lyric is short enough to leave plenty of "empty" space—"would you like some of my tangerine" consumes a full four bars—but not the kind of "space" that might otherwise fill a song representing psychedelic San Francisco. In any other hands, the instrumental break at the center of the song might have been an obvious place to bring the rest of the band forward to thicken the texture, but here Erik Jacobsen strips everything right back to just bass and piano. What was a light texture becomes even lighter; the dialogue between piano and bass shifts the melodic focus from the fullness of the upright piano to the walking bass, before the guitar interjections, drums, and hand claps recharge the ensemble in preparation for the return to the B section.

"Hello Hello" sounds like other Jacobsen productions, particularly the Lovin' Spoonful's hit "Daydream" (1966). "Daydream" also has an old-time feel about it, amplified by the saturation of John Sebastian's lead vocals and the gradual addition of instruments to the mix—acoustic guitar, bass, drums, harmonica, piano. Sebastian's vocal is a masterful example of bending notes and playing with the beat: a lyric about being lazy, sung lazily. "Hello Hello," by contrast, seems to be attempting an action, but lazily: we might be encouraged to visualize the singer sitting in the sunshine, eating a tangerine, but he is also trying to make a move on a pretty girl. The spaces between one line of lyric and another may just mean that she isn't responding to his advances.

One problem with "Hello Hello" is the popular assumption that it was in retrospect somehow a "message of welcome" to the Summer of Love, or that the "tangerine" on offer was code for some local lysergic product. But Sopwith Camel were playing "Hello Hello" before Jacobsen heard it, in the dancehalls around town, on bills with the other prominent local bands, at benefits for the Artists Liberation Front, on stage with the Mime Troupe. "Hello Hello" was not the only song Sopwith Camel knew, and it should not be interpreted as in any way "typical." Some of the other tracks on their debut album—"Frantic Desolation," for example—suggest a psychedelic undercurrent. While "Hello Hello" may have been the single that sold the band nationally, there is nothing to suggest that the rest of their output was similarly driven by a commercial impulse. Sopwith Camel did not enjoy the kind of rapturous local reception of some of their contemporaries—theirs was "not the kind of sound that grabs you"[7]—but "Hello Hello" is one of the few instances of contested fame to emerge from the scene, and for that reason it remains an interesting curiosity, worthy of occasional deep listening.

COUNTRY JOE & THE FISH, "SECTION 43"

(Joe McDonald)

Joe McDonald: guitar, harmonica
Barry Melton: guitar
David Cohen: Farfisa organ, guitar
Bruce Barthol: bass, harmonica
Gary "Chicken" Hirsh: drums, background sounds

Produced by Samuel Charters
Recorded at Sierra Sound Laboratories, Berkeley (Jan-Feb 1967)
Released on *Electric Music for the Mind and Body* (Vanguard, 1967)

> They're a warm open band, not a hard rock group, and they radiate the Berkeley hip-innocence when they play. . . . They give the impression of an unfreaked acidhead taking an outdoor trip in summer flowers: amazed when something works out, amused when it doesn't, because nothing serious ever goes wrong, and things work out unexpectedly fine often. Collectively they have no stage presence at all.[8]

> As far as [*Electric Music for the Mind and Body*] is concerned, there are some songs on there written on drugs. There are some songs written not on drugs. There are some songs written before I'd ever had illegal drugs, and there are some songs written after I had illegal drugs. And no one can tell. Including myself.[9]

Country Joe and the Fish were by 1967 regular fixtures at the Bay Area dancehalls. ED Denson's "folk scene" column in the *Berkeley Barb* often expressed a preference for the live experience of Country Joe over any of their local contemporaries, citing them as exemplars of political engagement and musical expression. This was in part due to geography—Country Joe and the Fish were a Berkeley band—but more probably because Denson was the band's manager. Denson had been deeply involved in folk and blues before moving to California, working with, among others, the guitarist John Fahey.[10] Fahey's influence is clear in "Section 43" stylistically, harmonically, and philosophically: his first recordings were subsumed by the identity of a fictional alter-ego, and it does not take an enormous interpretive leap to see Country Joe and the Fish in "Section 43" exploring the terrain of psychedelic consciousness in a similar act of ego loss.

"Section 43"

It is significant that "Section 43" is an instrumental journey. Although it can often seem that the most straightforward path to a song's essence is via its lyrics—as though the words alone convey all significance—in the case of the music created in and for a psychedelic environment, it was often the "instrumental spaces" that carried meaning:

> I believe what we all sensed was that whatever it was that was "high" about our music wasn't to be found in the words. Rather, it was in the improvisational interplay between the musicians and those magic moments when we really got into the "zone," that magical place of near-enlightenment, approaching pure experience, when we truly escaped the smallness of who we were into a place far more expansive and reflective of an altered state or other reality.[11]

"Section 43" was first recorded in June 1966 for a limited-issue three-track EP.[12] Although they were gaining a solid following around the Bay Area, in September 1966 Country Joe and the Fish announced that they were having financial trouble. The local dancehall scene was growing, which was undoubtedly a good thing, but it could only sustain a maximum of eight bands, and there were at least forty local bands already "trying to make it." Country Joe were moving toward more experimental music, a reflection of their artistic growth, but a potential limit to their appeal. Yet the surest means of financial security—a major-label contract, a Top Ten hit—was also the surest way of killing experimentation. They therefore sought patronage from the readers of the *Barb* to enable their journey of artistic freedom. Their sales pitch was provocative:

> Barry is working on a fugue (Porpoise Mouth) for bass, guitar, organ, conga drum, voice, and tape recorder, and both he and Bruce have begun using feedback during some of their songs. We are getting into improvisational forms, Joe is experimenting with his voice, and the songs themselves are beginning to get far enough out that it is conceivable that their subjects will be not just ire-inspiring, as our protest material has been, but bustable as songs dealing directly with sex are almost certain to be.[13]

"Section 43" was perhaps Country Joe and the Fish's first foray into this world of experimentation. The EP version of the song does "get far enough out" beyond the standard three-minute pop song, playing with effects and textures in novel ways, and the LP version, recorded in the early years of 1967, is remarkably similar. This presents an interesting problem in interpretation: either the band had refined their performance to a concise flow of ideas, which could stretch the listening experience "far enough out" beyond mainstream pop music, or the need to market their music via recordings set an artificial stricture on "Section 43," resulting in a mere glimpse of the prototypical "psychedelia" that came to define for some the music of the short 60s.[14]

Barry Melton described "Section 43" as comprising "four or five discrete movements."[15] On first listen it seems to meander in and out of thematic areas and into some rarefied musical spaces; in actual fact it follows what could be described as a loose Rondo form, with one primary idea (A) alternating with contrasting sections (B, C, D, etc.). Both recorded versions of "Section 43" follow an identical pattern, ABACADAB, but the LP version inserts transitional silences between the A and B sections.[16]

0:00	A	bass intro; Farfisa figure; guitar solo; first melodic block
0:55		second melodic block
1:27	B	arpeggiated guitar figure over slow-moving organ chords (x2)
2:39	A	return of repeated bass and Farfisa figures; harmonica solo
3:33	C	slightly accelerated; continued harmonica solo over full band groove
4:07	A	bass and Farfisa figure, with organ to fore
4:25	D	calliope-like ("fairground") passage
4:42	A	guitar assumes repeated organ figure; Farfisa solo
5:19		sitar-like guitar solo over static accompaniment
5:51		continued guitar solo; Farfisa more prominent in texture
6:13	B	arpeggiated guitar figure over static organ chords (x2) to end

It is easy to imagine how the structure of "Section 43" could lend itself to expansion and exploration in live performance. Provided the bass and organ were locked into the same groove at the return of the A sections, there would have been any number of directions the band could wander "out there." In a setting such as the Avalon or Fillmore, the band could have "played off the room," and let the audience direct the pace at which they moved from section to section, with the established structure determining the fluidity, or shock, of the transition.

The unique character of each section is defined by texture as well as by melody. The A section is signaled by the sinewy repeated bass figure and the shimmery Farfisa accompaniment. The bass and organ together create a grounding context for the roster of soloists—guitar, harmonica, organ, guitar—that assume primary melodic space. Texturally, the bass and organ leave a gap in the sound field that is filled by those soloists. With the arrival of the B section all sense of motion halts: the arpeggiated guitar pattern is woven through a fairly thick layer of slowly moving and occasionally dissonant accompanying chords. In the second A section the tonal area that the soloist explores shifts the listener's perception about what is the "right" and what is the "wrong" key. This is particularly acute in the playful "calliope" D section, a completely unexpected departure from the fluid characters of the preceding A, B, and C sections. In each section and across the song, harmonically and texturally, Country Joe and the Fish are playing with the listener's equilibrium.

"Section 43" crystallizes a moment defined by musical and pharmacological experimentation. The EP and LP recordings reveal minor differences in structural, musical, and technological detail, but the song's flow is the same in both instances. And there is another performance of "Section 43" that is worth mentioning here, as it codified a particular experience of the short 60s. Country Joe and the Fish performed "Section 43" at the Monterey Pop Festival in June 1967. If part of the intended effect of the existing recordings of "Section 43" was to replicate the environment and experience of a San Francisco dancehall, the sight of Country Joe and the Fish playing the song on a foggy Saturday afternoon disrupts that connection. The audience is seated, so there is no dancing for the band to "play off"; the sun is shining, so there is no light show; the setting is outdoors, so there is no artificial echo. The main psychedelic effect of the Monterey performance resulted from a broken bass amplifier, and the band "struggled on with its shaking and quivering only to be visually pleased" by the accidental effect.[17] That aural effect is not immediately apparent on the film, but the visual suggestions of altered states of consciousness are clear on the faces of the musicians and some members of the audience. That "Section 43" document is the soundtrack for a very particular, if hazy, moment in psychedelic time.

Notes

1. RJG, "Periodic Check of 'Serious' Music," *Chronicle*, February 22, 1967, p. 45.
2. Snoopy first fought the Red Baron in January 1966; the band's first dancehall appearance was at the Matrix on March 22, 1966. These two events may not be coincidental.
3. It should be noted that Erik Jacobsen's relationship with the Bay Area extended well into the long 60s: he produced a string of recordings for local musician Chris Isaak, including the ubiquitous "Wicked Game," from *Heart Shaped World* (Reprise, 1988).
4. Ben Fong-Torres, "Eric Jacobsen in Town with 'Hybridized Production Trip,'" *Rolling Stone* 15, August 10, 1968, p. 8.
5. Other "one-hit wonders" of San Francisco in the short 60s include the Mojo Men ("Sit Down, I Think I Love You," #36 in March 1967), Blue Cheer ("Summertime Blues," #14 in May 1968), Big Brother and the Holding Company ("Piece of My Heart," #12 in November 1968), and the Youngbloods (the re-issue of "Get Together" reached #5 in September 1969). Earning a solitary Top 40 "hit" therefore does not necessarily preclude a band from enjoying lasting impact or critical acclaim.
6. Jeremy Pascall, "The Big Pop Movement," *Rave!* (September 1967), p. 31.
7. RJG, "'Big Mama' Brings the Truth to UC," *Chronicle*, January 10, 1967, p. 41.
8. ED Denson, "The Folk Scene: Fresh Fish Only, a Berkeley Bag," *Barb*, June 10, 1966, p. 5.
9. Country Joe McDonald, quoted in Michael Goldberg, "The San Francisco Sound," *Rolling Stone*, August 23, 1990, p. 96.
10. Among the formative musical figures Denson worked with were Mississippi John Hurt, Bukka White, and Skip James. John Fahey recorded a number of influential albums in the mid-1960s, most notably in the guise of the fictional Blind Joe Death.
11. Barry Melton, interview with Richie Unterberger for *Eight Miles High* (San Francisco: Back Beat Books, 2003). Full transcript of the interview may be found at www.cjfishlegacy.com/meltoneightmiles.html (Accessed March 30, 2015).

12. The EP, *Country Joe and the Fish* (Rag Baby, 1966), was recorded at Sierra Sounds in Berkeley, produced by ED Denson, in June 1966. The band's personnel then were slightly different, featuring John Francis Gunning on drums and Paul Armstrong on tambourine and maracas. *Rag Baby*, the magazine run by Denson and McDonald, "carries local news and a complete directory of the coffee house and folk scene in the Bay Area. It also prints informative and instructive articles of and about folk music. It prints new songs by West Coast song writers." The "cover" of the first *Rag Baby Talking Issue* (October 1965) was a manila envelope with a photograph of war protesters in Berkeley. Inside the envelope were the single and sheet music of four songs, including the first recording of "The I-Feel-Like-I'm-Fixin'-to-Die-Rag."
13. ED Denson, "The Folk Scene: Fish High, Almost Dry," *Barb*, September 30, 1966, p. 6.
14. Barry Melton insisted that he entered into the job of mixing "Section 43" for the LP by taking an appropriate dose of LSD, to preserve the sense of liveness that they were trying to capture on vinyl. See his interview with Richie Unterberger.
15. Unterberger, *Eight Miles High*.
16. Apparently producer Sam Charters had the band record each section separately, which "made the total effect slightly less organic than that of the EP cut." See Alec Palao, liner notes to remastered mono and stereo mixes of *Electric Music for the Mind and Body* (Vanguard, 2015).
17. Al Kooper, "Hendrix Bobbed and Weaved; Paul and Art Fugued; and Otis Makes the Rescue," *Rolling Stone* 5, February 10, 1968, p. 17.

7. 1968

The inflated enthusiasms that rock is The New Art and the Far Out Thing are ridiculously out of perspective in terms of what has been and is still happening in the musical revolution. Those who are turned on by the modern phase of rock might well start exploring works like Elliot Carter's Piano Concerto, Takemitsu's *November Steps* or some late Penderecki for real earth-spinning experiences.

The commercialization of rock and the lack of discrimination and the lack of specific "whys" in its criticism make the effusive claims even more questionable. The dead earnestness and the unquestioning embrace of rock by its mass of devotees tend to negotiate its best aspect, the marvellous spoofing qualities that make rock a powerful break with the slack-jawed canned romance of the "top 40" pop tradition.[1]

Editor: Your Question Man asked where all the true hippies had gone and the responses expressed regrets at their departure because "everybody liked them."

Well, citizens, face it, you once had a gentle group of people among you who demanded nothing of you other than a little thought. They wanted to love you and they wanted to slow down the pace enough to pause, breathe a sigh of satisfaction and wonder at the infinite beauty of everything that surrounds us. You responded to them so viciously with your dirty names, your facetious comments, your perverted minds probing constantly for every bit of erotic behavior, your sensationalism and your sadism, your hatred and your hangups—that they either had to flee in panic simply to maintain their existence or you shattered their minds so badly that they now hate you. You couldn't tolerate anything out of the ordinary in your tidy little lives.[2]

For six weeks at the beginning of 1968 *Chronicle* workers were on strike. The biggest news from the hip community to report when the paper resumed production was the death of Neal Cassady in Mexico—"and only the Underground Press mourned this remarkable man."[3] The year 1968 was tumultuous, a year of global political unrest, but the *Barb* bemoaned the poverty of student activism. Compared with universities in Britain and Eastern Europe, the Berkeley student body was victim of "over-exposure by social scientists and the mass media . . . a categorized social aberration within the system, rather than a revolution against the system."[4]

A different revolution against the system was the "Alternate Society" embodied by intentional communities such as Morning Star Ranch. At the heart of this system was the belief that the simple "no trespassing" sign has wreaked untold damage on America and the rest of the world—the "territorial imperative" that has been the cause of so much war.[5] The "territorial imperative" in the Haight resulted in another casualty: the *Oracle* published its last issue in February 1968. In its pages poet Lew Welch reflected on the meaning of the movement and offered a blessing on the dispersing tribe:

> In the meantime, stay healthy, there are hundreds of miles to walk and work. Keep your mind. We will need it. Stake out your colively retreat. Learn the berries the nuts the fruit the small animals and plants. Learn water.
>
> Build whatever colively is your Way.
>
> For there must be good men and women in the mountains, on the beaches, in all the neglected beautiful places, that one day we come back to ghostly cities and set them right, at last.
>
> AND THERE MUST NOT BE A PLAN! It has always been the plan that did us in.
>
> In all that rubble, think of the beautiful trinkets we can wave above our heads as we dance!
>
> As we do right now. As we do RIGHT now!
>
> Meanwhile (1) Freak Out (2) Come back (3) Bandage the wounded and feed however many you can, and (4) Never Cheat.
>
> Lew Welch　　　　9-1-67

7.1 A final word from Lew Welch.

That same month, Jerry Rubin announced that 1968 would be the "year of the 'yippees'":

> The New Left created the teach-in, the hippy created the be-in, and the yippee is creating the do-in or live-in. America's first youth festival will be a do-in and it will take place Aug. 25 to Aug. 30 in Chicago in Grant Park.

The plan for this "do-in" was for hundreds of thousands of yippies to descend on Chicago in the week of the Democratic National Convention there, and create a "super-creative synthesis, energy explosion, information exchange . . . a total multi-media experience," with everything free. The intention to disrupt the Convention was certainly consistent with the spirit of radical protest, though details of the week's events were still somewhat hazy:

> The Chicago power structure, especially Mayor Daley, is not going to be thrilled about our using Grant Park. But with hundreds of thousands of us, what are they going to do? It is our human right. We are confident of receiving a permit to use Grant Park.

More worryingly, Rubin was daring the government, both civic and federal, to "bring thousands of troops, and the more troops, the better the theater. . . . Chicago will be an eye-opener."[6]

Michael Rossman, a leading figure of the Free Speech Movement, published a long and considered open letter to Jerry Rubin in a subsequent issue of the *Barb*, outlining his concerns over the "deeply and dangerously irresponsible" call for a Festival of Life:

> The brilliant formless Yippee publicity, in building the magical beckoning symbol of our Music, projects an image which is recklessly and dangerously slanted, however well it's meant. It promises grooving and warmth, and does not warn that joy there must be won from within—not absorbed from others—in a landscape of total hostility whose ground condition may well be the terror and death of one's brothers. . . .
>
> These aren't the kids from the Haight, now familiar with teargas and clubbings, who will go to Chicago wise and to express who they are . . . and who are the people you want there to fashion a symbol, the best of our people at joy. . . . Most of those whom YIPPIE itself will draw will be endangered and superfluous for the occasion. And this sort of organizing, however spectacular, is neither moral nor efficient, effective.[7]

Jann Wenner echoed Rossman's concerns in an extended *Rolling Stone* editorial, calling out the "recklessness and thorough lack of moral compunction" at the heart of the Yippies' Chicago plans: the Chicago protest "in methods and in means—is as corrupt as the political machine it hopes to disrupt." The main problem was that unsuspecting people would descend on Chicago in their droves, the only likely outcome being violence.[8]

Back home, the hippies continued to block traffic on Haight Street, and the police responded with tear gas and more than ninety arrests.[9] The *Barb* printed a number of eyewitness accounts of the police action against the "unsuspecting Sunday crowd," along with photographs documenting the police formation moving toward the Haight-Ashbury intersection, spraying mace into the crowd, "swinging riot sticks indiscriminately," saturating the area with tear gas; restraining a man and "methodically" beating him, a motorcycle cop "mow[ing] the sidewalk clean of people." Such excessive force formed the basis of an ACLU report on the police handling of demonstrations.

Attempts to contact Mayor Alioto to discuss this matter were unsuccessful.[10] The Peace and Freedom Party stepped into the fray, not only to defend the right to dissent, but to form a "special photographic unit to chronicle examples of police violence in the future." Their offices were compiling signed affidavits by witnesses to the events, presumably those whom Mayor Alioto branded as "Neo-Fascist punks and storm troopers." Around 200 Haight residents also marched to Park Station chanting "Peace! Peace!," though their message was lost on the on-duty officer.[11]

In the days following the Haight disturbances, Mayor Alioto's appointments secretary, Mike McCone, embedded himself in the community—first by visiting the Switchboard, then talking to neighborhood residents, merchants, and patrons, about the riot on Sunday night and their ideas for the peaceful coexistence of hippies and city officials. McCone returned the following Sunday, and arranged a closure of Haight Street from 3 p.m to 10 p.m. It began with the Litter Patrol, helped by volunteers and the mayor's aide, and soon the word spread:

> Ecstatic people now started coming back from the park to sing and dance on "their" street. Residents in apartments bordering Haight Street put their hi-fi speakers in the windows and turned the volume on full. . . . The street was becoming jammed now with happy celebrants playing bongo drums or sitting on the street and meditating or rapping or just walking along and grooving on the sights and each other. . . . When it came time to re-open the street to the vehicles, the Straight opened its doors for a free rock concert. . . . It was a stone groove . . .[12]

Several thousand people spent the day wandering, dancing, and watching as the officially sanctioned "happening" happened.[13] The Grateful Dead parked a flatbed truck on Haight Street, plugged into the Straight Theater's electricity supply, and gave their final street concert to the many thousands grooving peacefully.

All was not happiness and light, however: two days later, members of the Haight's straight community declared war against the hippies and challenged Mayor Alioto's "open street policy." At a community meeting attended by 70 residents, merchants, and property owners, the state of the street was discussed in graphic detail: "packs of hippie dogs running wild . . ., narcotics sold and used right in the street, property damage caused by hippies, blaring sound amplifiers and screeching motorcycles at all hours," not to mention the public sex witnessed at length by one offended resident.[14] One hip response was to call this "war" nothing more than "a conflict between the positive and the negative thinkers in this community,"[15] but the pressure was clearly on Mayor Alioto to listen to both sides. The mayor's office insisted that it had no plans to make Sunday's Haight Street closure a regular event, and expressed puzzlement at the hostile reaction of the local straight community.[16] The hippie community responded in kind by staging a "Freedom Festival Week," beginning with a parade from downtown to Haight Street, through the Park to the Polo Field.[17]

Discussions about a second Monterey International Pop Festival continued through the first quarter of 1968 and met with resistance from some Monterey residents. Gleason accused them of bigotry, but no matter; the chiefs of police in Monterey and neighboring areas stated that they would have no men available to serve as extra police on the intended festival weekend.[18] Considering the mutual admiration society established in 1967 between the Monterey Police and the hippies, this was an unexpected move. In April, John Phillips and Lou Adler announced that they had abandoned all plans to hold another festival in Monterey.[19]

In dancehall news, the Grateful Dead, the Jefferson Airplane, and other groups had jointly taken a lease on the old Carousel Ballroom on Market Street. The Carousel was owned by Bill Fuller, whose properties included similar ballrooms in Chicago, New York, Boston, London, Manchester, and locations in Ireland; one of the bands' intentions was to plan a summer tour of all these spots. The Family Dog were also planning operations at the Crystal Ballroom in Portland and the Coliseum in Salt Lake City, in addition to the Denver Dog and affiliated halls in Vancouver and Seattle. After its first promotionally haphazard, but musically brilliant, weekend, Gleason pronounced the Carousel "by far the best hall in town for rock groups in almost every imaginable way."[20] The ballroom scene was a booming business. Could it work in another city?

Denver Dog

On October 8, 1967, Chet Helms and Bob Cohen opened Family Dog operations at 1601 West Evans in Denver. Traveling with them to the Colorado outpost was

Diogenes Lantern Works, to replicate the Avalon's "total environmental theater." The *Berkeley Barb* asked Helms why he chose Denver for a second base of operations:

> "Denver is one of the most sophisticated towns we've visited," Chet replied. He includes the straights of the city in this statement. In comparison with the Avalon, Chet feels the Denver quarters are "more suitable, freer, and larger."[21]

There was also the potential in Denver for hippie hospitality: in addition to the forecasted recording facilities, art studios and workshops, the Denver Dog was set to include "a crash ranch" in the Rocky Mountain foothills, to welcome Family Dog employees, visiting artists, and musicians. How could it not succeed?

> MARC ARNO: If you want the irony of it, Chet took it as a positive cosmic sign that the ultra fascist governor of the State was named Governor Love.[22] I mean that was his real name: "It's a sign! It's a sign!" But when we got there in the Spring of '67? Now civil rights, that was a done deal, but you dig out some old newspapers from Denver and every month another black maid or Mexican gardener was being shot down in the street by police because they were in a white neighborhood after dark. They were outrageous and there was this one cop who was with the Vice Squad: Detective John, whose name strikes fear into the hearts of hippies, Gray. That's how he was referred to every time he was in the paper, which was a couple of times a week. And he'd just say shit and they'd print it like it was true. This guy had it in for us like nobody else. But a lot of people did because we weren't going to sell booze: that meant that sixteen-year-olds could come to our show.

The trouble with minors, curfews, and a lack of booze was certainly familiar to anyone following the Fillmore's ordinance saga, but establishment attitude to the hippies was much worse in Denver than it was in San Francisco. Detective John Gray was heard to say that he was going to "rid Denver of all long-haired people," and set to work in earnest at the Family Dog. Local sources called this what it was: a personal vendetta against the hippies. The Family Dog filed a restraining order against Gray for illegally searching and harassing their clientele inside the ballroom; Gray continued to do it regardless. This was in addition to arrests for vagrancy, hitchhiking, failing to carry ID, and possession of marijuana, throughout Denver Dog's area of the city.[23]

Gray's aggressive approach to the hippies included enforcing an ordinance requiring all minors to obtain parental permission to attend a Dog dance. The Denver Dog did not have the benefit of a Ralph Gleason or Bill Graham to argue on behalf of mixed-age dancing, so parents were unwilling to grant permission;

the Family Dog's income dwindled, and by April 1968 they were over $85,000 in debt. Many local San Francisco bands volunteered their services for a benefit at the Avalon, yet despite the evening's good vibes, the Family Dog's financial situation did not improve.[24] A few weeks later, *Rolling Stone* suggested that a "shake-up" in the Denver police department had reversed the Family Dog's fortunes. In Marc Arno's memory, this "shake-up" resulted from a last-minute intervention by a cunning insurance representative, who could itemize the many ways the city had infringed the constitutional rights of not only the Family Dog but also the members of the public who had attended their dances.

With dwindling audience numbers and dwindling funds, the Denver Dog closed in June, though plans continued for ballrooms in Portland, Vancouver, and Anchorage.[25] One enormous collateral loss from the venture was a proposed recording studio. Had Chet Helms invested the Denver money in proper recording facilities at the Avalon, the Family Dog might have established a cooperative record label for local bands. Instead, they were pressured into a political action that was anathema to the hippie philosophy:

> MARC ARNO: You must maintain the distinction: if it was political it wasn't hippie, it was yippie. Hippies could not, *could not* be political, they had to be apolitical. In fact in Denver when we ended up having to sue the city we won. It bankrupted us, but more importantly just the act of suing in Court was the death of hipness.

In the Haight, someone was trying to pit the new hippies against the old: the circulation of "a bogus handbill" announcing the mayor's order to close Haight Street one Sunday from 3 p.m. to 10 p.m. resulted in a stand-off between those who insisted on their right to take control of the street, and those who wished to avoid the heavy-handed police pressure of previous weeks. Even when hippies attempted to drive down Haight Street to encourage people back onto the sidewalks, a number of other hippies sat down in their path and refused to move.[26] The *Barb* couldn't confirm the provenance of the handbill, but they did note the attempts by the Straight Theater, by well-meaning hippies and local merchants, to convince the crowds that the handbill was a hoax, that the street was open to traffic, and that they needed to leave before the riot police arrived. A *Barb* reporter was among those attempting to clear the street, and spied a couple of "last year's Diggers (most of them, you remember, split early last summer when it got to be more of a work trip than an ego trip)," there to encourage the sitters, "delighted that the 'revolution in the streets' was finally here":

> Losers, of course, are the Haight Street Sunday mall and the woolly-headed, red-eyed, dim-witted kids who cheerfully turned into sociopaths for a day. Will

San Francisco and the Long 60s

7.2 Signs of the times.

they ever know they were screwed? Probably not. They're the same kids who smoke oregano and buy corn starch speed and sit among piles of dog shit all day convinced they're where the action is. Barnum, baby was a real prophet.[27]

Some weeks later the Haight-Ashbury Neighborhood Council requested that city officials close Haight Street once a month for an intensive cleaning, and the response was rather more positive. One city supervisor even saw potential in a city-community partnership to upgrade Haight Street "for the benefit of everyone."[28] Alas, the Department of Public Works testified that Haight Street already attracted seven times the street-cleaning services provided to other streets in the city; the answer, apparently, was for "those people" to realize that their litter and garbage was destroying the neighborhood.[29]

At 3 a.m. on Monday, March 18, the hippies at KMPX went on strike. The walkout party of about 500, plus Creedence Clearwater Revival, got a bit noisy for the station's neighborhood, so they moved en masse, but *sans* amplifiers, to Pier 10. By the morning the picket had started in earnest, with demands for greater artistic freedom and better pay.[30]

KMPX had changed the nature of FM radio programming across the country, yet despite the station's enormous local following and financial success, tension was bound to arise between the hip disc jockeys, "chick engineers," salesmen, and the "anti-hippie attitude" of the station's corporate management. The strike was backed by the station's hip advertisers, and a benefit for the strikers was held at the Avalon Ballroom.[31] Station salesman Whitney Harris wrote a letter to the editor of the *Chronicle* explaining why KMPX staff were on strike, thanking publicly the various sponsors and hip associates who had held benefit dances and dinners: "This is folk music and we are the folk."[32] One such benefit, the Super-ball, held at Winterland, was attended by everyone from hippies to business executives—everyone connected with the success of KMPX:[33] "It was like a family reunion," everyone united for the sake of local music, local hip business, and the desire for creative freedom.[34]

The KMPX strike finally ended on May 21. Most of the strikers moved to KSAN, and Gleason was left wondering who had won the dispute: Metromedia had recently switched the station's format from classical to "progressive." In 1968 there were already three adult rock stations, largely due to the success of KMPX; what Tom Donahue and the old KMPX crew were offering at the new call letters might not be that unique after all.[35]

Martin Luther King Jr. was assassinated on April 4. On the front page of the *Chronicle* two days later was an official proclamation from Mayor Joseph Alioto, "not of material substance but spiritual in content," expressing the shock and grief that King's death had caused the city, urging a future of nonviolence, and a reminder that King was "obviously . . . deeply moved by the teachings of our city's own patron Saint—Francis of Assisi—whose warm and gentle life fashioned so deeply the spirit of our citizens."[36] While clearly a heartfelt personal sentiment, it was also a subtle political maneuver aimed at stamping out unrest in the city, echoing the message of peace that was so often left out of the paper's exposés on the Haight community.

And the cultural divide in San Francisco remained as vast as ever. The Haight Clinic and the Atheneum Foundation for the Performing Arts applied for a permit to hold a benefit dance in the Palace of Fine Arts, featuring Quicksilver Messenger Service and Big Brother. At a meeting of the Recreation and Park Commission, the Palace of Fine Arts' benefactors and concerned patrons voiced their clear opposition to the idea, "appalled at the thought that the hippie community would show up in force," and worried that "you couldn't get them out once they got in. When it comes to hippies or anything having to do with hippies, we're dead against it." It all came down to class and culture, and apparently hippies had neither. The coexistence of all of the arts, classical and popular, at the heart of the Atheneum Foundation's charter was irrelevant: "Rock 'n' roll and hippies just don't mix with the Palace of Fine Arts; it's just common sense." The decision was deferred until a citizen's committee could be established with Mayor Alioto to write a policy for use of the Palace. In the meantime, Carousel Ballroom was donated for the cause.[37] The mayor soon announced his support of the Palace League's decision not to allow the hippies to use the venue, calling it "a reasonable exercise of discretion."[38]

All this took place amid an interesting change in dancehall culture. With the opening of the Carousel Ballroom, Bill Graham now faced new challengers. While the Fillmore had hosted performances by jazz artists in the past, Gleason was surprised to find that Cecil Taylor's Quintet was scheduled to open for the Yardbirds for a weekend in May, and that the Carousel had booked Thelonious Monk to headline a weekend with the Charlatans and Dr. John. Other jazz artists being considered for the ballrooms included Charles Mingus, Albert Ayler, and Archie Shepp:

> Among the things indicated by this is not only the development of a common audience for jazz and rock, but a recognition on the part of the ballroom operators that dancing is not a major factor any longer. Very few people dance at these ballrooms now, the events are really concerts in an informal atmosphere. Dancers go to the Avalon and the Straight Theater.[39]

These interesting programming decisions prompted the *Examiner* music critic to pronounce the very nature of genre divisions in local music moot:

> Most of our local groups are no longer definable simply as "rock 'n' roll" or "psychedelic" or "electronic rock." [Their music] falls into a category of creativity wholly apart from the 2-1/2-minute stuff which pumps from the 45-r.p.m. grist mills into high pressure, hit-conscious pop-rock radio stations.
>
> Other than the blues-oriented vocals by any of these groups and the occasional original themes of great beauty (like Grace Slick's "White Rabbit" or Joe McDonald's "Janis"), the primary impact of the San Francisco groups is composed of the most basic of ingredients: instrumental improvisations based upon original harmonic and rhythmic patterns.
>
> The same standards by which fine jazz renditions over the years have been judged can now be applied to the S.F. fringe-area of the national rock scene. And certainly it is high time that we have a revision of nomenclature within both contemporary "rock" and "jazz" areas of performance. . . .
>
> Cecil Taylor billed with It's a Beautiful Day . . . makes more sense than having him on the program with Al Hirt, although Hirt is still called "jazz" by many people. . . . [Jazz] promoters would be [wise] to realize that the jazz spirit

pervades the best of today's original electronic music and that San Francisco is the worldwide center of such creative spirit in "rock."

Rather than fighting "rock," jazz ought to join it, and perhaps create a new name for their combined creative efforts.[40]

Interesting programs often led to interesting posters advertising them, but *Rolling Stone* proclaimed the end of The Great Poster Trip: what began as a "phenomenon containing massive doses of camp" was now a "tourist fad," and the appearance of the Big Five in the pages of *Life* and *Time* heralded any number of bad imitations in the pages of lesser magazines across the nation. The maturing of the psychedelic vision into "serious" art ran "parallel to the post-drug phase that has opened in the 'hippie' movement, the exodus away from the Haight-Ashbury to Marin County, Mendocino and Big Sur."[41] There were still safe harbors in the Haight, however, even in 1968.

The Phoenix

Kurt "Crowbar" Kangas: Bob Stubbs owned a beatnik coffee shop before he opened up the Phoenix on Haight Street. His brother was Norman Stubbs. Norman made these musical instruments that nobody bought, so he opened up a leather company called East West Musical Instrument Company, which later turned into East West Leathers. So Norman opened up East West Musical, Bob opened up the Phoenix, and they were two businessmen to be reckoned with.

The Phoenix was at Haight and Masonic. Sundance Incense and Trading Company. We were the ones that sold all the incense, the oils, the cigarette papers, and of course the Indian Madras bedspreads. Beads were big. You buy the seed beads and string them up and you'd sell them to the suckers—the tourists, I'm sorry—who paid a dollar for a strand of beads that cost approximately five cents. That was a good way for a lot of people to make money.

I did a lot of mail orders for soldiers in Vietnam. They really liked bullet roach clips—you know, big bullets, and you pull out the end and there was a roach clip. They loved them, because you can take one and hook it on your clip, nobody would ever know. And we'd send them the *Oracle* and *Berkeley Barb*. I was just trying to support them and help them. And then these guys would come back from Vietnam—those were the days where you can stick a pound of pot in your gunny sack and just get on the plane—and then they would come up and knock on my door and go, "this is from Company C, man, thank you." I've always been proud that yes, I did my part for the war.

But we didn't have a blatant service, we were pretty much legal all the way down the line. We had a basement with a hidden dope room for our clients— that's the first thing they would do, was go down to the dope room and get twisted—in a hidden spot in our basement. If you were a cop you probably couldn't find it; you had to go around a lot of little labyrinths to get to it, and once you got in, it was this great lounge with a hookah in there. It was all beautiful. What can I tell you? Made out of bedspreads of course.

Underneath the table I had things called Pluto Bars and Cosmic Kisses, shaped like Hershey's Kisses, made with hash oil and pot oil. We had Bay Area Bombers, which were pre-packed little joints that sold for $10, $20, $50—the $100 joint was filled with five types of pot and three types of hash and lined with oils of all types. Exotic designer stuff. But I sold that under the table.

We also had a free box in there: come and dump your crap and let other people have it. So we were all-purpose stores and wholesaled to everybody in the country. The Hell's Angels had a store in Berkeley, so they would come in, wander around, say "is this for sale?" I'd say, "No." "Thanks"—and they'd take it and throw it in their bag. They didn't give a shit, they took anything and everything they wanted. And then I had to come up with a price for them!

We sold to the rest of the head shops around the country and you could see the movement happening everywhere. Because all of a sudden we're sending the stuff to Bumfuck Egypt, you know, and nothing was coming out of there. So we started thinking, "oh okay, now there's starting to be cool people everywhere."

On the steps of the Halls of Justice, surrounded by flower people and in full view of fellow policemen, Richard R. Bergess, aka "Sergeant Sunshine," lit up a joint. A former patrolman in the Haight, Sgt. Sunshine took it upon himself to understand local residents a bit better. After arresting one hippie, he "didn't turn in all the evidence," and discovered that marijuana was "a lot more fun than booze." He believed that "if more [policemen] smoked grass and . . . had the guts not to carry a gun, then people would start accepting policemen as protectors, not as oppressors."[42]

Chronicle readers' attention was briefly diverted to Big Sur, where hippies were developing new strains of venereal disease. Dr. Robert Fries, who had opened a weekly free clinic at Esalen, recommended abstaining from sexual contact for two weeks, or at least a couple of days. This was apparently met with complete bewilderment: "How can anything bad come out of anything so good?" The primary worry was that Big Sur would be a magnet for hippie migration from the Haight, and that communal living and the "quite unbelievable" array of cross-sexual relations practiced therein, would exacerbate the problem further.[43]

The hippies' "free" ethos extended to literature, with the publication of Richard Brautigan's *Please Plant This Book*, a paper folder containing eight envelopes of seeds, each bearing its own poem—calendula, sweet Alyssum Royal Carpet, carrots, squash, California native flowers, lettuce, parsley, Shasta daisy—distributed for free. In the simplest of ways, it was "a season-long happening, with Nature as producer."[44] Not all free poetry was well received, however. The Diggers' month of poetry readings on the steps of City Hall was curtailed abruptly and a press conference held in its stead. The Diggers had been trying to make arrangements for their projects in consultation with the mayor's office but had met with "no real response" to any of their proposals. On the contrary, the police had told produce markets not to supply the Diggers with free fruit and vegetables for distribution. The Diggers' five-point program—rent-free spaces in redevelopment areas, ten neighborhood free stores to distribute free food, neighborhood resources to celebrate "the city, the planet and free being," free use of parks and other public spaces, without need for permits—was never adopted; the press conference ended with five Digger arrests,[45] which led to further Digger protests against what they perceived as "gratuitous police trouble-making."[46]

> CHARLES JOHNSON: I think that the whole hippie idea was just a way of life predicated on what they thought was freedom. And freedom wasn't sleeping out under the stars; freedom was more of an attitude as to how *you* lived your life, whether or not you were living it well. If you weren't living it well, then you didn't consider yourself free. You lived your life well, you lived happily, then you were free.

Freedom versus commerce was a source of continual tension in the hip community. In 1968 the "stars" of the city's ballroom scene were reaping financial reward and finding widespread success in New York: Janis Joplin was featured in the *New York Times*, the Jefferson Airplane were rapturously received at Bill Graham's Fillmore East, the Grateful Dead were smuggled into Columbia University in a delivery van to play for striking students, LPs were due out by the Dead, the Airplane, Steve Miller, Quicksilver, the Loading Zone, and Sly and the Family Stone were steadily moving up the pop charts, with no sign of the momentum abating.[47] The richness of the free event—from Sunday afternoons at Provo Park in Berkeley, to the Free Folk Festival at Foothill College—did nothing to stop people from paying for dances and concerts, on the beach or in an auditorium, and only enhanced San Francisco's aura as a vital center for musical expression. Even the British musicians "go back to London and speak in awed tones of the fact that San Francisco bands play free concerts."[48] Still attempts at capturing the Monterey vibe in the city failed: a weekend festival in Golden Gate Park was mooted and dropped; and the Northern California Folk-Rock Festival was seen as crass and commercial.

The widespread unrest following Dr. King's assassination and the murder of Bobby Hutton earlier in the year prompted many ruminations on racial tension in the Bay Area, treated with due seriousness in the papers:[49]

> [The] economically deprived whites do not perceive their condition as the result of deliberate policy calculated to suppress them as a group—ethnic or racial. Many blacks do have such a view.
>
> Therefore, black people react differently, and that reaction is one of the reasons our cities are powderkegs of dynamite today. Blacks are becoming increasingly alienated. . . . Poor blacks are much more susceptible to mass acts

of rage and expressive violence. They are much more willing than poor whites to organize and to challenge the structures of power. . . .

Many black power groups are organizing black people in viable, constructive organizations in the ghettos.[50]

This was followed in May by a multipart profile of the Black Panthers. The first installment contextualized the party's direct action policy within the tense relationship between the Panthers and the Oakland police. The description of the racial divide in the East Bay was balanced, and the Panthers' own views on the local climate were presented without bias.[51] The second installment concerned the Panthers' "right now" philosophy and their ten-point plan: total self-determination, full employment, removal of all white businesses from the ghetto, decent housing, black history on the school curriculum, military exemption for all blacks, an end to police brutality and murder, freedom for all black men held in prisons and jails, trial of all blacks by black peers, "land, bread, housing, education, clothing, justice and peace."[52] With Huey Newton in the Alameda County Jail, the third installment featured an extended profile of Bobby Seale, working for the Panthers on the outside.[53]

In a revealing conversation, an anonymous intelligence agent offered a number of conclusions about the Panthers: that they had already been "penetrated" by at least one other intelligence agency, that their paramilitary training and the quality of their weapons were inadequate, that bail costs and legal fees were depleting any funds they may have, and that if the Panthers continued as a militant organization they would undoubtedly splinter into other Black Power groups and cease to exist. The interviewee spoke about the night of Bobby Hutton's murder, and said that the fact that Hutton was unable to shoot a policeman accurately from a distance of ten yards was evidence of a lack of training; but that it was "virtually impossible" for Black Panthers to train or arm themselves in the way that white paramilitary groups were able to do. The answer was for the Federal government to invest more money in the ghetto, as "you simply can't agitate happy people."[54]

"Happy people": at the beginning of the short 60s "happiness" seemed to come easily by chemical means or by ecstatic expression in the moment. The lingering sense of communion Ralph Gleason felt after one joyful and peaceful night at the Carousel, amid the Hell's Angels and hippies, black people and white, was shattered when the news broke of Robert Kennedy's assassination. On the night that Kennedy died, Joey Bishop was on television—"Mr. U.S.A., bewildered, patriotic . . . and anxious to be good"—with guests including a psychiatrist, a priest to lead the panel in prayer, the brother of Medgar Evers, and the governor of California, "spouting righteousness and morality and attacking 'our permissiveness' and assailing 'campus hoodlums,' the courts and in general offering a smooth version of the radical right line."

And all the while, as the talk went on and Joey struggled—a Hamlet strung between dreams and reality—the man slowly died and this terrible feeling came on again, the feeling of doom I had lost in the joy of the Carousel the night before, and the country seemed fated to keep spinning out of control down some grim spiral to madness, as the politicians talked about personal violence and not state violence, setting the stage for oppression and restriction, all in the name of liberty.[55]

The Airplane, the Dead, and 3,000 people went to Golden Gate Park to hold a Sunday wake for Robert Kennedy, but no one had asked the Park and Recreation Commission for a permit. The bands' management tried to reason with city police, whose reinforcements soon arrived on horseback and by the carload. The law was upheld, and the mourners dispersed quietly.[56]

The assassination of Robert Kennedy prompted an open letter in the *Barb* to Jerry Rubin, expressing doubts about the wisdom of the Yippie gathering at the Democratic National Convention. There was a very clear distinction between the pacifist hippies and the militant New Left, and concern that the "climate of violence" that caused Kennedy's death would be invoked more widely "to further curtail civil liberties." This led to an uncomfortable parallel between the chaos encouraged by the Yippies and the rise of Nazism in Germany, and the urgent call for a continuation of Martin Luther King's nonviolent course to prevent what would be "an unprecedented period of barbarism."[57]

In a dubious attempt at racial commentary, Jefferson Airplane appeared on the *Smothers Brothers Comedy Hour*, with Grace Slick in blackface. As she recalled:

> If you listen to the words of "Crown of Creation" and think about a spade singing it, it makes a lot of sense. Women wear makeup all the time, so why not black? . . . I did it because it was a trip; it's weird to have blue eyes and a black face. . . . There weren't any blacks on the show and the quota needed a little adjustment. I knew nearly everyone would object to it.[58]

Very quickly, and very quietly, in June the Carousel changed hands. While the joint committee running the ballroom—the Dead, Airplane, and other investors— were in discussions about future plans, Bill Graham flew to Ireland to meet the owner of the ballroom and signed a contract to take it over. The initial intention behind the Carousel was to showcase younger talent and to run it as a self-funding community project; Graham planned to honor this vision, but ultimately to run the Carousel as a business. A notice of this change appeared on the front page of the *Chronicle*, with word of the ballroom's new name: Fillmore West.[59]

Graham's primary interest in the Carousel was its size: the 2,000-seat hall held 500 more patrons than the Fillmore, which could alleviate the increased fees that bands were now charging to perform.[60] Gleason saw the end of the Carousel as an indication of the real death of the hippie. The youth movement, in thrall to the Digger ethic of "take it, it's yours, it's free," even with the best intention in the world, could not realize any substantial idea without its ending in "confusion [and] mismanagement." The Carousel also suffered from constant police attention. It was a painful lesson in "the ways in which ego trips, economic interest and a desire to avoid unpleasant reality" can ruin something intended for "the community."[61]

Bill Graham's New York operation, the Fillmore East, had gained some San Francisco press since its March opening. Of particular interest was the way in which Graham had transformed the former East Village Theater to a showcase for light and sound:

> The East Village itself is a natural home for rock music, as the neighborhood "is a hippie-crowded area which combines the old Bowery, the Lower East Side Jewish community and an odd mixture of the Haight-Ashbury and

7.3 Bill Graham takes over the Carousel Ballroom.

Berkeley's Telegraph Avenue." The inside of the hall might be more formal than its west coast counterpart, but Graham managed to replicate the vibe to great effect.[62]

Academic interest in the hippies had not yet waned: a group of psychologists, psychiatrists, and sociologists were awarded a research grant of $127,000 from the National Institute of Mental Health for a two-year project charting the long-term future of the Haight-Ashbury phenomenon: comparing the hippies with other youth subcultures, rural hippie communes, urban community organizations, and the long-term effects on drug use, psychologically and medically.[63]

Civic interest in the hippies had not yet waned either: two undercover police officers moved in on what they suspected was a drug deal at the corner of Haight and Clayton streets, and all hell broke loose. As the police led the arrestees away, they attracted an angry crowd that began pelting rocks and bottles at the patrol car. Police reinforcements arrived, the crowd backed off, traffic continued to move—but the hippies erected a barricade across Haight and set it on fire. When a policeman tried to stamp out the flames, he was pelted with bottles and then surrounded by peacekeeping hippies. Others began breaking nearby shop windows, and the police began a sweep up and down both sides of Haight Street. The crowd eventually dispersed, but some still tossed molotov cocktails in attempted arson at the Bank of America.[64]

According to Herb Caen, one of the many minor casualties of the incident was Dr. David Smith, who had tried to attend to a hippie who "had been beaten bloody." When he identified himself as a doctor to a nearby officer and said, "'I think this boy should be attended to before he is moved' . . . he got a club in the ribs and stomach, and had to be attended to himself."[65] But, of course, it was said that the police had used "patience and forbearance" and that false charges of police brutality needed to stop. Mayor Alioto blamed the incident on two young men from Oakland trying to sell drugs to minors, insisting that the incident was proof that the Haight had changed irreversibly.[66] The same scene replayed over the next three nights. Though the police might have been looking for LSD and marijuana traffic, the real problem on the street at this point was methamphetamine use, and unreported murders and rapes, and the fracturing of a once-strong community.[67]

The *Examiner* put a punctuation mark at the end of a week of tensions with their headline: "A New Hashbury":

The Haight-Ashbury is a year in time and a century in mood from the 1967 Summer of Love. . . . This summer, Mayor Alioto is saying, "We're not talking about flower children anymore."
    The mayor is right.
    Haight-Ashbury is probably the only truly integrated community in the country to riot.

> It is a tension-filled ghetto, simmering with hostility that bursts out in violence against the outside authority—i.e., the police—and turns inward to victimize its own people.
>
> Fights, holdups, muggings, rapes are common in the Haight.[68]

The *Chronicle* followed this report with an in-depth look at the rise of methamphetamine use in the Haight and the changing demographics of the neighborhood: the "speed" atmosphere was "infectious," the crowd now "purposeless," the young people no longer flower children, but "mentally ill in a way that makes them unreasonably challenge organized society," and the speed economy was attracting "underworld dealers, thrill-hunting motorcycle riders and hoodlums." A basic problem was the cost of speed as compared with the cost of LSD or marijuana: $10 would pay for enough marijuana for forty joints, but a speed habit cost a person $15 per day. The speed freak resorts to crime, the police lie in wait, the speed freak gets paranoid, violence breaks out, and the pattern is repeated endlessly.[69]

The dialogue in the papers turned to issues of addiction and illness, with the president of the Haight-Ashbury Neighborhood Council reminding *Chronicle* readers that "speed runs require injections, often with dirty needles," and that "any solution to the physical or social incoherence of Haight Street must rely on medical treatment for those severely damaged by methamphetamines."[70] The one place disposed to treating the effects of methamphetamine use and addiction, the Haight Free Clinic, announced its closure in September. Dr. Smith did not say whether the closure was permanent, but it was clear that the clinic had run out of funds, and was still receiving no public support via the city's Department of Health.[71]

Over in Berkeley, a group of Telegraph Avenue merchants began strategizing positive ways of avoiding the same fate that had befallen the Haight. A researcher for the Department of Social Planning suggested that police should "recognize the many differences in opinion and philosophy, and that all residents do not fall into any one group"; that the city should involve the hip community in civic decisions; and that the city should "provide confidential, genuine assistance to those who seek our help, and dry up the drug and narcotic suppliers of those who do not." Berkeley had already planned a health referral service for Telegraph Avenue, and Fred Cody announced that he would be providing stalls at his book store to rent to hippie artists. The plan was to raise money "to encourage arts and crafts among the street people." Such a positive approach to a complicated social problem was certainly radical, and illustrates the different philosophies behind the smaller East Bay communities and the greater San Francisco mentality.[72]

Psychedelic art had evolved, and the *Chronicle* couldn't really describe it. Reporting on an exhibition of drawings from *Zap Comix* at the Light Sound Dimension Gallery, art critic Thomas Albright described *Zap* as a new, "adults only" comic, headed by four contributing artists, R. Crumb, S. Clay Wilson, Victor Moscoso, and Rick Griffin:

> Crumb is nothing if not direct, but compared to Wilson he is the height of subtlety. Wilson uses a hard-line, Mad magazine style to draw epics of motorcycle gangs, pirates, and assorted goons and demons in orgies of excrescence and perversion. This is pretty brutal stuff.
>
> Like some of Crumb's cartoons, the obsessive and excessive degeneracy of Wilson's strips seem to reflect the decline of "Flower Power" into power of a more sinister, sick kind.[73]

And the success of San Francisco bands was enough to lure more industry people to the city. A New York booking agency installed a representative in San Francisco to recruit bands. Mercury Records moved its West Coast representative from Hollywood to San Francisco and was building a recording studio in the city, and the Bay Area would soon have a critical mass of over ten professional recording studios. Bill Graham was helping develop the local scene by featuring three new bands every Tuesday at the Fillmore West, followed by a jam session, all for a one-dollar admission price.[74] All together, signs that the San Francisco scene was only gaining momentum.

The second wave

> This week [June 28 1968] the Jefferson Airplane is all over Life from the cover onwards. The Quicksilver Messenger Service, Steve Miller Blues Band, Country Joe & the Fish, Moby Grape, and Blue Cheer are on the Billboard best selling LP chart. Creedence Clearwater Revival has an LP on Fantasy which is selling madly all over and there's more to come.
>
> Mercury has signed Mother Earth and the Melting Pot. Mad River has an LP coming out on Capitol. Columbia's Big Brother LP is due out this fall, the Airplane is finishing its new LP in Hollywood. The Loading Zone is on a national RCA promotion tour in between engagements, . . . Beautiful Day is negotiating with Columbia. Dino Valenti's Epic LP is due this summer, . . . and the new bands are springing up like healthy weeds. Not ON healthy weed. LIKE healthy weeds.[75]

Maybe it's just a coincidence that Santana and speed became popular at about the same time. Maybe not. At any rate their "long awaited" album is definitely a speed freak's delight—fast, pounding, frantic music with no real content. For those who hoped that the second generation of San Francisco bands would be an improvement over the first, this record along with those of the Sons of Champlin and It's a Beautiful Day should destroy such fantasies forever. In the post-psychedelic era all of the bands have their styles down pat. But like methedrine which gives a high with no meaning, the dazzling rock styles now offer us music with virtually no substance.[76]

A program on local public television station KQED in August listed all the bands then operating in San Francisco, capped at around 135.[77] Not all of those bands made records, not all of them appeared regularly in the local dancehalls, but all of them reflected the vitality of the local live music culture that circulated around the ballroom scene.

The term "scene" is important, for despite the city officials' attempts to close the ballrooms, the regularity of concerts, both formalized and free, was central to the development of a community united in the consumption of popular music. The music in this "post-psychedelic era" did not have a uniform sound, and the audience was by 1968 not unified in the consumption of a single type of drug; but the expectation of a certain kind of experience codified in the early years of the ballroom scene is a common thread right through the short 60s. The fact that San Francisco bands were gaining national recognition perhaps complicated matters somewhat. While it was reason enough to celebrate the success of a local movement, the live musical culture was lost on vinyl, and major-label interest in local bands would instill a commercial sensibility that might distance the musicians from their audience—and nowhere was that more clear than in the local papers' coverage of the careers of the "second wave" of San Francisco bands.

As early as May 1968, Steve Miller Band and Quicksilver were cited as leading this "second wave" of San Francisco bands into the recording studio.[78] Quicksilver had been around the scene since the beginning, of course, but were among the last of that "first wave" to be signed to a major-label contract. What their eponymous debut offered to an international audience was a version of their mature sound honed in the dancehalls and polished for a wider audience.[79] What other, newer, bands offered from 1968 onward was a multiplicity of styles and varied levels of acclaim.

In August 1968 Gleason was claiming that bands were still flocking to San Francisco—though San Francisco was no longer the "Liverpool of America," but "Kansas City all over again":[80]

> What did it in San Francisco was the ballroom scene. At one time, as many as four ballrooms operated. The ballrooms were rehearsal halls . . . and spiritual gathering grounds. Musicians came to the ballrooms not only to hear other bands but to meet other musicians. After a couple of years of this, the city became nationally known along the musical underground telegraph as the place to form a band.[81]

By this point, Creedence Clearwater Revival's first album was climbing the *Billboard* charts, and Sly and the Family Stone were soon "vying . . . for the honor of the San Francisco group with the greatest number of records to make the hit charts."[82]

Soon added to this mix was Santana, whose emergence from the San Francisco scene resulted in one of the longest careers in the long 60s. Put together, these three bands might "represent" the Bay Area in the late-60s pop charts, but this belies the fact that they had no common musical ground, and very little common cultural ground, between them. Creedence was "creating the most *vivid* American rock since *Music from Big Pink*";[83] Sly and the Family Stone were grounding psychedelia in a long history of rhythm and blues; and Santana, with their "wild conga drummer and an exciting guitarist" were drawing "a highly personal audience" to a different kind of musical hybrid.[84]

What was changing was the ballroom scene itself. A scene requires space to thrive, and the expansion of the ballroom circuit, from the Matrix to the Fillmore, Avalon, and beyond, was the most promising sign that the scene was being supported in a (literally) concrete way. But Gleason had recently begun wondering at the lack of dancing at these places. This was changing the dancehalls fundamentally from an environment where the audience and the performers melded, and where freedom of movement and freedom from musical structure could direct the length and pace of a given performance. This sense of freedom extended from the free concerts in the park to the more formalized, commercial settings of the dancehalls—but there was an inevitable by-product of outside interest in the scene from Monterey Pop onward, of the relentless pressure on concert promoters by city officials, expansion into other cities, changing demographics at home, the steady of flight of hippies from the Haight to outlying areas: with a "second wave" of musicians came a "second wave" of audience, and that in itself signaled a decisive shift. Gleason's comparison of San Francisco and Kansas City was barbed, and also had

> slightly ominous overtones. . . . The Swing Era ended with the star system, making the bands financially unwieldy and the audience changing to a listening one. San Francisco dances are more concerts all the time but the ballrooms are still the places to go.
>
> The next year or so ought to tell the story.[85]

A number of filmmakers had been coming to the Haight to cash in on flower power, with films such as *Petulia*, *Skidoo*, and *The Trip*, to varying success. Jack O'Connell's documentary, *Revolution*, was filmed in the Haight in the summer of 1967, and opened at the Straight Theater in autumn 1968. Despite its problems, John Wasserman saw it as essentially truthful, though he admitted that "a pall of doom" surrounds the film:

> Part of it is simply that the power structure will not tolerate this revolution. Part of it is the undeniable destruction caused by the hard drugs. And part of it is the knowledge that a lot of bad scenes have gone down in the Haight since June in 1967.[86]

There was one positive subtext in the recent glut of hippie-themed films like *Revolution* and *I Love You, Alice B. Toklas*: spirituality. Just as there were more hippie movies to come, with hippie music also taking over the *Billboard* Top 100, Gleason felt that perhaps the deeper message would be the movement's most important legacy.[87]

It was no doubt difficult to reconcile cinematic scenes from the optimistic early days of the Haight with the visual reminders of a more difficult reality. Shop fronts on Haight Street remained boarded up after one too many broken windows, deserted sidewalks offered proof that fear was the neighborhood vibe, and records at the Park Police Station showed a 300 percent increase in robberies, a 25 percent increase in rape, and 150 percent increase in aggravated assault from the same period the previous year. In the first eight months of 1968 there had been three murders in the Haight; there were none over the same period in 1967.[88]

In the midst of this, the Yippies and the Black Panthers announced a pact, and their intention to stage a "second Boston Tea Party" and change the political system from within:

> Let us join together with all those souls in Babylon who are straining for the birth of a new day. A revolutionary generation is on the scene.
> There are men and women, human beings, in Babylon today. Disenchanted, alienated white youth, the hippies, the yippies, and all the unnamed dropouts from the white man's burden are our allies in this human cause. The entire anti-capitalist, anti-imperialist world of mankind is with us.[89]

The White Panther Statement, published by the *Barb* at the end of November, cited "cultural revolution through a total assault on the culture" as their *modus operandi*. John Sinclair, minister of information, outlined the ten-point program, based on, and allied with, that of the Black Panthers, evoking the language of black revolutionary politics but with no clearly attainable goal: "Free food, clothes, housing, dope, music, bodies, medical care—everything! Free for everybody. . . . Free the people from their 'leaders'—leaders suck—all power to the people—freedom means free everyone!"[90]

The former manager of the Kingston Trio, Frank Werber, was arrested for marijuana trafficking and possession of narcotics. Federal agents had been interested in his extracurricular business dealings—the Trident Restaurant in Sausalito, Trident Studios, a land management firm, and his life of luxury on De Silva Island in Marin County—which led them to a delivery of 258 pounds of Mexican marijuana.[91] In all of the discussions about hard drugs in the Haight, one recurring theme was the regular scarcity of marijuana in the summer months, and clearly Werber's shipment would have gone some way to alleviate the problem.[92] The focus on marijuana possession and sale, however, led Ralph Gleason, among others, to comment on the gulf that existed between the law and social reality: people from all walks of life, in every income bracket, from the obscure to the famous, artists to government officials, smoked marijuana. It would be impossible, and pointless, to try to imprison every one of them. More danger was inflicted on society by the use of speed, sleeping pills, and alcohol than by marijuana; making an example out of "the first San Franciscan to build a fortune out of popular music" was merely a symbolic motion toward perpetuating "the mythology of prejudice."[93]

In a sign of festivals to come, the two-day San Francisco International Pop Festival, located twenty-five miles east of the city in Pleasanton, saw an interesting exchange between patrons and organizers. An audience 20,000-strong paid for the second day's lineup, but another 1,500 remained outside the gates, not wanting to pay the $5 admission. Some of the more vehemently anticapitalist in their number began heckling and taunting the police, who duly called for backup; but the promoters decided not to let the scene escalate further, and opened the gates to the outsiders, free of charge.[94] It might not have been entirely altruistic, however. The crowd—"an audience of suburbia, not metropolitan Bay Area, [looking] as if it was made up to play bit parts in a hippie flick"—had "knocked their way through the hurricane fence. THEN, they were let in free, ex post facto."[95]

At a time when San Francisco bands were filling the *Billboard* charts, when the music industry was moving into the city, when new bands were being showcased weekly, when psychedelic posters were plastered on walls across the country and abroad, when hippie fashion had permeated every aspect of popular culture, the city of San Francisco revoked the Family Dog's dance permit. The dances at the Avalon had been running peacefully and successfully for over two years, with no conflicts between the owners, the lessees, and the patrons; yet local witnesses to bad hippie behavior—public menace, urinating in doorways—were seemingly more important than the untold revenue that the hall had brought into the city since 1966.[96] These same witnesses would, however, welcome the Avalon hosting "conventional" dances—a loaded term suggesting a return to a culture long since passed on.[97] Earnest hippies presented their case, often in the clearest of terms:

> Editor—Save the Avalon. I want to dance. If the Board of Permit Appeals wants to sit at home and watch TV or shoot speed or balance sponges on their noses they have my blessing. I want to go to the Avalon.
> The Avalon on a good night radiates pure joy—people feeling free—people freeing themselves—people dancing. There are not the big money big band vibrations of Bill Graham's Fillmore West—it was always more like partying.
> So now the great plastic steamroller wants to do in the Family Dog. And since it's just a bunch of longhairs no sanity or justice will come—maybe. SF has been the musician—let it remain.[98]

The Beatles cabled their support and loaned Chet Helms a copy of the elusive *Magical Mystery Tour* for a number of benefit screenings around the city.[99] But the Family

Dog's appeals were rejected, despite the support of Mayor Alioto and one last effort at changing the minds of the Permit Board members.[100] Gleason put it plainly:

> The pattern really is the same no matter what protestations the authorities and the complainants make. Long hairs and hippie clothing added to amplified music equals mystery and mystery coupled with youth is dangerous. . . . I do not believe that the Family Dog case is without prejudice. No one talks at all about how to make them comply with the law in any point. Instead, they yank the permit and hear evidence to support and argue that. What they really want to do is to stop the dances at the Avalon.[101]

Rolling Stone was up in arms, telling its readers that "a hotel full of aged pensioners" had shut the Avalon down. The magazine spoke to the Board president and asked whether any new evidence might be put forward to change the decision, but heard that such evidence would be "irrelevant, because we already heard so much." This evidence included charges that "LSD was openly smoked there," and that the Avalon attracts "every kind of undesirable person" to the area.[102] The *Chronicle* reported that the Police Department "won its fight to suppress the Avalon Ballroom" but that Chet Helms had already found a new location for the Family Dog's dances.[103]

The numbers told an important story. A Bank of California vice president specializing in market research and planning conducted a survey of live performances, rock radio, recording studios, record sales, fees to artists and royalties, and found that in 1968 alone, the dollar value of the local industry was set to exceed $4 million, benefiting the city by anywhere from $8 million to $15 million. His prediction was that by the mid-1970s the local music industry would be the fourth largest business in the city, behind construction, manufacturing, and finance. These estimates were based solely on the "hard rock" centered around the Fillmore and Avalon, but clearly "the momentum has begun." The only problem was "any strong anti-youth political sentiment" that would impinge upon the growth of the scene—in obvious terms, the police focus on the Avalon.[104]

As the year closed, students at San Francisco State College were on strike. Around 3,500 students were urged by "various militants" to attack the university administration before it attacked them. Despite the students' chanting, hurling of "missiles" through administration building windows, and shouting profanity, the police did not act.[105] The ongoing tensions between hippie and straight, between younger and older generations, inspired a Christmastime parable in Gleason's column, wherein Christ was a hippie, and encountered many places up and down the coast of California, and right across the country, where he would be unwelcome—apart from "the Fillmore West and backstage among the rock bands at the Cow Palace and in the cell with Newton and on the lam with Cleaver and standing by the draft card burners and Muhammad Ali and singing Beatles songs with children of all ages."[106]

Notes

1. Robert Commanday, "Airwaves' Crucial Cultural Flip-Flop," *Examiner*, This World, p. 27. Commanday was bemoaning the loss of KSAN as a classical radio outlet, and citing the documentary evidence revealing Metromedia's violation of broadcasting principle and the FCC's investigation of the decision to change it to a rock format.
2. Greg Scandlen, Letter to the Editor: "Why Hippies Fled," *Chronicle*, September 20, 1968, p. 42.
3. RJG, "This Is the Way It All Happened," *Chronicle*, February 28, 1968, p. 53. The *Barb* tribute appeared as "End of the Road," February 9, 1968, p. 3. In it Cassady was described as "one of those persons who influences his generation by being." During the strike, *Chronicle* workers devised an hour-long television news magazine program, *Newsroom*, broadcast on local public television outlet, KQED—a new format then, but decidedly familiar to twenty-first-century television viewers. Gleason also had a ten-minute slot three times a week on KMPX on the days his column would otherwise have appeared in the *Chronicle*.
4. "ten days that shook the university" [*sic*], *Barb*, January 5, 1968, p. 2.
5. "Morning Star: No End in Sight," *Barb*, January 19, 1968, pp. 10–11. It is worth noting here that Woody Guthrie sang about the "no trespassing" sign in "This Land Is Your Land"—though in a verse generally deleted in its popular dissemination.
6. Jerry Rubin, "The Year of the Yippees," *Barb*, February 16, 1968, p. 4. For a full account of the Convention, see Norman Mailer, *Miami and the Siege of Chicago* (New York: Dell Publishing, 1971); see also Jerry Rubin, *Do It! Scenarios of the Revolution* (New York: Simon & Schuster, 1970).
7. "Rossman Raps Rubin," *Barb*, March 22, 1968, p. 10.
8. Jann Wenner, "Musicians Reject New Political Exploiters," *Rolling Stone* 10, May 11, 1968, p. 1.
9. "A Dreadful Crisis as Hashbury Crowd is Tear-Gassed by Fuzz," *Chronicle*, February 20, 1968, p. 1.
10. "Tales of the Terror," *Barb*, February 23, 1968, p. 4.
11. "Fuzz Go Berserk in the Hash," *Barb*, February 23, 1968, p. 5.
12. Thoms Benji, "Freed Street Stone Groove," *Barb*, March 1, 1968, p. 5.
13. Jerry Carroll, "Haight Street an Arcade of Pleasure," *Chronicle*, March 4, 1968, p. 3.
14. "Haight Street Straights Declare War on Hippies," *Chronicle*, March 6, 1968, p. 1.
15. "Denies Haight Hips 'War' With Straights," *Barb*, March 8, 1968, p. 3.
16. "No Permanent Haight Closing," *Chronicle*, March 7, 1968 p. 2.
17. "Hippie Parade—A Big, Noisy, Peaceful Doing," *Examiner*, March 10, 1968, p. 8.
18. RJG, "The Monterey Police and Pops Festival," *Chronicle*, March 13, 1968, p. 43.
19. RJG, "Sponsors Call Off the Pops Festival," *Chronicle*, April 19, 1968, p. 49.
20. RJG, "A Great Weekend at the Carousel," *Chronicle*, March 18, 1968, p. 41.
21. "Family Dog to Open Denver Ballroom," *Billboard*, September 16, 1967, p. 40.
22. John Arthur Love was governor of Colorado from 1963 to 1973, when he left to take a post as energy czar in the Nixon administration.

23. "John Gray and Long Hair: The Heat's On in Denver," *Rolling Stone* 2, November 23, 1967, p. 2. According to Marc Arno, police would "sit outside our club and follow kids home and arrest them for breaking curfew *on their front porch*, so the parents could be humiliated too." Diogenes Lantern Works were also accused of running a "sacrilegious light show," which they duly proved otherwise to the assembled ecumenical council of Denver.
24. See "Family Dog Just Misses the Pound," *Rolling Stone* 8, April 6, 1968, p. 6.
25. "S.F. Ballroom Circuit Grows," *Rolling Stone* 9, April 27, 1968, p. 10. Out of the rubble of Denver Dog emerged the career of local concert promoter, Barry Fey, whose Feyline productions began at the Denver Dog and continued for four decades, well into the long 60s, at venues like Red Rocks. See Barry Fey, *Backstage Past* (Lone Wolfe Press, 2011). And Denver Dog rippled to more unexpected places. As Marc told me: "The kid who used to park cars for us, who nearly lost all his fingers to frostbite, after the Dog left he went up into the mountains and started picking herbs and trying to smoke them all and make tea out of them just to see whether it gets you high. And that became Celestial Seasonings."
26. Jerry Carroll, "Hippies Close Haight St.," *Chronicle*, March 18, 1968, p. 1.
27. Thomas Benji, "Haight Hoax Riles Haightians," *Barb*, March 22, 1968, p. 3.
28. "Call for a Real Haight Scrubdown," *Chronicle*, April 24, 1968, p. 5.
29. "Trying to Keep Haight Clean," *Chronicle*, April 26, 1968, p. 19.
30. George Gilbert, "Rock Radio in the Streets," *Chronicle*, March 19, 1968, p. 3.
31. RJG, "Scorpions, Destiny and a 'Hippie' Strike," *Chronicle*, March 20, 1968, p. 41.
32. Whitney Harris, Letter to the Editor: "KMPX—What It's All About," *Chronicle*, March 29, 1968, p. 40. The quote was from Sandy Darlington in the *San Francisco Express-Times* [n.d.].
33. This included Larry Miller, who had just been offered, and promptly rejected, the station's program directorship. He was greeted at Winterland as a hero, though he did accept the position the following week.
34. RJG, "They All Came Out for KMPX Strikers," *Chronicle*, April 5, 1968, p. 47.
35. RJG, "Hippie Strikers Back at Work," *Chronicle*, May 22, 1968, p. 49.
36. "A Proclamation," *Chronicle*, April 6, 1968, p. 1.
37. "Arts Palace 'Defenders' Vs. Hippies," *Chronicle*, April 12, 1968, p. 1. The clash of "high" and "low" culture is a problem I explore in Chapter 9.
38. "Mayor Backs Ban on Rock Dance," *Chronicle*, April 13, p. 4. The *Barb* suggested that Alioto's decision stemmed in part from personal real estate interests in the Marina. "Haight Clinic Dies," *Barb*, September 13, 1968, p. 7. In July, Gleason mentioned that the Haight Clinic was planning a festival at the Palace of Fine Arts to be held over Labor Day, which would embrace musicians from all genres. "Popular Music—Quicksand World," *Chronicle*, August 5, 1968, p. 44. The permit was granted, despite the protestations of the Marina Civic Improvement and Property Owners Association, members of which claimed that "dozens of hippies pounded on Marina doors looking for bathrooms during a jazz festival" earlier in the summer, and because of descriptions of the Haight Clinic as "'filthy dirty' and a thorn in the community's side." "Jazz-Rock Festival OKd for Labor Day Weekend," *Chronicle*, August 23, 1968, p. 2. In the end the Festival was a bust: the audience was sparse, compared with the dancehalls, a formal indoor event did not have the right vibe, and the city's decision to install a police presence 150-strong added to the discomfort. See "The Time They Played the Palace," *Chronicle*, September 2, 1968, p. 47.

It is interesting to put this event into historical context: that same weekend the Democratic National Convention was held in Chicago, an event that pitted a city's law enforcement against the "radical agitators" who purposefully disrupted the convention. The police presence at the Palace of Fine Arts, and at the political rallies in Berkeley, were part of a much darker cultural climate than the hippies had endured in the Haight. For more on the Convention, see Mailer, *Miami and the Siege of Chicago* and the "Czechago, U.S.A." issue of the *Barb*, August 30, 1968. For more on the Chicago convention in the broader 1968 musical climate, see Beate Kutschke and Barley Norton, eds., *Music and Protest in 1968* (Cambridge: Cambridge University Press, 2014).

39. RJG, "Competition, Change at the Ballrooms," *Chronicle*, April 15, 1968, p. 42. In a letter to the editor of *Rolling Stone* (Issue 10, May 11, 1968, p. 3), Bill Graham denied that Archie Shepp had been invited to the Fillmore. Nonetheless, Gleason expanded on this point two months later, calling the Fillmore and Winterland "star-system shows."

> People come to see the scene. People come to see the bands, the singers and the audience. They stand in front of the bandstand and they sit on the floor. They do not dance. When the crowd is large, all the dance floor is covered with human bodies, prone, seated, etc. Since the Avalon and, in a sense, the Carousel, are basically not competing with the Fillmore (generally) in the star-system game, the attendance, most times, is proportionately smaller. Hence there is more actual room to dance. The vibes in both the Avalon and the Carousel are different, too. There is more a sense of audience involvement than at either the Fillmore or Winterland, both of which seem to make the audience into spectators rather than participants.

Dancers at the Fillmore now were mostly relegated to the side gallery; people brought chairs to the front of the auditorium to sit ten rows deep, with more audience seated on the floor behind them, struggling to see the stage—"an interesting study in social direction." See "Changing Role of Ballrooms," *Chronicle*, June 30, 1968, Datebook p. 27.

40. Philip Elwood, "S.F. Rock Sound Really Is Part of the Jazz Scene," *Examiner*, May 26, 1968, p. B4.

41. Thomas Albright, "Visuals: The Death of the Great Poster Trip," *Rolling Stone*, 11, May 25, 1968, p. 16.

42. Maitland Zane, "Cop Defies Pot Law," *Chronicle*, April 15, 1968, p. 1. Needless to say, the follow-up stories about Sgt. Sunshine painted a much different picture of the man—a number of careers before becoming a policeman, difficult family life, unexplained accidents while on duty at city prison, failure to report for psychiatric appointments, the obvious ill effects of marijuana on a man who had ascended to the rank of sergeant. Charles Raudebaugh, "Pot Cop Launches Great Campaign," *Chronicle*, April 16, 1968, p. 1. Sgt. Sunshine was ultimately found guilty of possession of marijuana, though the imposition of a sentence—either misdemeanor (one year in jail) or felony (up to ten years in prison)—was held up when Sunshine's lawyers moved for arrest of judgment and a new trial. See "Sgt. Sunshine Is Found Guilty," *Chronicle*, November 15, 1968, p. 3.

43. "The Big Sur Hippies—Sex and Strange Germs," *Chronicle*, May 3, 1968, p. 3.

44. Jeff Berner, "Astronauts of Inner Space," *Chronicle*, May 5, 1968, p. 24.

45. Jerry Burns, "Police Crush Diggers' Read-In at City Hall," *Chronicle*, May 8, 1968, p. 1.

46. Dick Hallgren, "Hippies Make Faces at City Hall," *Chronicle*, May 9, 1968, p. 3. It is interesting to note that around this time SF State University professor Leonard Wolf's *Voices from the Love Generation* was published by Little, Brown, providing

a much-needed, nonjudgmental historical record of the hippies of the Haight, in their own words. Peter Cohon, later Peter Coyote, a founding Digger, was one of the book's subjects, and his observations of the scene in its contemporary moment are worth comparing with his later autobiography, *Sleeping Where I Fall*. Wolf's book was reviewed favorably, albeit briefly, in the *Chronicle*: see William Hogan, "World of Books: Voices from the Love Generation," May 27, 1968, p. 43.

47. RJG, "A Beatles' Coup for KMPX Strikers," *Chronicle*, May 8, 1968, p. 48.
48. RJG, "Music for Free Is Very Special," *Chronicle*, May 10, 1968, p. 47.
49. Hutton's funeral was briefly mentioned in the *Chronicle* on March 13, 1968, p. 2, with more emphasis placed on the visible presence of the Black Panthers than the reason behind Hutton's death. For more information on this and other formative Black Panther events, see Howard Bingham, *Black Panthers 1968* (Ammo Books, 2009) and Julius Lester, *Look Out Whitey! Black Power's Gon' Get Your Mama!* (New York: Grove Press, 1968).
50. Charles V. Hamilton, "The Meaning of Black Power," *Examiner*, April 21, 1968, This World, p. 25.
51. Charles Howe, "Black Panthers—What They Want," *Chronicle*, May 15, 1968, p. 1.
52. Charles Howe, "The 'Right Now' Philosophy of the Panthers," *Chronicle*, May 16, 1968, p. 1.
53. Charles Howe, "Seale Spreads the Panther Message," *Chronicle*, May 17, 1968, p. 1.
54. Charles Howe, "Secret Agents' Analysis of the Black Panthers," *Chronicle*, May 20, 1968, p. 1.
55. RJG, "Strung Between Dreams and Reality," *Chronicle*, June 7, 1968, p. 49. Gleason's columns in the week between RFK's assassination and his funeral exhibited not only a tangible grief, but an unusual bitterness toward what he saw as hypocrisy and "the faceless thing that is destroying us." See in particular his "A Day of Love, Hurt and Sorrow," *Chronicle*, June 10, 1968, p. 49. "Campus hoodlums" refers to Ronald Reagan's unofficial policy as governor of California to "clean up Berkeley" and rid the state of the blight of "permissiveness."
56. Dick Hallgren, "Cops Stop a Rock 'Wake,'" *Chronicle*, June 10, 1968, p. 1.
57. Eugene Schoenfeld, "Hippocrates: Are Hippies Yippies?," *Barb*, June 21, 1968, p. 2.
58. Grace Slick, quoted in "It Happened in 1968," *Rolling Stone* 26, February 1, 1969, p. 18. See also Patrick Burke, "Tear Down the Walls: Jefferson Airplane, Race and Revolutionary Rhetoric in 1960s Rock," *Popular Music* 29/1 (January 2010): 61–79.
59. RJG, "The Future of a Ballroom," *Chronicle*, June 28, 1968, p. 49. Graham would be leasing the old Fillmore "to the neighborhood black community to stage its own programs."
60. Keith Power, "A Rock Landmark—End and Beginning," *Chronicle*, July 3, 1968, p. 1.
61. RJG, "Death and Life of the Carousel," *Chronicle*, July 7, 1968, Datebook, p. 23.
62. Philip Elwood, "Our Famed Fillmore Goes East—With a Difference," *Examiner*, October 27, 1968, p. 4. For more on the Fillmore East, see Graham and Greenfield, *Bill Graham Presents*.
63. David Perlman, "Through the Years With the Haight Drug Culture," *Chronicle*, July 10, 1968, p. 3.
64. "Rocks and Bottles Fly on Haight," *Chronicle*, July 17, 1968, p. 1. The *Barb* published firsthand accounts of the riots, clear in their suggestion that the police had effectively ambushed the area. See "Pigs Go Ape in Haight," *Barb*, July 19, 1968, p. 4.
65. Herb Caen, "Friday's Fractured Flicker," *Chronicle*, July 19, 1968, p. B25.

1968

66. "'Patience' in the Haight," *Chronicle*, July 18, 1968, p. 2.
67. See Keith Power, "Violence Waiting in the Haight," *Chronicle*, July 19, 1968, p. 1.
68. John Hurst, "A New Hashbury," *Examiner*, July 21, 1968, p. 1.
69. Donovan Bess, "The Haight—'Killer' on the Scene," *Chronicle*, August 5, 1968, p. 2.
70. James Browne, Letter to the Editor: "Haight Street Story," *Chronicle*, August 9, 1968, p. 42.
71. David Perlman, "Haight Medical Clinic Forced to Close," *Chronicle*, September 14, 1968, p. 2.
72. Don Wegars, "Haight St. Scene Feared in Berkeley," *Chronicle*, September 20, 1968, p. 4. The vibrant craft stalls have been a fixture on Telegraph Avenue ever since.
73. Thomas Albright, "Psychedelic Art—A New Model," *Chronicle*, August 23, 1968, p. 48. *Zap* was in the news later in the year when Moe Moskowitz was arrested at his bookstore on Telegraph Avenue for selling pornographic comic books, *Zap* and *Snatch* among them. See "An Obscenity 'Bust' at Moe's," *Chronicle*, November 15, 1968, p. 3. See also Thomas Albright, "Zap, Snatch & Crumb," *Rolling Stone*, 28, March 1, 1969, pp. 24–25.
74. RJG, "Learning to Talk With the Natives," *Chronicle*, September 20, 1968, p. 46.
75. RJG, "The Future of a Ballroom."
76. Langdon Winner and John Morthland, Review: *Santana*, *Rolling Stone* 44, October 18, 1969, p. 38.
77. *West Pole* was broadcast on Friday, August 16, 1968, at 10.00 p.m., and features performances by Ace of Cups, the Grateful Dead, Jefferson Airplane, Sons of Champlin, Steve Miller Band, and Quicksilver Messenger Service. Gleason acted as host, contextualizing the bands within the San Francisco scene, and the show as a whole portrays the musical culture of the city as a dynamic and varied soundscape. It is available on a commercial compilation with *Go Ride the Music*, which features live performances by the Airplane and Quicksilver (EV Classics DVD, 2008).
78. "The Quick on the S.F. Scene," *Examiner*, May 26, 1968, This World, p. 30.
79. The final track on the album, "The Fool," is one of the two songs I explore in greater depth at the end of this chapter, backed with Blue Cheer's "Summertime Blues," another representative of this "second wave."
80. "Today's Kansas City of Rock," *Chronicle*, August 11, 1968. Gleason is referring to the critical mass of nightclubs in the 1920s and 1930s housing artists such as Bennie Moten, Count Basie, Lester Young, and Ben Webster, who gave rise to a particular kind of big-band swing.
81. Ibid.
82. RJG, "Unique Series on Recording Business," *Chronicle*, June 4, 1969, p. 47.
83. Bruce Miroff, Review: CCR, *Green River*, *Rolling Stone* 44, October 18, 1969, p. 38.
84. RJG, "Reactions to the Rock Bands," *Examiner*, June 16, 1968, Datebook, p. 31.
85. RJG, "Kansas City."
86. John L. Wasserman, "'Revolution' One-Up on the Hippie Story," *Chronicle*, September 26, 1968, p. 54.
87. RJG, "The Surfacing of the Hippie Documentaries," *Examiner*, October 13, 1968, This World, p. 31.
88. Jerry Belcher, "Fear, Not Flowers," *Examiner*, September 29, 1968, p. 3.

89. Eldridge Cleaver, "Yipanther Pact," *Barb*, October 4, 1968, p. 9.
90. See John Sinclair, "White Panther Statement," *Barb*, November 29, 1968, p. 13.
91. Keith Power, "Showman Seized in Huge Pot Raid," *Chronicle*, October 16, 1968, p. 1.
92. Werber was ultimately found not guilty of the importation charge in August 1969, though he still faced county charges of possession of cannabis—which *Rolling Stone* maintained was "a set-up." See "Werber Innocent in Big Dope Bust," *Rolling Stone* 39, August 9, 1969, p. 12.
93. RJG, "Pot in the U.S.A.—Fact and Fantasy," *Chronicle*, October 16, 1968, p. 49.
94. "Noble Gesture at Pop Festival," *Chronicle*, October 28, 1968, p. 6. The expectation of free access to music at the later festivals at Woodstock and the Isle of Wight were rather less civilized, however.
95. RJG, "On the Edge of a Great Change," *Chronicle*, October 30, 1968, p. 44.
96. Gleason's response to the claim of public urination bears repeating: "I do not say it hasn't happened. . . . I have seen citizens urinating in Union Square, on Nob Hill and on Fifth Street but I do not regard this as the responsibility of the Fairmont, the St. Francis or the management of this publication." See "Young People See All the Paradoxes," *Chronicle*, November 20, 1968, p. 40. In advance of the hearing, Bill Graham offered to mediate discussions between the Family Dog and the Polk Street Merchants Association, stating that "Chet Helms puts on a damn good show." The music industry also publicly stated its support of the Family Dog, citing the business brought to the industry by shows at the Avalon. "Avalon Fate Up for Grabs Come Monday," *Barb*, November 15, 1968, p. 11.
97. RJG, "The Family Dog—A Big Business," *Chronicle*, November 13, 1968, p. 48.
98. Jack Wolf, Letter to the Editor: "My Love in Avalon," *Chronicle*, November 21, 1968, p. 46.
99. RJG, "Beatles Support the Family Dog," *Chronicle*, November 22, 1968, p. 44. The loan of *Magical Mystery Tour* is significant. The only other time the film had been shown in the United States was over two days in the spring of 1968, simultaneously at the Straight Theater and at a hall in Los Angeles. There were no plans to broadcast the film on television, as it had not fared well on its initial UK television broadcast on Boxing Day, 1967. Helms had plans to show the film at the Straight Theater, at the Palace Theater in North Beach, and two showings at the Avalon, all over one weekend.
100. Scott Blakey, "Avalon Ballroom Appeal Rejected," *Chronicle*, November 19, 1968, p. 1.
101. RJG, "All the Paradoxes."
102. "Family Dog Shot Down," *Rolling Stone* 25, January 4, 1969, p. 6.
103. "Cops Win Fight With Family Dog," *Chronicle*, December 10, 1968, p. 1.
104. RJG, "Tin Pan Alley Stretches to S.F.," *Chronicle*, December 16, 1968, p. 47.
105. "Sound and Fury at S.F. State," *Chronicle*, December 3, 1968, p. 10. For more on campus unrest in general, and dissent on the Bay Area campuses in particular, see *Rolling Stone*'s special issue, "American Revolution 1969," April 5, 1969.
106. RJG, "His Image in Today's World," *Chronicle*, December 25, 1968, p. 43.

BLUE CHEER, "SUMMERTIME BLUES"

(Eddie Cochran/Jerry Capehart)
Produced by Abe "Voco" Kesh
Recorded at Amigo Studios, North Hollywood (1967)
7" single released on Philips (BF 1646, 1967); highest chart position #14
From the album *Vincebus Eruptum* (Philips, 1968)

Dickie Peterson: vocals, bass
Leigh Stephens: guitar
Paul Whaley: drums

> The San Francisco Band of the Year in '68 was unquestionably Blue Cheer. Impossibly loud, unashamedly imitative, they carried the image of the egotistical methfreak to new extremes. They seemed to aim at creating, with musical instruments, the effect of a pack of motorcycle-riding Hell's Angels.[1]
>
> The fact that Blue Cheer sells doesn't alter the fact that they suck. Even they know it, and they probably get more laughs out of it than anyone. Luckily for Mercury, the Cheer rode in close enough behind Hendrix and the Cream to scrape up a bit of the stew. Being loud frequently helps sales. Being original also does. But though the emphasis is on "original material," just because it's original doesn't mean it can't be shit as well.[2]
>
> DICKIE PETERSON: There was a lot of friction between us and many of the bands in San Francisco. Not all of them—there were people there that were very nice to us, but we were sort of like the redheaded stepchildren from the back yard, you know.

"Summertime Blues" is a timeless rock 'n' roll single. Eddie Cochran first recorded it in 1958, and it has since enjoyed an extraordinary afterlife, representing every kid who has ever had to work over a summer vacation just to have enough money to go out and have a good time. The "struggle for fun" at the root of the song is a generational struggle:[3] why should a young person conform to his parents' work ethic if he cannot also be treated as an adult? "Summertime Blues" was one of many songs in the late 1950s and early 1960s that tapped into what was soon to be called the "generation gap," but it is one of the few such songs to have resonated across the decades in so many different stylistic contexts.

Blue Cheer was formed in San Francisco in 1967, amid the critical mass of incomers and seekers to the Haight. What distinguished them from other bands was their age: at nineteen, bassist Dickie Peterson was a good few years younger than most musicians in the established local bands. Blue Cheer may have shared common influences with other local musicians, but they honored those influences in a new way:

> DICKIE PETERSON: Well, there was an acid called Blue Cheer, which we took an awful lot of. Plus, our music was blues, and people—then and now—insisted that blues music must be sad. No, no, no! Hence "cheer," Blue Cheer. It was the blues but it was not sad. You know, there's blues music about driving in your Cadillac and picking up girls and dancing the night away, man, and getting drunk and carrying on and having a great time: this was the kind of blues that we were into.

The kind of blues that Blue Cheer were into was loud. With many of the other bands gaining notice for their solos and their musicianship, Blue Cheer's decibels seemed always to get the most press. They were invariably "loud, dissonant... full of feed back noises and screaming vocals,"[4] which could just as easily be read as the dismissal of the "new" rock 'n' roll back in the 1950s.

> DICKIE PETERSON: Nobody was doing what we were doing. And people liked it, it was exciting, it was brand new. We recorded a demo, and Abe Cash played it on his radio show on KMPX and started getting so many requests for it that the record companies couldn't ignore us. That's how we got signed, you know, is that people requested it. Even the people in the industry that we were working with did not understand what we were doing; they just knew they could sell it.

The "exciting, brand new thing" was the sound of the power trio, made famous by Jimi Hendrix and Cream, who had played local dancehalls and parks in the summer of 1967.[5] Blue Cheer had been playing in the city long before Cream and Jimi Hendrix showed up: in February 1967 they performed at a benefit for the Hell's Angels who were arrested in the Diggers' Parade—"a guaranteed PEACEFUL rock."[6] The connection between the Hell's Angels, Blue Cheer, and the word "peaceful" further sealed their reputation,[7] though any connections between Blue Cheer and their British power trio contemporaries were tenuous:

> DICKIE PETERSON: You know, there's no comparison, I don't think, other than there just happened to be three people in the band. I mean, Hendrix, Cream and us get compared all the time. I heard an interview with Clapton. They

"Summertime Blues"

said, "Wow, you guys created this heavy power metal music," and Eric says, "No, that wasn't us, that was Blue Cheer." And it wasn't just Hendrix, Cream and Blue Cheer; there was also the MC5, there was Iggy and The Stooges, there was The Savage Resurrection. I mean there were all kinds of people doing this. Maybe we got a lot of the kudos for it because we were the first American band to do it.

"Summertime Blues" is in a simple verse form. In Cochran's original recording there are three repetitions of a single, sixteen-bar section: six lines of text set over a static, chugging accompaniment, punctuated with a cadential pattern at the end of each line. Harmonically, the song follows roughly a typical blues structure (I-IV-I-V-I), and adheres in Cochran's version to a late 50s rockabilly aesthetic: country-influenced vocal delivery, acoustic guitar to the fore. Added to this is Cochran's over-dubbed electric guitar riff, electric bass, drums and handclaps, and a "novelty" vocal in the fourth line of every verse representing the dreaded voice of authority. In Blue Cheer's version each "novelty" response ("No dice, son, you gotta work late," "You can't use the car 'cause you didn't work a lick,'" "I'd like to help you son but you're too young to vote") is replaced with a solo line from one of the trio (guitar, bass, drums). With the addition of instrumental breaks and an extended outro, Blue Cheer transformed "Summertime Blues" from a light rockabilly classic into a "heavy, cosmic, kinetic" hippie beast:[8]

0:00	Intro	full band, half-time feel
0:12	Verse 1	guitar break at :37
0:46	Verse 2	bass break at 1:11
1:21	Verse 3	drum break at 1:45
1:55	Bridge	guitar solo shifting toward tonal area of Intro
2:15	Intro	
2:25	Transition	slow chromatic ascent (E♭-B) in bass and guitar; heavy distortion
2:57	Verse 3 reprise	full band break at 3:21
3:30	Intro	full band distortion from 3:39 to end

In Eddie Cochran's original version of "Summertime Blues," the chugging instrumental figure is almost imperceptible underneath the verses, and the repetitive handclapping figure provides the primary accompaniment underlying the vocals. In Blue Cheer's version the underlying accompaniment is similarly rhythmic, but full of static electricity. The bass is heavily distorted, and the drum emerges from that texture to amplify it even further at the end of each line of text. It is in those final phrases of punctuation that we get the sound of the full drumkit on top of the cadential phrase in the guitar and bass—cymbal crashes to match the wailing guitar.

The effect is one of emotional as well as musical amplification: the polite frustration of Eddie Cochran's original is here distorted to a level of constant high voltage, an internal buzz that erupts into an almost incoherent rage. This rage is also apparent in the double-tracked vocal, which shows its seams particularly at the ends of phrases when Dickie Peterson moves toward the outer edge of his comfort zone. Through its amplification alone, this performance of "Summertime Blues" suggests a departure from the Cochran original; with the added elements of distortion, pounding drums, and shouted lyrics, this ode to teenage angst reached a new generation of listeners who personified the growing generation gap.

Blue Cheer were not the only band covering "Summertime Blues" in the late 60s. The Who performed their version of the song at the Monterey Pop Festival, and later at Woodstock—similar in many ways to Blue Cheer's version, though with more fulsome drumming throughout, and an adherence to the "novelty" responses—and in 1970 T. Rex returned the song to its acoustic roots with an echo-laden and sympathetic version of their own.[9] For a song that had been released only ten years previously, it inspired a surprisingly high number of cover versions, proving the timelessness of the message and the adaptability of the music.

"Summertime Blues" was Blue Cheer's only chart hit, but it took them to unusual places. In February 1968 they appeared on *American Bandstand* to mime for the cameras. Judging from the post-performance interview, host Dick Clark was not entirely impressed by their music or their demeanor. Blue Cheer found a much more receptive crowd a bit further afield: in June 1968 they appeared at the Grande Ballroom in Detroit on a bill featuring the Psychedelic Stooges and the MC5.

> DICKIE PETERSON: That was the first power concert to happen in the world. And those three bands, we tore that place right to the ground, you know. And that's what they wanted. Detroit is really our kind of town.

QUICKSILVER MESSENGER SERVICE, "THE FOOL"

(Gary Duncan/David Freiberg)

David Freiberg: lead vocals, bass, viola
Gary Duncan: rhythm guitar, backing vocals
John Cipollina: lead guitar
Greg Elmore: drums

Produced by Nick Gravenites
Recorded in Los Angeles (1/68)
From the album *Quicksilver Messenger Service*, Capitol 2904 (5/68)

> The Quicksilver album is excellent. It is one of the best of the recent releases and is by far the best example on records of how a San Francisco band actually sounds when you hear it in person. This is the way it is. . . . The feeling on the album is beautiful.
>
> The Quicksilver play in a way that really projects the joy and the love these bands have at their best. . . . It turns out to be the kind of album that can be played over and over and over.[10]
>
> MARC ARNO: In fact in most instances live performances of whatever San Francisco group far exceeded the quality of their recording. The worst recordings of all, the least faithful to the group, was all the Quicksilver stuff. That was the thinnest, wateriest gruel—just the weakest representation of how strong they were live.
>
> The real importance of the QMS [sic] tour, however, is that they are playing free concerts in a number of cities. Instead of using their promotion budget from Capitol Records for big ads in trade papers and direct mailing to disc jockeys and the other traditional devices in the music business, they are using their budget to put on free concerts, aided by FM underground stations and newspapers, wherever they can. My intuition tells me it will pay off much better than the old ways and may change the whole business style.[11]

The Tarot was a familiar concept in the Haight, on the pages of the *Oracle*, in hippie pads and on street corners.[12] "The Fool" is named after the 0 card in the Tarot deck, which in some iterations shows our hero approaching a precipice, holding a rose in one hand and a wand in the other, with a dog happily walking alongside. He seems to be gazing skyward rather than beyond the precipice, suggesting an expectation of heavenly assistance should he take the next step. Whatever the motivation, "he is the spirit in search of experience."[13]

Searching for experience was a hallmark of life in the Haight in the short 60s, and a central aesthetic of the live musical event. Quicksilver Messenger Service, though living in Marin County, were fixtures on the city's dancehall scene, and played at some of the formative concerts at the Matrix, Fillmore, and Avalon that directed the development of psychedelic rock. By the time they signed to a major-label contract Quicksilver had honed their material and solidified their audience, and some of their songs had achieved legendary status. "The Fool" is one such song. It embodies the psychedelic approach to music-making, from its inception to its performance, as evidenced in guitarist John Cipollina's description of the compositional process:

> We wrote it with lots of chemicals and lots of butcher paper. We sat there and drew pictures, "Well, I don't know, so I'll give you this section now. I'm gonna make it go like this: here's a road and here's some trees and"—"oooh! Let me do the mountains! I'm gonna play mountains!" and stuff like that.[14]

These programmatic aspects of the song also place "The Fool" at an interesting intersection between psychedelia and progressive rock, with the psychedelic experience leading not only to new musical terrain, but also through cosmic revelation.

"The Fool" is what might be called a "single-movement sectionalized form" that "[expands] to enormous proportions by the inclusion of lengthy instrumental preludes, interludes, and postludes, as well as one or more contrasting bridge sections."[15] It presents a series of planned, or even programmatic, musical ideas, strung together with improvised sections, all embalmed in the twelve-minute studio version.[16] The tension here is felt in the subtle shifts of groove and texture, which alternate ultimately between what sounds like sunshine and darkness.

"The Fool" can be divided into distinct sections, each with contrasting melodic areas (A and B), and a "trip" comprising the central section. There is some repetition across sections, which gives the song a sense of inner coherence and meandering, yet logical, narrative:

0:00	Introduction	pentatonic guitar glissando; ad-lib to cadence (:43)
0:43	Section 1	A: guitar dialogue; viola countermelody
1:27		B: stepwise guitar ad-lib punctuated by jabs
2:00	Transition	
2:08	Section 2	A: lyrical viola line, disrupted by guitar jabs

"The Fool"

2:33		B: ascending guitar line, prefiguring vocal line
3:14	Bridge	extended guitar improvisation
4:31	Transition	
4:50	Section 3: Trip	transition: guitar effects, percussion, "whip" effect
5:16		A: pentatonic guitar passages
6:56		"choral" texture: entrance of wordless harmonies
7:17		B: vocal entrance, based on 2B melody. "Choral" texture continues
8:06		brief suggestion of 1B
9:24		shift to 6/8. vocal cadence; guitar arpeggios; final syllables of text spoken
9:52		Textural shift to viola over chordal guitar
10:31	Coda	Tempo change: guitar/organ interplay
11:09		Guitar ad-lib
12:04		Final cadence; dissonant feedback

If Country Joe & the Fish explored lysergic space in "Section 43," Quicksilver used the idea of lysergic experimentation to reveal metaphysical truths. The path that they take toward this revelation, in the first two sections of "The Fool," embody the character of the eponymous Tarot card, the "spirit in search of experience." With the arrival at the transition into Section 3 the texture changes: harmonically it is fairly static, with all focus turning to John Cipollina's guitar—rich with effects, disrupted by the sound of a whip, moving decisively from the "sunny" textures of the preceding four minutes into the "darker" textures of the psychedelic experience.

When the vocal enters for the B theme it is in a reprise of the melodic material from Section 2. The lyric here is cosmic: "Can you hear it in the morning, sings the golden sun/Life's song is moving ever onward, from and to the sound of one." It is a post-acid revelation, the Fool finally tuned in to the message: "one world, one truth." Singer David Freiberg strains at the limits of his range at the end of the verse, but is otherwise an effective conveyor of meaning and sensation. This vocal passage represents the post-trip epiphany, the chorus acting as an hallucinogenic reminder of the ecstatic state. There is a sense of time expanding and contracting, into and out of the trip, represented by a shift in tempo and groove, and an increase in, or absence of, studio trickery delineating the upward or downward trajectory of the experience. The text painting at the end of the lyric also suggests a revelation: a soaring upward line for "heaven's above," a descending cadential pattern for "life is love." In the end, the Fool realizes the most fundamental truth of the short 60s: "Life is love, love is life, it's love, love."

"The Fool" occupies a peculiar place in San Franciscan rock. It was clearly designed compositionally, just as "Section 43" had been, and like so many other songs in the repertoires of local bands playing in the dancehalls around the city, "The Fool" could have accommodated further sonic and improvisatory explorations. Invariably, those familiar with Quicksilver's live sets were often quick to dismiss the vinyl reproductions:

> "The Fool" takes up most of Side Two but, unfortunately, not very justifiably. It starts out carefully, waiting for the guitar to move out, spaced by some beautiful bass runs which cut into some hard-rock movements only to be lost in a series of impotent semi-buildups. Some very handsome guitar phrasing sneaks through but whatever good it does winds up buried halfway through the track. It digresses into some disappointing, ineffable routines, including a guitar-growling sequence, followed by a Claptonesque wah-wah pedal ritual. But with the addition of the vocal it picks up somewhat—the words are intoned in a middle-eastern, Hebrew cantor-like quaver. It closes out with some Yardbird "Still I'm Sad" declensions, culminating in an organ-anchored Bach-Procol Harum denouement.[17]

That reference to Procol Harum actually connects Quicksilver to the kind of prototypical "progressive rock" being developed in England by bands such as the Moody Blues, Pink Floyd, and the Nice. But where British bands were embarking on their lysergic journeys of self-discovery, Quicksilver had already done that work in the developmental years of the San Franciscan hippie scene. Quicksilver did not continue on their progressive trajectory, but "The Fool" remains a clear signpost for progressive psychedelia in the waning years of the short 60s.

Notes

1. "It Happened in 1968," *Rolling Stone* 26, February 1, 1969, p. 19.
2. Jef Jaisun, "Record Rap," *Berkeley Barb*, November 8, 1968, p. 12.
3. See Simon Frith's *Sound Effects: Youth, Leisure and the Politics of Rock* (London: Constable, 1983), p. 272.
4. RJG, "The Quick on the S.F. Scene," *Examiner*, May 26, 1968, This World p. 30. Gleason was plugging the band's *Vincebus Eruptum*, which included this very loud single—"remarkable for the fact that it is a hit"—and noted "that the liner notes are a poem written by Augustus Stanley Owsley III."
5. Bill Graham took the unprecedented step of booking Cream into the Fillmore for nearly two weeks in August 1967. Jimi Hendrix first played the Fillmore in June 1967 just before the Monterey Pop Festival, opening for Jefferson Airplane.
6. RJG, "Kingston Trio—In the Beginning," *Chronicle* February 3, 1967, p. 41.
7. Blue Cheer had another connection to the Hell's Angels: their manager was an ex-Angel named Allen "Gut" Turk, who also designed some of the band's early concert posters. The band rehearsed at the head shop that Gut ran in the Mission district.

8. Philips' ad for *Vincebus Eruptum* claimed that "Blue Cheer is heavy. Cosmic. Kinetic. It affects the visual and physical senses. Spiritually aware. Available now!" See *Rolling Stone* 8, April 6, 1968, p. 23.
9. The Who's performances of the song at Monterey and Woodstock provide interesting bookends to Blue Cheer's version, while the version captured on *Live at Leeds* (Polydor, 1970) is perhaps their definitive performance of the song. T. Rex released their version as the B-side to their single "Ride a White Swan" (Fly Records, 1970). When I asked Dickie Peterson what the difference was between Blue Cheer's version of "Summertime Blues" and the Who's, he replied, simply, "ours was better."
10. RJG, "The Quick on the S.F. Scene."
11. RJG, "Satire, Service and Sound," *Chronicle*, October 27, 1968, Datebook p. 31.
12. The practice of trusting intuition, central to the use of Tarot, was also part of the spiritual curriculum at Esalen, where for three years at the end of the 1960s Jack Hurley, Rae Hurley, and John Horler worked on reimagining the Tarot for what was eventually published as *The New Tarot Deck* (1974). Another obvious link here is the Ace of Cups, the all-female band that formed in the Haight in 1967 and who were also managed by Ron Polte. Ace of Cups were on the bill for some notable local performances: opening for Jimi Hendrix at his free concert in Golden Gate Park (1967), and along with the Sons of Champlin opening for the Band at their Fillmore residency (1969).
13. Arthur Edward Waite, *The Pictorial Key to the Tarot: Being Fragments of a Secret Tradition Under the Veil of Divination* (London: William Ryder & Son, 1911).
14. John Cipollina, quoted in William Ruhlman, "The John Cipollina Story," *Relix* vol. 14 (1987).
15. Edward Macan, *Rocking the Classics: English Progressive Rock and the Counterculture* (Oxford: Oxford University Press, 1997), p. 42.
16. Available contemporary live recordings may differ slightly from the studio version, but they are rarely much longer.
17. Barry Gifford, Record Review: *Quicksilver Messenger Service, Rolling Stone* 13, July 6, 1968, p. 20.

8. 1969

I don't know if what we were allowed to do here, we were allowed to experiment with, we could have done anywhere else. I don't think it would have worked anywhere else.[1]

There was no love in the Haight-Ashbury, even in its days of relative innocence, only the beginnings of hate, tentatively expressed in the rejection of loving parents. We have seen the hate grow, to be expressed in murder and sadism too shocking for description.[2]

For the last time: There *is* no "San Francisco Sound."[3]

Bucolic Marin and Sonoma Counties were by 1969 full of hippies, and no one expected them to be left alone. At Donald McCoy's Rancho Olompali compound, county, state, and federal narcotics agents discovered a stash of methamphetamine, LSD, hashish, and marijuana, and entered into what the *Chronicle* dubbed "the jolliest, happiest, least uptight raid in history." Some twenty-five children were there being taught by a former nun; among the children were two of Sgt. Sunshine's own.[4]

The compound's residents, the Chosen Family, moved into the same mansion where the Grateful Dead had lived for six weeks in the spring of 1966: the site of legendary house concerts, parties, and the photo shoot for the back cover of the band's *Aoxomoxoa* (1969). The Chosen Family had existed there in relative peace, baking hundreds of loaves of bread for the Diggers to distribute in the city, and—crucially—maintaining a "closed" commune. This was the key distinction between Olompali and Morning Star. The press interest in communal living, in alternative communal education, in the crossovers from establishment to hippie life, was never disinterested, and when the main house at Rancho Olompali burned down in February 1969 reports of the loss of the "celebrated hippie mansion" were emblematic of this.[5]

When, some months later, Lou Gottlieb deeded his Morning Star Ranch to God, questions about the commune's "hospitality" took on a more philosophical bent.[6] Gottlieb was facing more fines than he could pay out of his own bank account, and knew that the court would have difficulty seizing land from a divine being. Gottlieb resorted to offering his last earthly possession—his Bösendorfer piano—against the remaining debt.[7] Shortly thereafter, it was announced that the Chosen Family had fallen behind in their rent at Olompali, and the ranch had returned to the hands of its owner.[8] Late that summer it was left to Dr. David Smith to explain to delegates at the American Association of Planned Parenthood Physicians luncheon that flower children had not begun adapting to straight society, but rather had moved to communes, both urban and rural. The Haight might now be seen as a violent, "teen-aged ghetto," but, Smith said, "the hip movement has greatly increased." Smith and a research assistant had visited many of the communes in northern California and found that most people there were vegetarians, favored natural childbirth, eschewed marriage certificates, birth certificates, and Social Security numbers. And while those that were drug-free were the "most stable," that did not suggest a "revival of the Puritan Christian ethic."[9]

Other hippies stayed in the city and found a new (old) bohemia (again). The *Chronicle* found some former flower children disrobing in topless bars amid a rash of new shops along Grant Avenue catering to hippie fashions. Allen Ginsberg, Peter Orlovsky, and Lawrence Ferlinghetti now saw North Beach as "a mixture of the old-timers, the gentler kids and something new."[10] North Beach was unlikely to become another Haight, however: the rents were too high, if only to prevent hippies and "drug freaks" from descending in their droves.[11]

Dr. David Smith announced the temporary reopening of the Haight Clinic to deal primarily with the epidemic of speed abuse in the neighborhood. Having secured enough private funding, Smith again stressed that drug problems were a city-wide problem, and that his clinic had still received no funds from the City Hall. He called on city leaders to take "an intelligent, contemporary, humane approach" to the treatment of addiction, and to see speed abuse and attendant violence as a problem that extended far beyond the boundaries of the Haight.[12]

The hands-off attitude of the mayor and the Health Department prompted some to question whether the Haight could ever be restored. Long-time residents spoke of the "disaster area" that the neighborhood had become, of how "innocent people" were trapped in a cycle of violence and threat.

> Is it official policy, tacit or not, to write off the Haight? To let the depravity there burn itself out? To assume, for cold, administrative purposes, that everything in the Haight is vile, so the hell with it—just contain it?
>
> The Mayor and a retinue once made a dainty tour of flowerland and saw nothing, nothing! Dr. Ellis Sox's inspectors made a sweep and saw nothing, nothing! What will it take—a grand jury investigation?[13]

With a certain predictability, three months later the media turned its attention to the dangers of speed, by presenting stories about wayward young persons led to the Haight and injected with a drug so powerful they lose all control. Focus was on "a style of drug abuse unprecedented in its destructiveness of young, white, middle-class men and women," the violence associated with the drug culture, and the paranoia and psychosis caused by its use. David Smith was quoted extensively about the cases he had seen of methamphetamine abuse, and the Haight continued to be a byword for depravity.[14]

Out on the ballroom circuit, Gleason bemoaned the loss of a great opportunity: to go beyond the "calcified" structure of a weekend show into new uncharted territory. The Longshoremen's Hall had begun holding regular dances, but nobody was dancing any more; instead there was the standard rock concert, where people "come to look, not to participate."[15] Yet on February 19, heads responded to their elaborately printed invitations to something called the Frontiers of Science Celestial Synapse. According to *Rolling Stone* it was "the best vibrations and some of the best music the Fillmore West had seen in some time." The Grateful Dead's set, in particular, was "like one of the old Ken Kesey Acid Tests . . . only it's less hectic and confused. It's fucking amazing." The event was hosted by Don Hamrick and the Frontiers of Science, a commune based in Harbin Hot Springs in northern Lake County.[16] The commune used the term "synapse" to suggest "a mass meeting of minds, parallel to the linking-up of brain cells that makes thought possible." Whatever the reason, the Dead's four-hour show—"a flowing improvisatory set of new material"—recaptured all that Gleason had feared was lost from the scene.[17]

A few weeks later there was a different fear to reckon with, carried by the smell of tear gas along Telegraph Avenue, by state legislators' suggestion to "wall in the colleges and universities," by Hubert Humphrey's admission that "nobody knows the answer" to campus unrest—dangers to the very fabric of society.[18]

There were three different music stories to report in March. In what must surely be the first instance of a band giving away their music, the Sons of Champlin recorded a single called "Jesus is Coming" and sent it to 400 radio stations, "to be used by people any way they want to use it." The band also offered free copies to anyone writing in and asking for one, which elicited over 5,000 requests from around the world. This predated the release of their first major-label double-LP, a type of concept embracing their "vision of what paradise on this earth can be when people play music and love each other. We want to give away a vision of what life can be like. We're trying to find God."[19]

Second was the San Francisco debut of Janis Joplin and her new band. Big Brother's *Cheap Thrills* had been on the *Billboard* charts for months over the winter, during which time Joplin split from the band.[20] Though her career was the biggest industry news out of the city, reviews of Joplin's solo career never matched the heights of her time with Big Brother. Her first performance at Winterland was so underwhelming, the audience did not call her back for an encore, and Gleason found himself thinking

> of the other times in that hall when Janis, with the band the critics didn't like, the band the New York taste makers said was out of tune and couldn't keep up to her, brought the audience screaming to its feet with the kind of performance you remember all your life.
>
> It isn't like that now. Janis may still live here but the whole style of her thing has changed and is no longer San Francisco but New York.[21]

Third, the tale of a happy throng in the park listening to rock music and celebrating the return of spring. Immediately below it: the headline "Some Ugly Moments in the Sun," accompanying the tale of a "long-haired, whiskered youth wearing hippie beads," lighting firecrackers and resisting arrest, whereupon a crowd formed, sirens wailed, and a riot was broadly averted.[22] At least the paper saw the return of hippies to the park as "relatively benign," though the police presence kept an edge on things. The new gatherings in Speedway Meadow were organized by the nonprofit Thirteenth Tribe, both to give new bands a forum to perform, and to foster a revival of the kind of peaceful gatherings that marked the birth of the hippie scene two years previously. Bill Graham was there and was heard to say, "This is genuine. After all the tragedies of the Haight, thank God there is still some life left."[23]

And there was still dancehall news to report. Gleason's description of the Dead's Easter Sunday concert evoked a perfect night at the Avalon:

> The band went through one of those series of tension-and-release strictures leading up to searing climaxes and then relaxing to long, cooking kind of rhythmic sections which reminded me of the Dizzy Gillespie big band, when the whole group would get all kinds of indescribable goodies going on like a huge bubbling stew. Garcia lays those butter tones over the driving bass lines Lesh plays (which are not really bass lines at all in the ordinary sense, but a kind of bass counter line to Garcia's lead) while the two drummers and the rest whack out a rhythmically complicated but totally integrated pulse that just keeps driving like some great electrical machine.
>
> When it was over, the audience didn't want to stop. They cheered and whistled and clapped and then began stomping their feet on the floor.... When the Dead play like that, the audience dances. And when the hall has groups like that, the people come.[24]

Bill Graham began another protracted battle, this time over the proposed sale of the Fillmore West to the Howard Johnson Corporation, which planned to raze the building and open a motel-restaurant in its place. Gleason saw the Fillmore West as a cultural center and as worthy of protection as the beaches and redwood forests on the outskirts of the city. He reminded his readers that in the years since Graham began his operations—first in the old Fillmore, then on the site of the Carousel—millions of people attended dances, and there were "NO RIOTS, NO FIGHTS, NO SHOOTING. Think about that for a minute."

> Doesn't it really make you think the thing is worthwhile? Perhaps? Doesn't it seem odd that all the fears turned out to be groundless? Instead of letting the place be sold out from under him, the city should give Bill Graham a medal

for creating a recreational facility without peer in this country which has done a moral, a cultural and a practical good past measurement for this city and its young people.[25]

Out on the other side of town, Chet Helms announced the return of the Family Dog at the Great Highway, the former slot car raceway at Playland at the Beach. This was intended to be the country's "first musical environment sensorium," creating a party space not necessarily focused on the band, but "the ultimate environment" for audience enjoyment. Helms planned to book not only rock bands but also classical music and ballet, with admission charges set at $3.[26] The opening event was headlined by Jefferson Airplane and the Charlatans, in one of their final performances—a symbolic end to what had begun at the Red Dog Saloon four years earlier. When the hall finally opened, however, Gleason was underwhelmed:

> The new Dog house is really only the old Edgewater, the dance hall going back to the '40s. . . . The dance floor is now a squatting room for the audience. Nobody dances. There is a bandstand at each end so low you can't see the musicians. The patio in the back is pleasant and a great relief to the hot house atmosphere of the main room. The other lounges are resting places sans couches or chairs and occasionally with a clutch of conga drummers in action. . . . Inside, the sound was excellent on the main floor and rather spotty in the balcony where fans hung from the pillars and sat on the railings precariously.[27]

What Bill Graham was now doing at the Fillmore West went some distance beyond weekly dance concerts. On Tuesday nights, before the new bands showcase, there was a regular basketball game between the Fillmore West Wonders and a challenger; and in March, Graham began regular folk dancing sessions, led by a hoedown band.[28] But over at the Straight Theater, they were having trouble filling the house:

> There is nobody on Haight Street at 8:30 on a Friday night. Repeat. There is nobody on Haight Street at 8:30 on a Friday night. . . . Nobody, including hippies, goes on the street in the Haight at night. It's over because it's through.[29]

And then there was People's Park.

> While we sat in our rooms and played records and . . . watched the TV, they shot people in Berkeley, not in self-defense even, but for standing on a corner. . . . Can nobody stop the madness? Anywhere? There was not revolution in Berkeley. There was a muddy lot, let lie fallow by the University for months. Ordinary people . . . made it into a thing of beauty. Then in order to protect themselves from political attack, its legal owners erected a fence and called in the National Guard to play on the children's playthings. And they shot people in the street

in Berkeley on Black Thursday in a test to see how far the society would go to enforce a technical right.... An elected official on radio said "we'll fight them with guns" though God only knows what he was talking about.[30]

In a stark juxtaposition with the struggle for People's Park, over at the Berkeley High School auditorium Baba Ram Dass—formerly Richard Alpert, associate of Timothy Leary—was speaking to a large crowd about his existential odyssey in India, in a preview of the month-long workshop he would be leading at Esalen.[31] Echoing Ram Dass' signature phrase, "be here now," all around the Bay, artists and musicians and audiences gathered together for benefit concerts for the People's Park Bail Fund, and also, in Bill Graham's words, "to stand up and be counted. We have to say where we're at. This is important." Gleason tied this sense of urgency to the formation in 1965 of the Artists' Liberation Front and saw that the "spectre of a police state is haunting us." He said:

> The rock bands, the jazz groups, the park people and those who have been victimized by the state's force are my people. I stand with them. Art always wins because it is in favor of life. Force always loses because it is in favor of death. The concerts being held will be warm and loving affairs. They always are when the artists and the audience are one.[32]

In the end, Winterland wasn't big enough to hold the crowd,[33] and other benefits around the Bay Area further united the community in common purpose.

The horror of the Berkeley attack was nowhere more powerfully encapsulated than by a letter to the *Chronicle* from Professor Thomas Parkinson of UC Berkeley, who began quite simply:

> On Tuesday, May 21, 1969, Berkeley, a city in the United States, a university town with many suburban dwellers as well as the faculty, staff, and students of the University, was attacked from the air by toxic gas from a helicopter.
>
> It was the first city within the continental limits of the United States to be assaulted by a helicopter flown by a member of the National Guard and under the orders of an elected official, the sheriff of the county. The gas was sprayed into an area where 700 people were confined by the National Guard in close formation.[34]

This attack on an American city "by an arm of its own government," was the most extreme expression of the gulf between left and right, and a symbolic act that galvanized political activism in Berkeley well into the twenty-first century.[35]

To fill the gap left by the Monterey Pop Festival, representatives of the San Francisco pop scene announced plans for a Wild West Festival, to be held in San Francisco in

August.[36] Over a weekend there would be free concerts in Golden Gate Park and night-time concerts in Kezar Stadium. All local bands were said to be involved in the planning, and the musical offerings would include not only local rock bands but also "ethnic music" and cultural activities.[37] With such widespread cooperation, what could possibly go wrong?

The idea of "free" concerts had spread from San Francisco to London, New York, and Chicago as part of a new attitude toward commerce, and "a rejection of the value system of the Establishment." Moreover, free concerts—free admission, no payment to musicians—had historically worked as promotional tools, and not infringed on the success of the dancehall concerts, in San Francisco or elsewhere.[38] By the beginning of June plans for the Wild West Festival had begun to gel, and benefit concerts were duly held in the city's ballrooms. The San Francisco Music Council was looking to underwrite the festival's preliminary administrative costs, and could also promise that all of the city's major rock bands, along with about sixty minor ones, had agreed to take part.[39]

Not everyone could afford to work for free. The staff of the *Berkeley Barb* were on strike, and took the opportunity to seize the means of production from the paper's founder, Max Scherr, and publish *The Barb On Strike*, in which they called their erstwhile boss "a capitalist pig."[40] *Rolling Stone* couldn't really understand it:

> Here was the staff of an underground paper, *on strike*, carrying picket signs, demanding a better deal from the boss. Life often imitates bad art. This was the real thing—the staff of the Berkeley Barb, no less, on strike against Max Scherr, the grandest old man of underground publishing, whose four-year-old paper was one of the oldest and hardiest of its type, and perhaps—for better or for worse—*the* underground style-setter. . . . The Berkeley Barb was at the vanguard of the Revolution . . . on the side of the people, struggling to get them out from under the oppressive thumb of the *fascist/racist/capitalist pig AmeriKan system*.[41]

Not to be outdone, the light show workers went on strike against Chet Helms and Bill Graham, demanding a decent wage, publicity for their work, and a recognition of their newly formed Light Artists' Guild.[42] On their first night picketing outside the Family Dog, Chet Helms provided them with the electricity necessary to project lights on the outside of the building,[43] but the picketers' exchange with Bill Graham was rather less constructive. Graham argued that the audience paid to see the bands, not the light shows, and the loss of the light show would not impact his business. In hippie fashion the light show artists and representatives of the local rock industry entered into an open discussion at the Family Dog, which ended explosively. Stephen Gaskin accused Graham of having made "a choice between love and money. You've got our money, so you can't have our love.... You've used dramatics today to fuck over a lot of heads with your emotional trips." *Rolling Stone*'s report betrayed a certain bias: "Graham, long-ago ostracized from the hip community as a profiteer and the target of as much abuse as respect...," opposite "Chet Helms... the mystic/Texan who has tried... to move his operation away from the big-name band and dance/concert hall concept towards a free-form environmental theater, opened the meeting by casting the I Ching."[44] The end result was the resolution of the labor dispute, and assurance from Bill Graham that he would close his Fillmore West operations and leave the city on January 2, 1970.[45]

Graham's decision to leave was part of the "paranoia" seeping into every area of contemporary cultural life. The Wild West Festival had encountered similar problems, but managed to stave off disaster, at least temporarily. The headlining acts for the three evening shows at Kezar Stadium were finally announced: Janis Joplin, Jefferson Airplane, and Sly and the Family Stone.[46] Other details emerged about

> what may well be the world's farthest-out light show: Beamed into the sky by a bank of searchlights lined on one level of Twin Peaks, banked by a row of cars and *their* headlights topped by Moog synthesizers controlling the lights and horns, while pulsar wires connect the mountain to various large office buildings around the city. On signal from the Moogs, they too, will light up, some of them becoming light shows. And radio stations will wire the entire city into the mammoth display.[47]

Then, within days, the Festival was cancelled outright. The specter of commerce had reared its head, and some in the hip community—the Mime Troupe, anonymous people calling themselves the Haight Commune—wanted to know who was making money out of the festival, and how much; where the money was going, if not to the artists and craftspeople taking part; and called for a national boycott of the Wild West Festival. They charged that festival organizers had to all purposes colluded with the city's power structure, and exploited the hip community throughout the planning process. No matter that organizing committee members insisted that the festival was intended to help the hip community; the meetings between committee and public were ultimately held captive by radical groups purporting to speak for the hip community.[48] As Gleason, part of the Council, reported:

> [The Wild West] was designed to show the world that San Francisco could have a festival without a riot by being non-commercial, non-profit, and offering as much free entertainment in the park as possible. Artists of all kinds responded magnificently.
> Then the San Francisco Mime Troupe, boll weevils looking for an audience and a stage, attacked the Festival as a commercial middle-class shuck.... The

naïve organizers of the Wild West . . . tried to come to terms with the non-musical politicos . . . but could not, since the basic stance was "we want the festival to be free and we want the profits."

Apparently there is no place for dreams any more. The frustrations in this society have produced a situation where reason has been replaced by uncut paranoia, where the thrill is in the act of destruction, not of creation and where, since they don't believe in themselves or their own good intentions, some people cannot accept anyone else's.[49]

Rolling Stone was equally angry, calling the festival "the stillborn child of incompetence, paranoia, and half-baked political speed-freaks." There was certainly incompetent management at work and city officials were too slow and restrictive in their support of the event, but charges of profiteering from the hip community were wildly overstated: the festival owed $13,000 in loans, which would only be met by a series of benefit concerts. The "crazies" who accused the festival of acting as "the pimp merchants of bread and circuses" in the city were themselves "the rip-off artists" in this scenario.[50]

One positive result of the Wild West fiasco was the opening of the Family Dog seven days a week. By October, regular weekend dance concerts were supplemented by alternative entertainment, hosted by members of The Common—basically members of the hip community and associates of Chet Helms.[51] Each Tuesday at an open meeting members of the Common were invited to propose ideas for events, which were supported or rejected by other members of the Common, then hosted by whoever had the original idea. Some events were financially successful, such as the religious evening with Alan Watts, Malachi, Stephen Gaskin, and the Floating Lotus Magic Opera Company; others compounded the Family Dog's financial difficulties, such as the flea market that attracted only eight people. In the end, Helms had to insist on the power of hip veto, with energies directed not merely toward filling the weekly calendar, but toward finding a successful economic model for the venture.[52] "Hip community" and "successful economic model" are phrases not generally uttered in the same breath, particularly with reference to the event taking place on the other side of the country one August weekend.

The Bay Area at Woodstock

No one in this country in this century had ever seen a "society" so free of repression. Everyone swam nude in the lake, balling was easier than getting breakfast, and the "pigs" just smiled and passed out the oats. For people who had never glimpsed the intense communitarian closeness of a militant struggle—People's Park or Paris in the month of May or Cuba—Woodstock must always be their model of how good we will all feel after the revolution.[53]

BANANA: We were playing in some bar in Baltimore on the Woodstock weekend. And I have met people who have told me, "Hey man, you changed my life, man, your set at Woodstock, it was incredible, I've never been the same since." We were in *Baltimore*.

Three days of peace and music in Bethel, New York. The mythology of Woodstock is difficult to separate from its reality, and memories of the festival are often colored by memories of the film. The iconic performances preserved on celluloid—Richie Havens, Jimi Hendrix, Crosby, Stills & Nash, Country Joe McDonald—exist without a sense of the weekend's chronology.[54] The "triumph" of Woodstock, the sense that it realized a utopian dream and the promise of the flower children, denies evidence to the contrary—that it was a failed commercial enterprise and an often unpleasant experience for many of the performers and audience who were there.[55]

If the film of Monterey Pop launched the careers of Janis Joplin and Jimi Hendrix, the Woodstock documentary showed them as weary, older, and more ramshackle. Jimi Hendrix's performance of the Star-Spangled Banner may be a lasting moment of the 1960s, but it was part of an under-rehearsed set at a most unsociable hour of Monday morning. Woodstock did, however, provide a platform for established acts and emerging Bay Area talent.

The arc of the festival was initially envisioned as an acoustic first day, moving into an electric American second day, then a British third day.[56] Among those planning and building the festival were the Fillmore East's John Morris and Chip Monck, lighting designer for Monterey Pop and later for the Altamont Festival.[57] There were other connections between Woodstock's production office and the West Coast: the festival's head of security, Wes Pomeroy, was deputy sheriff of San Mateo County and later Berkeley's chief of police; he was aided by Wavy Gravy and the Hog Farm. Bill Graham remained resolutely distant, offering the most basic of advice if asked, though it was through his insistence that the little-known Santana was booked for the festival weekend.[58]

In the end, the festival didn't follow that three-day arc: Country Joe's acoustic set on the first day was entirely unplanned and fairly unremarkable until he launched into the "Fish cheer";[59] Carlos Santana took mescaline on Saturday morning, expecting to be on stage much later that night, and was still heavily psychedelicized when the band were pushed onto stage at 2:00 in the afternoon; the Grateful Dead's Saturday night show was stalled continually by equipment problems and it was, according to band lore, one of their worst performances; Creedence Clearwater Revival's set was delayed by the Dead, and John Fogerty subsequently refused to have any footage included in the documentary film; Janis Joplin was drunk before she hit the stage Saturday night; Sly Stone was already exhibiting a contrary disposition;[60] Jefferson Airplane expected to play on Saturday night, but didn't get onstage until 8:30 a.m. Sunday morning;

Country Joe and the Fish performed on Sunday afternoon, but it is Country Joe's solo appearance that is most remembered.

Rolling Stone duly summarized performances by the local bands:

> Grateful Dead . . . climbed out onto a limb with hopes that the audience would reach up to them; it didn't. Creedence Clearwater, clear and tight; a static Janis Joplin, . . . her back-up band just that; Sly and the Family Stone, apart in their grandeur, won the battle [of the bands], carrying it to their own majestically freaked-out stratosphere.[61]

When Gleason finally looked back on Woodstock, he stressed that one of the most important things that happened—and one of the things that the press did not comment on—was Pete Townshend booting Abbie Hoffman off the stage during the Who's set. Gleason heard that Hoffman intended "to appear at every festival he can get to to protest commerciality. This is more of the nonsense by the politicos about exploiting the people's culture. It should be interesting to see how successful he is."[62]

The impact of Woodstock on the subsequent careers of Sly and the Family Stone and Santana cannot be denied; the mythology of the Woodstock Festival has only increased since 1969, and it still remains shorthand for utopian bliss, for peaceful coexistence, and for the power of music to unify a population equal in size to the third-largest city in New York. The forces involved in its creation and execution could only have converged on Max Yasgur's farm, but it was a commercial enterprise, not an intentionally "free" festival; the incorporation of the "West Coast" vibe, and the performances by the Who, Jimi Hendrix, and Ravi Shankar added to the sense of a continuation of Monterey Pop, yet the beneficiaries of the film and recording rights were neither the musicians nor those in their communities.[63] And although it is rather less easily accessible than the Haight-Ashbury, Woodstock's mystique still draws pilgrims to Bethel, New York in search of the elusive hippie vibe well into the long 60s.[64]

There was reason to question the future of the "giant festival" in the wake of the collapse of Wild West and the "threats of violence by extremists who, despite the nonprofit nature of the affair, insisted on regarding it in the same light as the commercial festivals." Gleason maintained that the free festival was the best option for avoiding danger: "It is an interesting fact that activist elements consider all of the aesthetically valuable pop music as their personal property and feel defrauded when they have to pay to hear it."[65]

On what would have been Wild West weekend, the Fillmore West and Family Dog on the Great Highway held what amounted to a giant party. Early the next week at the Family Dog there was The Great S.F. Light Jam, featuring thirteen different light shows and, intriguingly, "taped music from three years of unissued tapes from the Matrix," including the Dead, Airplane, Quicksilver, Big Brother, and Steve Miller.[66] And the Big Sur Folk Festival brought thousands down the coast for a beautiful and peaceful weekend of music on the Esalen lawn.[67] In addition to organizer Joan Baez, it featured former Beau Brummel Sal Valentino, the Incredible String Band, Crosby, Stills, Nash and Young, and Joni Mitchell singing a new song she had written for Woodstock.[68] A free festival of another kind was headlined by Country Joe and the Sons of Champlin, held in the lower recreation yard of San Quentin prison. Not music for all, surely, but music for those who wouldn't normally get it:[69] music for free, but not for the free.

And what is the opposite of free? A concert tour grossing $2 million for the Rolling Stones. An unprecedented sum—but at a press conference in Hollywood, Mick Jagger played the innocent abroad, stressing that he was unaware the Stones' ticket prices were double that of other bands. Gleason wasn't buying it: bands had long been able to negotiate prices for seats or total gross, making Jagger's comments "a complete cop-out." The Stones' promise of a free concert at the end of the tour "doesn't do much for the people on the West Coast," however, and he was surely not wrong there.[70]

The House Select Committee on Crime heard four days of testimony on the pattern of drug use in the Haight. The primary message, relayed by Roger Smith from the Haight Clinic, was that the social use of marijuana and LSD had shifted to an upswing in the use of speed and heroin. Smith felt that it was "something of a paradox that the Federal government is quite willing to provide funds to do research, to identify the needs, but will provide almost nothing once the problem is clearly defined." The connection between drug use and crime was made similarly clear. Smith reserved his disdain for the city's Public Health Department, which was failing to address the problem in any meaningful way. In response Dr. Ellis D. Sox insisted that it was a problem of "community attitudes. I refuse to accept responsibility alone. . . . I think the community as a whole, and its attitude toward drug abuses, is at the heart of the situation." So he urged more federal funds be spent researching (again) the Haight's drug problem.[71]

Over Hallowe'en weekend a collection of hip "tribal chiefs" gathered in Jemez Springs, New Mexico, for a "Sympowowsium." Nearly sixty people, including Ken Kesey, Michael Lang (Woodstock), John Sebastian, Rock Scully (Grateful Dead), and Tom Law (Hog Farm) gathered together to discuss "the architecture of mass gatherings." Discussing the lessons that they had learned individually and collectively from Chicago and Woodstock, the group imagined ways in which to take the idea of a "festival" into more progressive directions—geodesic domes, "grace as opposed to efficiency," "garbage consciousness"—and the practicalities of feeding the thousands and comforting the freak-outs.[72]

On the same day that the transbay BART tube was opened to pedestrians for a sneak preview of the underground connector between the city and Oakland, fourteen Native Americans arrived on Alcatraz and "reclaimed" the island for the Indians. The fourteen successful squatters issued a proclamation offering to buy the prison for "$824 in glass beads and red cloth, a precedent set by the white man's purchase of a similar island 300 years ago." According to their proclamation, Alcatraz was well-suited to serve as an Indian reservation, as it "is isolated from modern facilities . . . has no fresh running water . . . has inadequate sanitation facilities . . . and [Native Americans have] always been held as prisoners and kept dependent upon others."[73] The invasion only lasted one night, after which the fourteen casually turned themselves in.[74]

In 1969 the former prison buildings on Alcatraz were in a state of acute disrepair, and the only inhabitants of the island were a contract security officer, his wife, and three patrolmen. When the same protesters headed a team of more than eighty Native Americans, representing more than twenty tribes, onto Alcatraz in the dead of night on November 20, and declared it "free Indian land," they were assisted by the island's inhabitants in finding suitable shelter and avoiding certain environmental hazards. They were allowed one delivery of food, in the assumption that they would agree to leave the island (again) the following day. The occupying force proceeded to spray-paint slogans around the island—"You are now on Indian land," "Warning: Keep Off Indian Property"—and scattered across the island to find hiding places, should Federal marshals come looking for them.[75]

The following day the "invaders" had been joined by more protesters.[76] What the occupation sought was something fundamental: for ships entering the Golden Gate to see Indian land, and "thus be reminded of the true history of this nation." The movement's proclamation stated:

> The choice now lies with the American government either to use violence upon us as before to remove us from the Great Spirit's land or to institute a real change in its dealings with the American Indians.[77]

The kinship the hippies felt with Native Americans extends back to the Trips Festival in 1966, when Stewart Brand announced that "America needs Indians." By 1968 Brand had directed his attention to more universal matters, publishing *The Whole Earth Catalog*, which marked its first anniversary with a thorough celebration in the pages of *Rolling Stone*.[78]

The Rolling Stones' concert at the Oakland Coliseum on November 9 had "interesting sociological implications." The Stones' crew apparently milled around encouraging people, in what Gleason saw as no uncertain terms, to dance in the aisles and crowd the stage. Bill Graham and one of the Stones' people entered into an altercation as a result, but clearly "Mick is so insecure that he cannot believe people dig him unless he is threatened by a mob at the lip of the stage. It really is a shame."[79] It is difficult to read that statement without a sense of foreboding, given the details of the Stones' subsequent concert in the Bay Area.

A rumor began circulating that the Stones had wanted to perform at the recent political rally in the Polo Grounds.[80] Some radicals believed the Stones to be politically engaged, but others felt that "it would be impossible to overestimate the lack of knowledge on the part of the Stones . . . of what actually is going on in this country. They have no connection with nor any demonstrated understanding of American youth or dissenting adults."[81] This led to Gleason's conveying disinterestedly the news that the Stones were planning to play a free concert in December at Golden Gate Park, perhaps to be filmed for cinematic release, though no plans had been confirmed.[82]

Within days of that piece the *Los Angeles Free Press* had announced that the Stones' free concert was on, and encouraged everyone to travel to San Francisco to enjoy it. Still no applications for permits had been filed, but the lineup for the concert had been announced as including the Dead, Dr. John, "possibly" The Band, and Ali Akbar Khan. Proceeds of the film, to be directed by Haskell Wexler, would go to "groups that do things free." The Hell's Angels were going "to staff a truck with free ice and free beer," and there would be appearances by the Mime Troupe and "representatives of ethnic groups." More pragmatic columnists thought it "curious that legalities have not yet been settled, since a representative of the Stones' management was in town for that purpose at the end of last week," reminding readers that the American Federation of Musicians would need to be involved in any negotiations for broadcast rights or film distribution, and so far had not been. These concerns were compounded by growing estimates of the crowd and lack of details about any arrangements for accommodation and food.[83]

One week before the intended concert Gleason was still asking if the Stones were "seriously going to appear free." His concerns stemmed from the "confusing" fact that their (late) request for a permit to the Park and Recreation People was withdrawn around the time that the Stones, in New York, were announcing their free concert. This coincided with a telegraph sent by The Mime Troupe to KSAN, the *Chronicle*, and Gleason, stating that they would not appear unless all the TV and film money went to the Weathermen Defense fund.[84] There were rumors of a 600-acre spot in Marin County that was available for the concert, but by this point there was surely not enough time to set up adequate facilities. The entire story "has really been masterfully mismanaged," and the many problems that had already befallen the Stones' current tour—delays, sound problems, ticket prices—were reason enough not to believe that a free concert would actually happen.[85]

City officials and Stones band management were due to meet to discuss the proposed free concert, but there was little chance that the concert would be held

1969

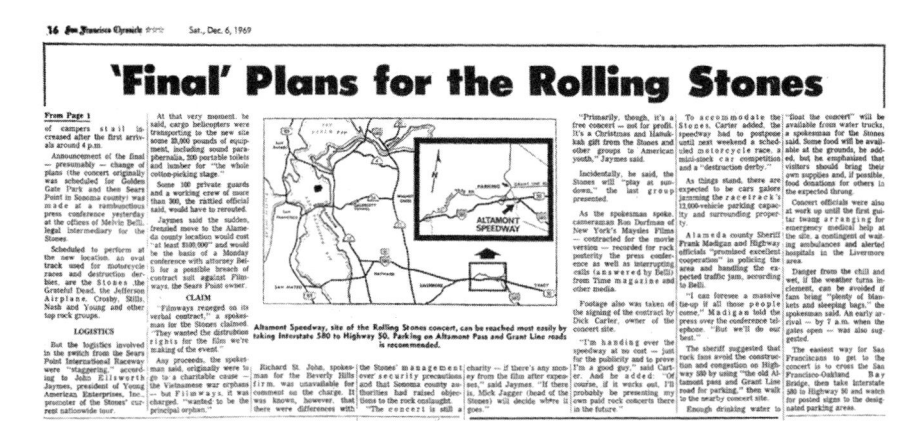

8.1 A map to the hinterlands.

in the park or the alternative Speedway Meadow: most of the Parks and Recreation Department were against the very idea, and in the absence of any formal application for permission, it was already too late to make other arrangements for a big enough outdoor venue. By December 1 the only other band confirmed for the Stones concert was the Grateful Dead.[86] Three days later the venue was confirmed as Sears Point Raceway in Marin County, featuring the Dead and Jefferson Airplane, with proceeds from the recording, TV, and movies going to "victims of the Vietnam War." With so little advance notice, the stage crews were facing a "three-day blitz," and organizers had appealed to the audience not to travel to Sears Point until the morning of the concert. The gates there would open at 7:00 a.m., overnight camping was prohibited, and no food would be available.[87] The next day, Gleason reiterated: "Be sure you have food, water and transportation, baby." He heard that Haskell Wexler would not be there to film the event, and that a sound system was being put together "by the pooled efforts of the Bay Area sound men," big enough for the music to be heard "over a site large enough to hold 250,000 people."[88] Then, finally, on the morning of the concert, the *Chronicle* published the news that the free concert had "shifted to a new location in the Alameda county hinterlands."

Despite the "staggering" logistics involved in transporting a stage and all sound equipment from one place to another, the final, definite, location for the Stones' free concert was Altamont Speedway, ten miles east of Livermore. The reason for the move was—according to Stones management—simply that Filmways, the corporate owners of Sears Point, had reneged on their verbal agreement, and demanded distribution rights for the concert film. The project would still benefit charity, but the direction of any revenue was now to be decided by Mick Jagger. The owner of Altamont Speedway, Dick Carter, offered the location in a magnanimous gesture, adding that "if it works out, I'll probably be presenting my own paid rock concerts there in the future."[89]

Altamont

Altamont. The word conjures up an event which was more costly to rock and roll than any single day in the history of entertainment. No other leisure-time activity has that dark a cloud over it. We've never been able to wipe that stain from our record.... It will always be something for the critics of rock and roll to use. You can't let all these people gather *here* for a concert. They may hurt each other. Look at *Altamont*.[90]

But for the stabbing, all appeared peaceful at the concert by the Rolling Stones and other members of the Rock 'n Roll Royalty, including the Jefferson Airplane and the Grateful Dead. The record-breaking crowd, probably the largest in the history of Northern California, was for the most part orderly, but enthusiastic.... When the charitable donation is made, the spectators yesterday will have the satisfaction of knowing they played unpaid extra roles in a motion picture.[91]

A lot depended on where you were sitting. The *Examiner*'s morning-after report on the Altamont concert marveled at the warm vibes and peaceful spirit of the audience, while a young photographer perched on the lighting rig witnessed Hell's Angels leap en masse into the audience and "pick out persons and clobber them to the ground," repeatedly—it was the one occasion when he actually hoped to see a Tactical squad.[92] People arriving for the concert in the morning were stuck in a thirty-mile-long traffic jam; the California Highway Patrol impounded over 200 cars parked illegally on roadways and private property. Denise Jewkes of the Ace of Cups, five months pregnant and standing on the stage, saw many beer bottles flying around, but not the one that fractured her skull. A hit-and-run driver plowed into a group of young people sitting around a campfire: two died, two were critically injured. Three babies were born at the concert site;[93] one man died in the Aqueduct canal. And the Hell's Angels killed a young man named Meredith Hunter.[94]

Ralph Gleason saw Hell's Angels beating people at the edge of the stage during Santana's set; saw Marty Balin leap off the stage to try to stop a fight during the Jefferson Airplane's set; and more stage area fighting that culminated in Meredith Hunter's death. Some stagehands still bear the scars:

> MARC ARNO: *Gimme Shelter* didn't show one one-hundredth of the violence that took place. The Jefferson Airplane, very progressive, had a black roadie. I found him lying beaten unconscious between two trucks behind the stage. I was trying to drag him out of there and a voice behind me said, "You leave our meat alone." And the Hell's Angels didn't beat me up; they kicked the shit out of me until I woke up being carried out of there myself.

The film crew saw it all:

> Maysles tapped the cameraman on the shoulder and said: "Don't shoot that. That's ugly. We only want beautiful things." The cameraman's response was quick: "How can you possibly say that? Everything here is so ugly."[95]

There was certainly enough to see offstage:

> There are the dancing beaded girls, the Christlike young men, and smiling babies familiar from countless stories on the "love generation," but the weirdos too, whose perverse and penetrating intensity no camera ever captures: speed freaks with hollow eyes and missing teeth, dead-faced acid heads burned out by countless flashbacks, old beatniks clutching gallons of red wine, Hare Krishna chanters with shaved heads and acned cheeks. Two young men in filthy serapes and scraggly beards lean against a crushed and brightly painted derelict veteran of the demolition derby. In the brims of their cowboy hats are little white cards: "Acid: $2."[96]

Blame it on money.[97] The Stones had been charging exorbitant ticket prices for their concert tour that year, and negotiations with Sears Point Raceway were focused on distribution rights for the Maysles Brothers' movie. Local high-profile lawyer Melvin Belli stepped in with talk of legal action, but hippies wanted a free festival, permits or no. As one said, "They can't stop it, we'll have a festival in the streets. Remember the fences came down at Woodstock."[98]

> "I know San Francisco by reputation," [Jagger] told *The Chronicle*. "It was supposed to be lovely here—not uptight. What happened? What's gone wrong?"[99]

> There was no love, no joy. It wasn't just the Angels. It was everybody. In 24 hours we created all the problems of our society in one place: congestion, violence, dehumanization.[100]

In the immediate aftermath everyone was on damage control. Sonny Barger of the Hell's Angels told the KSAN listening audience that the Rolling Stones had hired them as "security" and paid $500 in beer for their services;[101] local rock scenesters insisted that a local group "more familiar with the Angels" made the security arrangements; another Angel said they were asked just "to keep people off the stage."[102] Local ranchers estimated the cost of damages to their properties in excess of $500,000 and vowed to seek compensation from the Rolling Stones if necessary. Richard Carter, owner of the speedway, told reporters that the event was a "smashing success"; the Alameda County Board of Supervisors President sought background information on Carter to see whether he had violated his user permit in the past.[103]

8.2 Jack Casady sharing the Altamont stage.

The buck was certainly getting passed: the Maysles Brothers filmed the murder as part of the entertainment; Sonny Barger said that Mick Jagger used them "for dupes"; Sam Cutler, the Stones' road manager, said that Mick Jagger "wanted to thank people for everything that happened. The Angels did as they saw best. If people didn't dig it, I'm sorry."[104] But it was Cutler, along with Emmett Grogan and Rock Scully of the Dead, who were blamed for "[setting up] the deal to give the Hell's Angels $500 worth of free beer to be cheap rent-a-cops."[105] The Stones' manager, Allen Klein, safely ensconced in his New York office, insisted that it was "the San Francisco people" who were responsible for setting up the free concert: "All I can say is nobody contacted me." And Sam Cutler was "not part of the Stones management. . . . I did not hire Sam Cutler."[106]

The Rolling Stones' business manager had promised the bands at Altamont a cut of the film proceeds "to do with as they wish." He also insisted that Mayor Alioto's office had assured the Stones of a site for the free concert; the Mayor's office denied any conversations with anyone involved. Stones management claimed that Jagger was unaware the Angels would be on stage; and in what Gleason claimed was an attempt by the Stones' New York office to "shift responsibility" to the Grateful Dead, denied that Sam Cutler had made the arrangements for the beer payment, and that the Angels—the San Francisco and San Jose branches—were already drunk and arguing on the morning of the concert. Though the Stones' insurance would cover the damages of the day, the band were hesitant to make any gesture toward the family of Meredith Hunter, for fear "they would be hassled again by the media" for doing so.[107]

Speedway owner Richard Carter claimed that he was only expecting 50,000 people at the concert, and that Melvin Belli had assured him that all necessary services were arranged and all authorities consulted. The County Planning Director recommended Carter's event permit be revoked.[108]

> MARC ARNO: Since the very beginning the Hell's Angels—the *San Francisco* Hell's Angels—had voluntarily provided security for love-ins, be-ins, any kind of outdoor events, a lot of indoor events. And *never* was there *ever* any problem. Altamont was the turf of the *San Jose* Hell's Angels, who had never had any responsibility like that in their lives and were much more into mixing cheap wine with cheap drugs. And because there was no backstage area, they lined their bikes up across the front of the stage. If you ever watch *Gimme Shelter* again, you'll notice a bunch of Hell's Angels sitting up on top of buses behind the stage. Those are the Frisco Angels. They don't step in on other Angels' turf. They were just there to witness it all.

There may not have been fighting between branches of the Hell's Angels, but fighting happened nonetheless:

> Mid-morning on Saturday, Berkeley people laid what looked like a thousand tabs of sunshine acid on the Angels—not good sunshine: it had a lot of speed in it—and this was being dispersed both at the Angels' bus thirty yards uphill and on the stage. At one point, 500 reds were scattered on the front portion of the stage. The Angels were downing tabs of acid/speed and reds in huge gulps of Red Mountain wine. The more they took, the more fighting there was. The usual thing was to pick off non-Angels, but they were seen to turn on their own prospects (non-members who were trying to gain full status into the club). One prospect was soundly kicked—they were jumping on him—after Santana's set. He took a terrible beating, and, amazingly, was back on his feet ten minutes later, telling the full-fledged Angels he was their brother and everything was cool.[109]

But the Hell's Angels stood for a much bigger problem: "diabolical egotism, hype, ineptitude, money manipulation, and, at base, a fundamental lack of concern for humanity."[110]

> There is some of them lousy people ain't a bit better than the worst of us, and it's about time they realized it. They can call us all kinds of lousy dogs, and say

that we shouldn't be there. But you know what, when they started messing with our bikes, they started it.[111]

You could blame reds and liquor for the whole fucking mess. People just got themselves fucked up and wanted to fuck up everybody. You lose control of respect for yourself, and you lose control of respect for anybody else. That's what happened—reds and liquor did it.[112]

At the root of the problem was a lack of local knowledge:

Really, the difference between the open air show we held here [in London] and the one there is amazing. I think it illustrates the difference between the two countries. In Hyde Park everybody had a good time, and there was no trouble. You can put half a million young English people together and they won't start killing each other. That's the difference.[113]

In January 1971 Alan Passaro, the Hell's Angel identified on the Maysles' film as the man who stabbed Meredith Hunter, was found not guilty of murder. Passaro claimed self-defense; witnesses testified that Hunter had provoked the Angels guarding the stage; only one witness was found to testify against Passaro. Despite Passaro's acquittal, Melvin Belli announced his intention to sue the Maysles brothers for allowing footage of Hunter's murder to be shown as evidence in court—"for using Passaro as a movie star without his consent." Passaro claimed never to have met Belli.[114]

Within weeks the Grateful Dead were heard singing "Things went down we don't understand/but I think in time we will."[115]

Back in the city the year staggered to an ugly close. The Manson Family meted out unspeakable violence on innocent victims. Their connections with the Haight, their mysterious appearance at Esalen, and their musical aspirations, are part of the standard 60s tale.[116] But the media narrative—hippies, drugs, violence—short-circuited straight citizens' ability to distinguish the "true" hippies from the psychologically damaged hangers-on.[117] And remember the beatniks? The *Examiner* looked back on them with fondness: some had died, others still lived the bohemian life, and Lawrence Ferlinghetti was rumored to be rich from City Lights.[118]

Gleason looked back on the short 60s with mixed feelings:

The changes are happening, not all of them good. When I get discouraged, I go back to the music and it stands; from jazz to pop to folk to blues. When it is good it is great and when it is bad it's a bore. But the music is carrying a heavy weight these days. Not only Vietnam but a kind of disintegration of the American conscience. . . . A sad thing to end a decade on, but true I think.[119]

8.3 Altamont aftermath.

Yet when he looked back on the year 1969 he saw the national impact that local bands were having: well over half of the *Billboard* Album Charts that year had at least one album by a San Francisco band.[120]

Notes

1. Bill Graham, quoted in RJG, "The Rich and Rocky Odyssey of Entrepreneur Wolfgang Grajonka," *Examiner*, September 21, 1969, p. 47.
2. Dick Nolan, "Lesson of the Stones," *Examiner*, December 14, 1969, p. B3.
3. "Random Notes," *Rolling Stone* 38, July 26, 1969, p. 4.
4. Charlotte Risnik, "Jolly Raid at Hippie Mansion," *Chronicle*, January 9, 1969, p.1. The presence of harder drugs on the compound was disputed by members of the commune the following day, for the simple reason that there is "too much work to do on this ranch to be tripped out." Michael Grieg, "'Nicest' Pot Bust," *Chronicle*, January 10, 1969, p. 3.
5. See "Fire Guts Marin Hippie Mansion," *Chronicle*, February 3, 1969, p. 1. In the early 1980s the Olompali ranch was the site of an archaeological dig that unearthed, among other things, an interesting collection of LPs, some expected (Mike Bloomfield, Al Kooper, Stephen Stills), some unexpected (cast recordings of *South Pacific* and *My Fair Lady*). See E. Breck Parkman, "A Hippie Discography: Vinyl Records from a Sixties Commune," *World Archaeology* 46/3 (2014): 431–47.
6. "Gottlieb's Ranch 'Changes Hands,'" *Chronicle*, May 8, 1969, p. 3.

7. "Gottlieb Offers Judge a Piano," *Chronicle*, July 11, 1969, p. 4.
8. "Olompali Hippies Fade Away," *Chronicle*, August 14, 1969, p. 6.
9. Carolyn Anspacher, "New Life of the Flower Children," *Chronicle*, April 11, 1969, p. 3. See also Stephen Gaskin, *Haight-Ashbury Flashbacks* (Berkeley: Ronin Publishing, 1990).
10. Michael Grieg, "Renaissance in North Beach," *Chronicle*, February 24, 1969, p. 3.
11. Michael Grieg, "High-Rent Bohemians," *Chronicle*, February 25, 1969, p. 5.
12. Donovan Bess, "The Haight's 'Free Clinic' Reopens Fight on 'Speed,'" *Chronicle*, January 13, 1969, p. 3.
13. Dick Nolan, "Is Haight Hopeless?," *Examiner*, January 26, 1969, p. 3.
14. See Robert Gillette, "'Speed'—A Drug Destroying Young Lives," *Examiner*, March 9, 1969, p. 1.
15. RJG, "Reflections on the Ballrooms," *Chronicle*, February 9, 1969, Datebook, p. 31.
16. Hamrick had been a minister, but left the church after what he claimed was an alien abduction. The Harbinger Commune lasted about three years; the Harbin Hot Springs are now a New Age retreat and spa.
17. "Celestial Synapse at the Fillmore," *Rolling Stone* 30, April 5, 1969, p. 6. Incomplete recordings of this performance exist, according to Dead taping circles.
18. RJG, "A Fault Line for Everybody," *Chronicle*, February 24, 1969, p. 37.
19. RJG, "A Band's Gift—And a Search for God," *Examiner*, March 9, 1969, This World, p. 33.
20. See "Pop's Explosive Little Flower Girl," *Examiner*, March 16, 1969, for a sense of the excitement surrounding her every change in direction, and Alice Echols, *Scars of Sweet Paradise* (New York: Henry Holt, 1999), for a full account of what was propelling Joplin through the short 60s.
21. RJG, "No Opening Night Encores for Janis," *Chronicle*, March 24, 1969, p. 45.
22. See *Chronicle*, March 31, 1969, p. 7.
23. Steve Pelletiere, "Haight's High on Music and Spring," *Chronicle*, March 31, 1969, p. 1.
24. RJG, "Content at the Avalon Ballroom," *Chronicle*, April 13, 1969, Datebook, p. 31.
25. RJG, "The Malaise on the Spread," *Chronicle*, April 20, 1969, Datebook, p. 31. The *Chronicle* agreed, and published an editorial supporting the preservation of the "institution" that Graham had created, urging "public officials and private individuals with the musical interests and enthusiasms of young people" to give the Fillmore their fullest cooperation. See Editorial, *Chronicle*, March 8, 1969, p. 30. A letter to the editor in the same issue (p. 30) asked how the middle-class population of the city would feel if the Opera House were turned into a pancake shop, or Golden Gate Park into tract housing. Defining generational culture in these terms was necessary, but ultimately fruitless: the Grateful Dead played at the annual Black & White Ball a little later in the month, and the social gulf was in full view of Herb Caen. Having enjoyed an exchange with Jerry Garcia, Caen was approached by "a society matron" who "followed [Garcia] with her eyes and said, 'Oh, it talks, does it?' Yeah, it talks. 'What in the world do you find to SAY to people like that?' she asked. I couldn't find anything to say to her so I left." See "One Thing After Another," *Chronicle*, March 18, 1969, p. 19.
26. "The Return of Family Dog," *Chronicle*, April 25, 1969, p. 7. *Rolling Stone* later reported that the Avalon had been leased by a theater chain and was to open as a 600-seat cinema by Christmas. See "Random Notes," *Rolling Stone* 41, September 6, 1969, p. 4.

27. RJG, "Family Dog Back at 'New' Edgewater," *Chronicle*, June 16, 1969, p. 43.
28. RJG, "Florida Shuts Door on the Doors," *Chronicle*, March 7, 1969, p. 46.
29. RJG, "Jethro Tull an Interesting Combo," *Chronicle*, March 17, 1969, p. 50.
30. RJG, "There's Trouble Comin' Every Day," *Chronicle*, May 19, 1969, p. 46. See also *Rolling Stone*'s extensive report, "The Battle of People's Park," issue 35, June 14, 1969, pp. 24–30, for the firsthand accounts and photographs of the scene during and after the battle. Similar photographs were published in a two-page spread in the *Barb*, May 23, pp. 2–3, along with brutal firsthand testimony of the events and a leveled counterattack to the murder of James Rector. See "In Cold Blood," p. 4.
31. Dick Hallgren, "One Man's 'Incredible Journey,'" *Chronicle*, May 23, 1969, p. E6.
32. RJG, "Musicians Tune Up for Park Bail Fund," *Chronicle*, May 28, 1969, p. 49.
33. "A Jammed Benefit for 'Park People,'" *Chronicle*, May 29, 1969, p. 3.
34. Letter to the Editor: The Tragedy in Berkeley, *Chronicle*, June 2, 1969, p. 40.
35. For more on this and other struggles in Berkeley, see the documentary film *Berkeley in the 60s* (dir. Mark Kitchell, 1990) and W. J. Rorabaugh, *Berkeley at War: The 1960s* (New York and Oxford: Oxford University Press, 1989).
36. Among festival organizers were Bill Graham, Airplane manager Bill Thompson, Quicksilver manager Ron Polte, Tom Donahue, and Ralph Gleason.
37. RJG, "'The Wild West' Comes to S.F.," *Chronicle*, June 22, 1969, Datebook, p. 30.
38. RJG, "The Fascinating Free Concert Phenomenon," *Examiner*, June 29, 1969, This World, p. 31.
39. RJG, "Dual Benefits for Wild West," *Chronicle*, July 7, 1969, p. 42. John Wasserman printed a formalized list of the invitees—rock, theater, artists, poets, folk and jazz groups, opera and dance—and learned from organizer Ron Polte that they were aiming the festival "smack dab at six-year-olds in the sense that we're going to shoot for fantasy, free elephant rides, kites, water and boats and sails and ducks and kids' trips. We're figuring that if we can turn kids on it would be the most positive aspect of the festival." See "A Real Festival Is Like a Miracle," *Chronicle*, July 12, 1969, p. 35.
40. Don Wegars, "The Barb Rebels' Paper," *Chronicle*, July 11, 1969, p. 2. Tucked away in the *Barb on Strike* was a brief statement, "Where We're At" (p. 9): "We the people of the [Red Mountain Tribe for Berkeley] will work through our paper to keep the faith, to turn ourselves on, to get high, to live through the good times, the bad times, the bummers and the far out trips, with you." Subsequent issues were not so gentle: the July 11 issue featured a two-page spread entitled "Confessions of a Kosher Pig," with a Max Scherr byline; the front page of the next issue read "CIA Buys *Barb*." Though the tone mellowed over the next couple of months, the content was light on journalism and relied increasingly more heavily on advertisements for adult entertainments. Both *The Barb* and *The Barb on Strike* called each other "a scab-produced publication," and *Rolling Stone* left it to the readers "to determine which is the true Christ." See "Berkeley Barb on Strike," *Rolling Stone* 39, August 9, 1969, p. 12. Scherr sold the *Barb* to Allan Coult, who proceeded to publish anti-Semitic editorials, so Scherr tried to buy the paper back. Looking over the 1969 issues of the paper can certainly be trying: its "revolutionary" stripe was now a little ragged. Though the *Barb* had been on the forefront of the nascent gay liberation movement, it was decidedly less so with women's liberation, and in the latter half of the year featured a disproportionate number of photographs of naked women. The underground press had never censored content or turned down ad

revenue, however: sex classifieds and much more are explored in great depth in John Burks' cover exposé, "The Underground Press," *Rolling Stone* 43, October 4, 1969, Robert J. Glessing, *The Underground Press in America* (Bloomington: Indiana University Press, 1971), and Abe Peck, *Uncovering the Sixties: The Life & Times of the Underground Press* (New York: Pantheon Books, 1985).

41. Burks, "The Underground Press," p. 26.
42. Keith Power, "The Psychedelic Strikers," *Chronicle*, July 31, 1969, p. 2.
43. "Psychedelic Pickets," *Chronicle*, August 2, 1969, p. 2.
44. Ben Fong-Torres, "Bill Graham Explodes: 'Quitting San Francisco,'" *Rolling Stone* 41, September 6, 1969, p. 1.
45. RJG, "Why Bill Graham Is Leaving the City," *Chronicle*, August 8, 1969, p. 46. John Wasserman interviewed Graham for the *Chronicle* and perceived that he had mellowed slightly, but still maintained that the light show artists "will not accept . . . that they are not a draw. . . . Why do I have flowers and apples, and give away posters? For a very simple reason . . . I like to. It's my decision. It's part of the Fillmore totality. It's the same with light shows. Nobody COMES here because of the light show. Their only negotiating point is 'art'. It's not enough." See "Bill Graham—'Sick and Tired,'" *Chronicle*, August 22, 1969, p. 45. Bill Graham never actually left the city. He closed the Fillmore East at the end of June 1971, and the Fillmore West on July 4, focusing his energies on Bill Graham Presents at Winterland, and at other venues around the Bay Area. Bill Graham Presents promoted a variety of events ranging from straightforward one-night stands to the long-running summertime Days on the Green at the Oakland Coliseum, held regularly from 1973 until Bill Graham's death in 1991. This is detailed in *Bill Graham Presents*; for a contemporary look at his business, see Tim Cahill, "Bill Graham Drives His Chevvy [sic] to the Levee," *Rolling Stone* 107, April 27, 1972.
46. RJG, "A Pure S.F. Wild West Event," *Chronicle*, August 11, 1969, p. 41.
47. Ben Fong-Torres, "A Tidal Wave in the Wild West," *Rolling Stone* 39, August 9, 1969, p. 14.
48. For a comprehensive survey of the correspondence, meetings, formal protests, and underground reports of the Wild West Festival, see Michael Kramer, *The Republic of Rock* (Oxford and New York: Oxford University Press, 2013), pp. 94–129.
49. RJG, "The Cancellation of Wild West Show," *Chronicle*, August 15, 1969, p. 49.
50. "Fears and Follies Kill 'Wild West,'" *Rolling Stone* 41, September 6, 1969, p. 12.
51. RJG, "Black Music in the Bay Area," *Chronicle*, October 17, 1969, p. 43. This is a point that Kramer pursues further in *The Republic of Rock*, pp. 124–29.
52. See Ben Fong-Torres, "The Family Dog Becomes a Family," *Rolling Stone* 48, December 13, 1969, p. 20.
53. Andrew Kopkind, "The Woodstock Music and Art Fair," *Rolling Stone* 42, September 20, 1969, p. 30.
54. The Woodstock documentary does not present the performances in their actual running order, so there is no real sense that the Jefferson Airplane, for example, arrived on stage some nine hours after their scheduled slot, or that Country Joe McDonald was twenty minutes into an unscheduled (and unsucceessful) acoustic set before launching into "I-Feel-Like-I'm-Fixin'-to-Die Rag." For more on the problems of historicizing the Woodstock Festival, see Andy Bennett, ed., *Remembering Woodstock* (Aldershot: Ashgate, 2004).

55. See, for example, David Dalton, "Woodstock," *Gadfly* (August 1999) for a particularly vitriolic reminiscence, Grace Slick, *Somebody to Love? A Rock-and-Roll Memoir* (New York: Warner Books, 1998), Chris Salewicz's balanced retrospective, "Woodstock," in *Mojo* (July 1994), and Joel Makower, *Woodstock: The Oral History* (New York: Doubleday, 1989) for a more comprehensive, though still problematic, overview of the event.

56. See chapter 8 of Makower's *The Oral History* for reminiscences of the booking process. Michael Lang, one of the festival's producers, remembers wanting to "ease into" the opening day, with a lot of "folkish acts booked on Friday." The second day "was, as I recall, supposed to have been more of a getting-into-rock day and West Coast acts. And Sunday was just, blow it out." (p. 126)

57. Monck's recollection of the stage design at Woodstock provides a stark contrast to the stage construction at Altamont. At Woodstock the stage

> was about seventy-five feet across, with a sixty-foot turntable . . . about eleven-foot-six off the ground. The barrier fence was eight feet in front of that and was about six feet high. There was an eight-foot barrier behind that and upon that was the camera platforms. Two stairway accesses . . . and the bridge were upstage right to go cross the road to the performers' pavilion."

The stage at Altamont, by contrast, was at the bottom of an incline, only four feet off the ground, with no barrier. Bill Graham saw Chip Monck as partially culpable for the latter disaster, based on the amount of work involved in staging Woodstock and the lack of time available to build the environment for Altamont. See *The Oral History*, p. 142; Altamont is explored in greater depth later in this chapter.

58. Apparently, Graham pushed Santana as part of a package deal with the Grateful Dead. The collection of reminiscences of the Woodstock Festival included in *Bill Graham Presents* are worth reading as counterbalance to those in *The Oral History* and the documentary film. The vested interests of each of these sources are clear, and the truth behind the event probably rests somewhere in between them.

59. Simply put, this was the call-and-response cheer beginning with "Gimme an 'F'", continuing not onto "-I-S-H," but rather "-U-C-K."

60. According to John Morris, "Sly Stone was almost impossible to deal with in those days. . . . He was a real pain in the neck." See *The Oral History*, p. 195.

61. Greil Marcus, "The Woodstock Festival," *Rolling Stone* 42, September 20, 1969, p. 24.

62. RJG, "The Impact of Woodstock," *Chronicle*, September 1, 1969, p. 41. Hoffman's good works at Woodstock are often forgotten. See *The Oral History*.

63. The reiterations of the festival, on its twentieth and fortieth anniversaries, are testament to Woodstock's power as a cultural referent of the long 60s. At the time of writing, Michael Lang is rumored to be planning a fiftieth anniversary festival for 2019.

64. The opening of the Woodstock Museum at Bethel Woods in 2008 has codified the festival's mystique, with an additional commercial overtone.

65. RJG, "Can the Giant Ones Survive?," *Examiner*, August 24, 1969, Datebook, p. 29.

66. RJG, "A Giant Party with Rock Bands," *Chronicle*, August 25, 1969, p. 44. This came shortly after the August 1 burglary at the Matrix which saw the loss of sound equipment and a collection of recent and vintage live recordings from the club. "Burglars Clean Up at the Matrix," *Rolling Stone* 43, October 4, 1969, p. 36.

67. RJG, "A Special Quality at Big Sur," *Chronicle*, September 15, 1969, p. 46.
68. Jerry Hopkins' review of the Big Sur Festival in *Rolling Stone* 44 (October 18, 1969), pp. 20–22 is notable especially for Robert Altman's beautiful and evocative photographs.
69. "Quentin Rock Festival Turns on 2100 Inmates," *Examiner*, October 12, 1969, p. 2. Also see Jon Carroll, "San Quentin Rock Experience," *Rolling Stone* 46, November 15, 1969, pp. 20–21.
70. RJG, "What Price the Rolling Stones," *Chronicle*, October 29, 1969, p. 50.
71. Charles Raudebaugh, "Ominous Switch to Hard Drugs in the Haight," *Chronicle*, October 28, 1969, p. 2.
72. Jerry Hopkins, "Sympowowsium: What Comes After Woodstock?" *Rolling Stone* 49, December 27, 1969, p. 18.
73. Tim Findley, "Indians Invade, Claim Alcatraz," *Chronicle*, November 10, 1969, p. 1.
74. Tim Findley, "Invaders Say 'We'll Be Back,'" *Chronicle*, November 11, 1969, p. 1.
75. Tim Findley, "Invaders Claim Rock Is Theirs," *Chronicle*, November 21, 1969, p. 1.
76. Tim Findley, "Indians Reinforced—U.S. Delays Action," *Chronicle*, November 22, 1969, p. 1.
77. See Tim Findley, "Why They Want Island," *Chronicle*, November 25, 1969, p. 4.
78. Thomas Albright, "The Environmentalists," *Rolling Stone* 48, December 13, 1969, pp. 30–33; a newly rechristened Wavy Gravy features in John Burks, "Environmentalists," pp. 34–35.
79. RJG, "Second Thoughts on the Stones," *Examiner*, November 16, 1969, Datebook, p. 29.
80. The event was headlined by Crosby, Stills, Nash and Young. For details of the day's events, see Lynn Ludlow, "Establishment, Rebels and Rock at Great Rally," *Examiner*, November 16, 1969, p. 28.
81. RJG, "A Theme to Change the People's Heads," *Chronicle*, November 19, 1969, p. 48.
82. RJG, "Rolling Stones May Perform Free," *Chronicle*, November 21, 1969, p. 46.
83. RJG, "Stones' Plans for Free S.F. Concert," *Chronicle*, November 24, 1969, p. 46.
84. The Weathermen emerged in 1969 from Students for a Democratic Society. In 1970 they announced their revolutionary tactics based on "the classic guerrilla strategy of the Viet Cong" to fight "the insaity of Amerikan 'justice'" in Cambodia, at Kent State, and in the deep south. Their approach was a celebration of the fights waged by Eldridge Cleaver "and all black revolutionaries who first inspired us by their fight behind enemy lines for the liberation of their people." See "Communiqué #1," in David Horowitz, Michael P. Lerner, and Craig Pyes, eds., *Counterculture and Revolution* (New York: Random House, 1972), pp. 64–65.
85. RJG, "A Few Guesses on Rolling Stones," *Chronicle*, November 28, 1969, p. 50.
86. RJG, "Stones' S.F. Visit Still in Doubt,"*Chronicle*, December 1, 1969, p. 43.
87. "Rolling Stones on at Sears Point," *Chronicle*, December 4, 1969, p. 3.
88. RJG, "The Rolling Stones Are Right On," *Chronicle*, December 5, 1969, p. 46. The front-page item that same day itemized the on-again, off-again negotiations between the many factions with a vested interest in the concert, notably Sears Point's manager, who said that the Stones had "misrepresented" where the proceeds for the film and

recordings would go: Sears Point was only theirs on the condition that revenues went directly to help Vietnamese orphans. Negotiating powers were taken from Sears Point and given to Filmways, its corporate parent, who demanded the Stones honor their original commitment, once a mutually satisfactory charity was agreed upon. See "Rolling Stones Concert Is On, After Confusion," *Chronicle*, December 5, 1969, p. 1. Glimpses of these negotiations may be seen in *Gimme Shelter* (David Maysles, Albert Maysles, Charlotte Zwerin, 1970).

89. Michael Grieg, "New Site of Stones Concert," *Chronicle*, December 6, 1969, p. 1.
90. Bill Graham, quoted in *Bill Graham Presents*, p. 300.
91. Jim Wood, "Some Were Born . . . Two Died," *Examiner*, December 7, 1969, p. 1.
92. "Eyewitness to Chilling Violence," *Chronicle*, December 8, 1969, p. 4.
93. The *Chronicle* reporters were unable to find any confirmation of the births and discovered instead a "mammoth pile of folklore" already surrounding Altamont even just four days after the event. The SF General doctor who "ran the medical thing" at Altamont said that "as far as he knew, no babies were born at the speedway." The few women who went into labor there were taken to hospital, but whether by helicopter, cars, or ambulances was a matter of dispute, and no local hospitals reported any maternity cases connected with the event. One medic believed the rumor originated "by the management to whitewash the death," though the rumor had already begun long before the violence. See Julie Smith, "The Mystery of the Rock Babies," *Chronicle*, December 11, 1969, p. 19.
94. Jackson Rannells, "Cops Probe Four Deaths at Stones' Big Concert," *Chronicle*, December 8, 1969, p. 1.
95. "Let It Bleed," *Rolling Stone* 50, January 21, 1970, p. 31.
96. Michael Lydon, "The Rolling Stones Discover America," in *Flashbacks*, p. 177.
97. Weeks later, Gleason was still claiming that the cash generated by the Stones' tour—$2 million—set an unhealthy precedent for the materialistic and commercial impulses of the popular music industry, making a "free" concert all the more irresistible: "['Free'] assumes a dimension never anticipated by the Grateful Dead when they began the free music syndrome from a flat bed truck on Haight Street." In other words, "free" was commodified for a cynical end. "The Lesson of the Altamont Disaster," *Examiner*, December 28, 1969, This World, p. 28.
98. "Local people from the Grateful Dead office," quoted in RJG, "There Was a Tab, In Ego and Money," *Chronicle*, December 8, 1969, p. 49.
99. Michael Grieg, "A Forlorn Jagger Asks, 'What Went Wrong?,'" *Chronicle*, December 8, 1969, p. 1.
100. "A veteran of the whole rock scene," quoted in RJG, "There Was a Tab".
101. Much of Barger's conversation with KSAN program director Stefan Ponek is transcribed in Susan Krieger, *Hip Capitalism* (London: Sage, 1979), pp. 161–63, and can be heard briefly in *Gimme Shelter*.
102. Donovan Bess, "Angel's Altamont Story," *Chronicle*, December 9, 1969, p. 6.
103. George Murphy, "The Bleak Aftermath of Altamont," *Chronicle*, December 9, 1969, p. 1. The next day it was reported that Carter's permit only allowed the area to be used for races, rodeos and "limited spectator events." See "Big Concert Still Rocks East Bay," *Chronicle*, December 10, 1969, p. 3.

104. RJG, "Who's Responsible for the Murder?," *Chronicle*, December 10, 1969, p. 46.
105. Ibid.
106. "Let It Bleed," p. 36. See "'The Stones Have Not Acted Honorably,'" *Rolling Stone* 57, April 30, 1970, p. 1. Sam Cutler's memoir provides necessary detail regarding the aftermath of Altamont and his shift from the Rolling Stones to the Grateful Dead's orbit. See *You Can't Always Get What You Want* (Toronto: ECW Press, 2010).
107. RJG, "More Questions for Rolling Stones," *Chronicle*, December 12, 1969, p. 45.
108. Charles Howe, "Altamont Speedway's Battle for Permit," *Chronicle*, December 23, 1969, p. 3.
109. Carlos Santana, "Let It Bleed," p. 28.
110. Ibid., p. 20.
111. Ibid., p. 25.
112. Carlos Santana, quoted in Ibid., p. 30.
113. Keith Richards, quoted in John Burks, "In the Aftermath of Altamont," *Rolling Stone* 51, February 7, 1970, p. 7.
114. See Donovan Bess, "The Altamont Trial," *Rolling Stone* 79, April 1, 1971, pp. 28–30.
115. "New Speedway Boogie" (lyrics by Robert Hunter, music by Jerry Garcia) was first performed by the Grateful Dead at the Fillmore West in December 1969, and released on their album *Workingman's Dead* (1970).
116. See Vincent Bugliosi and Curt Gentry, *Helter Skelter: The Shocking Story of the Manson Murders* (London: Norton, 1974).
117. "The 'War on the Longhairs,'" *New York Times*, run in *Chronicle*, December 15, 1969, p. 1.
118. "Another Day, Another Broadway," *Examiner*, December 28, 1969, p. 3.
119. RJG, "A Glance Back at the Sixties," *Chronicle*, December 29, 1969, p. 33.
120. RJG, "Fantastic Impact of S.F. Pop Groups," *Chronicle*, December 31, 1969, p. 30.

SLY AND THE FAMILY STONE, "EVERYDAY PEOPLE"

(Sylvester Stewart)

Cynthia Robinson: trumpet
Freddie [Stewart] Stone: guitar, vocals
Gregg Errico: drums
Jerry Martini: saxophone
Larry Graham: bass, vocals
Rose [Stewart] Stone: piano, vocals
Sly Stone: vocals, guitar, keyboards

Produced by Sly Stone
7" single backed with "Sing a Simple Song" (Epic 1968)
Highest chart placement: #1 on the *Billboard* Hot 100 chart February 15-March 15, 1969
From the album *Stand!* (Epic BN 26456, 1969)

> ERIC CHRISTENSEN: On a lot of those Autumn sessions, Sly would play every instrument, and he could play them better than anybody in the band. He was certainly a musical genius, and certainly an innovator.
>
> The number one disc is "Everyday People," an Epic release by Sly & The Family Stone, the group that Sly Stewart formed when he was a disc jockey on KDIA.... Sly Stone's group is one of the hottest in the country, has had several hits and was the subject recently of a meeting at the Tamla-Motown headquarters in Detroit. It seems that the producers of the celebrated Motown music want to figure out what makes Sly Stone go![1]
>
> While all the Family Stone are competent musicians, their overall sound comes across more like a noisy clamoring street gang who just happen to have some musical instruments.... But ... they're [a] gang with a very evident sense of moral purpose.... Almost all their songs on *Stand!*, which includes their hit single, "Everyday People," are openly idealistic, telling of things as they *should* be, dealing with vast social problems in abstract terms, which is not usually within the scope of soul music. *Stand!* is not, however, simply a polemic. It's also extremely vital body music. It really can't be listened to [on] a low volume and communicate. *Stand!* depends on sheer energy more than anything else.[2]

San Francisco and the Long 60s

Sly Stone bookends this story of the short 60s, at the beginning as a producer, at the end as an international star. Though his career was derailed in the long 60s, the music that he and his Family Stone made, particularly from their debut, *A Whole New Thing* (1967) to *Fresh* (1973), remains untouchable. "Everyday People" represents here not only one sound of 1969, but a milestone for the band: their first #1 hit, and a rare song that topped both the pop and R&B charts.

Sly and the Family Stone were praised in *Rolling Stone* for being "the Bay Area's very first rhythm and blues group to go national."[3] This explosion onto the national airwaves came at the end of a grueling period of work for the band: in 1967 they had a regular gig at Winchester Cathedral in Redwood City, from 2 a.m. to 5 a.m. every weekend for five months. At first they filled their sets with cover versions, then gradually worked in original material. By all accounts they had an ecstatic following, which soon cleared the path to major-label recognition. They certainly presented the right image at the right time: a racially integrated, gender-balanced, socially conscious, extended family. Even when their songs were simple, the message was there:

> See, all Sly wants, all that makes him happy, is what's right. He cannot define what's right. He's said it through songs: Dancing is right. Togetherness is right. Getting higher is right. Family is right. Music is right.[4]

"Everyday People" is a simple song, rejoicing in a "superficial formlessness."[5] Its lyrics are a call for universal brotherhood, and its hook, "I am everyday people" an enactment of that call: an individual speaking for the collective, the collective represented in multipart harmony. The song is built on a great deal of repetition and minimal harmonic motion, which is not unusual for funk—James Brown could spin extended jams out of less material than Sly—but unusual for music in San Francisco in the short 60s. Here sections are not delineated by harmonic change but rather by lyrics and melody alone. There is no familiar blues progression to take the listener from one musical idea to the next, no sense of arrival at the chorus; the listener's interest is maintained through simple acts of tension and release, and through subtle textural changes. These textural changes are perceptible in the addition of voices through the song's first minute, and in the hook, which disrupts the gentle motion from A section to B section:

0:00	Intro	piano, bass, drums		4 bars
0:08	A	sax, vocal; female harmony	"Sometimes I'm right . . ."	8 bars
0:25	hook	multivoice harmony	"I am everyday people"	4 bars
0:34	B	female vocal; horns countermelody	"There is a blue one . . ."	8 bars
0:50	hook	"sha-sha" in lower voices; Sly above	"We've got to live together"	4 bars
0:59	A	"sha-sha" horns, vocal; female harmony	"I am no better . . ."	8 bars

1:15	hook	multi-voice harmony	"I am everyday people"	4 bars
1:24	B	female vocal; horns countermelody	"There is a longhair . . ."	8 bars
1:40	hook	"sha-sha" in lower voices; Sly above	"We've got to live together"	4 bars
1:49	B	female vocal; horns countermelody	"There is a yellow one . . ."	8 bars
2:06	A	to final cadence	"I am everyday people"	6 bars

The underlying rhythm of "Everyday People" is introduced by the piano in the second bar—the one sense of motion in an otherwise static soundscape. It is echoed in the second hook (:50) by a subtle "ooh, sha-sha" in the backing vocals; in the following A section (:59) the horns join in, but break up the pattern by playing only "ooh . . . sha." This gives the song the sense of a lopsided downbeat—the first horn stab comes on the downbeat; the second on the "and" of the next downbeat (**one**-and-two-and-three-and-four-and-one-**and**-two-and-three-and-four-and-**one**, etc.)—which contributes to its sense of groove.

Texturally, "Everyday People" is an exercise in additive process. On top of that prolongation of the tonic is a very simple tune that is passed from the voice in the A section to the horns in the B section. With the arrival at each new section, different voices are added to the mix, and the interaction between voices becomes increasingly complex, though never overtly busy or needlessly opaque. The characteristics of the various melodies are the primary reason why "Everyday People" retains its sense of simplicity—each is immediately familiar, like a nursery rhyme, and the listener is easily led through a subtly thickening texture without realizing it.

If "Everyday People" is an exploration of static consonance, the extraordinary instances of dissonance punctuate the song at crucial moments: at the first hook (:25), with the backing vocals in three-part triadic harmony, Sly Stone takes a vocal leap of a ninth. The resulting *appoggiatura*—the stressed dissonance on the downbeat—stretches over two beats, and resolves with a final embellishment.[6] This puts the "I" ("I am everyday people") at the absolute peak, melodically and gesturally, of the song. Philosophically, it emphasizes the self in the collective (*I* am everyday people), situating Sly Stone as the everyman, and his Family Stone as the integrated, harmonious, all-encompassing brotherhood. As he sang in the second line: "my own beliefs are in my song." How could we be surprised to discover that the message is really just as simple as it seems?

So much of the short 60s in San Francisco was about new modes of expression—philosophical, spiritual, political, social, sexual: "different strokes for different folks." Music was a vital factor in the exploration of these new modes of expression, both private and public—in communal homes, on the radio, in shops, in the park, in the ballrooms. Individual songs that correspond to the idea of "psychedelia," that seem to replicate or enhance the acid experience, might not have had a regular beat to dance to. Ralph Gleason, Tom Wolfe, Leonard Wolf, and others, all remarked on the types of dancing that they witnessed in the San Francisco dancehalls in the mid-1960s: it didn't look like the swim, it didn't look like the twist, it didn't look like the frug. What was it? It was freedom of physical expression, and it corresponded to the new psychedelic consciousness. When Sly and the Family Stone emerged from the Bay Area at the tail end of the short 60s, they presented to the world a psychedelicized dance music. Here were songs with an obvious beat, ready for the straight dances in cities not yet overrun with hippies. But though these songs were not outwardly psychedelic—yet—they were infused with the hippie ethos: love each other, be happy, dance. A medium and a message that rippled well into the long 60s.

IT'S A BEAUTIFUL DAY, "WHITE BIRD"

(David LaFlamme/Linda LaFlamme)

David LaFlamme: vocals, violin
Patty Santos: vocals, tambourine, percussion
Hal Wagenet: guitar
Linda LaFlamme: organ
Mitchell Holman: bass
Val Fuentes: drums

Produced by David LaFlamme
Recorded in Los Angeles (1969)
From the album *It's a Beautiful Day* (Columbia, 1969). An edited version was issued as Columbia single (9/1969). An earlier recording was issued as San Francisco Sound single 7 (1969).

> One of the most interesting and universally well received groups to appear on the local music scene in the past year is It's a Beautiful Day.... David LaFlamme is an excellent singer with a warm, moving voice and ... [his] violin playing is the outstanding instrumental feature of the band and gives it a unique tonal coloration. It is also used in conjunction with the guitar and bass to produce a raga-ish sort of sound on occasion. The songs are first class. I think the group has very definite possibilities of becoming a top pop unit. "White Bird" and "Hot Summer Day" are two of the best songs any group has come up with in this city in some time.[7]
>
> CHARLIE MORGAN: There is nostalgia in me. If I, say, put on It's a Beautiful Day, it gets to me, because the music is the thing that carries the emotional feeling of the times. Whether I like the words or not, the sound of the music is something that reaches into me in that emotional place.

The roots of It's a Beautiful Day stretch back to the Electric Chamber Orkustra, the band that featured five-string violinist David LaFlamme and Bobby Beausoleil.[8] The experimental sound of the Orkustra caught the ear of infamous local manager Matthew Katz, who designed a new five-piece "musical happening" around LaFlamme's prodigious talents. With the band membership established, Katz sent the band to Seattle to refine their material in a dancehall that he had recently opened there, which he called the San Francisco Sound.[9] Had It's a Beautiful Day remained in San Francisco they might have learned about Katz's managerial grip from the bands he sued—Jefferson Airplane and Moby Grape—and opted for a different career path. Instead, It's a Beautiful Day accepted Katz's offer of regular gigs and a place to stay, and entered into a long Seattle winter with no money, no transportation, and no momentum.

> DAVID LAFLAMME: We were penniless, dependent on people who were undependable and in an environment that was really not a friendly one. Really all we had left was our imagination and our talent. We were living in Seattle across from Volunteer Park in this old Victorian house. We had a little Wurlitzer piano in this attic room. Each room had the window seats and that little piano sat right in that window seat perfectly. We sat on two little chairs in front of that window with a little piano, and that's where we did our composing. And as you looked out that window you would see the long black road, the leaves blowing across it, you would see the bunch of seagulls who flew by. Quite frankly we were writing lyrics just describing what we saw out that window. I didn't think about it as a symbol of anything; it was just what we saw out the window.

The band played Katz's ballroom Friday and Saturday nights from December 1967 to January 1968, for which they earned the princely sum of twenty dollars each. They returned to San Francisco early in 1968, where they played all the local ballrooms with other local bands. With the addition of guitarist Hal Wagenet they became a sextet; their reach grew a bit wider and their local appearances a bit more regular, including one Fillmore bill where they were sandwiched between Cecil Taylor and the Yardbirds.

In October 1968 they were asked by Bill Graham at short notice to fill a twenty-minute slot at the Oakland Coliseum:

> DAVID LAFLAMME: Graham had a list. He called the Dead: no, of course not, Saturday. He called Quicksilver: no. He called the Sons: no. He called everybody until he finally got down to us at the very bottom of the list. And I called Bill back and said, "I just talked to everybody, it's on, we're on our way to the Coliseum." The only transportation we had was my old brown UPS truck. And we all piled in that thing with our amps and whatnot and went off to the Oakland Coliseum, a ragtag bunch of poor-ass hippies without two nickels to rub together, to go and open for The Cream at the Oakland Coliseum. Well, it was truly an amazing night.

It's a Beautiful Day were finally gathering momentum and name recognition. What they offered the local ballroom scene was a different sonic palate, one

"White Bird"

based in improvisation but not drawn from the same folk/blues/r&b well as their contemporaries. "White Bird" is one example of the directions the band could travel at the cusp of the long 60s.[10]

The most striking features of "White Bird" are textural: the multitracked violin, the instrumental interplay, and David LaFlamme's voice. This lends "White Bird" a richness unlike any of the other songs highlighted here from the short 60s:

0:00	Introduction	pizzicato violin	10 bars
0:20	Verse 1	"White bird in a golden cage . . ."	16 bars
0:53	Verse 2	"The leaves blow 'cross the long black road . . ."	16 bars
1:25	Refrain	"White bird must fly, she will die"	4 bars
1:33	Instrumental break	double-tracked violin	16 bars
2:05	Verse 3	"The white bird dreams . . ."	16 bars
2:37	Refrain x2		8 bars
2:53	Bridge	"The sunsets come, the sunsets go . . . /She must fly"	15 bars
3:23	Solos	acoustic guitar	16 bars
3:55		violin	16 bars
4:27		double-tracked violin, bird-like ascent	20 bars
5:04	Verse 1	"White bird in a golden cage . . ."	16 bars
5:36	Refrain x4	repeat to end; unresolved cadence; no harmonic resolution	14 bars

The song begins with an evocative pizzicato figure over a smooth, slowly moving acoustic undercurrent. These first ten bars create a sense of openness: there is an absence of drum and bass on the second beat of every bar, and the dialogue between the guitar and bass—one line ascending, the other descending—generates an undulating motion, a beating of wings and gentle coasting on the breeze. The listener's focus then turns to the vocal duet between David LaFlamme and Patty Santos. The effect of the two voices—often spaced over an octave apart, often in parallel perfect intervals, delivering the lyrics deliberately and slowly—is to open a space in the texture for the accompanying voices to appear and disappear. As the song progresses the sense of undulating motion becomes more apparent, by a more foregrounded strumming figure on the acoustic guitar and the emergence in the texture of the organ in the second verse. In among this is a more ornamental acoustic guitar line, weaving in and out of the texture underneath the vocals. Over the first two verses and refrain an energy has built up that finds release in the instrumental break: the violin, double-tracked in an echo of the two voices, represents the white bird, soaring up and down before returning safely to the third verse.

The middle section of "White Bird," from the bridge through the instrumental solos, is much more urgent, more unsettled. The violin solo (3:55) is again double-tracked, but the two voices do not move together in harmony; rather they seem to be pulling apart instead of working together. When they reconvene (4:30) it is to transition back to the first verse, spiraling ever upward (4:44) before finally settling back down for the voices to take over again. With the return of the verse (5:04) the song seems to resume its familiar course, but with every reiteration of the refrain the texture becomes thicker, the violin more insistent. The white bird never manages to take off again, however, and the song ends mid-cadence, with the violin grounded well below the voices.

> DAVID LAFLAMME: If you listen to my songs you will hear that they are about the same thing. They're all escapist songs: they're all about running away, running away from reality, running away from the real world. My songs either fly away, run away, get away, we got to get out of this place. Let's face it, the sixties was a terrifying time, most people didn't get along, all the people we loved either killed themselves or were killed or assassinated. It was just a terrible time.

There is a sense of fatalism in "White Bird" that chimed with the end of the decade. The urgency of flight, the need to escape in "White Bird" can be interpreted as reflecting a much broader social decline than the one in which It's a Beautiful Day found themselves that winter in Seattle. But Lester Bangs sure didn't like them. In his review of their self-titled album, he wrote that their vocal harmonies were "kind of ethereal and kind of lame," and that he could "*smell* them, and what they smell like to me is rotted posies pressed between pages of Tennyson." Put in plain English: "I hate this album ... for what it represents: an utterly phony, arty approach to music that we will not soon escape."[11]

Even if Bangs had known the story behind "White Bird," if he had known that David LaFlamme was taking an objective, not "phony," approach to its composition, his review would probably not have been any different. The transition to "arty" music was now fully engaged. The steps that Quicksilver Messenger Service had taken with "The Fool" toward extended structures and lyrics of mystical revelation reflected the motion in Britain toward progressive rock. It's a Beautiful Day were not a progressive rock band, but they shared stages with bands who were. The "arty" nature of progressive rock attracted criticism for its lack of "authenticity"; the "arty" nature of psychedelic rock in the short 60s was praised for its ability to capture a fleeting essence. Yet the "authentic" experience of psychedelic music was live, in a dancehall, in a park, in communion with thousands of other people. That experience was fleeting and could not survive. The flight that "White Bird" attempted was the same flight that many Haight hippies took out of the short 60s: upward and outward, to Marin, to Sonoma, to Mendocino, to Santa Cruz, to Big Sur, and on into the long 60s.

Notes

1. RJG, "Sly, Creedence—Two Best Sellers," *Chronicle*, March 5, 1969, p. 48. The second best-selling single that week was Creedence Clearwater Revival's "Proud Mary."
2. Alec Dubro, Review: *Stand!*, *Rolling Stone* 38, July 26, 1969, p. 37.
3. Review: *A Whole New Thing*, *Rolling Stone* 3, December 14, 1967, p. 20
4. Ben Fong-Torres, "Everybody Is a Star," *Rolling Stone* 54, March 19, 1970, p. 32.
5. Dubro, *Stand!*. It is not coincidental that the B side of "Everyday People" was entitled "Sing a Simple Song." No pretense here.
6. I am indebted to Richard Parfitt for the songwriter's perspective and Dave Marchant for his guitarist's ear. Huge thanks also to Rob Sivy, Kevin Holm-Hudson, Paul Carr, and Brian Robison for an extended and entertaining exchange on the nature of pentatonic arcs.
7. RJG, "LaFlamme and Co. Warm a Day," *Examiner*, June 8, 1969, This World, p. 43.
8. Beausoleil ("Bummer Bob") first entered this narrative in 1967 with the Anonymous Artists of America.
9. The San Francisco Sound was on 1214 E. Pike Street, at the historic Encore Ballroom. The venture barely lasted a year.
10. The band's trajectory into the 70s provides an exercise in "what if": when they traveled outside of the Bay Area in 1970–71 they were programmed with an eclectic range of bands: Frank Zappa and Love (San Diego and Atlanta), Pink Floyd, Fairport Convention, and Steppenwolf (Bath Festival of Blues and Progressive Music), the Who and Jethro Tull (Tanglewood), Poco, the Allman Brothers, and Little Richard (St Paul), and the Mahavishnu Orchestra (Carnegie Hall).
11. Lester Bangs, Review: *It's a Beautiful Day*, *Rolling Stone* 38, July 26, 1969, p. 37.

THE LONG 60s

We were dancing, and we were at the very edge of the world. The very edge. And it was so beautiful—and you could see forever! And I think that's one of the loneliest moments of my life. Because it was God, whatever that is, and nature, and lovely people, and music. And it made wonderful sense.

[Teresa Tudury]

But surely, everywhere, from whatever poem, choreographies extend into actual space.

[Robert Duncan, *Bending the Bow* (New York: Penguin, 1968), p. vi]

9. PSYCHEDELIA AND ITS HIGH OTHER

On October 7, 1964, the *San Francisco Chronicle* announced the opening concert of the San Francisco Tape Music Center's third season:

> The San Francisco Tape Music Center, where anything goes—except possibly the key of C major—will open its third season tonight at 321 Divisadero with a program titled "Music from the French Studios." . . .
>
> As local audiences know by now, there is no such thing as a "typical" Tape Center program. There is electronic and combined instrumental-tape music being written now which sounds no more wild, say, than Wagner nor Bruckner.
>
> There are also electronic tapes, and combined tape-and-visual effects which are enough to scare anyone out of his skull.
>
> And once again this season, the center's co-founders and other members promise nothing but infinite variety.[1]

The third season was notable for two single-composer concerts featuring the work of Terry Riley and Steve Reich. Riley's concert featured his new work, *In C*, which embodied "infinite variety" and perhaps a riposte to that opening snipe; and Reich's featured the premiere of *It's Gonna Rain,* full of tape effects to "scare" the audience out of its collective skull. These two works contributed to the larger contemporary musical map of San Francisco in fundamental ways, and both bear "high" and "low" traces.[2]

The long: *In C*

Terry Riley conceived of *In C* in March 1964 while traveling on a bus from his home in the Bernal Heights neighborhood to his job playing ragtime piano at the Gold Street Saloon in downtown San Francisco:

> *In C* just popped into my mind. The whole idea. I heard it. It was one of those things. I didn't want to go to work that night. And as soon as I got off work I came home and wrote it all down. . . . I had to revise a couple of the patterns, but it pretty much came as a package, you know. It was quite exciting; a this-is-the-answer experience. Because I *heard* it. Before, I was trying to calculate it. But when *In C* came, I heard these patterns of the beginning just unravel. About the first ten patterns just unraveled, and I thought, "Boy, what a great idea!"[3]

In C has been a significant marker of countercultural belonging and local legacy over the half-century since its premiere. It is a piece of fifty-three motives, scored for no specific instrumentation, and will last simply as long as it lasts. Along with Tape Music Centre colleagues Pauline Oliveros and Morton Subotnick, musicians in the first performance of *In C* included Steve Reich, who suggested to Riley that he incorporate a constant eighth-note C pulse throughout the work to keep the ensemble together.[4]

That first performance at the Tape Music Center was a pivotal event in the musical life of San Francisco, and was rapturously received by Alfred Frankenstein of the *Chronicle*:

> Terry Riley . . . is back after several years in Europe, and he reported in to the local public in a concert Friday night at the San Francisco Tape Music Center. During his sojourn abroad he has developed a style like that of no one else on earth, and he is bound to make a profound impression with it.
>
> He uses a variety of structural devices, but they all seem to eventuate in much the same effect. He begins with very simple melodic material, restricted in compass to only a few notes. This is very simply harmonized, at least at the start. The rhythms are as axiomatic as the other elements, the tempo is brisk and rigidly unchanging, and the volume level is consistently loud.
>
> This primitivistic music goes on and on. It is formidably repetitious, but harmonic changes are slowly introduced into it; there are melodic variations and contrasts of rhythm within a framework of relentless continuity, and climaxes of great sonority and high complexity appear and are dissolved in the endlessness.
>
> At times you feel you have never done anything all your life long but listen to this music and as if that is all there is or ever will be, but it is altogether absorbing, exciting, and moving, too. . . .
>
> The style discussed here reached its peak in a piece for instrumental ensemble called "On C," [*sic*] which stayed on C for the better part of an hour but left one refreshed rather than satiated. Riley does other things, too. . . . But "On C" [*sic*] was the evening's masterpiece, and I hope the same group does it again.[5]

Having been confronted with an otherwise unfamiliar musical experience, Frankenstein was careful to speak with composers from the Tape Music Center after the performance, to ensure that he understood exactly what had just happened, lest he write an uninformed review;[6] and his interest in the process and its effect is clear here. His suggestions of a loss of subjective time—inherent in the phrases "relentless continuity," "dissolved in the endlessness," "all there is or ever will be"—are significant, for they touch on a certain meditative ethos and, indeed, the psychedelic experience of "suspended time," which was then becoming a central aspect of the creative process in San Francisco.

When the piece was repeated some months later, *Examiner* critic Dean Wallace had a slightly different perspective:

Riley attacks the problem of organization [of sound] in a variety of ways. . . .

His results are usually pleasing, often tantalizing, sometimes intriguing, and on occasion, downright overwhelming. He is capable of building outlandish structures of pure, evanescent sound in a way that might make Wagner jealous; and he usually does this by means of the simplest of all devices: variations within a repeated pattern.

The best example of this trick was a piece which was . . . scored for electronic piano, a viola d'amore (or perhaps it was a centipede), a harpsichord, a fiddle or two, a flute, a piano, a piano accordion, a piccolo, and some sort of toy that resembled a . . . reed trumpet.

What does matter is that this weird assortment, playing an opus titled "In C," killed off the key of C major for good. It took them exactly 39 minutes. They did everything to C major, in all its extensions and inversions, that can possibly be done except grant it a pardon.

I'm glad C major is dead; now Riley can work on B-flat (Public Enemy Number Two). And, although you may think I am kidding, he does things like this in a way that is completely musical. The only element that may be missing is melody, and even this factor puts in a surprise appearance from time to time.[7]

What this review suggests is that *In C*, while clearly a significant shift in the local "art music" of San Francisco, nonetheless provoked different reactions in the audience. Some listeners were not quite willing to submit themselves to the potentially transcendent musical moment. And furthermore, the vocabulary for describing such music had not yet crossed over from "pop" to "art." Ralph Gleason, on the other hand, had been managing all along to describe jazz in exactly these terms. The birth of psychedelia a scant eighteen months later, if that, provoked similar flights of fanciful language in Gleason's regular columns—an early example of pop music being critiqued for its artistic and musical merits, in a language only later invoked for works of "art."

Tracing *In C* to the other side of psychedelia, to the very outer edge of the original hippie era, reveals the psychedelic signifiers common to both "low" and "high" music. The first recording of *In C* was released on Columbia Records in 1968, and was marketed very clearly to the countercultural audience.[8]

It was this version of the piece that reached the ears of San Francisco ballet master and associate choreographer, Carlos Carvajal. I met Carlos in 2009, to talk about his psychedelic choreography and to take a picture of his bathroom.[9] Carlos is a native San Franciscan whose entry to the world of classical ballet had come relatively late (he was eighteen when he began lessons) but remarkably swiftly (he was nineteen when he was given his first professional contract). As an adult, Carlos was introduced to

9.1 *In C*: "The only legal trip you can take. A hypnotic sound experience."

Buddhism in the early 1960s, and much of his work from that point on dealt in some way with his spiritual practice. He was contracted with ballet companies in France, Monte Carlo, and Venezuela, where he first met John Cage and Merce Cunningham:

> CARLOS CARVAJAL: I would see how sometimes they would interrupt the design. They would have this thing moving across the field of our view—you know, we're trying to see what was going on behind it. That's wonderful: the dance events, the words. And the fact that Cage made me know, made me *understand* that what I'm hearing out there could also be a musical sound, not just a car driving by, but I could use it as a musical sound. I could consider it music. I could consider the jets flying overhead music, I could consider the water dripping music. So the opening of that dimension was very helpful.

When he returned to San Francisco, Carlos enrolled in an MA program at San Francisco State College, and it was his seminars with poet Kenneth Rexroth that inspired one of his early works, the psychedelic ballet, *Voyage Interdit* (1968). Based in part on his experiences taking peyote at the Trips Festival in 1966, *Voyage Interdit* recounted a "simple, but archetypal" story of a novice attending a rock dance, being given a hit of acid, having a bad trip, then emerging as though through a purification ritual, into a new dimension of consciousness. Carlos assembled the score himself, mixing contemporary rock music with found sounds from local spots like Playland at the Beach. The work incorporated live music and light shows, and was well received by local critics.[10] By this point Carlos had bought his house in the Haight, and was a dedicated member of the local community. He and a group of dancers from the San Francisco Ballet would go to shows at the Avalon Ballroom, just to improvise and be part of the scene, to create uncredited dance "happenings" for the Family Dog.[11] These experiences also inspired *Totentanz,* Carlos' final MA project, a metaphysical and psychedelic dance of death.[12] In April 1970 he choreographed his final work for the San Francisco Ballet, *Genesis 70,* based on Terry Riley's *In C.*

Carlos' moment of revelation with *In C* mirrors Riley's own experience of composing it:

> CARLOS CARVAJAL: When the recording of *In C* came out it was panned. The critics hated it. Robert Commanday did not like it—but I listened to it and I just let my mind wander and I watched a ballet happening. I was able to construct a dance free of musical phrase, and just my own dance phrase on top of this wonderful, ever-varied tapestry of sound. It was never the same twice. So you could never count on hearing something thematic coming in to cue your dance.
>
> And we created a forty minute piece, starting in the rehearsal by doing dance moves and finally going into a little bit of a yogic ritual, and bit by bit changing and transforming into a lightshow, projections, dancers in white, dancers changing colors, spotted, dancers carrying around reflective discs or discs that would catch an image. We were playing with the visual imagery. I went through the elements: earth, air, fire, water, ether. We ended with the fifth element of ether, which was angelic—all my metaphysics were coming into play!
>
> It was a dance in which the dancers could not go on a theme. They had to look at each other, breathe together, start and then coordinate their movements by being conscious of each other. It was the whole company, a lot of dancers. I had groups at four corners of the stage. I gave them all a single movement, one movement that they did all in unison, coming right at each other, everybody converging on the center, passing through to the other sides—and the one instruction was: "don't touch anyone." So by watching they were able to cross without any mishaps. Plenty of time; you could take all the time you needed. It was like that: everyone turned, everyone would look at each other, everyone breathed together. That kind of pure dance was happening. The last image

actually—we had a big central screen—was the Da Vinci man in the middle. And it probably settled with everyone doing a large gesture, just standing there, that was about it: a yogic gesture.

And that caused a real sensation. People were cheering, people were booing. Since I had been involved in the Haight-Ashbury community and all of that, Chet Helms sent all of his friends, and everybody came to the performance dressed to the Ts in their best hippie garb, looking wonderful. But it upset the regular patrons who didn't like that, because they were afraid that hippies were—I don't know what they were afraid of. People are so afraid of change.

The ballet appeared to Carlos fully formed, then he allowed it to evolve, trusting the dancers to approach the choreography as one organism, much in the same way that musicians approach *In C* in performance. Although he had conceived of the choreography while listening to the Columbia recording, in order to perform *Genesis 70* at the San Francisco Ballet, Carlos had to work with live musicians: he could not use the recording, as he would have been in violation of the contract with the Local 6 chapter of the American Federation of Musicians. Coincidentally, six months earlier Gerhard Samuel had conducted the Oakland Symphony in the first performance of the orchestrated version of *In C*.[13] Samuel was the music director of both the Oakland Symphony and the San Francisco Ballet orchestras, so on one level *Genesis 70* was a natural extension of that earlier performance across the Bay.[14] Many local musicians, such as bassoonist Robert Hughes, played for both orchestras. Hughes recalled that the individual parts for the "orchestrated" version of *In C* were simply photocopied reproductions of the score that was printed on the back of the Columbia LP.[15] For the Oakland performances, Hughes recalled a xylophone playing the repeated "c" eighth notes;[16] in the SF Ballet performance that role was taken by a Moog synthesizer, which would have been loud enough to hear across the pit, and over the sound of the dancers. Bill Maginnis, composer/technician with the San Francisco Tape Music Center, was hired to set up the Moog for *Genesis 70*, but was not actually allowed to play it in the performance, though he was sitting next to it there in the pit, wearing concert dress.[17]

There are certainly a number of problems inherent in taking a work like *In C*, which although scored, was left entirely to the performers' intentions in the moment of its performance, and placing a forty-minute limitation on it. The idea of a conductor *directing* the piece is also anathema. Though Gerhard Samuel did not "conduct" the piece in any traditional sense, according to Hughes he did gesture to indicate the pace at which instrumental sections should move through the fifty-three individual cells.[18] Hughes remembers playing *In C* in the Oakland performances, but not in *Genesis 70*, which he attributes to a few basic facts: the stage at the Auditorium Theatre is big enough to accommodate a full-sized orchestra; the pit at the Opera House is rather smaller, with an entirely different acoustic. As a bassoonist Hughes can admit that instruments in the bass register would have muddied the texture, and "made it sound like Milhaud or something." Terry Riley's score, for reasons of shorthand if nothing else, was written entirely in the treble clef; the orchestra for *Genesis 70* would therefore have embodied that by default if not necessity.

If the story of the orchestral performances of *In C* is riddled with tensions between "high" and "low" critics and audiences, the same is true of *Genesis 70*. As Carlos told me, he began building the work within the framework of "traditional" ballet moves. The advance publicity for *Genesis 70* captured one of those moments, in retrospect rather far removed from the ultimate product.

The difference between the two stills (9.2 and 9.3) should be obvious: the expression on the face of the ballerina in the first photograph, while no doubt due to concentration and physical exertion, nonetheless suggests a certain detachment from Carlos' vision; the expression on the man in the second is, by contrast, ecstatic, if not sexual. The first embodies the "old, high art" aesthetic of the San Francisco artistic community; the second, the "new high" of the by-then dissipating hippie community. It also reflects an early insight into hippie dance:

> The music, art is not separate from life. [The hippie] plays and/or listens to music everywhere. He will dance anywhere. He is not ashamed of his joy. His dance is a prelude to sex, or a celebration of his existence: not a substitute for sex, or a tease, or a ritualistic (unsatisfactory) discharge of sexual energy. The dance has made him free. His freedom has made him dance.[19]

What Carlos did was expand the ballet experience to include referents of the psychedelic "happening": light shows, "metaphysical" gestures, free-form movement

9.2 Carlos Carvajal, Jocelyn Volimar and Bruce Bain in rehearsal for *Genesis 70.*

9.3 Michael Rubino in *Genesis 70*.

and—in short—freedom, which, though familiar to anyone engaged with the Haight community, were surely more disorienting to the Ballet audience at the Opera House than was the music.

The critics' reactions to *Genesis 70* were predictably mixed.[20] The *Palo Alto Times* noted the "strikingly avant-garde" nature of the new work, its "powerful visual and aural attack on the senses," with a "totally arresting," "almost hypnotic" end result. The reviewer did admit that

> "Genesis" can be a tough work to assimilate. The unrelenting intensity of the music and light show . . . took its toll at Saturday night's performance. Several persons walked out.
> But the majority, particularly a large contingent of bizarely [*sic*] dressed hippies, greeted the work with cheers. It's probably safe to say the Opera House

never before has had so many weirdly dressed patrons, and in many respects they were as interesting as the happenings on stage.[21]

Robert Commanday, longtime *Chronicle* classical music critic, was less forgiving:

> Where but in San Francisco is there a ballet company that will try so hard to freak out, and to so little avail? And where else find a vociferous element of the audience as eager to acclaim the effort?
>
> The scene and the evening were laid at the Opera House Saturday. The SF Ballet was fighting a desperate rear guard action, belated au-courantism, in Carlos Carvajal's new "Genesis 70." Activity for activity's sake was the sum of it.
>
> For music, it was one-track Terry Rileys [sic] cul de sac "In C," wherein the note "C" is machine gunned repeatedly (this time on the Moog Synthesizer) for an obsessive 40 minutes (or was it two hours?). Around it, the orchestra improvises a kaleidescope [sic] using 53 little C major motives.
>
> Vintage lights shows (ca. 1960) . . . played simultaneously on a great bull's eye and several other panels. . . .
>
> The dancers, keeping up with the unrelenting presto tom-tomming of the "C," carried on in a mad pace everything balletic that can be imagined, episodes thrown on in fast and overlapping sequences. It reached out to include even a De Mille hoedown, Limon circle dances, a brief Joffrey-Arpino business with two men crawling through long plastic tubes—but mostly, "Genesis 70" was a feverish montage that wouldn't quit.
>
> In one sense this was a stunning depiction of the crazed futility of the human race through modern times, the structuring of unstructured energies. Certainly it was an extraordinary demonstration of ensemble discipline, dancer memory and fantastic traffic plan. It was also terribly tiring, and I left wishing that daylight savings had come on two hours earlier.[22]

Carlos had mentioned that Commanday did not like the recording of *In C*, so one supposes that he was not disposed to liking any choreographic setting of it. And while it is true that some of Commanday's phrases here—"one-track Terry Riley," for example—jab at a compositional style that did not speak to him personally, the bigger artistic sin in Commanday's view was trying to recapture the spirit of a moment gone by—"belated au-courantism." Whether Commanday was unwilling to admit the validity of the freak-out as a cultural form, or merely heaving a great sigh at the Ballet's delayed appropriation of it, he nonetheless spoke to the general 1960s detachment between the hippies and straight San Francisco. The fact that the "real" hippies were anywhere but in San Francisco by the time of the premiere of *Genesis 70* makes Commanday's review all the more poignant.

And there was Carlos' final point: "People are so afraid of change." The Ballet guild met for a summer planning meeting shortly after this performance and said that while they had enjoyed Carlos' other work, they had not understood *Genesis 70*. When some guild members remarked pointedly on the changed audience demographics for Carlos' works, he decided there and then to resign.[23] This supports the theory that there were a certain number of rifts in the Bay Area musical community: hippie versus straight, experimental versus "classical," auditory versus visual, city versus East Bay. The centrality of dance to the psychedelic musical experience—"a prelude to sex, a celebration of existence"—may have influenced Carlos Carvajal's own choreography, and his own personal expression outside of the Opera House, but the "straight" audience for classical ballet, seated less than two miles away from Carlos' psychedelic bathroom, was slow to accept it.

The short: *It's Gonna Rain*

In C is the very embodiment of "the long 60s," both by virtue of Riley's connection to the counterculture in its quest for spiritual enlightenment, and in the work's capacity to evoke that quest even in contemporary iterations, in the meditative space that it creates for its performers and audience. As such *In C* stands in stark contrast to the "short 60s," and particularly to another piece premiered that same Tape Music Center season, Steve Reich's *It's Gonna Rain*. *It's Gonna Rain* is a tape piece in two movements, derived from a sermon delivered in Union Square by Pentecostal preacher Brother Walter that was recorded by Reich in November 1964, around the time of the premiere of *In C*. Each movement is based on a different phrase, or series of phrases, from Brother Walter's sermon: Reich uses uncut footage to open each movement, then the subsequent repetition of selected, edited text creates an internal rhythm and melody which Reich then exploits as a single phrase, looped against itself, to remarkable effect.

When comparing *It's Gonna Rain* and *In C*, it is tempting to hear in *In C* a certain sense of motion, or locomotion (the insistent "C" pulse propels the piece forward against the overlapping repetitions of the fifty-three motives) and in *It's Gonna Rain* a certain stasis (Brother Walter may have been moved by the spirit, but it's unlikely that he was physically *moved* by the spirit). *In C* is a mutable work, different in every performance; *It's Gonna Rain* is finite and unchanging;[24] but both works retain a sense of time and place, that is, mid-60s era San Francisco. These two works are often cited as seminal minimalist moments, the defining performances of the Tape Music Center's third season, yet despite any perceptible processural connections, the two works can provoke in the listener entirely different responses.

The recording process of *It's Gonna Rain* had its own synchronicity: Brother Walter's explosive phrase "it's gonna rain," in the moment of its enunciation, sent one of the manifold pigeons of Union Square into flight. As Reich looped the phrase, the sound of the pigeon's wings then became an unintentional pulse. The piece is therefore in a sense doubly situated: the pigeon's fluttering suggests its geographical

9.4 Birds in flight, Union Square.

site; the loop process a constant reminder of Reich's subjective presence, his finger manipulating the "record" button. Yet if in the first movement of *It's Gonna Rain* the listener is reminded subliminally via that pigeon of a certain expansiveness—the promise of the blue sky, a heaven above—the second movement of the work sounds progressively like a flock of birds shrieking menacingly, swooping down on the listener.[25] Alfred Hitchcock, of course, had captured that menace on celluloid: *The Birds* (1963), was filmed just up the coast in Bodega Bay, and maintains a certain place in the general Northern California psyche even now. The connection between geographical place and artistic affect are worth noting, for the claustrophobic second half of *It's Gonna Rain* sounds like nothing if not a horror movie, which might explain Reich's decision to play only the first movement at the work's premiere in 1965.

Reich has alluded to difficult personal circumstances during this period,[26] which are certainly perceptible in *It's Gonna Rain*:

> I was feeling very disturbed at that stage in my life. The latter part of *It's Gonna Rain* seemed so paranoid and depressing that I suppressed it. But it's the second half which really sticks it to you technically and musically.... You know, it's a heavy trip—bad vibes—but there's substance in there that gets to you.[27]

Reich's use of hippie jargon is interesting to note, for he is generally dismissive of his relationship to the contemporary 1960s San Francisco counterculture and its attendant recreational pursuits:

> In September 1965, Reich returned to New York, no longer easy with the cultural situation in California. The transformation of the Beat era into the

Hippie period was showing itself in many ways, including the emergence of a heavier drug scene.... "In the group of people I seemed to form a contact with, I did not feel on solid psychic footing," Reich says; he does not, though, find the question of the influence of drugs on his music to be "a profitable line of discussion."[28]

What interests me here is that Reich's statement is in fact antithetical to the creative ethos of his contemporary musical environment: he is distancing himself from the very process by which many of his peers "found their voice." *It's Gonna Rain* coincides with a general trend in the San Francisco Bay Area toward expanded consciousness, at the cusp of the beatnik/hippie transition, and it is fair to say that the majority of creative persons in San Francisco at that time were aware of, if not intimately familiar with, the ritualistic use of drugs such as mescaline and peyote. In fact, in March 1963 the California State Assembly's Public Health Committee approved a bill permitting Native Americans to use peyote in religious ceremonies, and Ralph Gleason remarked at the time:

> When I first came to town 15 years ago [1948], some of the local citizens were ordering the peyote buttons from a mail order house on the Texas border and others, with a more direct turn of mind, merely bought it at the cactus plant table in the horticultural section of a large downtown department store.[29]

As a musician involved with Mills College, the San Francisco Mime Troupe, and the San Francisco Tape Music Center, Reich would have known many such creative shoppers, as well as those simply open to new experience—Ramon Sender, for example, cofounder of the Tape Music Center, who recounted one fateful afternoon in 1963 spent in the company of Steve Reich:

> RAMON SENDER: I was at Mills College in 1962/63 driving over with Steve for Milhaud's seminars. Steve was living on Bernal Heights and I was living on Potrero Hill. And then about two blocks from me was Terry Riley and his wife. And one morning there's a knock on my door and there's Steve with a paper bag. And he said, "Where's your Waring blender?" He said, "I'm going to blend up this stuff." And we were each going to take 16 double-O caps. I said, "What is it?" And he said, "It's dried mushrooms." And I had never at that point even smoked a joint. And so we each took 16 caps of dried peyote and were fooling around at the piano and I'm having a wonderful time. And a couple of hours later he looks at me and says, "Well I'm going home now." And I said, "What? We're having such a great time!" He said, "No, no, no, go lie down. Just close your eyes." So I did, and I proceeded to live my life backwards all the way to the moment of conception and out into the white light. And the next morning

I called him up and said, "Do you have any more of those buttons? Can I buy them from you?" So I did, and then I called Pauline Oliveros and I said, "Pauline you've got to try this stuff."

Ramon has recounted this story to others;[30] it is very much a fact of his life, and clearly a formative experience. The point I wish to make here is that Reich acted as the "elder" in this situation, which suggests that he had already gained some experience with hallucinogens.

It would be easy simply to damn Reich by association with those of his friends who were notable, and celebrated, psychic travelers, but the significance of perceptual experimentation on local composers of "art" music cannot be overstated. Terry Riley has said:

> I was very concerned with psychedelia and the psychedelic movement of the sixties as an opening toward consciousness. For my generation that was a first look towards the East, that is, peyote, mescaline, and the psychedelic drugs which were opening up people's attention towards higher consciousness. So I think what I was experiencing in music at that time was another world. Besides just the ordinary music that was going on, music was also able to transport us suddenly out of one reality into another. Transport us so that we would almost be having visions as we were playing. So that's what I was thinking about before I wrote *In C*. I believe music, shamanism, and magic are all connected, and when it's used that way it creates the most beautiful use of music.[31]

Like any psychedelic blueprint, *In C* therefore has the potential to engender in its performance something akin to a transcendent experience, taking both performers and audience out of their bodies, to achieve a higher state of being.[32] But where *In C* is expansive, *It's Gonna Rain* is claustrophobic. Moreover, it is representative of Reich's uncomfortable position amid this community of seekers of higher consciousness, and his particularly parlous psychic state. By contrast, Riley's suggestion of the shamanistic potential of music is an evocative distillation of the countercultural ethos, and indeed was embodied by Carlos Carvajal's choreographic interpretation of *In C*.

Riley's own unashamed descriptors of his work—"magic through music"; "transcendence"; "an awakening"[33]—echo the key words generally used to describe contemporary popular music, particularly that of the Grateful Dead. The Dead are notable for the individual members' musical roots and influences: on the "low" side, Garcia's love of bluegrass and Pigpen's love of the blues balanced the broad sweep of Harry Smith's *Anthology of American Folk Music*; on the "high" side, Phil Lesh, Tom Constanten, and Steve Reich were colleagues in Luciano Berio's Mills College seminars and played in an ad hoc instrumental combo fused by a mutual interest in free jazz.[34] All of these sources accelerated the band's fluid genre-crossing. This fluidity was a central component of the Dead's experiences at the Acid Tests and was honed in their early performances. As Phil Lesh has noted:

> It was at the In Room [Belmont, 1965] that we first played one song for an entire forty-five minute set—in this case "In the Midnight Hour," the Wilson Pickett R&B classic. We had started out by expanding tunes through extended solos, mainly to make them last longer since there were so few of them. However, the longer the solo, the less interesting it became to play the same material as background, so those of us who weren't soloing began to vary and differentiate our "background" material, almost as if we were soloists, in a manner similar to jazz musicians. A good example of this technique is our version of the old Noah Lewis jug band tune "Viola Lee Blues," a traditional prison song. We electrified the song with a boogaloo beat and an intro lick borrowed from . . . Lee Dorsey's "Get Out of My Life Woman," and after each of the three verses, we tried to take the music *out* further—first expanding on the groove, then on the tonality, and then both, finally pulling out all the stops in a giant accelerando, culminating in a whirlwind of dissonance that, out of nowhere, would slam back into the original groove for a repetition of the final verse. It was after a run-through of this song that I turned to Jerry [Garcia] and remarked ingenuously, "Man—this could be *art*!"[35]

At this point Steve Reich was getting ready to leave San Francisco. His final musical contribution to local culture was the soundtrack to the Robert Nelson film *Oh Dem Watermelons*, played during the Mime Troupe's *A Minstrel Show, or Civil Rights in a Cracker Barrel*, which premiered on June 17, 1965, in Palo Alto. This work is an important example of Reich's early engagement with contemporary leftist and racial politics, and prefigures his subsequent disengagement from the counterculture.[36] It is also a means of placing Reich's mid-60s works on the larger developmental arc of the San Francisco "sound."

Oh Dem Watermelons offers an important example of the confluence of musical ideas that engendered in "pop" and "art" music a similar aesthetic in San Francisco's 1960s counterculture. While Nelson's work is occasionally hailed as a landmark of experimental film, the soundtrack has had a rather shorter shelf life.[37] Reich's contribution was essentially a riff on two minstrel songs, Stephen Foster's "Massa's in de Cold Ground" (1852) and Luke Schoolcraft's "Oh! Dat Watermelon" (1874), which Reich builds to a five-part canon that lasts about six minutes, then returns abruptly to a reprise of "Oh! Dat Watermelon," which lasts another minute until the end of the film. In other words, "Oh! Dat Watermelon" frames an extended suspension of time. I would argue that this—an insertion into the middle of a minstrel song of a five-part canon—is not dissimilar to the Dead's attempts at taking a blues or country standard *out further*. The fact that the Dead's forty-five-minute extension of "In the Midnight Hour" and Reich's soundtrack for *Oh Dem Watermelons* emerged in the same year is a chronological coincidence that deserves closer consideration. Both examples play with the idea of suspended time by stretching a simple musical idea beyond its natural limits, by extended repetition of short musical phrases, and in the tension between stasis and motion that these compositional devices create.

One other key to the Dead's improvisatory style deserves mention here. In 1964 Jerry Garcia went on a pilgrimage to bluegrass country, and took in, along the way, a performance at the Ash Grove in Los Angeles by fiddler Scotty Stoneman. As Garcia said about that performance:

> They did this medium-tempo fiddle tune like "8th of January," and it's going along and pretty soon Scotty starts taking these longer and longer phrases—10 bars, 14 bars, 17 bars—and the guys in the band are just watching him! They're barely playing, going ding-ding-ding, while he's burning. The place was transfixed. They played this tune for like 20 minutes, which is unheard of in bluegrass. I'd never heard anything like it. I asked him later, "How do you do that?" and he said "I just play lonesome."[38]

Garcia heard Stoneman incorporating a "double-bowing" technique: taking the short riff and "repeating it so that it phases out of synch with the prevailing rhythm of the piece."[39] Stoneman's double-bowing is clear in a contemporary live recording from the Ash Grove.[40] Like most reels, "Eighth of January" consists of two alternating sections (chorus, solo verse) of eight bars each. As the performance progresses, Stoneman stretches his solos slightly, from eight bars to ten, eleven, twelve, breaking the tune's larger note values into triplets, arpeggios, and shorter repeating figures.[41] Ultimately, against what Garcia called a "ding-ding-ding" accompaniment, Stoneman launches into a fast, repetitive, descending triplet figure—"breaking" from the underlying melody, "phasing out of synch," and prolonging the return to the chorus for ten seconds.[42]

Garcia employed this same technique to extraordinary effect in the Dead's early live performances of "Viola Lee Blues." One particularly striking example was recorded at the Dance Hall in Rio Nido, California, on September 3, 1967.[43] After two verses of the blues, Garcia begins a fairly straightforward solo that swiftly changes, in its second chorus, to an extended repetition of a three-note pattern. Under Garcia's phrasing each of the other band members can be heard exploring his own terrain "out there." Where there had been a familiar blues progression there is now stasis, and where there had been a solid backbeat there is now a series of irregular drum rolls: time is suspended for an extraordinary twenty seconds in the middle of an otherwise straightforward dance jam, before an abrupt return to the third verse of the blues. This performance embodies the same "suspension of time" as *In C* and *It's Gonna Rain*:[44] it has a clear link to the psychedelic moment, a gesture toward what Phil Lesh imagined as "art," a connection to the broader local musical climate, and roots in traditional music.

There is an interesting musical coincidence between Garcia's mimicked "double-bowing," Reich's *Oh Dem Watermelons* and his ultimate motion toward "phasing." That 1967 performance of "Viola Lee Blues" is not wildly different in either intention or affect to Reich's 1967 *Piano Phase*. *Piano Phase* is scored for two pianos or marimbas, both playing a composite figure (sixteenth-note pattern of E-B-D in the left hand, interspersed with F#-C# in the right hand), for an approximate number of repetitions as one player slowly phases out of sequence with the other. Though the process here is different to the "double-bowing"/"phasing" techniques deployed by the Dead, I believe that the chronological and geographical proximity of these musical developments is revealing of deep musical crosscurrents.

Minimalism and psychedelic rock both serve to suspend musical time, but—as most musical agents on both sides of the high/low divide would say—mind expansion provided the initial impulse; innate creativity did the rest. The career trajectory of the Grateful Dead proves the enduring popularity of that impulse, while Steve Reich's place in the canon of American music may rest on the fact that he played with the 60s aesthetic without buying into the attendant ideology.[45] Yet the longer life span of minimalism suggests a legacy inseparable from that initial mid-60s moment, that lingering dialogue between "high" and "low." This is embodied most strikingly in the extraordinary career of local composer, John Adams. His appointment as first composer-in-residence of the San Francisco Symphony (1982–85) was a gesture by the largest mainstream symphonic organization in the Bay Area toward the outer edges of youth and respectability, a blurring of the "high/low" divide, and a clear ripple from the short 60s.

Notes

1. Dean Wallace, "Tape Music Center Season," *Chronicle*, October 7, 1964, p. 42.
2. The contested terms "high" and "low" are often used to distinguish "art" and "popular" musics. For examples of the ways popular music scholars have challenged this binary, see Dai Griffiths, "The High Analysis of Low Music," *Music Analysis* 18/3 (October 1999): 389–435, and Simon Frith, *Performing Rites: On the Value of Popular Music* (Oxford: Oxford University Press, 1998). Needless to say, my use of the term "high" in this instance is intended to carry a double meaning.
3. Terry Riley, in Duckworth, *Talking Music: Conversations with John Cage, Philip Glass, Laurie Anderson, and Five Generations of American Experimental Composers* (New York: Schirmer Books, 1995), p. 277.
4. The extent to which Reich has inserted himself into the historical narrative of *In C*, and his relationship to the early minimalists, are interesting tangents. Much can be inferred from his discussions with Keith Potter in *Four Musical Minimalists* (Cambridge: Cambridge University Press, 2000), and in any of his more recent retrospective interviews.
5. Alfred Frankenstein, "Music Like None Other on Earth," *Chronicle*, November 8, 1964.

6. Morton Subotnick and Ramon Sender discuss this performance in Bernstein, ed., *The San Francisco Tape Music Center* (Berkeley and Los Angeles: University of California Press, 2008).
7. Dean Wallace, "Terry Riley's Sounds: An Electronic Concert," *Examiner*, May 23, 1965.
8. This ad appeared in the *Barb* on November 22, 1968, and as a full page in *Rolling Stone* 23, December 7, 1968, p. 31. In the wake of the television coverage of the Democratic National Convention in Chicago, particularly on the CBS network, Columbia Records, a CBS subsidiary, "re-appraised" its advertising strategies and restricted its advertising in the underground press. See Gleason, "'The Man Can't Bust Our Music,'" *Chronicle*, July 2, 1969, p. 47. In a letter to *Rolling Stone* Columbia president Clive Davis insisted that his company had tested advertising in various underground publications, and found that they were most successful with papers such as *Rolling Stone* that "are good for music," as opposed to "underground papers who have no connection with music at all." See "Correspondence, Love Letters & Advice," *Rolling Stone* 40, August 23, 1969, p. 3.
9. Carlos' bathroom was painted by Chuck Arnett, known locally as the artist who had decorated leather bars south of Market such as Ambush and the Tool Box. Arnett worked on the stage design for Carlos' ballet *Kromatika* in 1967, and on a whim painted Carlos' bathroom on the theme of the White Rabbit, using fluorescent paint for blacklight, to truly psychedelic effect.
10. See, for example, Henwell Tircuit, "Mad, Marvelous Ballet on the Psychedelic Side," *Chronicle*, April 19, 1968, p. 49:

    > It combines what would seem to be mutually exclusive elements—the swinging, intense All Men Joy rock group, electronic scores, music concrète, go-go, classical ballet and modern dance—places them within the concept on a double stage (which includes the auditorium as an activity area) and then uses strobe lights plus a marvelously controlled light show by the "Garden of Delights" as theatrical icing. But it was mad! But it was beautiful, balanced, convincing and utterly marvelous.

11. Carlos had met Chet Helms en route to Denver in 1966, where he was going to work on *The Way*, a ballet based on the Tao, choreographed by i-Ching. Though he was the only local choreographer to become an honorary member of the Family Dog, Carlos was not the only one to have engaged with contemporary local rock. Marc Wilde, for example, expressed an interest in the "poetic and religious" nature of the music, noting that "the new music and the new, big sound have given choreographers an entirely new literature to work with." Wilde's work, *Structures*, created for a Pacific Ballet gala, featured music from *Surrealistic Pillow*, to which the corps of 25 dancers "engaged in a series of free association dramatic sequences." See Marilyn Tucker, "Ballet Experts Look to Big Sound of Rock Music," *Chronicle*, May 13, 1967 p. 29. Furthermore, neither Wilde nor Carlos were the only classically trained dancers to express an interest in the hippies, as reports of the arrests of Fonteyne and Nureyev can attest.
12. *Totentanz* was premiered on April 1, 1967. For *Totentanz* Carlos had wanted to use music by Hans Werner Henze, but Henze refused, saying that his music was meant for love, not death. Carlos then commissioned Warner Jepson to produce a score of electronic music. It received rave reviews—"historical and momentous," "a major theatrical ballet," "a work of extraordinary modern impact"—and the KPFA arts review made a very important connection:

    > The source of the inspiration was the mixture of contemporary social phenomena—the Fillmore and Avalon Dance ballrooms; the pervading aura of living for the

existential moment; the unconscious fear of living in the ever present shadow of a nuclear cloud. All this tied into a medieval atmosphere—the dance mania of the middle ages; the deep fear of a hell. Which leads me to question whether anything has changed during the course of humanity. (Tom Borek, on KPFA, April 25, 1967)

13. *In C* for Orchestra premiered October 14, 1969, at the Oakland Auditorium Theater, now the Calvin Simmons Memorial Auditorium. The reviews of the premiere were mixed, one comparing it to the fracas at the premiere of *The Rite of Spring* (Paul Hertelendy, "C-Through Debut Roils Symphony," *Oakland Tribune*, October 15, 1969, p. 1), another calling it "the cleverest imaginable way of introducing an average audience painlessly to a far-out avant-garde piece of music" (Alexander Fried, "Clever Start for Oakland Symphony," *Examiner*, October 15, 1969). As for the audience, Fried said that it "talked, it laughed, it listened. . . . There was applause, some boos, some cheers, largely in fun," while Hertelendy stated that "the conclusion of the work was greeted with widespread boos. These in turn were countered by cheers of approval. The outspoken audience reaction overwhelmed the polite applause that normally provides the damnation by faint praise for such experiments. Portions of the orchestra joined into the fray by adding enthusiastic applause at the bows of the inscrutable conductor." A cursory listen to the archival recording from the first performance does reveal ambient audience noises as the piece begins (according to Fried, Samuel began conducting the piece as the audience took their seats), and finally a bit of early "whooping" before the end, with nothing but loud applause and shouts of "bravo" at the end. A later performance at Zellerbach Hall in Berkeley was more tempered, more *ordered* than the Oakland performance, with only fairly polite applause at the end and what might have been a solitary boo. Gerhard Samuel Collection, Box 4, Stanford University Archive of Recorded Sound.

14. Coincidentally, in the same week as the orchestral premiere of *In C*, Gerhard Samuel announced his resignation as musical director of the Oakland Symphony. Reasons for his departure included an increasingly busy performance schedule elsewhere; but he also cited pressures from "several board members who are disgruntled by my programming policy." Robert Commanday, "Samuel Quits Oakland Symphony," *Chronicle*, October 14, 1969, p. 1. The Oakland Symphony, and later the Berkeley Symphony, were renowned for their progressive and adventurous programming of new music. It is therefore surprising to learn of these tensions, especially at a time when the mainstream professional ensembles across the Bay were more determinedly conservative. My thanks to Maestro Kent Nagano for his insights into the historical profiles of Bay Area orchestral ensembles.

15. Indeed, in the brief written correspondence between Gerhard Samuel and Terry Riley, it is clear that Riley had already envisioned an orchestral setting of the work, and was preparing the parts himself, which he offered to the Symphony for a per-performance fee of $200 (July 8, 1969). Samuel's response (July 10, 1969) was that such a cost was beyond the capacity of any American orchestra, but that "with adequate communication I would have no trouble working out an interesting version myself." Riley's response (July 20, 1969) is missing from Samuel's archive, but the final letter from Samuel to the composer (no date) suggests that the financial details had been agreed: "If we could receive from you one sheet of the musical material, then we could have sufficient Xerox copies made of the various orchestral groups." Gerhard Samuel Collection, Box 50, Stanford University Archive of Recorded Sound.

16. The reviews of the Oakland performances note "an endless repetition of high C's [*sic*] in octaves on the piano" (Fried, "Clever Start") and "For 22 minutes, percussionist Jerome

Neff beat an oppressive and unvarying pulse on the two highest C strings of a piano." (Hertelendy, "C-Through Debut").

17. Bill's overriding memory of *Genesis 70* is not musical:

    From where I was in the pit, which was back up against the wall, slightly under the stage, all I could hear was the dancers. When you see a ballet and you're out in the audience they look like they're like floating like feathers. It sounds like a herd of elephants out there, man, it's just incredible. You know, you can't hear yourself think in there. But I had been hired to install and maintain and make sure everything was going right with the Moog synthesizer. And frankly I wasn't that familiar with it, you know, but it was enough like the Buchla [100 series Modular Electronic Music System, aka "The Buchla Box"] I figured out what was going on with it. But somebody got very upset because they didn't know what I was doing there and so they wouldn't let me touch it. After about the first two or three hours of being there and working with it and setting it up I sat there in the pit during the performance and didn't do anything. Somebody else was playing it and it was set up right supposedly in the way that they wanted to patch it so, okay.

    For more on the idiosyncrasies of the early Moog synthesizer, see Trevor Pinch and Frank Trocco, *Analog Days* (Cambridge, MA: Harvard University Press, 2002).

18. This is supported by contemporary reviews: "Instead of waving a baton, he held up a series of cards to guide his musicians through a mixture of written notes and their own off the cuff playing." See Alexander Fried, "S.F. Ballet Premieres a '70s Version of Genesis," *Examiner*, April 27, 1970.

19. Tulli Kupferberg, "The Hip and the Square: The Hippie Generation," *Berkeley Barb*, August 4, 1967, p. 8.

20. Advance notices of *Genesis 70* were optimistic, however, with reference often made to performances of the orchestrated *In C* as "the global village's first ritual symphonic piece." See "Five New Ballets Slated for Spring," *Livermore Independent*, April 5, 1970.

21. Paul Emerson, "Choreographer's Two Works Exciting in SF Premiere," *Palo Alto Times*, April 27, 1970.

22. Robert Commanday, "S.F. Ballet Performance of Carvajal's 'Genesis 70,'" *Chronicle*, April 27, 1970.

23. From this point Carlos and a small group of dancers left to form their own group, S.F. Dance Spectrum.

24. Reich has described the experience of *It's Gonna Rain* as "above all else, impersonal; *it* just goes *its* way. Another aspect is its precision; there is nothing left to chance whatsoever." See Reich, *Writings On Music 1965-2000* (Oxford and New York: Oxford University Press, 2002), p. 20.

25. Reich has claimed in recent recorded interviews that the first half of *It's Gonna Rain* could be heard as commentary on the Cuban Missile Crisis. I hear it rather as a more locally specific, and interior, work. The "birds" effect is apparent throughout the second half of *It's Gonna Rain*, but reaches a climax from about 5:30 to the end of the piece.

26. See Potter, *Four Musical Minimalists*.

27. Steve Reich in Duckworth, *Talking Music*, p. 297.

28. Potter, *Four Musical Minimalists*, p. 170.

29. RJG, "Narcotics and a Paradox," *Chronicle*, March 14, 1963, p. 43.

30. See Bernstein, ed., *Tape Music Center*, p. 74.
31. Terry Riley, in Duckworth, *Talking Music*, p. 269.
32. When asked if *In C* was a "drug piece," however, Riley replied:
    > Well, no, not specifically. But the drug experience leads towards some kind of *satori*, some kind of enlightening, and that was what I was after. And for a lot of people, the drug experience was the only way that they had of getting into that world. No, I don't think drugs are the answer and I don't advocate that. What I'm saying is that during the sixties that was the way a lot of us entered into a search for higher consciousness. (Ibid)
33. "I feel it's my field to try to create magic in sound. Magic in the sense of transcendence of this ordinary life into another realm. An awakening, you know. To use music to try to awaken ourselves." Ibid., pp. 270–71.
34. "I actually had, believe it or not, an improvising group in 1963 in San Francisco. Members of that group included Jon Givson, the reed player now with Phil Glass; Tom Constanten, who played with the Grateful Dead; and Phil Lesh, who plays bass with the Grateful Dead, but was occasionally a trumpet player in my group. What this group did, basically, was play what I called pitch charts, which were pieces influenced by Berio. . . . Everybody played the same note—free timbre, free attack, free rhythm. Then everybody played two or three notes, basically building up to the full twelve notes. The way we moved from one group to the other was that one player would play a kind of audible cue. That idea was taken from African music. The effect of these pieces was to hear the same chord atomized and revoiced in an improvisational way. Ultimately, I felt it was kind of vapid and didn't really have enough musical content." (Steve Reich in Duckworth, *Talking Music*, p. 294.)
35. Phil Lesh, *Searching for the Sound* (New York: Little, Brown, 2005), pp. 58–59.
36. See Sumanth Gopinath, "The Problem of the Political in Steve Reich's *Come Out*," in Robert Adlington, ed., *Sound Commitments: Avant-Garde Music and the Sixties* (Oxford: Oxford University Press, 2009), and "Reich in Blackface: *Oh Dem Watermelons* and Radical Minstrelsy in the 1960s," *Journal of the Society for American Music* 5/3 (2011): 139–93.
37. Indeed, Reich has disowned the soundtrack. See Gopinath, "Reich in Blackface."
38. Mark Rowland, "Strange Bedfellows: Jerry Garcia meets Elvis Costello," *Musician* 149 (March 1991): 48, quoted in James Revell Carr, "Black Muddy River: The Grateful Dead in the Continuum of American Folk Music," in Nicholas Meriwether, ed., *All Graceful Instruments: The Contexts of the Grateful Dead Phenomenon* (Newcastle: Cambridge Scholars Publishing, 2007), p. 134.
39. Carr, "Black Muddy River," p. 135.
40. Scotty Stoneman with the Kentucky Colonels, *Live in L.A. 1965* (Sierra Briar Records, 1978). This recording of "Eighth of January" does not reach the twenty minutes that Garcia claims to have heard, but at 5:20 it is the longest track on the record.
41. These solo choruses occur at 1:05, 1:49, and 2:06.
42. The descending figure (A-F#-E in the upper octave; F#-E-D in the lower) does not follow a regular pattern: the attacks on the upper-A occur at uneven intervals, magnifying this sense of suspended time.
43. Available on archive.org/details/gd67-09-03.sbd.backus.17272.sbeok.shnf (Accessed June 15, 2015). This recording fades in at the end of the second verse, just before the beginning

of the guitar solo (:08); the "minimalist" figure lasts from :32-:52. After the third verse, the extended improvisation begins at 1:27, making a brief suggestion of what became the "Dark Star" jam (21:30), before a final reprise of the third verse (22:17).

44. David Malvinni has described the Dead's improvisatory style as existing in a suspended time "that has transcended cause-and-effect relations—a belief in a now that is continually unfolding not as a linear point but as an instant that is under constant renewal with no sense of pastness." This is particularly true of improvisations over drones or ostinati, as in "Dark Star," but the description itself is also evocative of the type of slow harmonic motion typified by proto-minimalist works such as *In C*. See *Grateful Dead and the Art of Rock Improvisation* (Plymouth: Scarecrow Press, 2013), p. 9.

45. By contrast, composer Pauline Oliveros has mentioned "locals like Terry Riley, Steve Reich, eventually Janis Joplin and Big Brother and the Holding Company too, and Grace Slick. It was an amazing time. For me, I hesitate to think about what it would have been like not to have all that. It provided me with a platform for developing my work." See Bernstein, *Tape Music Center*, p. 104.

10. POSTLUDE: *THE DHARMA AT BIG SUR*

> I wanted to compose a piece that embodied the feeling of being on the West Coast—literally standing on a precipice overlooking the geographic shelf with the ocean extending far out to the horizon, just as I had done thirty-two years before on my arrival at the Pacific's edge.[1]

To commemorate the opening of the Disney Concert Hall in 2003 the Los Angeles Philharmonic commissioned a new work by John Adams.[2] Adams had moved to California from the East Coast at the end of the short 60s. His first sight of the dramatic Pacific coastline was a revelation—what he called a "shock of recognition."[3] Forty years into his compositional career, Adams returned to that profound experience in *The Dharma at Big Sur*, placing himself on the map of California's progressive aesthetic, and connecting with its musical lineage.

Twenty years earlier, Adams had been commissioned to write a very different piece for another Californian concert hall: *Harmonium*, scored for full orchestra and chorus, was performed at the 1981 inaugural season at the Davies Symphony Hall in San Francisco. Because Adams was known in the city for curating the New and Unusual Music series, early press tended to note his youthful "edge" and crossover appeal.[4] While his early compositions might bear a surface resemblance to the minimalism that grew out of the San Francisco Tape Music Center, the "high"/"low" balance in those pieces reflects his deeper influences: nineteenth-century symphonic works, jazz, rock.

Harmonium is marked by minimalism—incessant repetition, slow harmonic motion—and balanced by lush post-Romantic Mahlerian orchestral textures. Adams composed *Harmonium* while living in the Haight, which he described at the time as

> incredible—it has so much of that energy that I keep talking about. You know, if you're a college professor in Cambridge, Princeton, or Berkeley, the slice of life you eat every morning is in a very rarified atmosphere. I think that that aspect ultimately comes out in your music; whereas, if you tend to live in a more varied environment . . . with all sorts of crazies, gypsies, very rich and very weird people, it has to be reflected in your music.[5]

In a program note for the work Adams declared that "minimalism is a bore—you get those Great Prairies of non-event—but that highly polished, perfectly resonant sound is wonderful."[6] In the decades since, Adams' music has been described as minimal, post-minimal, and not-minimal, but the sonic palate that he exploited in *Harmonium*, among other early works, defined a compositional style at once immediately identifiable as Adams' own, and inseparable from his geographical placement in the Bay Area.

The Dharma at Big Sur was inspired by two Californian composers, Lou Harrison and Terry Riley. Harrison was a longtime resident of Santa Cruz County whose fascination with alternative tuning systems and Asian musics had an enormous impact on the musical life of the region.[7] Terry Riley's quarter-century of study with Indian vocal master Prandit Pran Nath instigated in his own work a quest for balance between formal composition and improvisation, of genre-crossing, "just" intonation,[8] and the exploration of different forms of repetition. Adams explores all of these influences in *The Dharma at Big Sur*, and the result is a piece deeply rooted in the history of Californian musical expression, its outward glance toward the East, and the spiritual importance of a very particular spot on the central coast.[9]

At the work's core is the sound of the electric violin. The experience of seeing Tracy Silverman—a classically trained, free improviser—perform at Yoshi's jazz club in Oakland, inspired Adams to explore "the expressive power [that] lies *in between the notes*."[10] Though *The Dharma at Big Sur* is meticulously notated, it is meant to sound improvised, spontaneous—"as if the solo violin were a seabird, riding the air currents as they shift direction and elevation in a high wind."[11] To achieve this effect, during the compositional process Silverman improvised on Adams' small motivic fragments to suggest directions outward. The result is a two-movement work balancing the "outward" influences of Harrison and Riley: the former in the first movement, "A New Day," the latter in the second, "Sri Moonshine."

Adams has described *The Dharma at Big Sur* in terms of an Indian raga: first "a long, dreamlike opening, similar to the *alap*, without pulse and with a feel of unpremeditated improvised lyricism," followed by "a lightly rhythmized *jor* section," and ending with "a pulse-throbbing virtuosic *jhala*."[12] Adams has also described the "jazz-infused melody" in the violin and the "dance-like effect" in the second movement as akin to "a gigantic, pulsing gamelan."[13] Whatever the intention, the result is a "wonderful pan-Asian-American polyglot of Indian and Persian melodic gestures and [Indonesian] gamelan-inspired percussion." And Adams makes "no pretense of being purist about it."[14] Rather, he invokes a broad, long-60s aesthetic—the shift toward Eastern spirituality as reflected in the work of Ginsberg and Kerouac, the shift in consciousness as explored in the prototypical "psychedelic" art music of early 1960s San Francisco—calling *The Dharma at Big Sur* simply his "California coastal-trance piece."[15]

The promontories and cliffscapes at Big Sur, where "the current pounds and smashes the littoral in a slow, lazy rhythm of terrifying power," are imprinted in Adams' piece.[16] As in the expanse of the Pacific, the activity underneath the surface gives the piece its texture. This is audible in the first movement, "A New Day," where a quiet bubbling in the strings and samplers, and subtle brass crests, underpin the violin's improvisatory opening.[17] The aural effect here belies its complexity, however: it may be "coastal-trance," but it is also a realization of Adams' desired "visceral effect of great emotional complexity."[18] At the first movement's climax, amid hints of Respighi's *Pines of Rome* in the cascading harps and keyboards, a brightened texture signals the "new day,"[19] transitioning to the "dance-like" second movement, "Sri Moonshine."[20]

There is much more surface activity in "Sri Moonshine" than there had been in the first movement, more textural variation, more sense of organic sonic expansion. The "gigantic, pulsing gamelan" emerges in the texture at 2:50,[21] but the more striking feature of "Sri Moonshine" occurs about eight minutes in, when the marimba introduces an insistent B pulse.[22] This remains constant for the final four minutes of the work, primarily in the samplers and percussion. The final minutes of *The Dharma at Big Sur* are filled with suggestions of *In C*, from the increasingly dense texture, to the repeated, overlapping fragments in the percussion. There is a brief shift to an E pulse,[23] but the overall effect is an obvious nod to Terry Riley, in what Adams has called "one enormous, ecstatic expression of 'just B.'"[24] "Just" refers to the tuning system, of course, but it also suggests a simplicity: this is "just B," much as Riley's 1964 piece was just "in C."

Adams' work derives its energy from the "shock of recognition" he felt when he first saw the central Californian coastline. *The Dharma at Big Sur* summons the power of the Pacific,[25] but it also suggests a return—of the tide, of history, of the seminal minimalist moment, of spiritual "good works." Adams may no longer be a minimalist, or post-minimalist, composer, but *The Dharma at Big Sur* reveals roots deep in the short 60s, its echoes of Harrison and Riley confirming a ripple of musical currents far beyond the long 60s.

10.1 Stillness at Esalen.

Notes

1. John Adams, *Hallelujah Junction: Composing an American Life* (London: Faber and Faber, 2008), pp. 233–34.
2. *The Dharma at Big Sur* premiered on October 24, 2003, conducted by Esa-Pekka Salonen, with Tracy Silverman on electric violin.
3. http://www.earbox.com/dharma-at-big-sur/.
4. Even in his own writing Adams has occasionally taken this tack: "On the album's back cover [*Harmonium*, ECM Records, 1984] is a photograph of the young composer, shoeless and in jeans, sitting with his dog on a sofa in his Haight-Ashbury apartment. Through the window behind him, Victorian rooftops are just barely discernible in the late-afternoon fog." John Adams, "Personal History: Sonic Youth," *New Yorker*, August 25, 2008.
5. David Landis, "New Audience for New Music," *San Francisco Symphony Magazine*, November 1980.
6. *Harmonium* program note, San Francisco Symphony, January 1984.
7. Upon his death Harrison's archive was bequeathed to the University of California, Santa Cruz, with costs of processing and curating the materials defrayed by grants from two Grateful Dead organizations, the Rex Foundation and Unbroken Chain.
8. "Just" intonation is a system of tuning based on pure ratios rather than an equal division of the octave. In *The Dharma at Big Sur* this presented extreme difficulties for the orchestra, so Adams specifies in the score "just" tunings only for the piano, harps, and samplers.
9. For more on Lou Harrison, see Leta Miller and Fredric Lieberman, *Lou Harrison: Composing a World* (Oxford and New York: Oxford University Press, 1998). For a history of Californian musical experimentation and spiritual consciousness, see Mina Yang, *California Polyphony* (Urbana and Chicago: University of Illinois Press, 2008).
10. Adams, *Hallelujah Junction*, p. 201. An obvious reference here is Sheila Whiteley's seminal work in psychedelic rock, *The Space Between the Notes: Rock and the Counterculture* (London: Routledge, 1992).
11. *Hallelujah Junction*, pp. 234–35.
12. Ibid., p. 235.
13. John Adams on *The Dharma at Big Sur*, available at http://www.earbox.com/dharma-at-big-sur/ (Accessed March 29, 2015).
14. Russell Johnston, "Electric violin virtuoso Tracy Silverman brings the Pacific Coast to Nashville with composer John Adams' *The Dharma at Big Sur*," *Nashville Scene*, March 18, 2010. Available at http://tinyurl.com/o69czb6 (Accessed March 29, 2015).
15. Adams, *Hallelujah Junction*, p. 234. For more on the Beats' connection to Big Sur and Eastern spirituality, see Henry Miller, *Big Sur and the Oranges of Hieronymus Bosch* (New York: New Directions, 1957), Michael McClure, *Touching the Edge: Dharma Devotions from the Hummingbird Sangha* (Boston and London: Shambhala, 1999), and Jack Kerouac, *Big Sur* (London: Harper Perennial, 2001), *The Dharma Bums* (London: Penguin Classics, 2006), and *Some of the Dharma* (London: Penguin, 1999).
16. http://www.earbox.com/dharma-at-big-sur/.

Postlude: *The Dharma at Big Sur*

17. I am deeply grateful to Daniel Nelson for his predictably rich insights into minimalism in general, and Adams' work in particular.
18. http://www.earbox.com/dharma-at-big-sur/.
19. This appears in the score at rehearsal letter Q, and in the Tracy Silverman recording at 12:15.
20. "Sri Moonshine" took its name from Riley's Moonshine Ranch in the Sierra foothills; Riley's record label is called Sri Moonshine.
21. This corresponds to rehearsal letter G1 in the score. The real "shock of recognition" here is in its clear echoes of the end of the second movement of *Harmonium*.
22. This corresponds to rehearsal letter S1 in the score.
23. This corresponds to rehearsal letter D2 in the score, and 10:55 in the Silverman recording. The E pulse lasts about one minute before returning to the "tonic" of B. The static harmony of much of *The Dharma at Big Sur* might therefore be heard in terms of what Adams called minimalism's "Great Prairies of non-event."
24. http://www.earbox.com/dharma-at-big-sur/.
25. I mean to suggest that the Pacific is actually inscribed in the music. *The Dharma at Big Sur* never made as much sense to me as it did when I took my iPod and a cup of coffee and sat on an Adirondack chair on the front lawn of Esalen, facing West, and listened to it in the predawn morning.

11. HIPPIES, INC.

Popular music was a fundamental feature of the Haight in the short 60s, and it is the connective thread of these final chapters. There are three aspects of popular music culture that I explore here via personal encounters with hippie historiography: consumerism (ephemera, style, myth), communitarianism (audiences, community), and archivism (industry machinery, career legacy). Though the relationship between "hippie historiography" and the long 60s might suggest an inherent nostalgia, the more evident trait is the continued tensions between "authentic" and "co-opted" hippiedom. This is in part what reveals the tangible borders between memory and nostalgia, idea and practice.

***

> It is of the essence of mystiques that they persevere long after the symbolic plots they harbor fall afoul of the actions of the players and the credibility of the props. Thus, they retain a potential for shaping the future, much as they are given to mythologizing the past. It is on this perhaps deceptive and Delphian note then that one is in the end constrained to still accord a measure of "reality" to the San Francisco mystique.[1]

> KURT "CROWBAR" KANGAS: You know, the whole culture was made for a certain type of mindset. It wasn't made for the lawyers out there that when the weekend comes they put on their little psychedelic shirts and call themselves a hippie. Uh-uh. A hippie's a state of mind.

The long 60s is about continuing the legacy, whether musical, cultural or social, of the short 60s. The subtext to the history of the short 60s was tension: between straight and hip, political and pacifist, mainstream and underground, traditional and experimental, "high" and "low" art, freedom and commerce. The narrative of San Francisco's hippie counterculture reveals its overground emergence around 1965, its peak in 1967, and dispersal shortly thereafter. The "ripple" effect emanating from the Haight-Ashbury to rural pockets of Northern California was made possible by the surface tension of civic society. Not every hippie left the city, of course, but the city was a changed place for the hippies' presence: in the long 60s, the "Haight" as hippie "source" was consolidated in the popular imagination.

By 1967 "the Haight" was already a construct: a place weighted with signification for "freedom" and "otherness." In a very short time Haight Street had gone from being simply a location for social interaction and for the purchase of goods and services into an idea—an "urban mythscape." The demographic changes in the physical space of the Haight-Ashbury neighborhood attracted visitors from across the city and across the country, drawn variously by reports of the good things and by morbid curiosity of the bad—it had become a "mediascape." The experiences of these visitors were shaped by the media narrative of the Haight: pictures of the concerts in the park, of beautiful people in ecstatic dress, of endless days of idleness—images of a utopian otherness, a mythical spot where everything is free and people love each other. Meanwhile the mythscape of the Haight existed almost to the exclusion of its reality: the people who created the community had left, the stores that originally serviced the hip community had closed, free concerts in the park were a sepia memory. The romantic myth of the Haight thus propagated, local rock music of whatever stripe could represent the myth, and listeners could "use" that music "as a means of mapping out the relationship between social and geographical landscapes."[2]

As an abstract idea, "the Haight" may just suggest acid rock and free love. The reality is complicated, however, by the historical attempts of city officials to deny Haight residents the freedom to conduct themselves in unconventional ways, from the tangible (rock dances, "obscene" language, narcotics use, public nudity) to the intangible (seeking truth and enlightenment, shunning established social norms of mainstream culture, visual and sonic explorations into the outer limits of consciousness). The tension within the Haight community between freedom and anarchism was similarly potent and nearly as destructive, as evidenced by the different tones of the *Oracle* and the Communications Company, and in the exchanges between the Haight Independent Merchants and the Diggers. Some of those tensions still exist, though they are tempered by distance and experience. In a *Guardian* retrospective on the Summer of Love, reporter Ed Vulliamy visited a number of former Haight figures, among them Bob Weir of the Grateful Dead and Peter Coyote of the Diggers. Weir explained that the Haight was "about exploration, finding new ways of expression, being aware of one's existence." The Haight hippies—and the Dead—eschewed the idea of leadership, whether political or cultural, which was one of their enduring legacies. Coyote, by contrast, showed that his Digger instincts were still well honed:

> "The Dead never did anything to remove a product from the market which by doing so may have diminished the cult. It's true that the Dead were the most familial of all the bands, but when Bob Weir accuses the Diggers of being ideological, he belies the Dead's participation in the mass culture of the late 20th century, which had a very pronounced ideology. We actually had no ideology—we were about practice." Then Coyote smiles: he and Bob had dinner only the other night. "Hey, we're on the same side. What the fuck."[3]

In the history of the "short 60s," the myth of a unified, shared, counter-mainstream-culture vision often makes the inter-Haight tensions difficult to understand. The distinctions in political ideology, or the different relationships that some hippies had with the notion of paying for goods and services, can seem obstructive to the greater movement toward cultural revolution. An awareness of those tensions, and the recognition that they represent sustained beliefs and lifestyle choices, is important to the understanding of the present day Bay Area. The fact that San Francisco now embraces that "same side" is perhaps one of the more inevitable outcomes of the short 60s. Part of this inevitability stems from that 1968 market research showing that popular music would be the fourth largest industry in the city by the mid-1970s.[4] Even with the collapse of the dancehall scene, the business of concert promotion continued unabated. The sense of "scene" might have dissipated and the sites for pop music consumption might have changed, but there was still a sense of ownership over the aesthetic. The hippie "moment" was tied into the development of the ideal concert environment, and this can be seen as San Francisco's "intangible heritage":

> *All* heritage is intangible, in that meanings and values attached to objects and sites of memory are socially and culturally negotiated. All heritage is, therefore, also political. The question becomes not what (or where or when) popular music heritage is in any given context, but rather what it does; how heritage discourses mobilise meanings, identities and performative enactments.[5]

The commercialization of the hippie aesthetic had crept into the mainstream well before the Summer of Love. The weekend hippie could buy a Love burger and a Madras bedspread on Haight Street; the social set could "hire" hippies to give their dinner parties a bit of color, or simply shop at the Union Square department stores for all the traditional trappings:

> VICKI LEEDS: My friend Deborah and I won a contest to be the Sonny and Cher models for Macy's. That was bizarre, just walking around like we were supposed to be there. We could go to all the different departments and get jewelery or hats or whatever we wanted as accoutrements to our outfits. We did that for about six months.

> TERESA TUDURY: You felt so trivialized and pigeon-holed and labeled. I remember coming home once to visit my family, and my mom and my dad were on their way to a masquerade party with their friends, and they were dressed as hippies! And my dad had this hideous long wig on, and a headband, and my mom was decked out in love beads and stuff, and it was like holy cripes, what a disconnect. It was hysterical to them, and yet I'm kind of standing there, you know? Very weird. It was kind of over.

And at the height of the Haight, from about 1966–67, the shift in culture was apparent on the street:

> ERIC CHRISTENSEN: When the vicarious people came in, you started to see people who weren't artistic, weren't contributing to the scene, were doing harder drugs, were being more negative in terms of the whole vibe. I guess back in the day we thought things were becoming co-opted, but in a way that's what happens organically—that things like yogurt would start appearing in Safeway, some of the big companies would start to do commercials with psychedelic art and that kind of thing. So it was getting co-opted, it was getting more mainstream. To stay on the cutting edge, and to stay avant-garde—it didn't mean as much to have long hair and a mustache and look that way. Before, it was like you could see somebody on the street and automatically say, oh that's a kindred spirit, believes the same things politically, believes the same things spiritually, socially. And you know, after a while it didn't mean much: a lot of people grew their hair long and didn't believe those things and didn't share those values.

"Co-opting" the scene and the arrival of "vicarious people" are indications of the Haight's mediascape. That some merchants catered for the vicarious people's sense of participation is unfortunate, but inevitable. The desire to grasp a moment is fundamental and connected to the recent impulse toward "pilgrimage, fandom, personal identity work, local pride, and the aim to participate in a 'tourist experience.'"[6]

In recent years the Haight myth has provided a feverish business for the local tourism trade. One weekend in December 2008 I took two guided walking tours of the Haight-Ashbury: the Flower Power Tour, $20 a head, and the SF City Guides tour, free of charge. The Flower Power walking tour was led by a woman who moved to the Haight as a teenager in the early 1970s. Her commentary was engaging and she served a basic function, pointing to buildings and mentioning famous names, ticking all the right boxes for the tourists: she had a lightness of historical touch that perpetuated the Haight's mediascape. To cite one example, our group eventually ended up in front of the house at 719 Ashbury, inhabited for a time by the Hell's Angels. Our guide retold the story of Chocolate George, the Hell's Angel who died in a head-on collision in the Haight in 1967. In her version of the story, the Hell's Angels were planning Chocolate George's funeral, and, looking to book some entertainment, went across the street to number 710 to coerce the resident Grateful Dead to play. The way our tour guide explained this bit of history—"you don't say no to the Hell's Angels"—implied that the Grateful Dead were somehow bullied into playing music for a bunch of thugs. The relationship was, in fact, more nuanced.[7] There is a contemporary insiders' account of Chocolate George's funeral that provides some inimitable local color:

> "In San Francisco, we play for free in the park. You can't find a better audience than that, they're beautiful," says Janis. . . .

"Chocolate George, one of the Angels, got killed, and they threw a free thing in the park. We got lots of beer, and they got the Dead and us. It was just a beautiful thing, all the hippies and Angels were just stoned out of their heads, passing DMT, you couldn't imagine a better funeral. It was the greatest party in the world," says Janis.

"We sent him off just like he would have wanted, man," says Sam.

"Everybody was fucking in the bushes," says Jim, the lead guitarist . . . who doesn't talk much, but has an eye for important details.[8]

What this shows is that certain narratives are imposed on events after the fact, and perpetuate another kind of myth—the Angels are known as bad guys, therefore they were always bad guys—when all it would take to improve the quality of the information, and provide a true link to the short 60s, would be to look through contemporary sources, or even just have a chat with someone who was there:

SUZI YOUNG: My daughter was about three when I turned her loose in the Avalon ballroom, all painted with day-glo paint that would show up in the black light, to dance. And it was a fabulous evening of watching her do that, and everybody dancing with her. And later on in the evening she came and fell asleep in the dressing room. As we were leaving, I was holding Julie in my arms, and Jesse [Colin Young] was right behind me—the stage was opposite the dressing room door, and all you could see was a sea of Angels' colors. Everywhere, cause they had their backs to you so you could see the backs of their jackets. And Jesse was afraid to ask them to move. So I had the baby in my arms, and I said excuse me, and they were perfectly wonderful gentlemen, and they moved. One of the Angels went tearing down the stairs behind us and threw open the door and said, "Don't ever let anybody tell you that Angels aren't gentlemen!" And he held the door as I carried the baby out. It's my remembrance of them.

By contrast, the San Francisco City Guide walking tour was rich in historical detail, and mentioned the hippies practically only in passing. This is significant, because it put the hippies in perspective: they were living on the fringes of the city, communally, for a pittance, in these lovely old Victorian homes. What was left were the remnants of the *after*-culture: the visual and sonic reminders of the importance that some people still invest in the place, of which there are plenty. On any given day there will be a handful of pilgrims standing outside 710 Ashbury to pay tribute to Jerry Garcia, to soak up any residual vibes from a half-century ago. Despite the conversion of the storied hippie pads into multimillion-dollar single-family homes, it is easy to juxtapose visual reality with remembered mediascape.

In the spring of 2011 I took a very different kind of guided tour: the Magic Bus, a multimedia "tour through time and space."[9] It is instantly recognizable—a psychedelic bus in the "Further" mold, guides in character as colorfully dressed hippies: this is tourism as performance art. The two long rows of seats in the middle of the bus face outward. While the bus is in transit screens are lowered and the movie takes over: documentary footage, modern voiceovers, music, environmental sounds. When the bus left Union Square the soundtrack was a 1950s transistor radio tuned to Fats Domino and Elvis. As the music leaped ahead to the Beatles' global *Our World* telecast of "All You Need Is Love" (1967) the screens lifted. As we watched the people outside in Chinatown move about their daily lives we heard about a "great awakening" that happened in the 60s, a new interest in philosophies of the East, the works of Alan Watts; moving along, we heard lines from Ginsberg's "Sunflower Sutra" and a Kerouac haiku before the bus stopped again and we found ourselves parked outside Kerouac Alley in North Beach.[10] From nineteenth-century immigration to 1950s Beats in six city blocks.

From there, our bus became a symbol of the 60s, immersed in documentary footage of the Freedom Riders, and of the Merry Pranksters' own magic trip: a reminder that one was either "on the bus or off it," and that the trip was open to all. The screens lifted for our trip up Haight Street toward the Park, a constant stream of 1967-era international pop hits adding sound to the mythscape. We heard snippets of hippie philosophy counterbalanced by clips of Governor Ronald Reagan demonizing the "gyrating" young people who congregated in public places; we drove to the Conservatory of Flowers, "the generator of Flower Power for all of San Francisco"; and stopped after a while at Civic Center. The context there was not the Diggers and Sgt. Sunshine; the context was the draft, the 1968 assassinations of Martin Luther King, Jr. and Robert F. Kennedy, and the 1978 assassinations of Supervisor Harvey Milk and Mayor George Moscone. The Magic Bus tour plays on the trappings of hippie San Francisco, but places the Haight in a long continuum of liberalism, of social freedom, of activism, and of cultural change.[11]

In the microhistory of the Haight community the bigger international picture of the 1960s can often seem remote. The political tensions in the local community, the struggles to maintain a commitment to free giving and receiving, and to nurture an environment of free expression, seem insignificant within the larger political upheavals of Chicago, Paris, and Prague. But predictions of doom and disintegration in the Haight leaned a grounding rhythm to the "short 60s," particularly in the pages of the *Oracle* and in the ComCo street sheets. From 1967, in the absence of those two voices, the pages of *Rolling Stone* relayed the messages from the countercultural epicenter:

> There's no denying that it's there: San Francisco was featured in more magazines and papers this summer than at any time since the earthquake of 1906. Why? The Haight-Ashbury. It was the summer's main topic of breakfast table conversation. To some it was the symbol of the New America; later, for others,

it became just another burned-out vision. Whatever it was, whatever it became and whatever it should have been, the impact of it on the American way of life has yet to be fully felt.[12]

Eight months later, Ben Fong-Torres wrote that:

> If bad-mouthing could kill, the San Francisco rock scene would have been long gone, eulogized, and forgotten by now. But, with all the liquidity and mysteriousness of a fistful of mercury, the seemingly amorphous "scene" has burst into lively new fragments with each blow from the nay-sayers. So the Jefferson Airplane, Grateful Dead, Big Brother, Quicksilver Messenger Service, Charlatans, and Great Society—these 1965–66 bands were, as events have proved, not so much fad-feeding pioneers as, together, the "first wave" of what has become the outfront concern of the pop music business: San Francisco rock. With the nationwide popularization of hippie-*nouveau* art, liquid light shows, and dance/concerts came the second San Francisco wave: Moby Grape, Steve Miller Band, Blue Cheer, Mother Earth, Lee Michaels, and the Loading Zone. And now, a year after the so-called "Death of the Hippie" rites in the Haight-Ashbury, followed by the violence-spurred transformation of Haight Street into a boulevard of boarded store windows, the third wave is upon us. And the San Francisco rock scene has never been healthier.[13]

In the same pages a scant four months later, the sociological side looked rather less rosy:

> In a most subtle, but quite obvious way, the hippie died in 1968. As foreseeable from the early part of 1967, slowly and surely that scene was through. Not that good things from it don't remain—because they most certainly do—but the cohesiveness and impetus faded. Whoever the "real" hippies were, the people currently freaking around the Haight-Ashbury and the East Village don't remind us of what the hip ethic was and what it still means, even though aged several years.[14]

In 1976 *Rolling Stone* published a ten-year retrospective, with a capsule history, a bit of oral history, a where-are-they-now segment, and a pilgrim's guide to the Haight. There was surely a touch of irony involved there: what would those 1969-era "pilgrims" have found in the Haight once they got there? The ballroom scene had ended, and Bill Graham was shifting his attentions to the Winterland Arena and to the promotion of larger-scale events in the Bay Area and further afield.[15] Yet less than a decade after the Gray Line's unwelcome "Hippie Hop" tours, *Rolling Stone* was offering a "hip" guide to the neighborhood for "hip" tourists.

Even in the late-60s, the "original" hippie community had an unusual relationship with the idea of the Haight. In 1969 the Grateful Dead appeared on *Playboy After*

Dark, and host Hugh Hefner spent some time chatting with Jerry Garcia about the band's connection to the city:[16]

> HUGH HEFNER: Jerry, the Grateful Dead have been a part of the San Francisco scene for four or five years. Is the hippie scene changing now?
>
> JERRY GARCIA: Yeah. Well, we're all big people now.
>
> HH: But I understand the Haight-Ashbury scene has changed a good deal.
>
> JG: Well the Haight-Ashbury is just a place, you know. It's just a street. It's not really the thing—it never was the thing that was going on.
>
> HH: It was just the thing that got the publicity.
>
> JG: Right, right. That's the thing people could talk about, because it's, like, easy to remember.

The Haight was "just a street" in 1969. Whatever vestiges of hipness remained, it was not enough to sustain a scene. The hippies had gone, and the emptiness on Haight Street was a stark reminder of the frantic pitch of the mediascape not two years previously.

These days it is possible to wander through San Francisco, Berkeley, and Oakland without being reminded of the Bay Area's radical history, but like the ubiquitous *tchotchkes* sold at Fisherman's Wharf, there are the inevitable reminders of the area's history to be found in shops on Haight Street and elsewhere. This is a clear reminder of the area's mythscape, the local agencies and souvenir merchants providing for the tourists what they expect to encounter: disembodied signifiers there for the "tourist gaze,"[17] foretold in the months before the Summer of Love:

> The hippies created a very groovy scene out in the Haight-Ashbury. They kissed cops, gave flowers to drunks, invaded downtown department stores with lovely bright balloons, and turned on with strange drugs. Everything they did was brilliantly merchandised under the name of love. . . .
>
> [But] the merchants of love . . . are another matter. . . . They are debasing the currency of brotherhood. They are the carnies who follow the missionaries into uncharted land. They rightly stink.
>
> Out in the Haight you can buy a "Love Guide," which turns out to be a street map and directory to shops making an honest buck out of the hippie movement.
>
> A couple of months back the Diggers and other Haight militants picketed at "Love Dance" on account of it cost three bucks fifty to get the body in. A jewelry store called "Happiness Unlimited" has a window sign: "We love you; we hope you love us."
>
> About the same time a bar on Haight street converted itself into a hot dog and hamburger establishment. The hamburger is called, naturally, a LOVEburger. The hot dog is a LOVE dog. And this cuddly establishment has applied for permission to change its name to "THE LOVE CAFE."

And you may be sure this is only the beginning....

In the end, the punishment of the hippies will be brutal and biblical. Their own imagination and talent for self-advertising will do them in. Their love, and their flowers and their balloons will bring the creeps. The creeps will prove unendurable. And this too will pass.[18]

Back in 1967 local heads decided to engage with hippie tourism, and took an active role in the Gray Line Bus Tours: in the spirit of the Diggers they took to "freeing" the tourists, inviting them to the Dead house at 710 Ashbury, or holding up mirrors to the bus windows to blow the surprised minds. The tourist became an actor in his or her own play.[19] And some enterprising souls published a tourist map of the Haight-Ashbury, which they sold for $1. It's a proper fold-out number, with a detailed map of Haight Street on one side and a handy hippie glossary on the other.

The map itemizes every business on the street, from dentists' offices to laundromats to liquor stores to banks; in other words, it shows Haight Street as the heart of a business community, head and straight. The marginalia hints at a countercultural presence and the more free-form recreation at Golden Gate Park, but otherwise, it simply states that the Haight is just a neighborhood like any other.

After my Flower Power Walking Tour in 2008 I paid $5 for a color photocopy of a "star map" of the area. Lurid tie-dye effect and faux-psychedelic lettering aside, what is notable about this "star map" is the inclusivity of it. Here the Haight is extended

11.1 Haight tourist map, 1967.

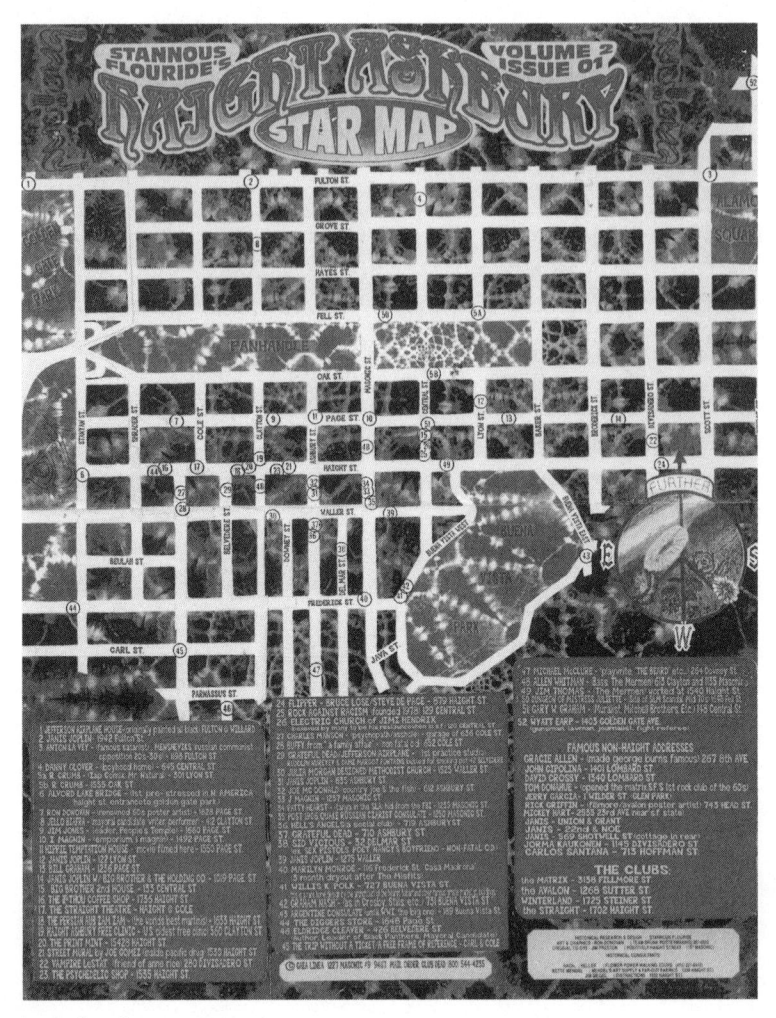

11.2 Haight "star" map, 2008.

geographically to neighboring areas, and temporally beyond the 60s to encompass the homes of Wyatt Earp and Jello Biafra (Dead Kennedys), the Dungeon of Mistress Juliette, the office of Rock Against Racism, and the bar with "the world's best martinis." The Dead, Big Brother, Jefferson Airplane, and the rest are present and accounted for, but comprise a relatively small percentage of the suggested sites of interest. The hippie mythscape is present in its visual design, but it maps a larger countercultural history including more recent iterations, the neighborhood's changing demographic, and the subtle encroachment of "establishment" hippiedom, located on the northeast corner of the Haight and Ashbury intersection.

Ben & Jerry's is an embodiment of the long 60s. From the opening of their first Vermont store in 1978, social activism has been an integral part of the Ben & Jerry's

11.3 Cherry Garcia, Karamel Sutra, Hazed & Confused.

mission. They foregrounded the short 60s in their business model, in their marketing, and in their commitment to grassroots activism. Theirs is a playful engagement with 1960s signifiers, perhaps never more successfully imprinted than Cherry Garcia, the first ice cream flavor to be named after a rock musician.[20]

> BEN COHEN: I was touched profoundly by the spirit of the 60s. In the 60s people were taking those values of peace and love—you know, that's all over the Bible, and as near as I can tell, all over every major religion—but they were taking it out of the houses of worship, and they were taking it into the streets. And I think that's really what we're supposed to be doing. I mean the idea is not just to have those values on Saturday or Sunday when you're in church or temple, but to take those values into your everyday life. And people were doing it. And there was another part to 60s values besides peace and love, which was: fun. And, yeah, that's part of it too. We are put here on earth I think to have a good time, and to spread joy and peace and love. I mean, what better thing is there to do?

The embodiment of that approach to life is found in another Ben & Jerry's flavor, named after the clown and humanitarian, Wavy Gravy. The proceeds from his eponymous flavor—resurrected for a brief time in 2005—support Camp Winnarainbow, a training ground for the hippies of tomorrow.[21] Wavy Gravy is a living reminder that the long 60s are viable, and the charitable work that he has done, quietly, individually, and in his larger collective, is a continuation of the ideals of the short 60s.

So is ice cream a tangible, or intangible, heritage? Do consumers enjoy a deeper "tourist experience" if they buy a cone of Cherry Garcia on the corner of Haight

11.4 Rainbow Warriors, Union Square 2005.

and Ashbury? Playing with the myth of the short 60s while connecting to the larger social revolution of the long 60s allows for a certain "vicarious nostalgia,"[22] but also captures the sense of "fun" that was a central value of the times. The long 60s are about more than tie-dyed bedspreads and photos of 710 Ashbury; they are about a certain kind of hip capitalism and consumerism, about little pockets of quiet activism and local engagement in communities throughout the Bay Area and beyond. Rather than marketing a vibe, as in the tourist traps of the Haight, aimed at embalming the short 60s, the long 60s are about letting history breathe in everyday life.

Notes

1. Fred David, "The San Francisco Mystique," in Howard S. Becker, ed., *Culture and Civility in San Francisco* (New Brunswick: Transaction Books, 1971), p. 162.
2. Andy Bennett, "Music, Media and Urban Mythscapes: A Study of the 'Canterbury Sound,'" *Media, Culture and Society* 24/1 (January 2002): 87–100.
3. Ed Vulliamy, "Love and Haight," *The Guardian*, May 20, 2007, available on theguardian.com/music/2007/may/20/popandrock.features8 (Accessed March 31, 2015).
4. See RJG, "Tin Pan Alley Stretches to S.F.," *Chronicle*, December 16, 1968, p. 47.
5. Les Roberts, "Talkin Bout My Generation: Popular Music and the Culture of Heritage," *International Journal of Heritage Studies* 20/3 (2014): 271.

6. Marion Leonard and Robert Knifton, "Engaging Nostalgia: Popular Music and Memory in Museums," in Sara Cohen, Robert Knifton, Marion Leonard, and Les Roberts, eds., *Sites of Popular Music Heritage: Memories, Histories, Places* (Abingdon: Routledge, 2015), p. 164.
7. See *The Electric Kool-Aid Acid Test* (New York: Farrar, 1968), chapter 13.
8. Michael Thomas, "Rock-and-Roll Woman," from *Ramparts* [no date], in Jonathan Eisen, *The Age of Rock: Sounds of the American Cultural Revolution* (New York: Vintage Books, 1969), p. 284.
9. See their website, magicbussf.com.
10. Kerouac Alley spans the short distance between Columbus (North Beach) and Grant (Chinatown) avenues, and is nestled on the North Beach side between City Lights and Vesuvio bar. "Sunflower Sutra" (Berkeley, 1955), from Allen Ginsberg, *Collected Poems 1947-1980* (New York: Harper & Row, 1984); Jack Kerouac, *Book of Haikus* (New York and London: Penguin, 2003).
11. Good resources for the city's alternative histories are David Talbot, *Season of the Witch: Enchantment, Terror and Deliverance in the City of Love* (New York: Free Press, 2012), and Rebecca Solnit, *Infinite City: A San Francisco Atlas* (Berkeley and Los Angeles: University of California Press, 2010).
12. *Rolling Stone* 6, February 24, 1968.
13. *Rolling Stone* 20, October 26, 1968.
14. *Rolling Stone* 26, February 1, 1969.
15. This was the same year that the Band performed their final concert at Winterland Arena. An interesting ripple in itself—the Band were the primary progenitors of "country-rock" at the crucial 1968 musical crossroads. The preservation of their legacy in the documentary film from this final performance, *The Last Waltz* (dir. Martin Scorsese, 1978), situates San Francisco firmly on the border between "short" and "long" 60s: a last great night at the ballroom, a musical aesthetic grounded in the past, preserved for the future.
16. The Grateful Dead's appearance on *Playboy After Dark* was filmed in January 1969 and broadcast in spring of that year (season 1, episode 23). Members of the Grateful Dead spiked the coffee on set, and Hefner's private mug of Pepsi. See Dennis McNally, *A Long Strange Trip: The Inside History of the Grateful Dead* (London: Transworld Publishers, 2002), pp. 285–86.
17. John Urry, *The Tourist Gaze: Leisure and Travel in Contemporary Societies* (London: Sage, 1990).
18. Charles McCabe, "Love and the Buck," *Chronicle*, May 17, 1967, p. 24.
19. This is an interesting inversion of the audience/performer dynamic in *City Scale*, for example, which involved disrupting the city's natural rhythm by incorporating theatrical and musical elements where they would otherwise not obviously exist. As the short 60s progressed, one of the "more and more explorative" aspects of the Haight involved uncovering those theatrical and musical elements and incorporating them into the neighborhood's daily rhythm.
20. The marketing campaign for Cherry Garcia presented a gentle jab at 1960s stereotypes. In one animated commercial a conservative-looking man, dressed in a shirt and tie, is walking along a path, eating a bowl of cherries. He trips and falls down a cliff face, hitting

rocks all the way, flipping and tumbling, cherries flying everywhere. He stands up slowly, woozily. His shirt is now tie-dyed, his face covered in a moss beard, his necktie now a headband, his glasses askew, and his fingers bent into a peace sign: the fifteen-second transformation of a square into a hippie.

21. I interviewed Ben Cohen and Jerry Greenfield at the resurrection of Wavy Gravy ice cream, a public celebration held at Union Square on August 24, 2005.
22. Sara Cohen, Les Roberts, Robert Knifton, and Marion Leonard, "Introduction: Locating Popular Music Heritage," in *Sites of Popular Music Heritage*, p. 9.

12. GATHERINGS OF THE TRIBE

Aging turns many of us into totally different people. If we confront the experience with full awareness, aging can prepare us to learn what so many great sages have tried to teach: to be mindful of our mortality, to honor the needs of the soul, to practice compassion. Conscious aging opens us to these truths; it is a mighty undoer of the ego.[1]

Let's make Haight Love together, and then move to the country where love is hanging out waiting. Love-Ashbury will then exist as our trade capital, our funnel to the world, and we can occasionally share a natural sunset together, steadying our lives with both the active and the passive changes.[2]

The Peanut Gallery was the studio space in San Rafael shared by artists Stanley Mouse, Alton Kelley, Victor Moscoso, Pat Ryan, David Sheridan, Tim Harris, Larry Noggle, Linda Miller, and Enid Hansen. The artists had held three joint shows in the Bay Area in the late 1970s under the banner Concrete Foundation of Fine Arts. The announcement for each show featured some version of a dragon, designed initially by Pat Ryan and Dave Sheridan. In July 1979 they were evicted from the Peanut Gallery, so the building could be refashioned into offices. The actual meeting-space was gone, but their virtual identity survived, and by the early 1980s that dragon—rainbow-hued, holding a lightning rod—had been embroidered on the back of black satin jackets worn proudly by 700 members of what became known as the Artista Gang.

A "gang" is meant to forge a common identity, a recognizable belonging to a larger group united in a shared ethic. In the case of the Artistas, the "gang" is an ironic play on the adolescent culture of the 1950s, philosophically light years before the dawn of the psychedelic. As one contemporary commentator suggested, bands like Quicksilver Messenger Service, the Dead, and Charlatans were part of this aesthetic, and the Artistas "commemorated" the Hot Rod influence in their adoption of a mysterious group moniker and visual signifiers: the "individual member name on the front and the name of the club on the back."[3]

Although the Artistas were founded by artists, Alton Kelley insisted that theirs was not "an artist co-op or league. We don't talk about Picasso and organize shows. We aren't together for any commercial purpose. That takes the fun out of it. This is strictly for fun."[4] Membership in the Artista gang was

> open to painters, printers, photographers, filmmakers, musicians, mimes, authors and actors. It is also open to truck drivers, soda jerks, bartenders,

certified public accountants and gas station attendants. Just as long as you are an artist at what you do.[5]

There are important generational ideas to note here as well. By the time the Artistas were formed most had passed the artificial threshold of the time—"don't trust anyone over 30." There was a long decade separating them from the short 60s, and musical tastes had shifted as well. Maintaining a sense of youthful "fun" (with the knowledge that the music of one's youth was now "classic rock") was eased by irony, hence the satin jackets and the "gang" names. This also coincided with a general trend in the 1970s toward 1950s nostalgia, evidenced by the musical *Grease* (1971), Elton John's pop single "Crocodile Rock" (1972), the film *American Graffiti* (1973), and the television series *Happy Days* (1974–84).[6] Yet the Artista gang played with 1950s signifiers within a deeply 1960s sensibility: the "gang" nucleus was a creative community, part of a progressive social movement that changed the paradigm of artistic culture in the Bay Area.

In the decades since the first Artista party the group's mission is still "fun," but the parties carry a deeper meaning—of community, history, and belonging.

> KURT "CROWBAR" KANGAS: These are our last years; we're all in our 60s now. About ten years ago we saw a need to try to bring back a family again. You know, because the economy is so bad, nobody's going anywhere, nobody's doing anything, a lot of people are getting older, our friends are dying, people are becoming alone. The Family Dog is gone, Bill Graham has gone, all these supposed families are gone, dispersed; they've gone all over the world. So I started Artista up again, and people are actually calling me up and saying, "Thank you. Thank you. It feels good to belong to a family again."

The most recent resurrection of Artista is not an exercise in nostalgia, or in grabbing the embers of a culture; on the contrary, it is a renewal of cultural purpose and an enaction of the beliefs that were forged back in the short 60s. The Artista members that I have encountered embody a local demographic of

> the best educated, most socially conscientious, most politically savvy older generation the world has ever seen. They grew up entertaining (if not always endorsing) countercultural values, reveling in their willingness to search beyond the limits of convention.[7]

The awareness that hippies had in their youth of their social responsibilities has inspired them

> to do good things with the power that history has unexpectedly thrust upon it in its senior years. What boomers left undone in their youth, they will return to

take up in their maturity, if for no other reason than because they will want to make old age *interesting*.[8]

What made youth interesting in the short 60s in San Francisco was the Haight's soundscape. There were the Sunday jams at the Panhandle, bigger concerts in the Park, and formalized rock concerts at dancehalls like the Avalon and Fillmore. Regardless of setting, in the early days of local rock culture the overriding sense was one of community: the lines between performer and audience blurred, there was no "star" system, and there was a freedom to express oneself in the moment. Attempts to "capture" that essence elsewhere led to a commodification of the culture. The free events that Ralph Gleason felt best represented the new musical culture in San Francisco were attempted elsewhere by others—at Altamont, for example—but never really succeeded. As the audiences got bigger, bigger halls were needed to accommodate them, and the nature of "rock promotion" shifted beyond the limits of the hippies' capabilities.[9] The original audience had largely dispersed, but Bill Graham tried to maintain the sense of intimacy and community that he had established at the Fillmore (a community bulletin board, a barrel of free apples) by designing the new concert experience around the aesthetic and sensibility of the short 60s:

> In San Francisco, there was a long history of free shows in the park and an honorable, non-money relationship between the people and the bands.
> That was why I came up with the name. "Day on the Green." I wanted to make these events *special*. I wanted to create giant outdoor sets so the bands would be going into a space that was like a theater piece. I wanted to keep the posters and the balloons and make the backstage area special for the artists who were coming in....
> We started hiring people from the Haight-Ashbury Medical Clinic run by Dr. David Smith, to take care of the kids. We used the third-base dugout for a clinic....
> It was a time when there was an ongoing extension of the sixties into the seventies. The concert-goer was living in the real world now, not the world that had existed in the Haight-Ashbury when the original Fillmore was still going.... But there was still an element of the society that wanted to come together to enjoy one another.[10]

This desire to maintain the vibe of a late-60s free concert in the park is a recognition of what worked, not only musically but socially. The Days on the Green were one ripple from the short 60s, and they begat another: the establishment of Rock Medicine, an offshoot of the Haight Free Clinic.

Two of the philosophies propounded by the Haight Free Clinic—"health care is a right, not a privilege," and "love needs care"—resonate well into the twenty-first century. The initial purpose of the Haight Clinic was to treat local residents without charge, in a nonjudgmental environment, but they struggled continually for financial security and lacked any formal support from the city. Like many smaller local endeavors, the Haight Clinic was funded largely from donations and from moneys raised by benefit concerts: as Dr. David Smith told me, "The Haight-Ashbury Free Clinic was built on rock 'n' roll, and Bill Graham was our patron saint." Music and social responsibility were therefore fused from the beginning of the Haight's short 60s, formalized in the continued legacy of Bill Graham Presents, and reflected in the informal events such as those sponsored by the Artista Gang. Well into the long 60s, the marriage of music and community is inviolable.

According to Eyerman and Jamison, the sense of community embodied by a particular music,

> when linked to social movements . . . can have lasting effects on individuals and society. Social movements not only provide temporary spaces for the mobilization of tradition and the reconfiguration of identity, they also effect major cultural shifts, as they interact with the institutionalized practices of a dominant culture.[11]

The Haight was a temporary space for the engenderment of safety and community, and existed within the dominant, straight, culture of mainstream San Francisco. The interactions between straight and hip were occasionally tense, but undeniably transformative. In the long 60s, at those moments when the Haight community re-emerges, the "temporary space" they inhabit aligns with the local history perpetuated by its mediascape, but now reinvigorated by collective purpose. Some "major cultural shifts" enacted by the hippies in the short 60s are by now mainstream and global: Apple computers, environmentalism, yoga, organic, sustainable, seasonal produce.[12] For a native northern Californian, these are fundamental aspects of local culture, as familiar as the "Bill Graham Presents" imprint on a ticket stub. Tapping into the deeper current of the long 60s reveals the simple structures upon which this ethos was formalized. There are four events in the long 60s that illustrate this point, all Artista ripples.

In July 2005 we attended Chet Fest, the memorial concert at the Great American Music Hall for Chet Helms, who had died about a month earlier.[13] Outside, the vibe was much the same as at any sold-out concert—people milling around, hoping for tickets, selling t-shirts—but the entry gates were a portal to another time. The Great American Music Hall is an ornate and intimate old place, and at Chet Fest the light shows were authentic 60s-era liquid projections, the audience and the bands were multigenerational, and there was a feeling throughout the night of renewed purpose. This was forged most notably by the presence of Wavy Gravy, acting as master of ceremonies for the night, but also by our subjective place in the audience. Just to our right was an altar, and throughout the evening people walked past us, always smiling, to add flowers, candles, pictures, to it. There was a good concert going on, but this was a social event—talking, dancing, being in a shared moment, on a level removed from the people there just to hear the music. This was the event where Wavy Gravy announced "we're still a tribe. We'll *always* be a tribe." It was, in Eyerman and Jamison's words, a "reconfiguration of identity"—a gathering-together for the Haight community, and an insight into their culture for those of us on the outside of it.

Crowbar held his sixtieth birthday party at a little club in the Mission in spring 2007. Outside the club we saw a proliferation of hippie signifiers—tie-dye, diaphanous skirts, long gray hair on both sexes; but also their significant others—the ironic suits, conservative haircuts, and an occasional walking stick. Inside the club there was an indefinable yet palpable feeling of family, of living history, and, in local parlance, of good vibes. There was a sense of normality as well as a sense of event about the evening. Guests floated in bearing plates of food and bottles of wine, just showing up for another potluck dinner with the usual crowd. On stage were Blue Cheer and It's a Beautiful Day, just musicians playing for a friend's party, nothing to do with industry executives or singles promotions. Crowbar's birthday party was one more iteration of community, still carrying on quietly in its work.[14]

Shortly after Crowbar's birthday was the official celebration of the fortieth anniversary of the Summer of Love, held at Speedway Meadow in Golden Gate Park. The field was a sea of color, a multigenerational gathering, soundtracked by everyone from Country Joe to a reformed Moby Grape. Lined along the perimeter were Artista jackets, crafts stands, food stalls, and poster artists holding court. For the 50,000 people present that day there was a feeling of expanse and celebration, a city-endorsed recognition of an enduring historical moment. But the crowd were not there just to hear the music; they were there to *relive* a moment, to recreate the feeling of one of the "sacramental gatherings" in the park that ignited the temporary space of the short 60s.[15] At the end of the day, returning from the outerlands to downtown, the East Bay, the suburbs, the audience might have felt transformed, if only briefly.

In early September 2011 we rented a Volkswagen Westfalia Camper and headed up to Sonoma for the Artista Joyfest, arriving on a Friday night to a gentle buzz of activity. The weekend was built around two solid days of music, a mini-festival held in the shady enclosed backyard of the Sonoma Sanctuary. The generations came together for the Joyfest: on stage Lester Chambers and his son Dylan sang "Time Has Come Today" for a transcendent ten minutes,[16] while in the audience the age span between the youngest hippie and the oldest was ninety-two years.[17]

Joyfest was a celebration—the Artista Gang are still about "fun"—but it was a weekend for community support, a fundraiser for members in need. As with benefit concerts in the short 60s, at Joyfest there was no division between "them" on stage and "us" in the audience; everyone was one. It is a fundamental aspect of the Haight culture which Artista have nurtured well into the long 60s.

> LiAnne Graves: There's a core of people, Artista and people from the Haight, who still carry the values. This is one thing that I do see in the people of my age

12.1 The youngest and oldest hippies at Joyfest.

from that time, is the core values are still alive—love and caring, just the good values of helping, being connected with your people and reaching out more to keep those principles alive.

I spent the Sunday morning at Joyfest talking with people who had traveled to Sonoma about what Artista meant to them. The same words kept recurring: friends, family, belonging, memory. Not everyone there had lived in the Haight in the 60s, but all were connected through a web of association: people who wanted to pay tribute to lost friends, people who wanted to reconnect with a shared past.

There was another ripple that weekend that connected Joyfest back to the original Artista mission statement, and further back into the short 60s. Just outside the stage area was a mural that was being painted progressively, bit by bit, across the weekend. As I discovered, it was also "progressive" across Artista events, an exercise in memorializing a moment and casting it into the future. One of the women working on the mural Sunday morning was Ann Cohen. Ann had been sitting in the audience on Saturday, drawing the musicians as they played, the crowd as they reacted. The Joyfest mural was also in a sense "live drawing," a continually changing canvas, always in process. I asked Ann to explain how the mural came to be.

> Ann Cohen: It started off last year—we stretched the canvas and we put it in the barn. And I painted some of these guys, and the judge is over there with Lauren.[18] They put it up by the pool and it fell over so we now have "windows of opportunity." Now this year people are participating, which is wonderful: they

12.2 Painting the Joyfest mural. Yana Zegri Soder on right.

> are putting what they feel that they really want to express out on the canvas. It's sharing—it's one way of starting a community again, through us having a job to do and being together in one space. We've kind of forgotten what a community is, but we're all working on it again, which is beautiful.
>
> SH. How do you feel a weekend like this moves forward without being too nostalgic, without searching for something that happened before?
>
> AC: I think just being in the moment. That's what most of us are doing—we're playing and that's how it moves forward. How we feel from our heart in the creative community; opening up and bridging and going forward is what we are talking about now.

The "windows of opportunity" that Ann mentions require an enactment of the "in the moment" ethos, of not dwelling in the past, but rather moving forward. But because there were reminders on the canvas of the previous year's community, I asked Ann whether it was difficult to take something that had been created in another moment and see it covered up—to see living history become a palimpsest.

> AC: We're just not worrying about it. I'm not worrying about where it's going or what I have to do or anything. We're just doing one spot and moving on, just the way we were talking about our philosophy on life. Living in the moment you don't miss much.

12.3 Evolution in a rainbow, at Haight and Cole.

The Artista mural also stretches back to a moment in the short 60s and obliquely back to the idea of hippie tourism. One of the other women working on the mural was Yana Zegri Soder, an artist whose work is familiar to anyone visiting the corner of Haight and Cole: the Evolutionary Rainbow, which she painted in 1967. I asked her what her vision had been back then.

> YANA ZEGRI SODER: Evolution in a rainbow. When I was in art school Escher was very big, so it was just a bunch of geometric shapes that all kind of fit together. So it starts out with the amoebas in the indigo and the purple is dinosaurs and blue is the fishes and the aquatic life. And then it turns into the green with the reptiles and then the yellow has all the animals and the orange is cities and civilization and the red is dancing people that turn into redwood tress and then clouds. So it's like the future—I don't foretell the future because it's whatever you think.

Although Yana originally sketched it, the secret of its execution, she told me, was "a hit of some really good acid. It was early in the morning, nobody's on Haight Street. The sun was shining; I just knew it and I just did it." Yana's approach here echoes other creative expression in the short 60s—the immediate visualization of an idea (musical, visual, physical) enabled by personal access to the psychedelic experience.

When some years later the wall was scheduled for demolition Yana's mural was dismantled, piece by piece, and she was given a clean slate to paint her mural again once the wall was rebuilt. With the help of friends and family she carefully traced over the original pattern, hoping to reproduce it exactly. What happened next was an echo of that earlier experience:

> Well, somebody gave me a hit of acid. Through the teeth, over the gums, there it went—and I saw it. There was this blank wall and I just saw it finished. It was early in the morning, nobody was around. That was the last time I've painted on acid. I did it that day because it just took me right from the "I've got to trace all this and do this all the traditional 'right' way." It just overrode that: it was like, "*this* is the right way."

The mural painting at the Joyfest weekend worked as a continuation of the Artista narrative: a communal effort, a work of collaborative memory. The approaches to "live art" that Ann Cohen and Yana Zegri Soder described are rich with significance, and in the case of Yana's contributions, reference directly that "short 60s" moment in the figures dancing along the edge of the Artista canvas. This is about capturing a moment, whether the fleeting instant of a musical gesture, or the image of a friend now passed, or the vision of a future landscape colored by the acid experience in the short 60s. The coexistence of these impulses imbue the texture of an Artista celebration—or any other gathering of the tribes—with a gentle ripple of meaning from the Haight half a century ago.

"The Haight" is a moment in time, a myth, and just another neighborhood. In the long 60s the Haight community is geographically dispersed and brought together for public parties and private celebrations out of a common sense of purpose. Artista events are vibrant reminders of a very basic ethos: love one another, care for one another. They are an exercise in what Roszak calls "practical nostalgia": mining the past to find solutions for the future:[19]

> Start with what you have. That was among the key ideas of countercultural protest. Start here—in this neighborhood, this house, with these people. Don't waste time on blueprints and head trips. Start with the means, the wit, and the resources at hand and build out from where you stand toward something better.[20]

Notes

1. Theodore Roszak, *The Making of an Elder Culture: Reflections on the Future of America's Most Audacious Generation* (Gabriola Island, BC: New Society Publishers, 2009), p. 39.
2. Tom Law, "The Community of the Tribe," *Oracle* 6 (February 1967), p. 15.
3. Hank Harrison, *The Dead Book: A Social History of the Haight-Ashbury Experience*, vol. 1 (San Francisco: The Archives Press, 1973), p. 11.
4. Brian Williams, "Call Them Artistas," *Examiner*, July 27, 1981, p. B1.

5. Ibid.
6. For more on this, see Kenneth Gloag, *Postmodernism in Music* (Cambridge: Cambridge University Press, 2012), especially pp. 46–52.
7. Roszak, *Elder Culture*, p. 8.
8. Ibid.
9. Even Bill Graham was hesitant about opening the floodgates to stadium shows. See *Bill Graham Presents* (New York: Delta, 1992).
10. Bill Graham, quoted in Ibid., p. 354.
11. Ron Eyerman and Andrew Jamison, *Music and Social Movements: Mobilizing Traditions in the Twentieth Century* (Cambridge: Cambridge University Press, 1998), p. 173.
12. See Andrew G. Kirk, *Counterculture Green: The* Whole Earth Catalog *and American Environmentalism* (Lawrence: University Press of Kansas, 2007), Thomas McNamee, *Alice Waters and Chez Panisse* (London and New York: Penguin, 2007), and Fred Turner, *From Counterculture to Cyberculture: Stewart Brand, the Whole Earth Network, and the Rise of Digital Utopianism* (Chicago and London: The University of Chicago Press, 2006).
13. The Tribal Stomp, a free concert in honor of Chet Helms, was held on October 30, 2005 in Speedway Meadow at Golden Gate Park. Featured bands included Blue Cheer, It's a Beautiful Day, the Jerry Miller band, and many others.
14. On a smaller scale the Artista gang have held benefit concerts to help pay medical bills and to celebrate lives, most recently that of Sam Andrew of Big Brother and the Holding Company, who passed away early in 2015.
15. Timothy Miller, *The Hippies and American Values* (Knoxville: University of Tennessee Press, 1991), p. 82.
16. The Chambers Brothers, "Time Has Come Today," from *The Time Has Come* (Columbia, 1967).
17. Artista member Joe Buchwald, Marty Balin's father, was ninety-four at the Joyfest; my younger daughter was two.
18. Judge Murphy was a fixture on the San Francisco scene, who played in college and garage bands through the 60s, collaborated with lyricist Robert Hunter, sang with John Cipollina, and later formed Lansdale Station with his wife, Lauren. In 2011 the Artista Gang held a fundraiser for the Judge's Wellness Fund, but Judge Murphy passed away in 2013.
19. Roszak, *Elder Culture*, p. 12.
20. Ibid., p. 14.

13. THE GRATEFUL DEAD ARCHIVE

>TERRY HAGGERTY: There's got to be, like, ten experiences in the history of mankind where there's an opening of a whole new paradigm, a whole new thing. I've got great respect for the Dead and the place that they play in the history of the world, in communications and psyche and spirituality.

Jerry Garcia passed away on August 9, 1995; in an official statement four months later the Grateful Dead officially disbanded.[1] In April 2008 the remaining members of the Dead announced their decision to donate the band's archive to the McHenry Library at the University of California, Santa Cruz.[2] The idea of a Grateful Dead Archive met with some bemusement—anything as concrete as a university library housing the band's legacy in perpetuity seemed an unusually mainstream solution for a countercultural remnant.[3] But the Dead had historical links to Santa Cruz.[4] Professor Fred Lieberman of the UCSC Department of Music had collaborated with Mickey Hart on three books,[5] and he was one of the first musicologists to teach an undergraduate survey course on the Grateful Dead. His professional association with the band gave him "street cred" among the UCSC students, though some might have found his outward appearance at variance with how they thought a Dead "insider" should look.[6]

UCSC was founded in the same year as the Grateful Dead, and both institutions are embodiments of the long 60s. The alternative sensibilities fostered by UCSC since the short 60s make the location of the Grateful Dead Archive a natural fit. This sentiment was echoed by Bob Weir at the band's press conference: "It seemed to all of us that the stuff really belongs to the community that supported us for all those years," he said. "And Santa Cruz seemed the coziest possible home for it."[7]

The Grateful Dead had other potential homes for their archive, at larger universities in California and in the Ivy League. But UC Santa Cruz was able to commit to curating the archive without making any additional financial demands on the band. They also committed to appointing a specialist archivist, and to developing a dedicated exhibition space for Archive materials. Yet even before the establishment of the Archive, the Grateful Dead were already the best-documented band in the history of popular music: every set list, every concert, every specification of every sound system over a thirty-year performing career, was documented, circulated, and now posted online for anyone to access.[8] The Dead fostered in their community a unique sense of common ownership that goes beyond fandom and into the realms of tradition, myth, and ritual. For the Dead in the long 60s, "memory is not just the province of individuals; it is institutionalized, socially managed and performed by whole communities."[9]

At the core of the Grateful Dead is the band's mindfulness not only of their fans, but of the fleeting moment. David Letterman once suggested to Bob Weir and Jerry Garcia that allowing, and even encouraging, their audiences to tape shows defeated the industry's main goal of selling records, of commodifying their product. Weir explained that the concert tapes "bring back memories" for the people who were there; Garcia was more philosophical: "The shows are never the same, ever. Not even ever. And when we're done with it, they can have it."[10] This is a beautiful articulation of the meaning of musical creation—it exists in the moment—and explains in part the band's failure to adhere to the industry's formula—recording and touring; selling records, tickets, and merchandise through "establishment" channels. The live performance creates the memories; the memories are then "performed" by the Deadhead community, physically and virtually.

To make this system work over three decades of performances necessitated consensus, some agreement regarding the ongoing project of concerts, interviews, marketing, and so on. This presents challenges to UCSC's Grateful Dead Archivist, Nicholas Meriwether, and to the people who might believe the band's operations to have been haphazard or underdefined.

> NICHOLAS MERIWETHER: What would be some examples of things that might surprise people? Well, on one hand you could say that they might be surprised at the degree to which the Dead were enormously thoughtful, reflective and careful businessmen. When they were having internal organization issues in 1979/80/81, Alan Trist did this remarkable analysis of their business structure, of who people were, what they did, the challenges that they faced. Earlier they had decided, "Okay, we have big meetings and those meetings often have as many as fifty people. We actually need to have some sense of how to organise meetings." Well what did they do? They picked up *Roberts Rules of Order*, they read it, they figured out what they liked about it, what they didn't like about it, they came up with their own rules: remarkable.

This suggests an element of historical forethought. In the contemporary view of the hippies, the idea that they would have any sense of their future selves was anathema—living in the moment, rejecting established norms, pursuing alternative modes of expression, were not necessarily promising business models.

Stories of the Dead's interactions with Warner Brothers in their early recording career certainly suggested a *laissez-faire* approach to formalizing their music. But the band understood the industry and knew what they did not want to happen to their musical legacy, which is significant. Because Warner Brothers owns the masters of their early studio albums, in subsequent negotiations for their next major-label contract with Arista the Dead ensured that they retained those rights. So despite their Haight-honed individualist attitude they used their experience with the industry to inform their future decisions.

The Dead's musical legacy has its own amateur archivists. Whether or not the band ultimately donates their original masters, this raises the question of how formalized the UCSC Archive needs to be in its curation of the Dead's performing history:

> NICHOLAS MERIWETHER: Basically you don't need 40 or 100 different audience recordings of every show. What you do need is a good range. So if I knew that I had access to a really good front-of-soundboard recording, I would get it. If I knew that there were three or four high-end microphones at a show, I would be interested in targeting those mics. There is a wonderful taper who recorded shows with two 30-foot mic stands, 100 feet apart, with really, really expensive mics. They're great. Nobody's got ears 30 feet up and 100 feet apart so they have this incredibly, wonderfully rich, deep sound field. Any 1966 audience recordings I will collect; they will be horrible, sonically, but interesting for other reasons. But I would use a sampling approach when I've got an abundance of riches.
>
> Would I collect a couple of truly wretched but representative audience recordings? Maybe, but probably not. I have a limited amount of resources to conserve and curate materials and I'm not in a position right now to cast a net that wide. I'm not convinced that approach would skew the record. I think as long as I do a good enough job with the discography, I can just say, "I preserved the best sounding audience recordings. We should not believe that those are by any means the ones that most commonly circulated."

The Grateful Dead Archive Online (gdao.org) is remarkable in this regard. Enabling a "socially constructed collection" of materials to complement the official Dead Archive deepens the resource and continues the Deadhead community's sense of ownership of, and belonging to, the material. There is a level of bureaucracy for contributors to negotiate—copyright and licensing agreements, validation, consistent with the codes of the Board of Regents of the University of California—but the Archive Online throws into relief the "architecture of heritage" constructed around Deadhead culture: "We're done with it, [so] they can have it." The community memory work of the Deadheads serves as a process of music heritage—its "practices, spatialities, performativities, and instrumental functionality." The "archive" thus works as

> both the tangible object: the institution, collection or digital resource . . ., but also in the more generic sense of an intangible repository or (potentially) limitless databank of cultural memory from which threads, fragments and traces of popular music pasts are gleaned and crafted.[11]

The level of amateur archiving also presents the formal Dead Archive, and the field of Grateful Dead Studies, with interesting intellectual problems. So much of the information surrounding the live legacy of the Grateful Dead has been documented already, online and in print. The attention to historical and technical

327

detail represented on sites such as archive.org is, according to Nicholas, "every bit as good as anything coming out of a library school." The information that Dead scholars and fans may require about any given performance over a thirty-year history is freely available, or available for correction; it needs to be exacting and authoritative. What the UCSC Archive can do is illuminate all that material from underneath—to show the machinery at the heart of the Dead's business, the library that informed the band's worldview, the communication that the band maintained with its fanbase, and documentary evidence of the band's care with its media narrative.

The field of Dead Studies presents a dimension to the legacy of the band that was perhaps unimaginable back in the short 60s. Even a brief glance through the collections of essays drawn from Dead Caucus meetings shows a variety of perspectives and approaches unique in contemporary scholarship:[12]

> NICHOLAS MERIWETHER: It's useful for graduate students to have a sense of what kinds of papers have already been given: "Hey, I'm interested in Nietzsche and the theory of the eternally recurring same; has anybody done that? Oh cool, there's been three conference papers; can I get a draft of that, or can I bounce off of this?" I've conducted good oral histories with former Area Chairs of the Caucus to help situate some of the broader issues involved, too. We're taking methodologies and critical and theoretical perspectives that have been refined and honed in other fields and bringing them to bear on something that has never had to withstand that kind of scrutiny, and never been able to before.

From Fred Lieberman's Grateful Dead survey course at UCSC to the creation of Dead Central,[13] the Grateful Dead have enjoyed a long presence in the academy, if surreptitious at first, then more determined and forward-looking now. The more casually enshrined memories of the Grateful Dead—the lyrics to "Ripple" hanging at Black Oak Books, for example—are symbolic of the importance of a particular cultural moment to an extended community of Deadheads. But this should not suggest that the Dead are ready to be suspended in aspic:

> NICHOLAS MERIWETHER: All of them are still very active creatively, artistically, professionally. They are not looking back. They are delighted that David Lemieux is taking care of their recorded legacy and that I'm taking care of their literary, historical, cultural legacy. They couldn't be more supportive and pleased, but they are not nostalgic. They are very much wrapped up in what they are doing now.

***

In January 2015 the remaining members of the Grateful Dead announced a weekend of shows to be held at Soldier Field in Chicago in celebration of the band's fiftieth anniversary. Tickets were distributed initially via mail order, a throwback to the Dead's long-running system. The online debates about the venue (why Chicago?), cost (why not a free concert in Golden Gate Park?), and limit (why not a farewell tour?) were predictable and animated. As this book went to press the cost of tickets on the secondary market had reached unfathomable heights: $15,000 for an obstructed view, upwards of $100,000 for more desirable seats.[14] For thirty years Grateful Dead concerts were the most obvious ripples from the short 60s, "Brigadoon" moments of countercultural community. The thousands who will flock to the "Fare Thee Well" shows will be experiencing something *like* a cultural moment from the 60s, but one firmly embedded in a twenty-first-century music industry framework.[15] There will be Deadheads, tapers, and dancers, but there will also be merchandisers, concessioners, and scalpers whose pockets will be lined with hippie money. Twenty years after the Dead disbanded, this particular ripple will be amplified by celebration, expectation, and regret.

Any backward glance to the short 60s, and every demarcation of the long 60s, is complicated by memory and nostalgia. The history I have offered in these pages, multilayered and multivoiced, records some of those complications. The newspaper and hip press accounts of the Haight in the short 60s were rarely disinterested, and remain calcified in an environment of cultural and generational tension long since dissipated. Fifty years later, Haight hippies still can only view the short 60s through the lens of the long 60s, their memories authenticating their experiences. Our access to the short 60s, via newspapers, recordings, celebrations, guided tours, and memorabilia are just variations on those stories of a brief time when something special happened.

DICKIE PETERSON: Since the 60s I've carried with me a very strong belief in peace. A very strong belief that it's my responsibility, as a human being, to take care of my brothers and sisters. If I don't, I'm an asshole, you know. I spend more time with younger musicians than I do older ones, and I do that because, as an elder statesman, it's my obligation. If I don't do that, I don't deserve what I have. I feel that very strongly. Once a week I go up to Camp Meeker, where there's young players, and I play with them, and I help them organize, I help them sort their songs out. I help them understand that simplicity is how you shine. You make too much noise, it's just noise, you know. Things like this I feel are my responsibility. This is what I got from the 60s.

ERIC CHRISTENSEN: I'll walk down Haight Street, and the denizens of Haight Street will look at me like some older straight guy with relatively short hair. And I'll kind of see this look—not necessarily of disdain, but of one that I don't belong. And I'll think, forty years ago I was here, looking a lot more radical than you were at the time. So it's kind of funny to me. I've often thought maybe we should have a "former hippie" ID card that you wear. A lot of it's internalized now. I don't need that external expression of radicalness.

Vicki Leeds: I asked my mother once if she was sorry that I had not finished college and bless her heart, she said, "You got a better education on the streets than most people I have ever met got in school. You have a sense of the world, you have a sense of people and know just who you are. And what you've learned is very useful in life." And indeed it seems to have been.

Ken Irving: I've known a lot of people over the years that were involved with dope in the Haight-Ashbury, and I call them good friends. They're good friends, you know. I would have liked to have met them back then to see what the difference is.

LiAnne Graves: How can you process the 60s in a few years? You process it over a lifetime and you either love what you went through, accept what you went through and see the thread or, like many people, don't even want to talk about it. And that's sad. It was colorful, man, it was wonderful, it was a trip and a half. And I'll tell you, there's nothing like surfing on acid.

Suzi Young: There's a kind of an innocence in the belief that you can change things. The stark reality of what you're up against is very difficult. I heard in an interview a priest talking about what Jesus wanted from the people that followed him. To paraphrase this person, he didn't want their money, he didn't want them tithing; he wanted their lives. And the price asked for activism, for bringing about real, meaningful, constructive social change and justice, is your very life. Most people have a hard time giving that. You have to be pushed up against a very severe wall to say, there is no other alternative for me except to act in this manner. And the great desire of most of us who came out of the 60s was to be able to change things without picking up arms, to do it by sheer force of numbers. The idea that love can't change everything is really hard to mature to. Maybe it's the lesson of old age, that keeping the faith is really keeping the faith; is, in the face of adversity, being able to continue to believe.

Terry Haggerty: I keep telling people, the only thing we really have is our freedom and our freedom to be happy, and I think we're going to go back to what the great hippie ethic was: live simply, communicate more, love more, live with less. You don't need that much. It's better for the world, it's your responsibility as free humans to be able to live with less. It's an inherent part of your responsibilities, you know.

Art Rogers: It's about tolerance, it's about joy, it's about acceptance. It's about putting good out. It's about love. All that. Just to make a better world. That's what this movement was all about back then. People would say hey, why not just be nice to everybody, why not *not* make war? Why sweat the small stuff? Now, that's an idealistic world.

Teresa Tudury: I think we were really interested in change and openness—and we were also hedonistic and foolish, and self-absorbed, and all the other things, too. But when I look at where our main interests lay as a generation, I don't feel terribly apologetic.

Charlie Morgan: I was thinking about how there was such a sweetness to that time, about how when you actually go around talking about love all the time, even if you don't know what it is, and even if you're just sort of searching for it, it really does change a society. I'm not saying that the soul of the human race has abandoned love, but you know, it's one thing, say, to love a person, and it's another thing to love them and tell them about it. And that kind of expressiveness was really right there. It's something that I really miss, and I think that the way the wheel of life turns is that we're probably going to get back to that. I think that people are going to get lonely for that.

Notes

1. The statement read: "Although individually and in various combinations [members of the Dead] will undoubtedly continue to make music, whatever the future holds will be something different in name and structure." See Dennis McNally, Stephen Peters, and Chuck Wills, *Grateful Dead: The Illustrated Trip* (London and New York: DK Publishing, 2003) p. 447.

2. To formalize the announcement, Mickey Hart and Bob Weir met with the press at the Fillmore Auditorium, and Chancellor George Blumenthal was there to speak on behalf of the university.

3. In the opening news item on *The Daily Show*, November 11, 2009, host Jon Stewart summarized the job description of the Grateful Dead archivist: "They're looking for someone who loves the Grateful Dead, yet somehow also has exceptional organizational skills. . . . You know, basically, UC Santa Cruz is saying, 'I need a miracle.'" Poking what was meant as good-natured fun at the field of archive studies and the requirements for the job, Stewart closed the segment with the observation: "There you have it. Four years of undergrad, two years of graduate school and now you can spend your days picking blotter acid out of Phil Lesh's underwear from the *Blues for Allah* tour."

4. As I noted in Chapter 10, the Dead also enabled the acquisition of Lou Harrison's archive. And the band's engagement with "academic" music took them to other unexpected places: while on the music faculty at the University of Southampton I was surprised to discover that my colleague, composer Michael Finnissy, had been the recipient of a Rex Foundation grant. His explanation of the process went something like this: "They called me up and asked if I would like £10,000. I said yes, thanks."

5. *Drumming at the Edge of Magic* (Novato: Grateful Dead Books, 1990), *Planet Drum: Celebration of Percussion and Rhythm* (San Francisco: HarperSan Francisco, 1992), and *Spirit into Sound: The Magic of Music* (Petaluma: Grateful Dead Books, 1999).

6. Some UCSC music students in the late 1980s, myself included, found the relationship between Lieberman and the Dead an odd one: of all the department faculty, Fred seemed the least *hip*. Through my brief conversations with Fred much later in my academic career, however, his engagement with the Dead made perfect sense, philosophically as well as musically.

7. Jesse McKinley, "A Deadhead's Dream for a Campus Archive," *New York Times*, April 24, 2008.

8. See, for example, the three-volume *Deadhead's Taping Compendium*, ed. Michael M. Getz and John A. Dwork (New York: Henry Holt, 1998, 1999, 2000), and setlists.net. One possible exception might be Bob Dylan, though it is doubtful that he would condone the level of intrusion into either his personal life or his business dealings that the Dead have done. Dylan's fanbase have been dedicated "archivists" of his setlists and (illegal) concert recordings, but he has never encouraged them to do so. Deadheads, on the other hand, have occupied fairly free territory in just those endeavors. My thanks to Lee Marshall for his Dylanological insights.

9. Mark Duffett, "Why I Didn't Go Down to the Delta: The Cultural Politics of Blues Tourism," in Sara Cohen, Robert Knifton, Marion Leonard, and Les Roberts, eds., *Sites of Popular Music Heritage: Memories, Histories, Places* (New York and London: Routledge, 2015), p. 241.

10. Jerry Garcia and Bob Weir, on *Late Night with David Letterman*, April 13, 1982.

11. Les Roberts, "Talkin Bout My Generation: Popular Music and the Culture of Heritage," *International Journal of Heritage Studies* 20/3 (2014): 274.

12. The Grateful Dead Scholars Caucus meets at the annual Southwest Popular/American Culture Association conference, and represents the full cross-disciplinary scope of Grateful Dead Studies.

13. Dead Central is the dedicated exhibition space for the Grateful Dead Archive at the McHenry Library.

14. Stubhub.com. The entirely predictable demand for tickets to the Chicago shows prompted an announcement in April 2015 of two further shows, to be held at Levi's Stadium in Santa Clara on June 27 and 28. Ticketing for those shows was run by Ticketmaster, which, as members of the Dead explained in an open letter to their fans, would ensure that tickets got "into the right hands" and "give each of you an equal opportunity to obtain tickets at the most affordable possible prices." See www.dead50.net. In advance of the Santa Clara shows, *Rolling Stone* (issue 1236, June 4, 2015) planned a feature retrospective on the Grateful Dead, with a suitably psychedelic cover designed by poster artist Wes Wilson.

15. One also enabled by twenty-first-century technology: live telecasts of all five shows would be available on pay-per-view (single concerts, $19.95; all three Soldier Field shows $79.95; all five shows $109.95) and as video-on-demand for a period of weeks following the concerts. For those seeking a more communal experience, all three Chicago shows would be broadcast live to cinemas nationwide. Deadheads outside the United States would be able to see the final concert "as live" in a delayed broadcast on July 6, 2015: a mediated experience, to be sure, but a relatively affordable one (£15 at my local Cardiff cinema).

NOTES ON INTERVIEWEES

Sam Andrew moved to the Haight in 1964 and began playing guitar with Big Brother and the Holding Company the following year. Interviewed August 4, 2005, Berkeley and April 29, 2011, San Rafael.

Marc Arno [Richardson] grew up in San Francisco. A self-styled audiovisual nerd, he began working light shows in 1966 and was a regular backstage presence throughout the 60s. Interviewed January 17 and February 27, 2012, Skype.

Banana [Lowell Levinger] was raised in Santa Rosa but began his musical career on the East Coast. He moved back to Marin County as a member of the Youngbloods in 1967. Interviewed September 7, 2005, Inverness.

Carlos Carvajal is a native San Franciscan. In 1971 he received the first San Francisco Art Commission Award of Honor for his work in choreography and dance, and in 1986 he received the Isadora Duncan Award for a lifetime of significant work. Interviewed January 9, 2009, San Francisco.

Eric Christensen was born and raised in San Francisco. While still in high school he worked for Tom Donahue at Autumn Records. Eric's first documentary film was *The Trips Festival* (2007). Interviewed March 22, 2007, Mill Valley.

Ann Cohen is an artist and musician. Her live art drawings have appeared in magazines and other publications; she also illustrated two books of poetry by her late husband, *Oracle* editor Allen Cohen. Interviewed September 11, 2011, Sonoma.

Jhiani Fanon [John Fannin] moved to San Francisco from Atlanta. He lived at 1626 Haight Street in 1967 and enjoyed a colorful long 60s. Interviewed March 23, 2007, San Francisco.

Rusty "Professor Poster" Goldman grew up in Daly City. He began collecting handbills and posters from the Haight while still in high school. Interviewed September 15, 2011, Pacifica.

Notes on Interviewees

LiAnne Graves grew up in Marin County, and began surfing in 1963. She is a skilled photographer and still surfs around the Bay Area. Interviewed December 15, 2011, Skype.

Wavy Gravy entered the world as Hugh Romney. Among his many good works is the foundation of Seva, the charity dedicated to combating preventable and curable blindness in the Third World. Interviewed August 30, 2005, Berkeley.

Terry Haggerty played his first professional gig on the guitar at the age of five. He played with the Sons of Champlin from 1963 to 1978. Interviewed September 2, 2005, San Rafael.

Glenn Howard grew up in Palo Alto and was a childhood friend of Ron "Pigpen" McKernan. He is the founder and curator of the American Musical Heritage Foundation. Interviewed August 11, 2010, Santa Cruz.

Robert Hughes moved to California in 1960 to study with Lou Harrison; they established the Cabrillo Music Festival in 1962. Bob founded the Oakland Symphony Youth Orchestra in 1963. Interviewed September 29, 2013, Skype.

Ken Irving was a homicide inspector from the Marin County Sheriff's Office. In 1967 he worked with the San Francisco Police Department on the Superspade case. Born and raised in Nicasio, he has been neighbor to everyone from dairy farmers to the Grateful Dead to dotcom millionaires. Interviewed September 6, 2005, Nicasio.

Charles "CJ" Johnson attended the University of California, Berkeley (1967–71) on a basketball scholarship. He played for the Golden State Warriors on two NBA championship teams (1975, 1978). For twenty-five years CJ was a regular attendee at Grateful Dead shows, which he enjoyed from his privileged spot offstage. Interviewed July 30, 2005, Oakland.

Kurt "Crowbar" Kangas returned to the Bay Area from Denver in 1966. He worked at Sundance Incense and Trading Co from 1967 to 1978. Interviewed May 3, 2007 and August 14, 2011, Petaluma.

David LaFlamme moved to San Francisco in 1962 from Salt Lake City, where he had established a career as a classical violinist. Interviewed May 3, 2007, Petaluma.

Linda LaFlamme was raised in New York. After attending the Woodstock Festival she moved to California. She met David LaFlamme in 1973 and has been a part of It's a Beautiful Day ever since. Interviewed May 3, 2007, Petaluma.

Notes on Interviewees

Vicki Leeds graduated from Lowell High School in 1967 and moved into the Blue Cheer house. She settled in Point Reyes Station in 1974, where she runs Cabaline Country Emporium & Saddlery. Interviewed September 8, 2005, Point Reyes Station.

William Maginnis began working at the San Francisco Tape Music Center in 1964. His career as a jazz drummer is still in full swing. Interviewed August 20, 2010, San Francisco.

"Country" Joe McDonald grew up in Los Angeles. He moved to Berkeley in the early 1960s, where he played in folk bands until the formation of Country Joe and the Fish in the fall of 1965. Interviewed May 26, 2007, Cardiff.

Nicholas Meriwether is archivist of the Grateful Dead Archive, UC Santa Cruz. As a Dead scholar he has published extensively in band fanzines, in the *Deadhead Tapers Compendium*, and in essay collections. Interviewed April 27, 2011, Santa Cruz.

Charlie Morgan was born and raised in San Francisco, and as a high school student had a moment of epiphany at City Lights Books. He played baseball for San Francisco State and studied sitar with Ali Akbar Khan. Interviewed September 7, 2005, Inverness.

Albert Neiman grew up in Los Angeles and moved to San Francisco in 1961 where he was involved with renovating the Straight Theater. Along with running the Straight Ashbury Viewing Society he ran a visual effects store on Haight Street. Interviewed August 10, 2005, Oakland.

Dickie Peterson grew up in North Dakota and moved to San Francisco in the mid-1960s. Blue Cheer formed in 1966 and gave its last performance in 2008. Interviewed March 23, 2007, Guerneville.

Art Rogers moved to San Francisco from Raleigh, North Carolina. He worked as a photojournalist, taught photography at the San Francisco Art Institute, and was awarded a Guggenheim Fellowship for his work. Interviewed September 7, 2005, Point Reyes Station.

Ramon Sender was a cofounder of the San Francisco Tape Music Center. He was one of the first residents at Morning Star Ranch, where he took his compositional expertise into new realms. Interviewed August 20, 2010, San Francisco.

Dr. David E. Smith studied medicine at UC Berkeley and moved to the Haight in 1960. He is the founder of the Haight-Ashbury Free Medical Clinic. Interviewed August 23, 2010, San Francisco.

Notes on Interviewees

Yana Zegri Soder moved to San Francisco from Kansas City in 1967. Her biggest piece of work is on the corner of Haight and Cole streets. Interviewed September 2011, Sonoma.

Teresa Tudury was born in San Francisco and fell into the folk music scene as a teenager. Her band, The All-Night Apothecary, was short-lived, but her solo career continues. Interviewed July 17, 2005, Sebastopol.

Wes Wilson was working as a lithographer when he was asked to design the handbill for the Trips Festival in 1966. He became known as one of the "Big 5" poster artists in the San Francisco Renaissance. Interviewed December 1, 2011, Skype.

Suzi Young moved to San Francisco in 1967 with the Youngbloods. She was married to singer Jesse Colin Young but is a musician in her own right. Interviewed September 6, 2005, Inverness.

BIBLIOGRAPHY

Aaronson, Bernard and Humphry Osmond, eds. *Psychedelics: The Uses and Implications of Hallucinogenic Drugs* (Garden City: Anchor Books, 1970).

Adams, John. *Hallelujah Junction: Composing an American Life* (London: Faber and Faber, 2008).

Adams, Rebecca. "Inciting Sociological Thought by Studying the Deadhead Community: Engaging Publics in Dialogue," *Social Forces* 77/1 (September 1998): 1–25.

Adams, Rebecca and Robert Sardiello, eds. *Deadhead Social Science: You Ain't Gonna Learn What You Don't Want to Know* (Walnut Creek: AltaMira, 2000).

Adlington, Robert., ed. *Sound Commitments: Avant-garde Music and the Sixties* (Oxford: Oxford University Press, 2009).

Anderson, Terry. *The Movement and the Sixties: Protest in America from Greensboro to Wounded Knee* (New York and Oxford: Oxford University Press, 1995).

Anson, Robert Sam. *Gone Crazy and Back Again: The Rise and Fall of the* Rolling Stone *Generation* (Garden City: Doubleday, 1981).

Anthony, Gene. *Magic of the Sixties* (Layton, UT: Gibbs Smith, 2004).

Anthony, Gene. *The Summer of Love: Haight-Ashbury at Its Highest* (San Francisco: Last Gasp, 1995).

Armstrong, Don and Jessica Armstrong. "Dispatches from the Front: The Life and Writings of Ralph J. Gleason," *Rock Music Studies* 1/1 (2014): 3–34.

Baker, Deborah. *A Blue Hand: The Beats in India* (New York: The Penguin Press, 2008).

Bareiss, Warren. "Middlebrow Knowingness in 1950s San Francisco: the Kingston Trio, Beat Counterculture, and the Production of 'Authenticity'," *Popular Music and Society* 33/1 (2010): 9–33.

Becker, Howard, ed. *Culture and Civility in San Francisco* (New Brunswick: Transaction Books, 1971).

Bennett, Andy. *Cultures of Popular Music* (Maidenhead: Open University Press, 2003).

Bennett, Andy. "'Heritage Rock': Rock Music, Representation and Heritage Discourse," *Poetics* 37 (2009): 474–89.

Bennett, Andy. "Music, Media and Urban Mythscapes: A Study of the 'Canterbury Sound'," *Media, Culture and Society* 24/1 (January 2002): 87–100.

Bennett, Andy. ed. *Remembering Woodstock* (Aldershot: Ashgate, 2004).

Berger, Harris M. *Metal, Rock, and Jazz: Perception and the Phenomenology of Musical Experience* (Hanover: Wesleyan University Press, 1999).

Bernstein, David W., ed. *The San Francisco Tape Music Center: 1960s Counterculture and the Avant-Garde* (Berkeley and Los Angeles: University of California Press, 2008).

Bess, Donovan. "LSD: The Acid Test," *Ramparts* 4/12 (April 1966): 42–8.

Bingham, Howard L. *Howard L. Bingham's Black Panthers 1968* (Los Angeles: Ammo Books, 2009).

Bisbort, Alan. *The White Rabbit and Other Delights: East Totem West, A Hippie Company 1967-1969* (San Francisco: Pomegranate Artbooks, n. d.).

Bloom, Alexander and Wini Breines, eds. *"Takin' It to the Streets": A Sixties Reader* (New York: Oxford University Press, 1995).

Bibliography

Boon, Marcus. *The Road of Excess: A History of Writers on Drugs* (Cambridge, MA: Harvard University Press, 2002).

Boyd, Joe. *White Bicycles: Making Music in the 1960s* (London: Serpent's Tail, 2006).

Brackett, David. *The Pop, Rock, and Soul Reader: Histories and Debates* (New York and Oxford: Oxford University Press, 2005).

Brandelius, Jerilyn Lee. *Grateful Dead Family Album* (New York: Warner Books, 1989).

Brandellero, Amanda and Susanne Janssen. "Popular Music as Cultural Heritage: Scoping Out the Field of Practice," *International Journal of Heritage Studies* 20/3 (2014): 224–40.

Braunstein, Peter and Michael William Doyle, eds. *Imagine Nation: The American Counterculture of the 1960s & 70s* (New York and London: Routledge, 2002).

Brautigan, Richard. *Trout Fishing in America, The Pill versus The Springhill Mine Disaster; and In Watermelon Sugar: Three Books in the Manner of their Original Editions* (Boston: Houghton Mifflin/Seymour Lawrence, 1989).

Brennan, Matt. "Down Beats and Rolling Stones: the American Jazz Press Decides to Cover Rock in 1967," *Popular Music History* 1/3 (2006): 263–84.

Brightman, Carol. *Sweet Chaos: The Grateful Dead's American Adventure* (New York and London: Pocket Books, 1998).

Bromell, Nick. *Tomorrow Never Knows: Rock and Psychedelics in the 1960s* (Chicago and London: University of Chicago Press, 2000).

Burke, Patrick. "Tear Down the Walls: Jefferson Airplane, Race, and Revolutionary Rhetoric in 1960s Rock," *Popular Music* 29/1 (January 2010): 61–79.

Cándida Smith, Richard. *Utopia and Dissent: Art, Poetry, and Politics in California* (Berkeley and Los Angeles: University of California Press, 1995).

Cándida Smith, Richard. ed. *Text & Image: Art and the Performance of Memory* (New Brunswick and London: Transaction Publishers, 2006).

Cantwell, Cathy. *Buddhism: The Basics* (New York and London: Routledge, 2010).

Carl, Robert. *Terry Riley's In C* (Oxford: Oxford University Press, 2009).

Caserta, Peggy, as told to Dan Knapp. *Going Down With Janis: Janis Joplin's Intimate Story* (New York: Dell Publishing, 1973).

Cavallo, Dominick. *A Fiction of the Past: The Sixties in American History* (New York: Palgrave, 1999).

Chapple, Steve and Reebee Garofalo. *Rock'n'Roll is Here to Pay: The History and Politics of the Music Industry* (Chicago: Nelson-Hall, 1977).

Charters, Ann, ed. *The Portable Sixties Reader* (New York: Penguin, 2003).

Childs, Marti Smiley and Jeff March. *Echoes of the Sixties* (New York: Billboard Books, 1999).

Clayton, Martin, Trevor Herbert and Richard Middleton, eds. *The Cultural Study of Music: A Critical Introduction* (New York and London: Routledge, 2003).

Clover, Joshua. *1989: Bob Dylan Didn't Have This to Sing About* (Berkeley and Los Angeles: University of California Press, 2009).

Coates, Norma. "If anything, blame Woodstock: The Rolling Stones: Altamont, December 6, 1969," in Ian Inglis, ed., *Performance and Popular Music: History, Place and Time* (Aldershot: Ashgate, 2006), pp. 58–69.

Cohen, Katherine Powell. *Images of America: San Francisco's Haight-Ashbury* (Charleston: Arcadia Publishing, 2008).

Cohen, Robert and Reginald E. Zelnik, eds. *The Free Speech Movement: Reflections on Berkeley in the 1960s* (Berkeley and Los Angeles: University of California Press, 2002).

Cohen, Sara, Robert Knifton, Marion Leonard, and Les Roberts, eds. *Sites of Popular Music Heritage: Memories, Histories, Places* (London: Routledge, 2015).

Cohn, Nik. *Rock from the Beginning* (New York: Pocket Books, 1970).

Connell, John and Chris Gibson. *Sound Tracks: Popular Music, Identity and Place* (London and New York: Routledge, 2003).
Conners, Peter. *White Hand Society: The Psychedelic Partnership of Timothy Leary and Allen Ginsberg* (San Francisco: City Lights Books, 2010).
Constanten, Tom. *Between Rock and Hard Places: A Musical Autobiodyssey* (Eugene: Hulogosi, 1992).
Cook, Nicholas and Anthony Pople, eds. *The Cambridge History of Twentieth-Century Music* (Cambridge: Cambridge University Press, 2004).
Coyote, Peter. *Sleeping Where I Fall: A Chronicle* (Berkeley: Counterpoint, 1999).
Crosby, David and David Bender. *Stand and Be Counted: Making Music, Making History: The Dramatic Story of the Artists and Events that Changed America* (San Francisco: HarperSanFrancisco, 2000).
Cubitt, Geoffrey. *History and Memory* (Manchester: Manchester University Press, 2007).
Cutler, Sam. *You Can't Always Get What You Want: My Life with the Rolling Stones, the Grateful Dead and Other Wonderful Reprobates* (Toronto: ECW Press, 2010).
Dalton, David. *Piece of My Heart: A Portrait of Janis Joplin* (New York: Da Capo Press, 1991).
Darnovsky, Marcy, Barbara Epstein and Richard Flacks, eds. *Cultural Politics and Social Movements* (Philadelphia: Temple University Press, 1995).
Dass, Ram. *Remember: Be Here Now* (San Cristobal, NM: Hanuman Foundation, 1978).
Dass, Ram and Ralph Metzner. *Birth of a Psychedelic Culture: Conversations about Leary, the Harvard Experiments, Millbrook and the Sixties* (Santa Fe: Synergetic Press, 2010).
Davidson, Michael. *The San Francisco Renaissance: Poetics and Community at Mid-Century* (Cambridge: Cambridge University Press, 1989).
Davis, R. G. *The San Francisco Mime Troupe: The First Ten Years* (Palo Alto: Ramparts Press, 1975).
DeGroot, Gerard. *The Sixties Unplugged* (London: Pan Books, 2009).
Denisoff, R. Serge. *Great Day Coming: Folk Music and the American Left* (Baltimore: Penguin Books, 1973).
Denisoff, R. Serge and Richard A. Peterson, eds. *The Sounds of Social Change: Studies in Popular Culture* (Chicago: Rand McNally, 1972).
de Rios, Marlene Dobkin and Oscar Janiger. *LSD, Spirituality and the Creative Process* (Rochester, VT: Park Street Press, 2003).
Dettmar, Kevin J. H. *Is Rock Dead?* (New York: Routledge, 2006).
Didion, Joan. *Slouching Toward Bethlehem* (New York: Farrar, Straus, Giroux, 1968).
Dodd, David. *The Complete Annotated Grateful Dead Lyrics* (New York: Free Press, 2005).
Dodd, David and Diana Spaulding, eds. *The Grateful Dead Reader* (Oxford and New York: Oxford University Press, 2000).
Doggett, Peter. *There's a Riot Going On: Revolutionaries, Rock Stars and the Rise and Fall of 60s Counter-Culture* (Edinburgh: Canongate, 2008).
Doukas, James N. *Electric Tibet: The Chronicles and Sociology of the San Francisco Rock Musicians* (North Hollywood: Dominion, 1969).
Doyle, Michael. *Radical Chapters: Pacifist Bookseller Roy Kepler and the Paperback Revolution* (Syracuse: Syracuse University Press, 2012).
Draper, Robert. Rolling Stone *Magazine: The Uncensored History of the Greatest Rebel Journal, Featuring Jann Wenner, Hunter S. Thompson, Lester Bangs, John Lennon, Greil Marcus, Mick Jagger, and a Host of Hippie Renegades* (New York: Harper Perennial, 1991).
Duckworth, William. *Talking Music: Conversations with John Cage, Philip Glass, Laurie Anderson, and Five Generations of American Experimental Composers* (New York: Schirmer Books, 1995).

Bibliography

du Noyer, Paul. *In the City: A Celebration of London Music* (London: Virgin Books, 2009).
Echols, Alice. *Scars of Sweet Paradise: The Life and Times of Janis Joplin* (New York: Henry Holt, 1999).
Echols, Alice. *Shaky Ground: The Sixties and Its Aftershocks* (New York: Columbia University Press, 2002).
Edelstein, Andrew J. *The Pop Sixties: A Personal and Irreverent Guide* (New York: Ballantine, 1985).
Editors of *Esquire*, eds. *Smiling through the Apocalypse: Esquire's History of the Sixties* (New York: Crown, 1987).
Editors of *Ramparts*, eds. *Conversations with the New Reality: Readings in the Cultural Revolution* (San Francisco: Canfield Colophon, 1971).
Eisen, Jonathan, ed. *The Age of Rock: Sounds of the American Cultural Revolution* (New York: Vintage Books, 1969).
Eymann, Marcia A. and Charles Wollenberg, eds. *What's Going On? California and the Vietnam Era* (Oakland: Oakland Museum of California, 2004).
Farber, David, ed. *The Sixties: From Memory to History* (Chapel Hill and London: The University of North Carolina Press, 1994).
Farber, David and Beth Bailey, eds. *The Columbia Guide to America in the 1960s* (New York: Columbia University Press, 2001).
Farren, Mick. *Give the Anarchist a Cigarette* (London: Pimlico, 2002).
Fink, Robert. *Repeating Ourselves: American Minimal Music as Cultural Practice* (Berkeley and Los Angeles: University of California Press, 2005).
Fitzgerald, Joseph M. "Vivid Memories and the Reminiscence Phenomenon," *Human Development* 31 (1988): 261–73.
Fletcher, Tony. *All Hopped Up and Ready to Go: Music from the Streets of New York 1927-77* (New York: Omnibus Press, 2009).
Fong-Torres, Ben. *Becoming Almost Famous: My Back Pages in Music, Writing and Life* (San Francisco: Backbeat Books, 2006).
Frank, Thomas. *The Conquest of Cool: Business Culture, Counterculture, and the Rise of Hip Consumerism* (Chicago and London: University of Chicago Press, 1997).
Franklin, Adrian. *City Life* (London: Sage Publications, 2010).
Frith, Simon, ed. *Facing the Music* (New York: Pantheon Books, 1988).
Frith, Simon, ed. *Performing Rites: On the Value of Popular Music* (Oxford: Oxford University Press, 1998).
Gair, Christopher. *The American Counterculture* (Edinburgh: Edinburgh University Press, 2007).
Garcia, Jerry. *Harrington Street* (New York: Delacorte Press, 1995).
Garcia, Jerry, Charles Reich and Jann Wenner. *Garcia: A Signpost to New Space* (Cambridge: Da Capo Press, 2003).
Gaskin, Stephen. *Haight Ashbury Flashbacks* (Berkeley: Ronin Publishing, 1990).
Gastaut, Amélie a Jean-Pierre Criqui. *Off the Wall: Psychedelic Rock Posters from San Francisco* (New York: Thames & Hudson, 2005).
Gitlin, Todd. *The Sixties: Years of Hope, Days of Rage* (New York: Bantam, 1993).
Glatt, John. *Rage & Roll: Bill Graham and the Selling of Rock* (New York: Birch Lane Press, 1993).
Gleason, Ralph J. *The Jefferson Airplane and the San Francisco Sound* (New York: Ballantine Books, 1969).
Glessing, Robert J. *The Underground Press in America* (Bloomington and London: Indiana University Press, 1971).
Gloag, Kenneth, *Postmodernism in Music* (Cambridge: Cambridge University Press, 2012).

Bibliography

Goffman, Ken. *Counterculture Through the Ages, from Abraham to Acid House* (New York: Villard, 2004).

Goodman, Mitchell. *The Movement Toward a New America: The Beginnings of a Long Revolution* (New York: Alfred A. Knopf, 1970).

Gopinath, Sumanth. "Reich in Blackface: *Oh Dem Watermelons* and Radical Minstrelsy in the 1960s," *Journal of the Society for American Music* 5/2 (2011): 139–93.

Gottlieb, Annie. *Do You Believe in Magic? Bringing the 60s Back Home* (New York: Simon & Schuster, 1987).

Graebner, William, ed. *True Stories from the American Past, Vol. II: Since 1865* (New York: McGraw Hill, 2003).

Graham, Bill and Robert Greenfield. *Bill Graham Presents: My Life Inside Rock and Out* (New York: Dell, 1992).

Gravy, Wavy. *Something Good for a Change: Random Notes on Peace thru Living* (New York: St Martin's Press, 1992).

Green, Jonathon. *All Dressed Up: The Sixties and the Counterculture* (London: Pimlico, 1999).

Griffiths, Dai. "The High Analysis of Low Music," *Music Analysis* 18/3 (October 1999): 389–435.

Grogan, Emmett. *Ringolevio: A Life Played for Keeps* (Boston: Little, Brown, 1972).

Grunenberg, Christoph, ed. *Summer of Love: Art of the Psychedelic Era* (London: Tate Publishing, 2005).

Grunenberg, Christoph and Jonathan Harris, eds. *Summer of Love: Psychedelic Art, Social Crisis and Counterculture in the 1960s* (Liverpool: Liverpool University Press, 2005).

Hall, Stuart. "The Hippies: An American 'Moment'," in Julian Nagel, ed., *Student Power* (London: Merlin Press, 1969), pp. 170–202.

Harrison, Hank. *The Dead Book: A Social History of the Haight-Ashbury Experience* (Menlo Park: The Archives Press, 1973).

Henke, James with Parke Puterbaugh. *I Want to Take You Higher: The Psychedelic Era 1965-1969* (The Rock and Roll Hall of Fame and Museum/San Francisco: Chronicle Books, 1997).

Hicks, Michael. *Sixties Rock: Garage, Psychedelic & Other Satisfactions* (Urbana and Chicago: University of Illinois Press, 1999).

Hill, Sarah. "When Deep Soul Met the Love Crowd. Otis Redding: Monterey Pop Festival, June 17, 1967," in Ian Inglis, ed., *Performance and Popular Music: History, Place and Time* (Aldershot: Ashgate, 2006), pp. 28–40.

Hoberman, J. *The Dream Life: Movies, Media and the Mythology of the Sixties* (New York: The New Press, 2003).

Hoffmann, Albert. *LSD: My Problem Child: Reflections on Sacred Drugs, Mysticism and Science*, trans. Jonathan Ott (Sarasota: Multidisciplinary Association for Psychedelic Studies [MAPS], 2005).

Hopkins, Jerry, ed. *The Hippie Papers: Trip-Taking, Mind-Quaking, Scene-Making Word from Where It's At* (New York: Signet Books, 1968).

Horowitz, David, Michael P. Lerner, and Craig Pyes, eds. *Counterculture and Revolution* (New York: Random House, 1972).

Hoskyns, Barney: *Beneath the Diamond Sky: Haight-Ashbury 1965-1970* (New York: Simon & Schuster, 1997).

Hoskyns, Barney. *Hotel California: Singer-Songwriters and Cocaine Cowboys in the LA Canyons 1967-1976* (London: Fourth Estate, 2005).

Huxley, Aldous. *The Doors of Perception* (London: Vintage Books, 2004).

Huxley, Aldous, ed. Michael Horowitz and Cynthia Palmer. *Moksha: Writings on Psychedelics and the Visionary Experience 1931-63* (London: Penguin, 1983).

Bibliography

Hjortsberg, William. *Jubilee Hitchhiker* (Berkeley: Counterpoint, 2012).
Irwin, John. *Scenes* (Beverly Hills: Sage, 1977).
Jackson, Blair. *Goin' Down the Road: A Grateful Dead Traveling Companion* (New York: Harmony Books, 1992).
Jackson, Blair, Dennis McNally, Stephen Peters, and Chuck Wills. *Grateful Dead: The Illustrated Trip* (London and New York: DK Publishing, 2003).
Jerome, Judson. *Families of Eden: Communes and the New Anarchism* (London: Thames and Hudson, 1974).
Johnson, Troy R. *The Occupation of Alcatraz Island: Indian Self-Determination and the Rise of Indian Activism* (Urbana and Chicago: University of Illinois Press, 1996).
Jones, Steve. *Rock Formation: Music, Technology, and Mass Communication* (London: Sage, 1972).
Joseph, Peter. *Good Times: An Oral History of America in the Nineteen Sixties* (New York: William Morrow & Co., 1974).
Joynson, Vernon. *The Acid Trip: A Complete Guide to Psychedelic Music* (Todmorden, Lancs.: Babylon Books, 1984).
Kaiser, David. *How the Hippies Saved Physics: Science, Counterculture, and the Quantum Revival* (New York and London: W. W. Norton and Company, 2011).
Kaliss, Jeff. *I Want to Take You Higher: The Life and Times of Sly & the Family Stone* (New York: Backbeat Books, 2008).
Kandel, Lenore. *The Love Book* (San Francisco: Superstition Street Press, 2003).
Kaplan, Geoff, ed. *Power to the People: The Graphic Design of the Radical Press and the Rise of the Counter-Culture, 1964-1974* (Chicago and London: University of Chicago Press, 2013).
Keith, Michael C. *Voices in the Purple Haze: Underground Radio and the Sixties* (Westport, CT and London: Praeger, 1997).
Kelly, Karen and Evelyn McDonnell. *Stars Don't Stand Still in the Sky: Music and Myth* (New York and London: New York University Press, 1999).
Kelly, Linda. *Deadheads: Stories from Fellow Artists, Friends, and Followers of the Grateful Dead* (New York: Citadel Press, 1995).
Keniston, Kenneth. *Young Radicals: Notes on Committed Youth* (New York: Harcourt, Brace & World, Inc., 1968).
Kerouac, Jack. *Big Sur* (London: Harper Perennial, 2001).
Kerouac, Jack. *Book of Haikus* (New York and London: Penguin, 2003).
Kerouac, Jack. *The Dharma Bums* (London: Penguin Classics, 2006).
Kerouac, Jack. *Some of the Dharma* (London: Penguin, 1999).
Kesey, Ken. *One Flew Over the Cuckoo's Nest* (London: Penguin, 2005).
Kirk, Andrew G. *Counterculture Green: The Whole Earth Catalog and American Environmentalism* (Lawrence: University Press of Kansas, 2007).
Kornbluth, Jesse. *Notes from the New Underground* (New York: Ace Books, 1968).
Kostelanetz, Richard. *The Fillmore East: Recollections of Rock Theater* (New York: Schirmer Books, 1995).
Kramer, Michael J. *The Republic of Rock: Music and Citizenship in the Sixties Counterculture* (Oxford: Oxford University Press, 2013).
Krassner, Paul. *One Hand Jerking: Reports from an Investigative Satirist* (New York: Seven Stories Press, 2005).
Krieger, Susan. *Hip Capitalism* (London: Sage Publications, 1979).
Krim, Seymour, ed. *The Beats: A Gold Medal Anthology* (Greenwich, CT: Fawcett Publications, 1963).
Krims, Adam. *Music and Urban Geography* (New York and London: Routledge, 2007).

Bibliography

Kripal, Jeffrey J. *Esalen: America and the Religion of No Religion* (Chicago and London: University of Chicago Press, 2007).

Kubernik, Harvey and Kenneth Kubernik. *A Perfect Haze: The Illustrated History of the Monterey International Pop Festival* (Solano Beach: Santa Monica Press, 2011).

Kutschke, Beate and Barley Norton, eds. *Music and Protest in 1968* (Cambridge: Cambridge University Press, 2014).

Lattin, Don. *Following Our Bliss: How the Spiritual Ideals of the Sixties Shape Our Lives Today* (New York: HarperCollins, 2003).

Leary, Timothy, Ralph Metzner, and Richard Alpert. *The Psychedelic Experience: A Manual Based on the Tibetan Book of the Dead* (New York: Citadel Press, 1993).

Lee, Martin A. and Bruce Shlain. *Acid Dreams: The Complete Social History of LSD: The CIA, the Sixties, and Beyond* (New York: Grove Weidenfeld, 1985).

Leitch, Donovan. *The Autobiography of Donovan: The Hurdy Gurdy Man* (New York: St Martin's Press, 2005).

Leland, John. *Hip: The History* (New York: Harper Perennial, 2005).

Lemke, Gayle and Jacaeber Kastor. *The Art of the Fillmore: The Poster Series 1966-1971* (New York: Thunder's Mouth Press, 1999).

Lemke-Santangelo, Gretchen. *Daughters of Aquarius: Women of the Sixties Counterculture* (Lawrence: University Press of Kansas, 2009).

Leonard, Marion and Robert Strachan, eds. *The Beat Goes On: Liverpool, Popular Music and the Changing City* (Liverpool: Liverpool University Press, 2010).

Lesh, Phil. *Searching for the Sound: My Life With the Grateful Dead* (New York: Little, Brown, 2005).

Lester, Julius. *Look Out Whitey! Black Power's Gon' Get Your Mama!* (New York: Grove Press, 1968).

Levy, Shawn. *Ready, Steady, Go! Swinging London and the Invention of Cool* (London: Fourth Estate, 2002).

Lewis, George H., ed. *Side-Saddle on the Golden Calf: Social Structure and Popular Culture in America* (Pacific Palisades: Goodyear Publishing, 1972).

Lipton, Lawrence. *The Holy Barbarians* (New York: Grove Press, 1959).

London, Herbert I. *Closing the Circle: A Cultural History of the Rock Revolution* (Chicago: Nelson-Hall, 1984).

Lydon, Michael. *Flashbacks: Eyewitness Accounts of the Rock Revolution 1964-1974* (New York and London: Routledge, 2003).

Lydon, Michael. *Rock Folk: Portraits from the Rock'n'Roll Pantheon* (New York: Dell Publishing, 1971).

Macan, Edward. *Rocking the Classics: English Progressive Rock and the Counterculture* (Oxford: Oxford University Press, 1997).

Mailer, Norman. *Miami and the Siege of Chicago* (New York: Donald I. Fine, Inc., 1986).

Makower, Joel. *Woodstock: The Oral History* (New York: Doubleday, 1989).

Malkin, John. *Sounds of Freedom: Musicians on Spirituality and Social Change* (Berkeley: Parallax Press, 2005).

Malvinni, David. *Grateful Dead and the Art of Rock Improvisation* (Plymouth: Scarecrow Press, 2013).

Marcus, Greil, ed. *Rock and Roll Will Stand* (Boston: Beacon Press, 1969).

Martin, Bill. *Avant Rock: Experimental Music from the Beatles to Björk* (Chicago and LaSalle: Open Court, 2002).

Martin, Bradford D. *The Theater Is in the Street: Politics and Public Performance in Sixties America* (Amherst and Boston: University of Massachusetts Press, 2004).

Bibliography

Marwick, Arthur. *The Sixties: Cultural Revolution in Britain, France, Italy, and the United States, c. 1958-c.1974* (Oxford and New York: Oxford University Press, 1998).

May, Thomas, ed. *The John Adams Reader: Essential Writings on an American Composer* (Pompton Plains: Amadeus Press, 2006).

McCleary, John Bassett. *The Hippie Dictionary: A Cultural Encyclopedia of the 1960s and 1970s* (Berkeley: Ten Speed Press, 2002).

McClure, Michael. *Huge Dreams: San Francisco and Beat Poems* (New York and London: Penguin Books, 1999).

McClure, Michael. *Touching the Edge: Dharma Devotions from the Hummingbird Sangha* (Boston and London: Shambhala, 1999).

McDonough, Jack. *San Francisco Rock: The Illustrated History of San Francisco Rock Music 1965/85* (San Francisco: Chronicle Books, 1985).

McLuhan, Marshall. *Understanding Media* (London: Abacus, 1973).

McNally, Dennis. *A Long Strange Trip: The Inside History of the Grateful Dead* (London: Transworld Publishers, 2002).

McNally, Dennis. *Desolate Angel: Jack Kerouac, The Beat Generation, and America* (Cambridge, MA: Da Capo Press, 2003).

McNamee, Thomas. *Alice Waters and Chez Panisse* (London and New York: 2007).

Melechi, Antonio. *Psychedelia Britannica: Hallucinogenic Drugs in Britain* (London: Turnaround, 1997).

Meriwether, Nicholas, ed. *All Graceful Instruments: The Contexts of the Grateful Dead Phenomenon* (Newcastle: Cambridge Scholars Publishing, 2007).

Meriwether, Nicholas, ed. *Reading the Grateful Dead: A Critical Survey* (Lanham: Scarecrow, 2012).

Mertens, Wim. *American Minimal Music* (London: Kahn & Averill, 1983).

Merwin, W. S. *The Second Four Books of Poems: The Moving Target, The Lice, The Carrier of Ladders, Writings to an Unfinished Accompaniment* (Port Townsend: Copper Canyon Press, 1993).

Middleton, Richard. *Pop Music and the Blues: A Study of the Relationship and its Significance* (London: Victor Gollancz Ltd., 1972).

Miles. *Hippie* (London: Cassell Illustrated, 2004).

Miles, Steven. *Spaces for Consumption* (London: Sage Publications, 2010).

Miller, Henry. *Big Sur and the Oranges of Hieronymus Bosch* (New York: New Directions, 1957).

Miller, Timothy. *The Hippies and American Values* (Knoxville: University of Tennessee Press, 1991).

Mills, John 'Mojo', ed. *Shindig! Annual Number Two* (Maidenhead: Volcano Publishing, 2009).

Morrison, Craig. "Psychedelic Music in San Francisco: Style, Context, and Evolution." PhD diss., Concordia University, 2000. http://spectrum.library.concordia.ca/1163.

Nagel, Julian, ed. *Student Power* (London: Merlin Press, 1969).

Nettl, Bruno. *The Study of Ethnomusicology: Thirty-One Issues and Concepts* (Urban and Chicago: University of Illinois Press, 2005).

O'Brien, Glenn, ed. *The Cool School: Writing from America's Hip Underground* (New York: The Library of America, 2013).

O'Neill, William L. *Coming Apart: An Informal History of America in the 1960s* (New York: Quadrangle Books, 1980).

Orenstein, Claudia. *Festive Revolutions: The Politics of Popular Theater and the San Francisco Mime Troupe* (Jackson: University Press of Mississippi, 1998).

Pearson, Mike and Michael Shanks. *Theatre/Archaeology* (London and New York: Routledge, 2001).

Peck, Abe. *Uncovering the Sixties: The Life & Times of the Underground Press* (New York: Pantheon Books, 1985).

Perks, Robert and Alistair Thomson, eds. *The Oral History Reader*, 2nd edn. (London and New York: Routledge, 1998).

Perry, Charles. *The Haight-Ashbury: A History* (New York: Vintage, 1985).

Perry, Helen Swick. *The Human Be-In* (New York: Basic Books, 1970).

Perry, George, ed. *San Francisco in the Sixties* (London: Pavilion, 2003).

Perry, Paul. *On the Bus: The Complete Guide to the Legendary Trip of Ken Kesey and the Merry Pranksters and the Birth of the Counterculture* (London: Plexus, 1990).

Pichaske, David. *A Generation in Motion: Popular Music and Culture in the Sixties* (New York: Schirmer, 1979).

Pinch, Trevor and Frank Trocco. *Analog Days: The Invention and Impact of the Moog Synthesizer* (Cambridge, MA: Harvard University Press, 2002).

Potter, Keith. *Four Musical Minimalists* (Cambridge: Cambridge University Press, 2000).

Powers, Devon. *Writing the Record: The* Village Voice *and the Birth of Rock Criticism* (Amherst: University of Massachusetts Press, 2013).

Price, Roberta. *Huerfano: A Memoir of Life in the Counterculture* (Amherst and Boston: University of Massachusetts Press, 2004).

Reich, Steve. *Writings On Music 1965-2000*, ed. Paul Hillier (Oxford and New York: Oxford University Press, 2002).

Rich, Alan. *American Pioneers: Ives to Cage and Beyond* (London: Phaidon Press, 1995).

Roberts, Les. "Talkin Bout My Generation: Popular Music and the Culture of Heritage," *International Journal of Heritage Studies* 20/3 (2014): 262–80.

Robins, Wayne. *Behind the Music: 1968* (New York: Pocket Books, 2000).

Rorabaugh, W. J. *Berkeley at War: The 1960s* (New York and Oxford: Oxford University Press, 1989).

Roszak, Theodore. *The Making of a Counter Culture: Reflections on the Technocratic Society and its Youthful Opposition* (Garden City, NY: Anchor Books, 1969).

Roszak, Theodore. *The Making of an Elder Culture: Reflections on the Future of America's Most Audacious Generation* (Gabriola Island, BC: New Society Publishers, 2009).

Rothschild, Amalie R. with Ruth Ellen Gruber. *Live at the Fillmore East: A Photographic Memoir* (New York: Thunder's Mouth Press, 1999).

Rowbotham, Sheila. *Promise of a Dream: Remembering the Sixties* (London and New York: Verso, 2001).

Rubin, Jerry. *Do It! Scenarios of the Revolution* (New York: Simon & Schuster, 1970).

Sander, Ellen. *Trips: Rock Life in the Sixties* (New York: Charles Scribner's Sons, 1973).

Sandford, Mariellen R., ed. *Happenings and Other Acts* (London and New York: Routledge, 1995).

Sayres, Sohnya, Anders Stephanson, Stanley Aronowitz, and Fredric Jameson, eds. *The 60s Without Apology* (Minneapolis: University of Minnesota Press, 1984, in association with *Social Text*).

Scherzinger, Martin. "Curious Intersections, Uncommon Magic: Steve Reich's *It's Gonna Rain*," *Current Musicology* 79/80 (2005): 207–44.

Schwarz, David. "Listening Subjects: Semiotics, Psychoanalysis, and the Music of John Adams and Steve Reich," *Perspectives of New Music* 31/2 (Summer, 1993): 24–56.

Schwarz, K. Robert. "Process vs. Intuition in the Recent Works of Steve Reich and John Adams," *American Music* 8/3 (Autumn 1990): 245–73.

Sculatti, Gene and Davin Seay. *San Francisco Nights: The Psychedelic Music Trip 1965-1968* (London: Sidgwick & Jackson, 1985).

Bibliography

Scully, Rock with David Dalton. *Living with the Dead: Twenty Years on the Bus with Garcia and the Grateful Dead* (New York: Cooper Square Press, 2001).

Selvin, Joel. *Monterey Pop* (San Francisco: Chronicle Books, 1992).

Selvin, Joel. *San Francisco: The Musical History Tour* (San Francisco: Chronicle Books, 1996).

Selvin, Joel. *Sly and the Family Stone: An Oral History* (New York: Avon Books, 1998).

Selvin, Joel. *The Summer of Love: The Inside Story of LSD, Rock & Roll, Free Love and High Times in the Wild West* (New York: Cooper Square Press, 1999).

Shapiro, Harry. *Waiting for the Man: The Story of Drugs and Popular Music* (London: Helter Skelter, 2003).

Shenk, David and Steve Silberman. *Skeleton Key: A Dictionary for Deadheads* (New York: Main Street Books, 1994).

Slick, Darby. *Don't You Want Somebody to Love: Reflections on the San Francisco Sound* (Berkeley: SLG Books, 1991).

Slick, Grace, with Andrea Cagan. *Somebody to Love? A Rock-and-Roll Memoir* (New York: Warner Books, 1998).

Snyder, Gary. *The Real Work: Interviews & Talks, 1964-1979* (New York: New Directions, 1980).

Snyder, Gary. *Turtle Island* (New York: New Directions, 1974).

Solnit, Rebecca. *Infinite City: A San Francisco Atlas* (Berkeley and Los Angeles: University of California Press, 2010).

Stanley, Rhoney Gissen, with Tom Davis. *Owsley and Me: My LSD Family* (Rhinebeck and New York: Monkfish Book Publishing Company, 2013).

Stevens, Jay. *Storming Heaven: LSD and the American Dream* (New York: Grove Press, 1987).

Talbot, David. *Season of the Witch: Enchantment, Terror, and Deliverance in the City of Love* (New York: Free Press, 2012).

Tamarkin, Jeff. *Got a Revolution! The Turbulent Flight of Jefferson Airplane* (New York: Atria, 2003).

Tendeler, Stewart and David May. *The Brotherhood of Eternal Love: From Flower Power to Hippie Mafia: The Story of the LSD Counterculture* (London: Cyan Books, 2007).

Thompson, Hunter S. *Hell's Angels: A Strange and Terrible Saga* (New York: Ballantine Books, 1995).

Torgoff, Martin. *Can't Find My Way Home: America in the Great Stoned Age, 1945-2000* (New York: Simon & Schuster, 2004).

Trager, Oliver. *The American Book of the Dead: The Definitive Grateful Dead Encyclopedia* (New York: Fireside, 1997).

Troy, Sandy. *One More Saturday Night: Reflections with the Grateful Dead, Dead Family, and Dead Heads* (New York: St Martins Press, 1991).

Turner, Fred. *The Democratic Surround: Multimedia & American Liberalism from World War II to the Psychedelic Sixties* (Chicago and London: University of Chicago Press, 2013).

Turner, Fred. *From Counterculture to Cyberculture: Stewart Brand, the Whole Earth Network, and the Rise of Digital Utopianism* (Chicago and London: The University of Chicago Press, 2006).

Unger, Irwin and Debi Unger, eds. *The Times Were A-Changin': The Sixties Reader* (New York: Three Rivers Press, 1998).

Unterberger, Richie. *Eight Miles High: Folk-Rock's Flight from Haight-Ashbury to Woodstock* (San Francisco: Backbeat Books, 2003).

Unterberger, Richie. *Turn! Turn! Turn! The '60s Folk-Rock Revolution* (San Francisco: Backbeat Books, 2002).

Vincent, Rickey. *Party Music: The Inside Story of the Black Panthers' Band and How Black Power Transformed Soul Music* (Chicago: Lawrence Hill Books, 2013).

Bibliography

von Bothmer, Bernard. *Framing the Sixties: The Use and Abuse of a Decade from Ronald Reagan to George W. Bush* (Amherst and Boston: University of Massachusetts Press, 2010).

von Hoffman, Nicholas. *We Are the People Our Parents Warned Us Against* (Chicago: Elephant Paperback, 1989).

Warner, Simon. *Text and Drugs and Rock 'n' Roll: The Beats and Rock Culture* (New York and London: Bloomsbury, 2013).

Wasserman, Abby. *Praise, Vilification & Sexual Innuendo or, How to Be a Critic: The Selected Writings of John L. Wasserman 1964-1979* (San Francisco: Chronicle Books, 1993).

Watts, Alan W. *The Joyous Cosmology: Adventures in the Chemistry of Consciousness*, 2nd edn. (Novato: New World Library, 2013).

Watts, Alan W. *The Way of Zen* (New York: Vintage, 1989).

Weir, Rob. "Tie-Dye and Flannel Shirts: The Grateful Dead and the Battle over the Long Sixties," *Journal of Popular Music Studies* 26/1 (March 2014): 137–61.

Weir, Wendy. *In the Spirit: Conversations with the Spirit of Jerry Garcia* (New York: Three Rivers Press, 1999).

Whalen, Jack and Richard Flacks. *Beyond the Barricades: The Sixties Generation Grows Up* (Philadelphia: Temple University Press, 1989).

Whiteley, Sheila. *The Space Between the Notes: Rock and the Counterculture* (London: Routledge, 1992).

Willis, Paul E. *Profane Culture* (London, Henley and Boston: Routledge & Kegan Paul, 1978).

Williams, Paul, ed. *The Crawdaddy! Book* (Milwaukee: Hal Leonard, 2002).

Wolf, Leonard, ed. *Voices from the Love Generation* (Boston and Toronto: Little, Brown, 1968).

Wolfe, Burton H. *The Hippies* (New York: Signet Books, 1968).

Wolfe, Tom. *The Electric Kool-Aid Acid Test* (New York: Farrar, 1968).

Zak, Albin. *The Poetics of Rock: Cutting Tracks, Making Records* (Berkeley and Los Angeles: University of California Press, 2001).

Zimmerman, Nadya. *Counterculture Kaleidoscope: Musical and Cultural Perspectives on Late Sixties San Francisco* (Ann Arbor: University of Michigan Press, 2008).

INDEX

Page references in bold refer to figures.

Ace of Cups   186, 231 n.12, 248
acid, *see* LSD
Acid Graduation   94, 123
acid rock   109, 302
Acid Tests   4–5, 7, 9, 12, 34–8, 40, 45, 57, 58, 59, 64, 66, 235, 286
Adams, Carolyn "Mountain Girl"   62–3
Adams, John   288, 295–8
  The Dharma at Big Sur   295–7
  Harmonium   295–6
Adler, Lou   147–8, 197
Albin, Peter   44
Alcatraz   245
alcohol   26, 33, 43, 47, 75, 77, 80, 123, 162, 174 n.52, 198, 215
Alioto, Joseph (Mayor of San Francisco, 1968–76)   196–7, 201–2, 209, 216, 218 n.38
All-Night Apothecary   11, 28
All Saints Episcopal Church   128, 155
Alpert, Richard (Ram Dass)   15 n.10, 59, 60 n.10, 73, 74, 151, 238
Altamont Festival   6, 242, 247–52, **250**, **253**, 257 n.57, 259 n.93, 317
Anderson, Chester   116–17, 125–6, 135–6, 145, 157, 176 n.91, 181 n.180
Anderson, Signe   111
Andrew, Sam   43–4, 64–6, 78, 148–9, 305
Anonymous Artists of America   123
Arista Records   326
Arnett, Chuck   289 n.9
Arno, Marc   77, 82, 84, 85, 86, 87, 139, 142, 198, 199, 218 n.23, 218 n.25, 227, 248, 251
Artista Gang   315–23
Artists Liberation Front   88, 173 n.36, 187, 238
Astronauts of Inner Space   137, 151
Atheneum Foundation for the Performing Arts   201–2
Autumn Records   54, 55, 56, 57, 58, 59, 70, 108, 111, 130, 186
Avalon Ballroom   4, 61, 67, 69, 82, 113, 123, 133, 140, 143, 199, 201, 213, 228, 236, 277, 289–90 n.12

as business   79, 117, 128, 140, 219 n.39
closing of   215–16, 222 n.96, 99
as space   81, 84, 86–7, 162, 190, 198, 202, 305, 317
Ayler, Albert   202

Babbs, Ken   35, 37, 124
Baez, Joan   27, 38, 88–9, 244
Balin, Marty   39–40, 49 n.43, 248
Ballard, Roy   128, 136
ballroom (dancehall) scene   22, 40, 41, 43, 197, 202, 205, 212–13, 219 n.39, 235, 239, 266, 268, 289 n.12, 307, 313
Banana   69, 84, 242
The Band   6, 246
  Music from Big Pink   6, 213
Barger, Sonny   39, 249–52
Barthol, Bruce   188, 189
The Beard   97
Beard, Martin   185
Beatles   54, 55, 56, 58, 86, 215, 216, 306
beatnik   11, 28, 31, 32, 34, 35, 44, 62, 65, 68, 70, 71, 95, 121, 203, 249, 252, 284
the Beats   27, 28, 96, 306, *see also* beatnik
The Beau Brummels   54–6, 244
  "Laugh Laugh"   54–6
Beausoleil, Bobby "Bummer Bob"   123, 172 n.26, 267
"be here now"   59, 238
Belli, Melvin   249, 251, 252
Ben & Jerry's   310–12
Bergess, Richard R. "Sgt. Sunshine"   204, 219 n.42, 233, 306
Berio, Luciano   285, 292 n.34
Berkeley, *see also* People's Park
  drug culture   88, 93, 251
  gigs in   70, 95, 115, 123, 205, 290 n.13
  political culture   27, 117, 119, 192 n.12, 219 n.38
  protests in   38, 44, 95, 193
  progressive culture   70, 81, 97, 188, 210
Berkeley Barb, strike   239, 255 n.40

Index

Big Brother and the Holding Company   3, 64, 66, 78, 92, 113 n.2, 121, 124, 130, 162, 166, 191 n.5, 201, 211, 235, 244, 307, 310
   at Monterey Pop   147, 148–9
Big Sur   11, 28, 32, 134, 203, 204, 244, 270, 296
Billboard magazine   130, 158, 185, 211, 212, 214, 215, 235, 253
Black Oak Books   1, 2, 9–10, 12, 13 n.1, 328
Black Panthers   137, 173 n.45, 176–7 n.99, 206, 214
Black Power   94, 128, 205–6
Blue Cheer   84, 160, 166, 191 n.5, 211, 223–6, 231 n.9, 307, 319
   "Summertime Blues"   191 n.5, 223–6
bluegrass   28, 58, 285, 287
blues   13, 30 n.16, 39, 40, 70, 81, 82, 188, 202, 224, 225, 252, 264, 268, 285, 286, 287
bohemia, defining beatniks and hippies   32, 48 n.5, 70, 125, 173 n.40, 234, 252
Brand, Stewart   61, 62, 66–7, 73, 100 n.4, 245
Brautigan, Richard   124, 173 n.36, 204
British Invasion   41, 54, 186
Brown, Willie   136
Bruce, Lenny   27
Buchla, Don   66, 101 n.19, 123
Buchla Box   66, 101 n.19, 123, 291 n.17
The Byrds   39, 55, 127

Caen, Herb   28, 98, 124, 133–4, 154, 168–9, 209, 254 n.25
Cahill, Tom (San Francisco Chief of Police, 1968–70)   98, 122, 128, 168
Cain, Tim   107
Camp Winnarainbow   12, 17 n.37, 311
Capitol Records   93, 170, 211, 227
Carousel Ballroom   4, 69, 197, 202, 206, 207–8, 208, 219 n.39, 236
Carter, Dick   247–52
Carvajal, Carlos   275–82, 279, 285, 289 n.11, 12
Casady, Jack   **250**
Cassady, Neal   4, 26, 48 n.22, 193
Champlin, Bill   107, 109, 114 n.8
The Charlatans   40, 41–3, 44, 50 n.51, 50 n.55, 186, 202, 237, 307, 315
Chocolate George (Charles Hendricks)   98, 161–2, 304–5
Christensen, Eric   65, 76, 77, 82, 121, 261, 304, 329–30
Church of All Saints   128, 155
Cipollina, John   228, 229
City Lights Books   1, 22, 34, 138, 173 n.36, 252
Clapton, Eric   224–5, 229
Cleaver, Eldridge   176–7 n.99, 216
clothing, hippie style   36, 44–5, 47, 73, 88, 302

Cochran, Eddie   223–6
Cohen, Allen   90–1, 96–7, 138, 184 n.225
Cohen, Ann   320–1
Cohen, Ben   311
Cohen, Bob   162, 197–8
Cohen, David   188
Columbia Records   113, 143, 144, 185, 211, 275, 276, 278, 289 n.8
Commanday, Robert   277, 281
The Committee   12, 37, 97
communes (intentional communities)   37, 68, 89, 154, 194, 209, 233–4, 235,
Communications Company (ComCo)   91, 116–17, 119–20, 124–5, 133, 135–6, 148, 171 n.8, 173 n.39, 181 n.180, 302, 306
consciousness, psychedelic   5, 6, 12, 13, 33, 63, 64, 74–9, 82, 91, 97, 121, 188, 191, 266, 277, 284, 285, 292 n.32, 296
Constanten, Tom   285, 292 n.34
Country Joe and the Fish   3, 101 n.25, 142, 188–91, 211, 229, 243
   Electric Music for the Mind and Body   142, 188
   "Section 43"   188–91, 229
Cow Palace   56, 216
Coyote, Peter   220 n.46, 302
Crawdaddy!   159, 174 n.50
Cream   130, 223, 224–5, 268
Creedence Clearwater Revival   29 n.9, 142, 201, 211–13, 242–3
Crosby, Stills and Nash (and Young)   6, 12, 14 n.3, 242, 244
   "Teach Your Children"   12, 14 n.3
Crumb, Robert   211
Cutler, Sam   250–2

dancehall ordinance   80, 95, 117, 155, 222 n.96
dancing
   and community   46, 81, 305, 319
   as self-expression   36, 44–5, 63–4, 215, 279
   stylistic descriptions of   4, 35, 36, 46, 63, 79, 81, 85, 155, 266
   under-age   79–80, 198
Davis, Ron (R.G.)   45
Days on the Green   256 n.45, 317
Deadheads   9, 16 n.34, 326–9, 332 n.8
Death of Hippie   9, 158, 164, 166–8, 184 n.225, 307
Democratic National Convention (Chicago, 1968)   195, 207, 218–19 n.38, 244
Denson, ED   101 n.25, 188, 192 n.12
Denver Dog   162, 197–9, 218 n.25
Didion, Joan   11, 176 n.91

350

Index

Diggers 91, 92, 97, 98–9, 116, 126, 127–8, 133, 134, 135, 168, 180 n.159, 199, 204–5, 207, 224, 233, 302, 306, 308, 309
Diogenes Lantern Works 198–9
DMT 34, 153, 305
Donahue, Tom "Big Daddy" 54, 56, 111, 128, 130–1, 159, 201
Dow Chemicals 141, 180 n.162
Duncan, Gary 227
Duncan, Robert 44, 272
Dylan, Bob 6, 14 n.3, 39, 127, 332 n.8

Electric Chamber Orkustra 161, 267
Elliott, Ron 54
Elmore, Greg 227
The Emergency Crew, *see* The Grateful Dead 57
Enrico's 26, 27, 28
Errico, Gregg 261
Esalen Institute 32, 37, 59, 231 n.12, 238, 240, 244, 252, 297

Family Dog 43, 44–5, 46, 67, 83, 124, 132, 134, 145, 162–3, 197–9, 277, 289 n.11, 316
    dance permit 215–16, 222 n.96
    Great Highway 237, 239–40, 241, 243–4
Fanon, Jhiani 69, 75, 77–8, 121, 126
Fantasy Records 29 n.9, 211
Fariña, Mimi 88–9
FDA, *see* US Food and Drug Administration
Ferguson, Mike 41, 42
Ferlinghetti, Lawrence 1, 44, 234, 252
Fillmore Auditorium 4, 46–7, 61, 66, 67, 69, 70, 81, 82, 84, 85–6, 87, 88, 95, 97, 113, 117, 146, 161, 190, 202, 213, 219 n.39, 228, 267, 289 n.12, 317
    as business 86, 128, 140, 162, 207, 216
    dance permit for 46–7, 71, 79–80, 127, 174 n.52, 198, 256 n.45
Fillmore East 205, 208, 242, 256 n.45
Fillmore West 2, 207, 211, 215, 216, 235, 240, 243–4, 256 n.45, 236–7, 254 n.25
Finnissy, Michael 331 n.4
folk music, scene 11, 39, 95, 101 n.25, 107, 153, 192 n.12
folk music, style 28, 38, 39, 40, 43, 70–1, 101 n.25, 125, 161, 188, 201, 252, 268
folk-rock 28, 40, 55, 108
Fong-Torres, Ben 144, 307
Fonteyn, Dame Margot 155, 289 n.11
Frankenstein, Alfred 124, 274
free concerts 3, 61, 115, 140, 153, 196, 212, 227, 239, 244, 246–52, 259 n.97, 302, 304, 317, 329
free events 61, 171 n.17, 195, 205, 215, 240–1, 243, 244, 305, 317

Free Frame of Reference 98
free love 70, 126, 138–9, 140, 204
Free Speech Movement 26, 27, 195
Freiberg, David 227, 229
Fuentes, Val 267

Garcia, Jerry 2, 5, 7, 13, 14 n.3, 14 n.5, 14 n.6, 15 n.18, 57, 162, 254 n.25, 326
    and the Haight 136, 308
    musical style 3, 57, 236, 285–8
    post-death 16 n.32, 305, 325
Gaskin, Stephen 239–40, 241
Gimme Shelter 248, 251, 258–9 n.88
Ginsberg, Allen 1, 15 n.10, 38, 44, 119–22, 123, 234, 296, 306
Howl 1, 28
Gleason, Ralph **26**, 26–7, 28, 29 n.9, 30 n.10, 38, 40, 87, 99, 102 n.53, 128, 132, 140, 144, 151, 153, 201, 202, 206–8, 214, 217 n.3, 218 n.38, 235, 238, 240–1, 243, 245–6, 275, 284, 317
    on Altamont 244, 246–52
    and dances 44–5, 46–7, 79–80, 95, 174 n.52, 198, 212, 213, 216, 219 n.39, 222 n.96, 236–7, 266
    on the free event 97–8, 117, 120, 140, 240–1, 243, 244, 259 n.97
    on Monterey Pop 134, 146, 147, 148, 197
    and *Ramparts* 145
    and *Rolling Stone* 159
Glide Memorial Foundation Church 124–5
Golden Gate Park 3, 10, 28, 31, 86, 144, 254 n.25, 329
    and hippies 162, 309
    use for gatherings 117, 121, 132, 144, 158, 205, 207, 239, 246, 319
Goldman, Rusty "Professor Poster" 41, 78, 83
Gottlieb, Lou 100 n.4, 153, 167, 233
Grace Cathedral 38
Graham, Bill 45, 94, 97, 99, 127, 211, 236, 238, 242, 245–6, 268, 307, 316, 317–18, *see also* Fillmore, Fillmore East, Fillmore West
    and Altamont 248, 257 n.57
    as businessman 66–7, 71, 81, 83, 85–7, 128, 145–5, 240
    and the Carousel Ballroom 202, 207, 208
    and curfew 95
    and dancehall ordinance 71, 79–80, 198, 222 n.96
    and drug use 64, 100–1 n.15
    and light show strike 239–40
    and Matthew Katz 144, 161, 178 n.125
    and Mime Troupe 45–7, 66–7

351

Index

and programming 85, 202, 256 n.45
Graham, Larry 261
Granelli, Jerry 99, 124
Grateful Dead 9, 10, 13, 36, 40, 64, 66, 85, 92, 93, 94, 99, 107, 113 n.2, 119–20, 121, 142, 162, 182 n.185, 197, 205, 207, 233, 259 n.97, 236, 244, 268, 302, 304, 305, 307–8, 310, 315
  and Acid Tests 4–5, 7, 9, 36, 235, 286
  and Altamont 246–252
  American Beauty 2, 13, 14 n.6
  Anthem of the Sun 6, 13, 15 n.18
  Aoxomoxoa 13, 233
  and commerce 302
  "Dark Star" 6–9, 16 n.27, 293 n.44
  early style 57–9
  final performances 329
  From the Mars Hotel 13
  history 2–9
  "In the Midnight Hour" 286
  Live/Dead 7
  at Monterey Pop 147
  "The Only Time Is Now" 57–9
  "Ripple" 1–3, 9–10, 12–13, 14 n.5, 14 n.6, 142–3, 328
  "Scarlet Begonias" 10
  and 710 Ashbury 154–5, 158, 166, 309
  and the Straight Theatre 163, 166, 168, 196
  and suspended time 285–8
  "Truckin" 16 n.33
  "Uncle John's Band" 6, 8–9
  "Viola Lee Blues" 286, 287–8
  at Woodstock 242–3
  Workingman's Dead 13
Grateful Dead Archive 325–8
Graves, LiAnne 43, 65, 70, 77, 85, 122, 139, 319–20, 330
Gravy, Wavy 12, 37, 86, 101 n.16, 242, 311, 312, 318–19
Gray Line Bus Tours 133, 134, 307, 309
Great American Music Hall 12, 318–19
The Great!! Society!! 44, 46, 110–13, 307
  "Someone to Love" 110–13
Griffin, Rick 211
Grisman, David 3, 14 n.6
Grof, Dr. Stanislav 33
Grogan, Emmett 145, 184 n.225, 250
Guaraldi, Vince 38, 99

Haggerty, Terry 74, 77, 78, 107, 109, 325, 330
Haight-Ashbury 3, 10, 27, 41, 115, 122, 124, 137, 158, 186, 208, 227, 228, 236, 243, 252, 270, 301, 315, 323, 329
  arrests in 122
  communal living in 68, 89

  as community 4, 10, 11, 65–6, 68, 74, 111, 119, 123, 128, 130, 152, 156, 201, 278, 280, 318–19
  as culture 43, 46, 61, 63, 81, 86, 90, 91, 98, 109, 111, 115, 131, 134, 151, 209, 219–20 n.46, 227, 228, 301, 319
  drug culture 6, 93, 130, 135, 140–1, 150, 153, 168, 180 n.162, 197, 204, 210, 214, 234, 244, 330
  end of scene 132, 136, 152–3, 155, 162, 166–8, 194, 203, 213–14, 233, 237, 270, 304, 307
  infectious disease in 131–2, 133, 140–1, 150–1
  inter-scene tensions 126, 145, 148, 176 n.91, 199–200, 240–1, 302–3
  mystique of 208–9, 243, 301–2, 304, 306–10, 323
  as neighborhood 31, 44, 68–70, 88, 109, 116, 131, 133, 152, 155, 173 n.45, 224, 234, 236, 277, 295, 302, 304–6, 309, 317
  as personal history 68–70, 316, 317–23, 326, 329–31
  police attention 95, 99, 122, 155, 157, 166, 168–9, 169, 170, 195, 196, 209–10, 218–19 n.38
  runaways in 137–8, 154, 168
  as slum 131, 137, 175 n.71, 234
  speed use in 135, 210, 234
  as tourist destination 5, 133–4, 137, 303–12
Haight-Ashbury District Merchants' Association 97, 122, 135
Haight-Ashbury Free Clinic 131, 141, 150–1, 158, 168, 169, 210, 234, 244, 317–18
  benefits for 201–2, 218 n.38
Haight Ashbury Neighborhood Council 140, 175 n.78, 200, 210
Haight Independent Proprietors (HIP) 97, 302
Haight Street 28, 31, 67, 68–70, 89, 91, 92, 95, 96, 98, 116, 120, 126, 132, 155, 157, 162, 166, 181 n.177, 197, 200, 203, 237, 252 n.97, 303, 308–9, 322, 329
  disturbances on 169, 196, 209–10, 213–14
  as social center 43, 122, 132, 146, 200, 301–2, 308
Haight Switchboard 131, 154–5
Ham, Bill 42, 50 n.52, 99, 124, 172 n.33
Hammond, Phil 41–2
Happening House 128–9, 150, 168
"happenings" 21–2, 38, 44, 63, 92, 95, 98, 120, 124–5, 134, 161, 162, 196, 204, 267, 277, 279
Harrison, George 157, 181 n.177

352

Index

Harrison, Lou   296–7, 331 n.4
Hayward, Claude   116, 145, 181 n.180
head shops   41, 131, 203–4, 230 n.7
Hell's Angels   88–9, 98–9, 116, 119–20, 145, 146, 162, 204, 206, 223, 224, 230 n.7, 304–5
  at Altamont   246–52
  and Pranksters   35, 49 n.27
  tensions with hippies   38–9, 120
Helms, Chet   12, 25, 44, 67, 94, 124, 145–6, 215–16, 222 n.96, 222 n.99, 237, 241, 277, 278, 318, *see also* Avalon Ballroom
  arrest of   133
  as businessman   81, 86–7, 128, 145, 162–3, 240
  and Denver Dog   162, 197–9
  and light show strike   239–40
Hendrix, Jimi   130, 223, 224–5, 242
heroin   32, 157, 244
Hinckle, Warren   145, 159
hippie
  and black community   125–6, 173 n.45
  and commerce   69, 71, 128, 131
  commercialization of   137–8, 303, 308–12, 329
  culture   27, 83, 115, 301
  definitions of   32, 48 n.11, 95, 301
  diet   158, 318
  discrimination against   131, 201–2, 215–16
  "free" ethos   91–2, 204–5, 207–8, 214, 249, 303, 306, 330
  as heritage   243, 303–6, 316–18, 326
  as hype   5, 133–4, 140, 150, 162, 166–8, 213–14, 307
  in the media   32, 115, 120, 134–5, 137–8, 144–6, 153–4, 166, 204, 233, 252
  and Native American cultures   12, 132, 151–3, 245
  and nostalgia   301, 315–23
  and police   96, 97, 98, 120, 168–9, 170, 196, 198–9, 209–10
  and political action   117, 195–6, 201, 214
  and political disengagement   91, 117, 169–70, 207
  as seekers   8, 120
  and spirituality   88, 119–20, 123, 154
Hirsh, Gary "Chicken"   188
Hoffman, Abbie   243
Hog Farm   12, 17 n.38, 37, 77, 242, 244
Holman, Mitchell   267
Howard, Glenn   59, 65, 77
Huckleberry House   168
Hughes, Robert   278–9
Human Be-In   9, 11, 117–22, 127, 171 n.17, 195
hungry i   27, 28, 40

Hunter, George   41, 42
Hunter, Meredith   248–52
Hunter, Robert   1–3, 6, 6–8, 10, 12–13
Hutton, Bobby   205–6
Huxley, Aldous   25

Iggy and the Stooges   225
Invisible Circus   124–5, 126, 173 n.39
Irving, Ken   82, 157, 330
I/Thou   92, 167
It's a Beautiful Day   161, 178 n.125, 202, 211, 267–70, 319
  "White Bird"   267–70

Jacobsen, Erik   185–7, 191 n.2
Jacopetti, Ben   61, 100 n.4
Jagger, Mick   244, 247, 249–52
jazz   5, 26, 27, 28, 31, 38, 108, 125, 151, 161, 202–3, 218 n.38, 238, 252, 275, 285, 286, 295, 296
Jazz Workshop   27, 87
Jefferson Airplane   3, 14 n.6, 39–40, 44, 46–7, 49 n.43, 88, 107, 111–13, 121, 129, 142, 174 n.50, 185, 197, 205, 207, 211, 237, 240, 244, 307, 310
  at Altamont   246–52
  Jefferson Airplane Takes Off   111
  and Matthew Katz   144, 161, 178 n.125, 267
  "Somebody to Love"   111–13
  Surrealistic Pillow   40, 111, 142, 185, 289 n.11
  "White Rabbit"   111, 113, 202
  at Woodstock   242, 256 n.54
Job Co-Op   128, 131
Johnson, Charles   35, 77, 85, 107, 130, 205
Johnson, President Lyndon B.   110–12
Joplin, Janis   108, 113 n.2, 146, 202, 205, 235, 240, 242, 243, 293 n.45, 304–5

Kandel, Lenore   96–7, 120, 138
  The Love Book   96–7, 138
Kangas, Kurt "Crowbar"   68, 75–6, 82, 86–7, 101–1 n.15, 68, 203–4, 301, 316, 319
Katz, Matthew   142, 144, 160–1, 178 n.117, 178 n.125, 267
Kelley, Alton   315
Kennedy, Robert F.   206–7, 306
Kepler's Books   34
Kerouac, Jack   4, 48 n.22, 296, 306
  On the Road   4, 28, 48 n.22
Kesey, Ken   12, 14 n.10, 26, 27, 34, 44, 49 n.27, 62–3, 64–5, 77, 101 n.16, 123, 124, 186, 244
  and Acid Tests   4–5, 35–6, 37, 66, 94, 235
  arrest of   62–3

353

Index

Kezar Stadium   239, 240
King, Martin Luther   201, 207, 306
Kingston Trio   60 n.5, 108, 214
Kirshna Consciousness   123, 154, 249
Klein, Allen   250–1
KMPX   56, 129, 129–31, 174 n.66, 201, 217 n.3, 224
Kraemer, Peter   185, 186
Kreutzmann, Bill   57, 66
KSAN   201, 217 n.1, 246, 249
KYA   44, 56, 130

La Honda   26, 31, 34, 35, 49 n.27
LaFlamme, David   70, 172 n.26, 266, 267–70
LaFlamme, Linda   75
Laughlin, Chandler   41, 50 n.49
Leary, Timothy   15 n.10, 25, 29 n.3, 72, 73, 76, 78, 101 n.16, 123, 127, 135, 151, 171 n.17, 238
Leeds, Vicki   69, 121, 139, 158, 160, 303, 330
Lesh, Phil   3, 57, 59, 146, 236, 285–6, 287, 292 n.34, 331 n.3
Lewis, Peter   142, 143
Lieberman, Fred   325, 328, 332 n.6
light show   22, 44–5, 50 n.52, 63–4, 87, 99, 110, 124, 129, 191, 218 n.23, 239–40, 256 n.45, 277, 280, 281, 289 n.10, 307, 318
  as psychedelic experience   63, 81–2, 83–5, 90, 191, 279
Light Sound Dimension   124, 210
"Liverpool of America"   31, 45, 140, 212
Loading Zone   205, 211, 307
London   124, 162, 172 n.35, 197, 205, 239, 252
Longshoremen's Hall   44, 46, 61, 65–6, 79, 113, 235
Los Angeles   12, 227, 246, 266, 287, 295
  tension with San Francisco   14 n.8, 97, 147–8
Love Circus   126, 157
Love Pageant Rally   92, 94
Lovin' Spoonful   186–7
LSD   4–5, 9, 14 n.10, 25, 29 n.3, 29 n.4, 33, 34, 50 n.49, 61, 83, 87, 94, 123, 141, 153, 224, 233
  and American drug culture   73
  "bad trips"   73, 98, 123, 151, 153
  black market   33, 71–3, 92–3, 140, 141, 168, 170, 210
  common use of   69, 216, 244
  communal experience   36, 49 n.27, 63, 74–8, 88
  "dangerous drug"   29 n.3, 71–3
  "dosing" of unsuspecting persons   64–5, 76, 77, 101 n.16, 116–17, 123
  illegality of   72–3, 92–3, 157, 209
  and media   32–3, 120, 134
  and music-making   78–9, 92–3, 192 n.14
  psychiatric treatment with   33
  and rock music   73, 127, 161, 188–91
  toward spiritual enlightenment   29 n.4, 33, 73–8, 89, 101 n.16
  studies regarding efficacy of   71–3
  and violence   157
LSD Rescue   98

McCabe, Charles   62, 155, 169–70
McClure, Michael   44, 97, 155
McDonald, Country Joe   20, 158, 188, 192 n.12, 202, 242, 243, 244, 256 n.54, 318, 319, 256 n.54
McKenzie, Scott   148–50
  "San Francisco (Be Sure to Wear Flowers In Your Hair)"   148–50, 179 n.145
McKernan, Ron "Pigpen"   4, 57, 59, 88, 124, 166, 285
MacNeil, Terry   185
Magic Mountain Festival   146
The Magic Theatre for Madmen Only   41
Maginnis, William   43, 65, 66, 101 n.20, 278, 291 n.17
Magoo's Pizza Parlor   59
Mailer, Norman   38
Mamas and the Papas   55, 127, 148
Manson Family   49 n.34, 123, 252
marijuana   25, 31, 32, 33, 34, 46, 62, 68, 75, 88, 123, 127, 142, 143, 153, 155, 157, 166, 169, 198, 204, 209, 214–15, 233, 244
  market value of   25, 33, 210
The Marina (district)   31, 115, 218 n.38
Marin County   6, 69, 77, 107, 108, 113 n.2, 115, 119, 129, 143, 146, 157, 162, 203, 214, 228, 233, 246, 247, 270
Marshall, Fred   99, 124
Martin, Tony   21, 85, 129
Martini, Jerry   261
The Matrix   39–41, 45, 69, 110, 111, 112, 113, 166, 186, 191 n.2, 213, 228, 244, 257 n.66
Mayell, Norman   185, 186
MC5   225, 226
Meagher, Ron   54
Melton, Barry   189–90, 192 n.14
Mendocino   12, 28, 203, 270
Mercury Records   211, 223
Meriwether, Nicholas   326–8
Merry Pranksters   4, 26, 35–7, 44, 64, 66–7, 77, 94, 186, 306
mescaline   69, 74, 76, 242, 284, 285
methamphetamine   209–10, 233, 234

Index

methedrine 88, 93, 157, 212
Meyers, Dr. Frederick 153, 180 n.162
Meyers, Jim 107
Milhaud, Darius 279, 284
Miller, Jerry 129, 130, 142, 143
Miller, Steve, *see* Steve Miller Blues Band
Mills College 128-9, 284, 285
Mill Valley 88
Miner, David 110, 112, 113
Mingus, Charles 202
minimalism 288, 295-6
The Mission (district) 31, 158, 319
Mitchell, Bob 54, 57
Moby Grape 113 n.2, 142-4, 177 n.116, 185, 211, 267, 307, 319
   "8:05" 142-3
   and Matthew Katz 144, 267
   Moby Grape 142-4
   "Omaha" 143
Monck, Chip 242, 257 n.57
Monk, Thelonious 202
Monterey Folk Festival 28
Monterey International Pop Festival 134, 146-50, 159, 179 n.138, 180 n.156, 191, 197, 205, 213, 226, 230 n.5, 231 n.9, 238-9, 243
Monterey Pop (film) 148, 242
Moog synthesizer 240, 278, 281, 291 n.17
Morgan, Charlie 68, 74, 75, 82, 121, 267, 331
Morning Star Ranch 100 n.4, 154, 167, 183 n.215, 194, 233
Moscoso, Victor 211, 315
Moskowitz, Morris "Moe" 92, 115, 221 n.73
Mosley, Bob 142, 144
Mother's Nightclub 56, 111, 113
Mothers of Invention 79
Mouse, Stanley 124, 315
Muir Beach 35, 37
Mulligan, Dec 54
Murphy, Michael 37-8
mushrooms, magic 69, 74, 95, 100-1 n.15, 284
The Mystery Trend 46, 108, 114 n.6

Neiman, Albert 42, 43, 81-2, 87, 121, 149, 166-7
Newton, Huey 137, 176 n.99, 206, 216
New York 11, 26, 36, 113 n.2, 127, 185, 186, 197, 205, 208, 211, 235, 239, 246, 250, 283
New York Times 31, 127, 205
North Beach 1, 11, 22, 26, 28, 30 n.10, 31, 32, 40, 54, 56, 62, 88, 95, 97, 100, 108, 111, 125, 234, 306
   topless bars in 100, 168, 234
Nureyev, Rudolf 155, 289 n.11

Oakland 38, 39, 88, 95, 128, 170, 178 n.117, 206, 209, 245, 296, 308
Oakland Coliseum 245-6, 256 n.45, 268
Oakland Museum 99
Oakland Symphony 278-9, 290 n.13, 290 n.14
Oliveros, Pauline 128, 274, 285, 293 n.45
The Oracle 11, 89-91, 93, 116, 119, 120-1, 134, 135, 138, 149, 151, 152-3, 157, 166, 171 n.8, 194, 203, 227, 302, 306
Owsley acid, *see* Stanley, Augustus Owsley III

Palace of Fine Arts 201-2, 218 n.38
Panhandle (Golden Gate Park) 61, 68, 69, 92, 95, 115, 116, 122, 128, 140, 141, 146, 317
Park and Recreation Commission 127-8, 158, 201, 207
Park Police Station 68, 89, 98-9, 120, 127, 155, 196, 214
Peninsula 28, 35, 54, 57, 58, 115, 123
People's Park 237-8, 241
Peterson, Dickie 76, 78, 79, 82, 89, 122, 223-6, 231 n.9, 329
Peterson, John 54
peyote 29 n.2, 74, 76, 151, 277, 284-5
Phillips, John 147-50, 179 n.145, 197
The Phoenix 203-4
Point Reyes 156
Polo Field (Golden Gate Park) 117, 121, 197, 246
poster art 42, 44, 66, 81, 82, 83, 89, 90, 99, 121, 128, 159, 161, 203, 215, 256 n.45, 317, 319, 332 n.14
progressive rock 228, 230, 270
Prosser, John 107
psychedelia (musical style) 27, 28, 79, 143, 189-91, 213, 227-30, 266, 270, 275, 285, 288, 296
psychedelic experience 5, 13, 61, 63, 73, 74-9, 82, 189, 228, 229, 274, 285, 322
The Psychedelic Experience (book) 48, n.13, 74
Psychedelic Shop 89, 96-7, 138, 166
psychedelic time 90, 229-30, 274, 285-8, 293 n.44

Question Man 28, 183 n.211, 193
Quicksilver Messenger Service 40, 113 n.2, 121, 170, 201, 205, 211-13, 227-30, 244, 268, 270, 307, 315
   "The Fool" 227-30

Ram Dass, *see* Alpert, Richard
Ramparts Magazine 144-5, 159, 176-7 n.99
Rancho Olompali 113 n.2, 233, 253 n.5

355

Index

Reagan, Ronald (California Governor, 1967–75)   26, 29 n.8, 206–7, 220 n.50, 306
Redding, Otis   85
Red Dog Saloon   41–3, 45, 64, 85, 186, 237
Reich, Steve   273, 274, 282–8, 292 n.34, 293 n.45
   It's Gonna Rain   273, 282–6, 287
   Oh! Dem Watermelons   286–8
   Piano Phase   288
Resner, Bill   155
Resner, Hillel   155
Rexroth, Kenneth   88, 277
Rifkin, Danny   162, 166
Riley, Terry   273–7, 279, 281, 282, 284, 285, 290 n.15, 292 n.32, 293 n.45, 296–7
   In C   273–82, 285, 287, 290 n.13, 292 n.32, 293 n.44, 297
rock music (style)   31, 40, 44, 46–7, 64, 66, 70–1, 81, 109, 110, 111, 114 n.5, 125, 130, 161, 193, 202–3, 213, 228, 229, 270, 307
Rogers, Art   37, 69, 74, 75, 84, 138–9, 167, 330–41
Rolling Stone Magazine   7, 11, 29 n.9, 143, 147, 148, 158–60, 173 n.36, 182 n.197, 195, 199, 203, 214, 216, 235, 239, 240, 241, 243, 245, 264, 289 n.8, 306–7
Rolling Stones   108, 127, 186, 244, 245–52, 258 n.88
Rubin, Jerry   38, 94–5, 195, 207
Ryan, Pat   315

Samuel, Gerhard   278–9, 290 n.13, 290 n.14, 290 n.15
Sandoz Pharmaceuticals   14 n.10, 71–2
San Francisco Ballet   275, 277, 278, 279, 280, 281–2
   Genesis 70   277–82, 291 n.17
San Francisco Health Commission   32, 98, 131, 132, 133, 150–1, 210, 234, 244
San Francisco Mime Troupe   21, 32, 38, 45–7, 57, 66, 91–2, 100, 114 n.6, 187, 240–1, 246, 284, 286
   Candelaio   32, 45
   A Minstrel Show, Or Civil Rights in a Cracker Barrel   50 n.59, 286
San Francisco Opera House   87, 155, 254 n.25, 278–9, 280–2
San Francisco "sound"   55, 56, 107, 113, 142, 161, 178 n.117, 233, 266, 267
San Francisco State College   27, 33, 54, 94, 97, 99, 152, 216, 277
San Francisco Symphony   288, 295
San Francisco Tape Music Center   21–2, 64, 66, 101 n.19, 123, 273–5, 278, 282, 284, 295
   City Scale   21–23, 49 n.26, 313 n.19

San Jose   4, 35, 57, 151, 251
San Mateo   34, 242
San Quentin Prison   244
Santa Cruz   31, 35, 36, 49 n.28, 135, 270, 296, 325
Santana   211–13, 242–3, 248–52
Santos, Patty   267, 269
Sausalito   108, 113 n.2, 157, 214
Savio, Mario   27
Schulz, Charles   185
Scully, Rock   6, 166, 244, 250
Seale, Bobby   137, 206
Sears Point Raceway   247, 249, 258–9 n.88
Sebastian, John   187, 244
Sender, Ramon   21, 22, 49 n.26, 61, 65–7, 76, 100 n.4, 101 n.20, 183 n.215, 284–5
710 Ashbury   3, 154, 158, 162, 166, 304–5, 309, 312
Shankar, Ravi   31, 130, 243
Shelley, John (Mayor of San Francisco, 1964–8)   80, 95
Shepp, Archie   202, 219 n.39
Sievers, William   185
Silverman, Tracy   296–7
Slick, Darby   110, 111, 112, 113
Slick, Grace   110–13, 178 n.125, 202, 207
Slick, Jerry   110, 111, 113
Sly and the Family Stone   56, 205, 212–13, 240, 242–3, 261–6
   "Everyday People"   261–6
Smith, Dr. David   141, 150, 153, 157, 209, 233–4, 317, 318
Snoopy   185, 191 n.2
Snyder, Gary   1, 119, 138
Soder, Yana Zegri   322–3
Sonoma County   100 n.4, 153, 233, 270, 319, 320
Sons of Champlin   107–9, 211, 231 n.12, 235, 244, 268
   "Sing Me a Rainbow"   107–9
Sopwith Camel   86, 185–7
   "Hello Hello"   185–7
Sox, Dr. Ellis D. (SF Health Commissioner)   131–2, 234, 244
Speedway Meadow   236, 247, 319
Spence, Alexander "Skip"   142, 143–4
spirituality   2, 32, 38, 74, 91, 154, 213–14, 235, 296, 325
Stanford University   72, 73
Stanley, Augustus Owsley III   37, 93, 122, 141, 162, 170, 171 n.15,
Stephens, Leigh   223
Stern, Gerd   73
Steve Miller Blues Band   146, 170, 205, 211, 212, 244, 307

Index

Stevenson, Don   142, 143
Stewart, Sylvester (Sly Stone)   54, 56, 108, 110, 111, 261–6
Stockhausen, Karlheinz   182 n.185
Stone, Freddie (Stewart)   261
Stone, Rose (Stewart)   261
Stone, Sly, *see* Stewart, Sylvester
Stoneman, Scotty   287
    "Eighth of January"   287
STP   141, 150, 153, 167, 180 n.162
Straight Theater   134, 155, 163, 166, 168, 196, 199, 202, 213, 222 n.99, 237
Subotnick, Morton   274
Summer of Love   5, 150, 158, 162, 170, 187, 209, 302, 308
    anniversary of   11, 144, 302, 319
    hippie invasion   115, 127–8, 136–8, 224
    as hype   162, 303
Summer of Love, Council for a   134, 135, 140
Superspade, *see* Thomas, William

tarot   227–9, 231 n.12
Taylor, Cecil   202, 267
Telegraph Avenue   88, 93, 98, 99, 115, 209, 210, 235
Thelin, Jay   97, 138, 184 n.225
Thelin, Ron   89, 96, 122, 166
Thomas, William "Superspade"   99, 157–8, 162, 181 n.179
1090 Page Street   43–4, 64, 186
Tribute to Dr. Strange   44–5
Trident Records   108, 114 n.5
Trident Studios   107, 108, 214
Trips Festival   9, 37, 61–7, 70–1, 73, 94, 100 n.4, 101 n.20, 102 n.53, 245, 277
Tudury, Teresa   11, 28, 69, 74, 139, 272, 303, 331

Union Square   25, 88, 101 n.20, 222 n.96, 282–3, 283, 303, 306, 312
United Fruit Company   126–7, 173 n.47
University of California, Berkeley   33–4, 72, 95, 153, 193, 237–8
University of California, Santa Cruz   325–8
Unobsky, Mark   41, 42, 50 n.49
US Food and Drug Administration (FDA)   33, 71–2, 141

Valentino, Sal   54, 244
Van Gelder, Peter   110, 113
Velvet Underground   80, 102–3 n.53
Vietnam War   29 n.8, 38–9, 137, 162, 169, 170, 203, 247, 252, 259 n.88
Virginia City   31, 40–3, 50 n.49, 186
von Hoffman, Nicholas   11, 130, 170

Wagenet, Hal   267, 268
Warhol, Andy   36, 80, 102–3 n.53, 123
The Warlocks   35, 36, 47, 57–9, *see also* The Grateful Dead
Warner Brothers Records   14 n.8, 55, 326
Wasserman, John   39, 79, 123, 213, 255 n.39, 256 n.45
Watts, Alan   241, 306
Weir, Bob   3, 14 n.5, 57, 166, 302, 325, 326
Welch, Lew   132, 194
Wenner, Jann   145, 158–9, 195
Werber, Frank   108, 214–15
Whaley, Paul   223
The Who   186, 226, 231 n.9, 243, 270 n.10
Wild West Festival   238–9, 240–1, 243, 255 n.39
Wilson, Wes   62, 83, 332 n.14
Winterland Arena   4, 94, 126, 201, 219 n.39, 235, 238, 256 n.45, 307
Wolf, Professor Leonard   11, 128, 158, 167–8, 266
Wolfe, Tom   4, 11, 15 n.11, 36, 160, 266
    The Electric Kool-Aid Acid Test   4, 11
Wolman, Baron   159–60
Woodstock Festival   12, 226, 241–3, 244, 249, 257 n.57

The Yardbirds   202, 267
Yippies   195–6, 199, 207, 214
yoga   74, 89, 91, 119, 128, 152, 183 n.215, 318
Young, Jesse Colin   305
Young, Suzi   76, 139, 305, 330
Youngbloods   113 n.2, 191 n.5

Zap Comix   210–11
Zellerbach, Merla   25, 29 n.4, 32, 95–6, 158, 171 n.17
Zen   61, 73, 74, 151

357